DUMONT

BERND POLSTER

# GERMAN DESIGN
## FOR MODERN LIVING
# THE CLASSICS

# Contents

# Contents **Milestones**

5

# Contents **Designers and Manufacturers**

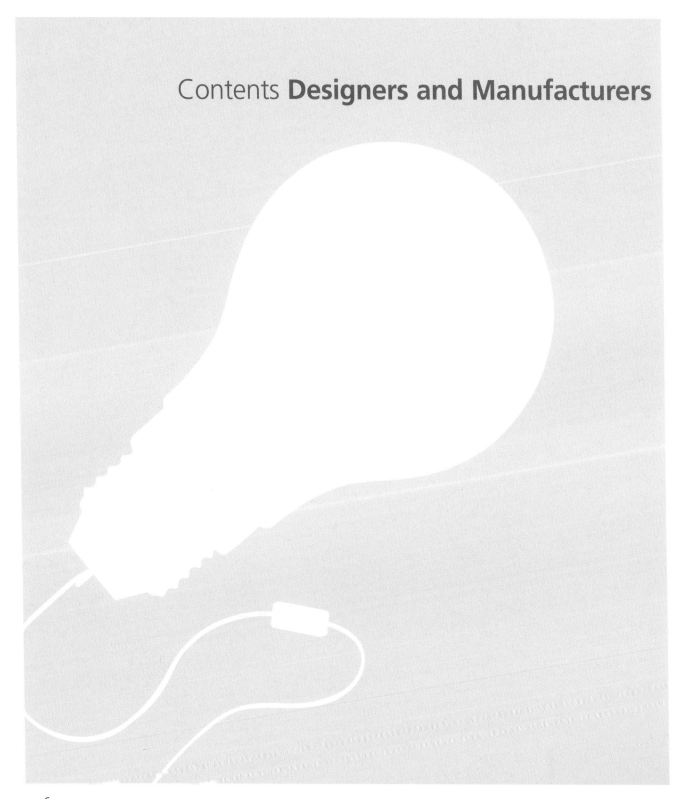

Foreword **Systematization and Freedom**

**Neuschwanstein Castle and the Bauhaus** are German myths that are virtually carved in stone, and yet they represent visions of domesticity that could hardly be more opposite. Between them lies a revolution – a political one of course, but also a cultural one. In the course of this turnabout, dusty romantic props that had been accumulating all through the 19th century were all at once swept aside. This left behind a shocking void and a grandiose free space for creativity. The innovation engine that was cranked up back then is still driving German design today. Whether we think of the cantilevered chair, the functional lamp, the tableware service or flexible sofa arrangements, at the heart of it all is nothing less than the intention to create a whole new system of objects for daily use.

When in 1927 in Stuttgart-Weissenhof people stood back to take stock of the results of this major clean-up campaign, a small scandal ensued. Architect Josef Frank had dared to furnish his model home with a cosy corner full of soft cushions. This was evidently an affront to the taboo against all too much comfort. Purists caught a whiff of the "old German" living room rearing its ugly head, shown on the exhibition poster as a cautionary image – crossed out with thick brushstrokes, naturally in red.

The domestic scene in Germany had become a cultural battlefield. Liberation from the petty bourgeois milieu was already forthcoming during the contradiction-riddled days of the Kaiser, when various forces came together to cause fresh winds to blow through the world of design. The artist was now also an inventor of form, industry was running at full steam and an alternative scene was asserting itself. Esoteric groupings created islands of authenticity around 1900 and came up with a slogan meant to signalize an abrupt departure from the Wilhelminian goose step: "Lebensreform" – lifestyle reform. Without the workshop movement associated with this sub-culture and its arcadian culmination in Dresden-Hellerau, the Bauhaus would hardly have been conceivable.

But design's "big bang" had to wait until after the apocalypse of the First World War. Domestic lifestyles continued to be politicized, a development that came to a head under the Nazi regime. The fact that pure form – which was now considered the "good" kind – then ruled so rigorously after 1945 was almost an inevitable counter-reaction. In Germany, abstract art and modern furniture acted as a cultural catharsis. The last rebellion in domestic living, in the 1980s, had two different thrusts. It took aim at both the functionalism of the forefathers as well as at great-grandfather's deer head, which still hung proudly over the sofa.

Perhaps one reason for the Germans' intimate connection with their own four walls can be found in this historical rollercoaster ride. Nowhere else do people spend so much money on the home. In no other country did a series of upheavals and breaks with the past take place in such quick succession, forcing people each time to make a fresh start. The connection between an eventful history and an abundance of domestic innovations documented here cries out for further attention and would certainly form a fascinating topic for future studies.

The caesuras in style are reflected as well in the biographical collages of many Germans. For a short period during the 1960s, four generations of my family lived in the same town. I remember that my great-grandparents' house was dark during the daytime. When I visited them, I sat on a cosy sofa that dated from the days of the Kaiser, just like they did. My grandparents on the other hand had a flat chaise longue that did not survive my jumping experiments unscathed. It came from the "production", as they called the companies that made moderately modern furniture for workers' households. At home we soon had a modern sofa suite with a lightweight wooden frame and square foam upholstery. My children still sit on this early seating system today, exploring the seemingly endless cushion-stacking and reclining options it offers.

In the chip-controlled revolution of late, mobility and flexibility are more pertinent than ever. Old design virtues thus shine all the more brightly in the wake of the many cultural battles, demonstrated for instance by the astounding renaissance of the transformable sofa. Even a few taboo topics such as the German oak cabinet are undergoing a contemporary metamorphosis. Thus, the final demise of the heavy wooden furniture of old, fondly referred to as "Gelsenkirchener Barock", is nothing more than a marginal note, but one that fits in well with our vision of the future.

Bernd Polster

# 1815

# **Design for modern living** A history

# 1815–1918 The invention of simplicity

**1815** In the wake of the Congress of Vienna, there is a new focus on the home. A simpler domestic style finds its way into German living rooms. As a countermove to French elegance, the art of omission blossoms for the first time in these climes. Shaped by Romanticism and Classicism, this epoch, which would later be derisively labelled "Biedermeier", becomes the prototype for German bourgeois culture and at the same time a herald of modern lifestyles. The modern division of rooms in the home is developed. – Karl Friedrich Schinkel is Prussia's head architect as well as an inventor of original furniture and an authority in matters of taste.

**1830** Furniture that imitates the styles of bygone eras is shown at exhibitions. Historicism takes root and with it the fruitless search for a "German style".

**1835** Pioneer Michael Thonet applies his bentwood technique to a chair in Boppard (Rhineland) and with it develops the first series furniture. Chair *No. 14* from 1859 is the first piece of furniture to be produced over a million times and an early example of industrial design.

**1871** Germany is united as an empire. The "delayed nation" experiences two industrial revolutions in quick succession and becomes a leading industrial power. The population increases by more than half by 1910, to 65 million. This incredible dynamism is countered by an entrenched system in which the military sets the spirited pace. – As elsewhere in Europe, the nouveau riche accoutre themselves and their surroundings in lavish historicism. The domestic salon becomes a theatre setting for social life.

**1875** Berlin now has one million inhabitants and is developing into a metropolis with enormous magnetism. Industrial centres such as the Ruhr Valley emerge. Furnishings for workers' apartments are usually limited to the bare essentials.

**1876** The *German Art and Industry Exposition* in Munich makes the Neo-Renaissance popular, a massive style that is today considered "old German" and which epitomizes our image of German furniture. – At the World Exposition in Philadelphia, Germany shines with nationalist kitsch. With its show "Germania, Prussians, Kaiser, Crown Prince and Bismarck", the economic upstart reveals its stylistic deficits.

**1883** Friedrich Nietzsche's *Also sprach Zarathustra* comes out. This work by a social outsider becomes the bible of the civilization-weary.

**1884** King Ludwig II of Bavaria moves into Neuschwanstein, the last of the 19th-century fantasy castles. Lavishly decorated with the dream world of German mythology, the architectural and artistic realization of which nearly exhausted the state coffers, this scheme takes historicism to absurd extremes. The same romantic themes recur in the popular tapestries that hang over so many German sofas.

**1887** As a strategy against cheap imports, England introduces the label "Made in Germany".

**1888** Wilhelm II, a fan of pomp and uniforms, becomes the new Kaiser. His handlebar moustache sets the ideal for male beauty while also coming to symbolize uselessness. – The *Arts and Crafts* exhibition in London puts a name to the movement whose design reforms are earning great respect throughout Europe. – The first department store chains open their doors. One of their advantages is the "fixed prices" that have not yet become common practice.

**1890** Sigmund Freud inaugurates psychoanalysis. The first Institute for Experimental Psychology was founded in Leipzig in 1879. The individual is discovered.

**1891** Prosperity produces novelties. **WMF**'s sleek cocktail shaker *No. 1/2* looks like a foreign body in the product catalogue.

**1892** Artists turn their backs on the established art market to found the

"Munich Secession". A few of the apostates, such as **Peter Behrens**, soon turn their attention to applied arts (further secessions follow in 1897 in Vienna and 1898 in Berlin).

**1893** At the *World Exposition* in Chicago, German artists are inspired by the English arts and crafts on display. – Hermann Obrist's embroidered "Peitschenhieb" ("Whiplash") is regarded as an early Jugendstil work. The new sensuous artistic style, applied to objects of everyday use in an effort to create Gesamtkunstwerke, or total works of art, gives rise to the inventor of form as new artist type.

**1895** An economic boom sets in that will continue almost until the outbreak of the First World War. During this period, the population of the cities quadruples. Opponents of what is often merciless urbanization come together to form "homeland preservation" associations. – In the artists' colony in Worpswede, Heinrich Vogeler designs the Barkenhof compound as a total work of art.

**1896** Architect Hermann Muthesius goes to London as Prussian cultural attaché in order to get an idea of whether England's design reform might be applicable to conditions in Germany. He later affirms this possibility in several books. – The new magazine *Die Jugend* gives the reformed art its German name, Jugendstil, which is at first meant to be derogatory, but also comes into use in other countries.

**1897** The *International Art Exhibition* in Dresden spells the breakthrough for Belgian **Henry van de Velde** and Jugendstil furniture. – At the *VIIth International Art Exhibition* in Munich's Glass Palace, "modern minor arts", although shown only in two rooms, cause a sensation. – Magazines like *Deutsche Kunst und Dekoration*, *InnenDekoration* and *Dekorative Kunst* propagate the new curvaceousness in design. – Biedermeier is rediscovered and now appraised positively.

**1898** The Vereinigten Werkstätten für Kunst im Handwerk (United Workshops for Art in Craftsmanship) in Munich and the Dresdner Werkstätten für Handwerkskunst (Dresden Workshops for Handicraft Art) are founded based on the English model. The two successful enterprises merge a good decade later to become the **Deutsche Werkstätten** (German Workshops). They mark the beginning of a workshop movement that aims at a "room art" inspired by Jugendstil. A number of creative talents come together in Munich, including Peter Behrens, August Endell, Hermann Obrist, Josef Maria Olbrich, Bruno Paul and **Richard Riemerschmid**. In Dresden, artisan and idealist Karl Schmidt sets out to turn his company into a real-life utopia. He relocates to a suburb called Hellerau and erects his enterprise in a garden town designed by architect Riemerschmid. (other foundings: in 1899 the Werkstätten für angewandte Kunst [Workshops for Applied Art] by Henry van de Velde in Berlin, in 1900 the Saalecker Werkstätten [Saaleck Workshops] by architect and "homeland preservation" pioneer Paul Schultze-Naumburg, in 1902 the Königliche Lehr- und Versuchswerkstätten [Royal Teaching and Experimentation Workshops] in Stuttgart, in 1903 the Wiener Werkstätte. – The scandal set off by the Jugendstil facade of the Elvira photo studio in Munich shows how strongly Jugendstil is polarizing the public. – The first association for Freikörperkultur (nudist society) is established in Essen. – Following Bismarck's death, hundreds of commemorative towers are erected, resulting in nothing less than a standardized "serial product."

**1899** An artists' colony is established in Darmstadt on the Mathildenhöhe. Its initiator, Grand Duke Ernst Ludwig of Hesse, a close relative of the Queen of England, is familiar with the art reform movement in Britain and a friend of the Viennese Secessionists. – Dresden creates its own variation on the theme of the ideal home. In the *Volksthümlichen Ausstellung für Haus und Herd* (Folk Exhibition for Home and Hearth) the focus is on the simple things in life. The *Deutsche Kunstausstellung* (German Art Exhibition) achie-

| | |
|---|---|
| 1747 | Nymphenburg founded |
| 1748 | Villeroy & Boch founded |
| 1763 | KPM founded |
| 1817 | Duravit founded |
| 1819 | Sauter founded |
| | Thonet founded |
| 1830 | Schinkel Garden Chair |
| 1831 | Wilde + Spieth founded |
| 1844 | Kahla founded |
| 1853 | WMF founded |
| 1859 | *No. 14* Chair |
| 1869 | Müller Möbelwerkstätten founded |
| 1870 | Martin Stoll founded |
| 1871 | Sedus Stoll founded |
| 1879 | Bofinger founded |
| | Rosenthal founded |
| 1881 | FSB founded |
| 1882 | Renz founded |
| 1883 | Vorwerk founded |
| 1887 | Arzberg founded |
| 1889 | Deutsche Werkstätten founded |
| | Drabert founded |
| 1891 | *No. 1/2* Cocktail Shaker |
| 1892 | Poggenpohl founded |
| 1895 | Mono founded |
| 1897 | Helit founded |
| | Rasch founded |
| 1899 | Music-Room Chair |
| | Fish Service |
| | Miele founded |
| 1900 | Wilkhahn founded |
| 1901 | *Behrens House* Chair |
| | Hansgrohe founded |
| 1903 | Service with Leaf Decor |
| | Pott founded |
| 1906 | Flötotto founded |
| 1908 | Eggersmann founded |
| 1909 | Behrens Kettle |
| 1912 | Behr founded; WK Wohnen founded |
| 1914 | Alfi founded |
| 1918 | Kaldewei founded |

ILLUSTRATIONS:
above: Kitchen by Bruno Paul for Haus Feinhals, around 1910
below: Vase by Josef Maria Olbrich for Villeroy & Boch, 1895

ves fame based on a music room designed by Richard Riemerschmid. His **Musikzimmerstuhl** (Music Room Chair) is regarded as an early turning point in formal innovation.

**1900** At the otherwise mostly conservative World Exposition in Paris, the German reformists walk off with several gold medals. The turbulent Jugendstil, which is already beginning to ebb, has put an end to historicism. But the transformation of taste is not yet complete. The motto is now reason and Sachlichkeit – objectivity. – The magazine *Kunstwart* publishes *Ten Commandments for Furnishing the Home*. Number one: "Furnish your home practically!" – Monte Verità in the Swiss canton of Ticino serves as refuge for "life reformers", a colourful bourgeois subculture which, based on an urge for more naturalness, develops counter-concepts to the Wilhelminian spirit of subjugation. These range from expressive dance and nudism to natural medicine and reform dress, vegetarianism and rambling romanticism. The Werkstätten are also part of the sphere of influence of this alternative scene. – Henry van de Velde moves to Berlin. At the German Tailors' Conference, the artist, whose works are now in high demand, speaks on the topic of "reform dress". – A reformhaus health food store opens in Wuppertal.

**1901** The model colony founded two years earlier on the Mathildenhöhe in Darmstadt shows furnished homes as total works of art in an exhibition titled *A Document of German Art*. Peter Behrens' house is deemed particularly successful. – The first volume of *Kulturarbeiten* (Culture Works) by Paul Schultze-Naumburg strikes a chord with his contemporaries. In his book, the conservative designer denounces the excesses of historicism.

**1902** The Dürer Association in Dresden demands the "aesthetic education of the people" and picks up some 300,000 followers in only ten years, who at the same time form the readership of the magazine *Kunstwart*. – Henry van de Velde relocates to Weimar, where he soon becomes director of the Kunstgewerbeschule (School of Arts & Crafts), which will give birth to the Bauhaus. – The Jugendstil pavilion designed by Peter Behrens at the International Exhibition of Applied Art in Turin makes headlines. – Architect Alfred Grenander, Berliner by choice like Behrens and van de Velde, founds the Werkring, an association for progressive applied arts.

**1903** In the course of a design reform from above, Peter Behrens becomes director of the Kunstgewerbeschule (School of Arts & Crafts) in Düsseldorf. – The thermos and sparkplug are just two of his many inventions. – A black dance troupe from the USA introduces the Cakewalk to Berlin. Ragtime rhythms bring swing to the entertainment industry and start to rock the rigid rules of etiquette.

**1904** At the World Exposition in St. Louis, Germany and its reformists are once again a hit. The presentation conceived by Alfred Grenander is a major success for the "artists of the interior", some of whom first make each other's acquaintance on American soil.

**1905** Vehement debates take place in Germany on what a "beautiful home" should look like. – Richard Riemerschmid, by now a prominent figure, works for the Meissen porcelain factory, the Villeroy & Boch earthenware industry in the Westerwald and for WMF. – Kitchen maker **Poggenpohl** produces furniture in simple Werkstätten style. – **Ludwig Mies van der Rohe** moves to Berlin. – In Dresden, the artists' group Die Brücke begins to paint in a more "straightforward and genuine" manner. – Einstein formulates his theory of relativity.

**1906** At the *III. Deutsche Kunstgewerbe-Ausstellung* (Third German Applied Arts Exhibition) in Dresden, Riemerschmid's *machine-made furniture* is displayed, an extensive program designed for the first time for factory production.

**1907** The Deutscher Werkbund is the first German design association to bring artists and manufacturers together – a model that is then adopted in other countries such as England and Sweden. This educational initiative is driven forward by means of publications and exhibitions, which take place in 1912 in the USA, 1914 in Cologne and 1927 in Stuttgart. Since the aim is also to promote exports, chauvinism is rampant, as demonstrated by fighting words such as "Deutsche Wertarbeit" – high-quality German craftsmanship. – Peter Behrens, a co-founder of the Werkbund, becomes artistic adviser to AEG in Berlin. For the electric company, whose state-of-the-art products have up to that time been cloaked in historicizing styles, the pioneer of industrial design develops a simply designed product range that lend it a more streamlined corporate identity. This comprehensive program is a world premiere.

**1908** Bruno Paul designs the first *Typenmöbel*, or modular furniture, a term the reformers adopt as their own. – In how-to books such as Wohnung und Hausrat. Beispiele neuzeitlicher Wohnräume und ihrer Ausstattung (The Household and Its Contents. Examples of Modern Interiors and Furnishings) Werkstätten products are recommended. – The book Das Haus in der Sonne (The House in the Sun), in which Swedish painter Carl Larsson idealizes the rural family lifestyle, reflects the state of the German psyche.

**1910** A furniture exhibition of the functional "German school" at Paris' Grand Palais receives kudos in the local press. Only France's government reacts negatively and, fearing the dominance of the neighbouring country, postpones the applied arts exhibition scheduled for 1915. – Historicism survives in the form of "Stilmöbel", such as that on view in the German contribution to the Word Exposition in Brussels.

**1911** The Deutsche Werkstätten commission 20 artists to create designs for Das Deutsche Hausgerät, a modular furniture program of a scope never before witnessed. The furniture is designed to appeal to all layers of society. – The Bildungsanstalt für Musik und Rhythmus (Educational Institute for Music and Rhythm) established in Hellerau becomes the cradle of Modern Dance. – **Walter Gropius** receives a contract from the Fagus Works in Alfeld near Hanover to build a factory that will come to be considered the archetype of functionalism. – The Tango wave sweeps Europe.

**1912** The *Werkbund Annuals book* series is launched (until 1920). – An exhibition of over 1,000 objects organized by the Werkbund tours the USA. This is the largest-scale design campaign to date. – The **WK** association for "Wohnungskunst" (home art), inspired by the Werkstätten and supplied by the **Behr** company, provides stylistic reform with a further commercial foothold. – Exhibitions such as *Gediegenes Gerät fürs Haus* (Tasteful Home Furnishings) in Dresden-Hellerau or the *Wohnungsausstellung* (Home Exhibition) in Bielefeld convey the new reserve in home furnishings.

**1914** The *Werkbund Exhibition* in Cologne, an imposing showcase of the new wave in design, has to close early due to the outbreak of world war. Many intellectuals are infected with war fever. – The steel helmet, a remarkably functional design, comes to symbolize the German military.

**1915** The *Deutsches Warenbuch* (German Book of Goods), which is like a travel guide to exemplary products, ennobles basic forms. – In the midst of the war, the Werkbund puts on a show of German furniture in London, and later in Basel, Bern and Copenhagen.

**1917** Werkbund co-founder Paul Schultze-Naumburg designs the Cecilienhof in Potsdam for the Crown Prince and his wife, a 176-room palace in the English cottage style. The Werkstätten have now made it to the top – the imperial household. However, in a population forced to subsist on starvation rations, this multimillion-mark project prompts indignation rather than admiration. – Henry van de Velde leaves Germany after being subject to xenophobic indignities.

**1918** The First World War ends with capitulation and revolution.

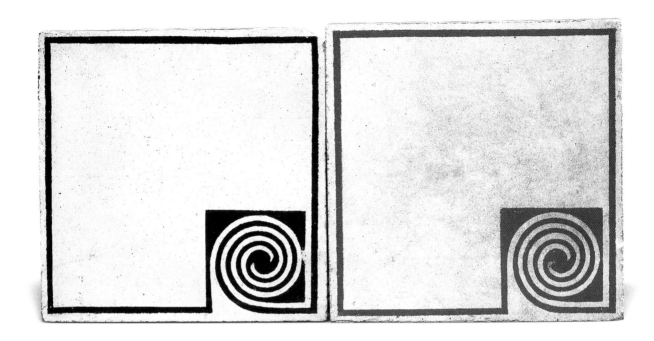

ILLUSTRATIONS:
above: Wall tiles by Peter Behrens for Villeroy & Boch, 1904
below l.: Desk by Bruno Paul, 1908
below r.: Chair ("Hellerau-Stuhl") by Richard Riemerschmid
for Deutsche Werkstätten Hellerau, 1918

15

# 1919 – 1945 A clean slate

**1919** The first German republic and the state-run Bauhaus are established in Weimar. Founding director **Walter Gropius** sets up his academy in the Werkstätten tradition. – Along with the Kaiser and the German Reich, the old values have also been swept away. Censorship has been abolished. Feelings are mixed – a new awakening takes place against the backdrop of an apocalyptic mood. Dance fever breaks out in Berlin. The magazine *Dada* shocks the citizenry.

**1920** Gropius designs the cubic *F 51* chair for his director's office at the Bauhaus – tantamount to a manifesto of interior design. **Josef Albers** and **Marcel Breuer** join the Bauhaus, which acts like a magnet for young, future-hungry artists. Expressionist Johannes Itten, now a master at the Bauhaus, brings 15 female students with him from Vienna. Abstract carpets are produced in the weaving mill. – Jazz rhythms and pageboys are all the rage. A military putsch is warded off through a general strike. The young, deeply cleft democracy is left reeling. – In the Expressionist film *The Cabinet of Dr. Caligari*, in which light and scenery play leading roles, there is not a right angle in sight.

**1921** Dutch architect Theo van Doesburg, co-founder of the artists' group "de Stijl", holds guest lectures for the Bauhaus, to which the formal ascetic contributes vital impulses. Reduction to essentials is now the order of the day. The Bauhaus sees itself as a laboratory for industry and endeavours to develop "types" exemplifying whole groups of products.

**1922** The magazine *die form* published by the Werkbund is the ancestor of all design magazines. – In his book *Die Schöne Wohnung* (The Dwelling Beautiful), Hermann Muthesius shows models for interiors in Werkstätten style. The book soon attains the status of required reading for interior designers and is brought out more than a dozen times until the end of the 1960s, frequently in completely revised editions. – The Schauburg opens in Cologne, a large cinema like the ones that will soon spring up in all the major cities.

**1923** The model home "Am Horn", with which the Bauhaus presents its work for the first time, is an experiment in "Neues Wohnen", New Design for Living. The furnishings are based on concepts in which mechanics and modularity play an important role, such as in the innovative children's room by **Alma Buscher**. But the truly sensational aspect of the show is the shocking simplicity of the interiors. – In Hamburg **Karl Schneider** designs Villa Michaelsen, an early work of the "Neues Bauen" (New Building) and "Offenes Wohnen" (Open Living) movements. – Currency depreciation reaches a climax. Bread distribution begins. The first entertainment show is broadcast on the radio.

**1924** The economy begins to recover. Berlin becomes the world's cultural capital. – *Form ohne Ornament* (Form Without Ornament) is the title of a touring exhibition of the German Werkbund, which provides the Modernists with a motto. – **Marianne Brandt** revolutionizes the dining table with her ornament-free *Tee-Extrakt-Kännchen* (Tea Extract Pot). – Now ennobled as the "Bauhaus Lamp", the *WA 24*, a joint work by Carl J. Jucker and **Wilhelm Wagenfeld**, is one of the first products to become a type, but fails to catch on immediately. – The Georgsgarten colony is established in Celle. Its architect, **Otto Haesler**, anticipating Zeilenbau (linear building), already incorporates combined living/dining rooms and small kitchen niches that will become the model for the functional Frankfurt Kitchen of 1926.

**1925** In the *B3* tubular steel easychair designed by Marcel Breuer, which is reduced like a bicycle to a simple frame, the aimed-for fusion of industrial and creative forces finds incisive expression. – Socialist Ernst May, now chief city planner for Frankfurt, heads up the most ambitious residential project of classical Modernism. Well over 10,000 apartments are built, for which **Ferdinand Kramer** develops simple type-based modular furniture. The

*Frankfurt Bed*, which can be tilted up into the wall during the day, is one of his space-saving accomplishments. In the midst of the "New Frankfurt", which has now become a further avant-garde mecca, the **Braun** company erects its new factory. – Public residential building projects get underway. In the suburb of Britz, the first large residential development in green surroundings is built according to plans by Bruno Taut. Two years later, Taut presents his ideas on furnishings in the book *Ein Wohnhaus* (A House to Live In), including a dining table in which a black rubber coating replaces the white tablecloth. – Exhibitions reflect the spirit of the times. In Dresden the theme is *Wohnung und Siedlung* (House and Housing Development), one of the hot topics of the day. *Neue Sachlichkeit* (New Objectivity) in Mannheim shows the crystal-clear realism that has taken shape in Germany. The title becomes a headline for Modernism. The *Exposition des Arts Décoratifs* in Paris gives the Art Deco style its name.

**1926** The Bauhaus moves to Dessau into a new building that approaches quite closely the ideal of a functionalist total work of art. The event is lent drama by, for example, the use of the new tubular steel furniture, tangible symbols of the anti-cosiness aesthetic. The school encompasses seven master studios in which a cool ambience is displayed for the benefit of visiting journalists. Favourite words bandied about by the domestic rebels are "air" and "light". These qualities are achieved through large windows and the monochrome white of the walls, which make the rooms seem all the emptier. – The magazines bauhaus and Das *Neue Frankfurt* become mouthpieces and discussion forums for the movement. – In Weimar **Erich Dieckmann** continues to design modern furnishings at the ex-Bauhaus, now dubbed the Bauhochschule (University of Architecture). – Mart Stam from the Netherlands, later a guest lecturer at the Bauhaus, invents the Freischwinger, or cantilevered chair, a furniture genre that will become a major hit the following year with Mies van der Rohe's *MR 10* easychair. – Margarete Schütte Lihotzky rationalizes cooking in her *Frankfurt Kitchen*. It becomes the prototype for all compact linear kitchens. – Functionalism, writes Hermann Muthesius in the second edition of his book *Die Schöne Wohnung* (The Dwelling Beautiful) is, as Jugendstil before it, merely an "eccentric" intermezzo. – In Europe Charleston fever rages. The "Roaring 20s" are off to a wild start.

**1927** The model housing development in Stuttgart-Weissenhof attracts an array of young architects who represent "Neues Wohnen", the new style of domesticity, including Josef Frank, Walter Gropius, Le Corbusier, Ludwig Mies van der Rohe, Hans Scharoun and Mart Stam. A radical break with all that has gone before, their domestic concepts seem more uniform than they actually are. Although, or perhaps precisely because, the project is just as controversial as the Bauhaus, it gives the modern movement a decided push. – Huge apartment blocks are built in Hamburg, such as the Heidburg, whose 470 units are decorated by architect Karl Schneider. In Hamburg's Gewerkschaftshaus (Union House), the exhibition *Neues Wohnen* shows how existing furnishings can be transformed to "look modern", i.e. freed of ornament. The reform of domesticity and living has made inroads into society under the Social Democrats, even though workers often take a sceptical view of the proposed changes. – **WK** brings the first wall unit system onto the market with its modular furniture program *Aufbaumöbel*. The furniture can be purchased piece by piece. A wall unit that costs around 300 marks is a major purchase for a working-class family earning a maximum of 100 marks per month. – Berlin theatre director Erwin Piscator, who turns performances into media spectacles drawing on the assistance of constructivist artist László Moholy-Nagy, has Marcel Breuer redecorate his apartment. The provocatively barren interior attracts tremendous attention in the press. – The young English artist Francis Bacon travels to Berlin to experience the libertine lifestyle there first-hand and sets off a tubular furniture mania upon his return to London.

**1928** The *Frankfurter Register* is published. This catalogue of products

| | |
|---|---|
| **1919** | Berker founded |
| **1921** | Braun founded |
| **1920** | *F 51* Easychair<br>Bauhaus Carpets |
| **1922** | Bauhaus Door-Handle |
| **1923** | Loewe founded |
| **1924** | *WA 24* Table Lamp<br>Tea-Extract-Pot |
| **1925** | Albers Nesting Tables<br>*B 3* Club Chair<br>König + Neurath founded<br>Walter Knoll founded<br>Weko founded |
| **1926** | *HMB 25* Hanging Lamp<br>*B 9* Nesting Tables<br>*Frankfurt Kitchen* |
| **1927** | *Kramer Chair*<br>*MR 10* Chair<br>Alno founded<br>Koziol founded |
| **1928** | *B 35* Easychair |
| **1929** | *MR 90 / Barcelona* Easychair<br>*B 32* Chair<br>Hewi founded |
| **1930** | Bauhaus Wallpaper<br>*MR 50 / Brno* Chair<br>*1930* Light Switch<br>*6632* Desk Lamp<br>Interstuhl founded |
| **1931** | *Urbino* Porcelain Tableware<br>*ST 14* Chair<br>*Form 1382* Porcelain Tableware |
| **1932** | *Eiermann* Shelf |
| **1933** | *S 179* Serving Trolley |
| **1934** | *S 285* Desk<br>Erco founded<br>Vitra founded |
| **1936** | *2200 Olympic Chair* |
| **1937** | Interlübke founded |
| **1938** | Haba founded |
| **1939** | Kusch + Co founded |

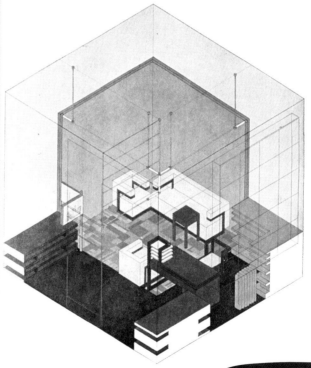

ILLUSTRATIONS:
above: Furniture by Marcel Breuer, 1927
mid: Director's room by Walter Gropius, 1919
below: Table by Ludwig Mies van der Rohe, 1927

exemplifying the "new objectivity" is a treasure trove for architects. The first edition shows lamps by Christian Dell. – The Opel "Rocket Car" breaks speed records at the Avus track in Berlin.

**1929** The German pavilion at the World Exposition in Barcelona, built by Ludwig Mies van der Rohe and furnished with his own designs, declares Neue Sachlichkeit as the official style of the republic. – In Frankfurt the exhibition *The Chair* shows modern seating from various countries. – The *Neue Typografie* is exhibited in Magdeburg. There is no need to visit a museum to see it, however: clear-cut typefaces are now also being used in advertising. Frankfurt graphic artist Robert Michel, for example, designs typefaces for Esso and Shell that lend the companies a clear, streamlined corporate style. – *Befreites Wohnen* (Liberated Living) by Siegfried Giedion is published – yet another educational reference work in design. – At an international conference in Frankfurt, attendees discuss "Living at Subsistence Level". – The first *Cologne Furniture Fair* is held in the new trade fair building. – The stock market crash in New York plunges the world into an economic crisis.

**1930** The **Bauhaustapeten** (Bauhaus Wallpapers) are the first products to be branded with the school's name. – Two modernists put their designs on the market: Otto Haesler with *celler volks-möbeln* (celle folk furniture) and Karl Schneider with *Typenmöbeln* (type-based furniture). – Bruno Paul develops the *Wachsende Wohnung* (Growing Home), another additive furniture system. – The last scene of the musical film *Die Drei von der Tankstelle* (Three Good Friends) takes place in a corporate headquarters office that bears all the marks of the Neue Sachlichkeit. The actual model used for the film is the new Shell Building in Berlin.

**1931** The completely revised edition of *Die Schöne Wohnung* is a panorama of "Neues Wohnen" (New Design for Living). – Neue Sachlichkeit reaches its zenith – and department store shelves. Porcelain dishware such as the service *1382* by Hermann Gretsch and **Urbino** by Trude Petri show that the new style has also found a place on the dining table. Clarity is the code for progress. – A Jewish synagogue is built in Plauen in the style of the "Neues Bauen" (New Building).

**1932** Six million Germans are out of work. The economic and political situation comes to a head. – At the Berlin summer show *Sonne, Luft und Haus für alle* (Sun, Air and House for Everyone) 24 architects present entries in the competition *Das wachsende Haus* (The Growing House), small-format model homes that can be expanded. Represented are Erich Mendelsohn, Hans Scharoun and **Egon Eiermann**. – The exhibition *Architecture: International Exhibition* at New York's Museum of Modern Art introduces German functionalism on US shores.

**1933** Democracy is abolished under Reichs Chancellor Hitler. As a symbol of so-called "cultural Bolshevism", the Bauhaus must close its doors, not least due to its excessively international orientation. – The repression of dissidents prompts a wave of emigration among intellectuals, including almost the entire Bauhaus faculty and numerous proponents of Neue Sachlichkeit. – Hitler forges contacts with the Vereinigte Werkstätten (United Workshops), which decorate a number of rooms for prominent Nazi figures. The vestibule of the "Führer's Apartment" in the Old Reichs Chancellery is the first "Third Reich" interior designed to inspire awe and fear.

**1934** The book *Die Schöne Wohnung* is issued yet again in the 1931 edition. – Hitler demands "simplicity" and a "dignified stance" as features of a "German style", which never actually comes into being due to general confusion as to who is in charge.

**1935** Wilhelm Wagenfeld is the first artist to join corporate management, at the Lausitz Glassworks. The functionalist, who made glass popular in the household, is the most prominent example of the astounding continuity of Modernism during the Nazi period. Numerous Bauhaus students also find a niche in the regime. – Sales figures for tubular steel furniture rise significantly during the 1930s. Zeppelins, as emblems of the Reich, continue to be furnished with these modern pieces. – Hitler's "Berghof" on Obersalzberg Mountain is praised as an ideal "German home". The interior was designed by the Vereinigte Werkstätten in a style oscillating between farmer's parlour, symbols of power and a relapse into historicism. Echoes of Neuschwanstein are hard to overlook.

**1936** At the *Olympic Games* in Berlin, the regime makes a show of cosmopolitanism. Swing music sets the scene in the Berlin bars. The athletes sit on the lightweight plywood chair **2200 Frankfurter Stuhl**. – Most filling stations and rest stops along the new, aesthetically orchestrated autobahns are built in "homeland preservation style". The interiors look just as rustic. – The blood and earth ideology leads to a preference for arts & crafts, which however remain a marginal phenomenon. The numerous feature films produced by UFA and Hollywood are more to the public's taste.

**1937** The German Pavilion at the World Exposition in Paris is a prime example of the brute architecture of dictatorship.

**1939** In *Deutsche Warenkunde* (The Book of German Goods), a comprehensive almanac of exemplary objects of daily use published by the Ministry of Propaganda, products by émigré artists are also recommended, such as the Oranier Stove by Walter Gropius. The authors include modernists like Hermann Gretsch and Hans Schwippert. – An accompanying show at the Leipzig Trade Fair once again shows *Deutsches Wohnen* (German Design for Living), for a long time giving this descriptor a Nazi tinge and rendering it unusable. – The Second World War begins.

**1940** In a mood of sure victory, Germany launches a domestic education offensive. How-to guides recommend a moderate form of Modernism. The five-volume work *Hausrat, der zu uns passt. Ein Wegweiser für alle, die sich zeitgemäß einrichten wollen* (Today's Household. A Guide to Contemporary Home Furnishing) is published by Hermann Gretsch, who holds several official posts and also furnishes the training compounds of the Deutsche Arbeitsfront (German Labour Front). – Construction begins on the concentration camp in Auschwitz. – The first air attacks destroy residential areas.

**1941** Various state offices publish how-to guides for domestic surroundings, such as *Deutscher Hausrat* (German Household Goods), a model collection from the Reichsheimstättenamt (Reichs Department of Housing), which also receives the seal of approval of the Deutsche Arbeitsfront. – In the new edition of *Die Schöne Wohnung*, the standard work for interior designers, a veiled Modernism likewise prevails. With some exceptions: On a tubular steel table by Josef Hillerbrand stand *Urbino* dishes by Trude Petri.

**1945** World War II is over. In Berlin alone, over half a million homes have been destroyed.

ILLUSTRATIONS:
left: Desk lamp by Christian Dell for Römmler, around 1930
below l.: *273/10* night table by Bruno Paul for
Deutsche Werkstätten Hellerau,1931
below r.: Handle for the *Frankfurt Kitchen*
by Margarete Schütte-Lihotzky, 1926

**1946** Living space is a luxury in Germany's ruined cities.

**1947** Interior designer **Michael Bayer** invents a swivel-out sofa. This kind of space-saving furniture is needed more than ever. – After a long cultural drought, people come out to exhibitions and the theatre in droves. American jazz and Boogie-Woogie provide the soundtrack for the new turning point in Germany.

**1948** The émigré German avant-garde resumes the modernist trend in exile. With *Mechanization Takes Command*, Siegfried Giedion chronicles their progress, as does Nikolaus Pevsner one year later with *Pioneers of Modern Design*. – In the western occupation zones, the "D-Mark" revs up the economy. – The West German Constitutional Convention meets in Bonn in the auditorium of the former Teaching Academy. The later parliament building is erected in the style of "Neues Bauen".

**1949** Lively exhibition activities reflect the contemporary dilemma: *Wie Wohnen?* (How to Furnish the Home?) is one of the most frequently asked questions of the day, finding its answer in an exhibition in Stuttgart and Karlsruhe. The solution lies in lightweight, often folding multifunctional furniture pieces. – At the *Cologne Furniture Fair*, which now resumes for the first time since the war, heavy-set "Stilmöbel", old-fashioned pieces in historical styles, still dominate. The Deutscher Werkbund responds with its own counter-showcase; furniture prototypes are put on display under the old familiar title *Neues Wohnen*. – Finally, Max Bill of Switzerland sets down the first commandment for the next design reform in his exhibition *Die Gute Form*, which is at heart about domestic lifestyle. The second modern period has begun. – The swivel chair *S 41* is one of the first furniture pieces manufactured by **Wilde + Spieth**, on the initiative of architect **Egon Eiermann**. His designs make the company one of the main suppliers of post-war Modernism. – With the introduction of FM radio, the clumsy "standard radio set" oriented on the style of Stilmöbel makes its way into German homes. As the first major purchase by many households, it is at once a symbol of the "Economic Miracle" and of the restoration of the country. – The Federal Republic of Germany and the German Democratic Republic are created and become hostile siblings in the Cold War. West Berlin is now a geographic island. Although in the GDR there are some initiatives to forge a connection to the modernist style that is making inroads in the West, these can be realized only sparingly under the "social realist" dictatorship. Even Mart Stam and **Marianne Brandt** as executives at the new Institute of Industrial Design in East Berlin are ultimately unable to toe the Stalinist line.

**1950** Young Philip **Rosenthal** is named head of advertising in the family enterprise and proceeds to mould it into the epitome of "good form" while inventing the idea of "designer as product author". One of the firm's employees is the young artist **Hans Theo Baumann**, who made a spectacular debut with a plexiglass chair for **Vitra**, at the time still called Fehlbaum.

**1951** A new generation sets the course for the future. Following the death of company founder Max **Braun**, his sons Erwin and Artur take over the helm of the Frankfurt phonograph firm, albeit not entirely voluntarily. The changing of the guard proceeds in similar fashion at Rosenthal, **Bofinger** and **Wilkhahn**. Young, forward-looking entrepreneurs, who also include Heinz Röntgen, founder of **Nya Nordiska**, are disillusioned by the experience of war and set off on a quest for something different. Design, jazz and modern art are just the thing.

**1952** Heinrich Löffelhardt becomes artistic director of **Arzberg**. 13 services bring "good form", now also featuring the fashionable organic flow of line, to West German tables. – Archrival Rosenthal engages **Wilhelm Wagenfeld**, who simultaneously delivers designs to **WMF** and various lamp manufacturers. The amazingly productive old master, together with **Hans Gugelot** and **Herbert Hirche**, counts among the great mentors of the second new beginning in design. – In yet another completely revised edition of *Die Schöne Wohnung*, American and Scandinavian interiors are included for the first time.

**1953** Instruction commences at the Hochschule für Gestaltung Ulm (Ulm Academy of Design), which views itself as successor to the Bauhaus. It likewise has a strong international focus and is just as magnetic an attraction for a young avant-garde. The students draw using the new *Rapidograph* ink pen from Rotring and sit on the *Ulmer Hocker* (Ulm Stool, 1955) in which a few of the academy's most fundamental concepts are incorporated. It is simple as can be and astoundingly versatile. Hans Gugelot will later develop a furniture system for children based on this stool. – The Rat für Formgebung (German Design Council) is founded in Frankfurt and the Industrieforum (Industry Forum) in Hanover, two custodians of exemplary design. Both adopt an Italian invention: the design award. – The Museum of Modern Art in New York shows **Thonet** furniture, the first solo exhibition for an industrial enterprise.

**1954** New building developments spring up everywhere. – Along with etiquette guides that teach people how to act properly, the number of publications that counsel reason and good taste when furnishing a new apartment is on the rise. The invitation *Wir richten eine Wohnung ein* (Let's Furnish a Home) comes from the pen of Michael Bayer. His words of wisdom make a good impression not only on readers, but also on the company **Interlübke**, at the time still known as Gebrüder Lübke. Senior head Leo Lübke hires the young modernist as art director, an occupation that hasn't even been invented yet. Most people discover via radio that Germany has become world champion in football.

**1955** At the *Funkausstellung* (Radio Exhibition) in Düsseldorf, the Braun company presents its new devices, designed with help from Ulm. The crystal-clear forms betray a spiritual kinship with the Bauhaus and make the common "radio furniture" look hopelessly old-fashioned. The modular trade fair stand, designed by **Otl Aicher** to impress, causes a sensation. A basic idea behind Braun's strategy is to build a product range that goes with modern-day furniture. This is why the company enters into a liaison with the German-American furniture maker Knoll International. – Architect Georg Leowald creates the first "designer chairs" for Wilkhahn. – The **Behr** furniture series *Zerlegbar* (Take-Apart, known as *BMZ* for short – Behr Möbel Zerlegbar) is one of the early wall unit systems, and one of the best-selling. A German innovation catches on. – At the *documenta 1* art exhibition in Kassel, a city that was heavily bombed in the war, people can view abstract art in the original, with the name Picasso as derogatory code word. The newly gained freedom of expression is practiced en masse in kidney-shaped tables, shell chairs and slanted chair legs. Even Thonet lends its chairs and tables the popular expressionist touch. – **Peter Raacke** develops cubic combi-stoves, forerunners of the appliances that will become standard in fitted kitchens.

**1956** The friendship between Philip Rosenthal and Erwin Braun gives rise to a circle of like-minded manufacturers who start a design initiative, among them Knoll International, **Rasch** and **WMF**. One of their major triumphs is the exhibition *form, farbe, fertigung* (form, colour, fabrication), which tours Germany for three years, confronting a quarter of a million visitors with exemplary design. – The phonograph combination *SK 4*, which Hans Gugelot develops for Braun, is the first radio made of metal, with a see-through cover, and makes just as shocking an impression as **Marcel Breuer's** tubular steel furniture three decades before. The scandalously naked device ushers in a new era in both industrial and domestic design. – Also to Gugelot's credit, the trailblazing *M 125* wall unit system, which he spent six years fine-tuning, goes into production in a completely revised form at a new Bofinger plant. – In Kronberg, **Otto Zapf** and **Dieter Rams**, interior designer at Braun for the past two years, are busy brooding over new furniture ideas. – The exhibition *Künstlerisches Schaffen*, Industrielles Gestalten (Creative

| | |
|---|---|
| **1946** | JAB Anstoetz founded<br>Planmöbel founded |
| **1948** | *E 10* Basket Chair<br>Brühl founded |
| **1949** | *SE 42* Chair<br>Bulthaup founded |
| **1950** | *SE 68* Chair<br>*M 125* Cabinet System |
| **1952** | *1034* Door-Handle<br>Dornbracht founded |
| **1953** | *SE 18* Folding Chair<br>Deep Easychair with Footstool<br>*Max and Moritz* Salt and Pepper Shakers<br>Table Base with Cross-Bracing<br>Keuco founded |
| **1954** | S 664 Chair<br>COR founded |
| **1955** | Ulm Stool |
| **1956** | *SK 4 / Phonosuper* Phono Combination<br>*369* Easychair<br>*GB 1085* Bed<br>*Bar Trolley* |
| **1958** | *HF 1* Television Set |
| **1959** | *Berlin* Porcelain Tableware<br>*Quinta* Upholstered Furniture System<br>*mono-a* silverware<br>*studio 2* Hi-Fi-System<br>*TC 100* Stacking Tableware |
| **1960** | *606* Shelf System<br>Gaggenau founded<br>Schönbuch founded |
| **1961** | Mobilia founded |
| **1962** | *RZ 62* Easychair<br>*Britz* Wall Lamp |
| **1963** | *SL* Closet System |
| **1964** | *K 4999* Children's Chair<br>*BA 1171* Bofinger Chair<br>Nya Nordiska founded<br>Rolf Benz founded |

ILLUSTRATIONS:
above: Drawing (advertisement) of an early furniture
programme by Michael Bayer for Interlübke, 1959
below: *SK 1* radio by Artur Braun and Fritz Eichler
for Braun, 1961

# 1946 – 1965

Work, Industrial Design) in Osnabrück, which is opened by German President Theodor Heuss, displays modern art against a backdrop of abstract wallpapers made by **Rasch**.

**1957** Numerous modernist projects are undertaken in the adolescent years of the republic. The *Interbau* show in West Berlin features a model housing development in the new Hansa quarter for which a circle of international architects were recruited, among them Alvar Aalto, **Walter Gropius** and Oskar Niemeyer. In the city on the front lines of the Cold War, the elaborate event is also a boastful gesture on the part of the West. Just like back in 1901 at Darmstadt's Mathildenhöhe and 1927 in Stuttgart-Weissenhof, the model homes are the true attraction for visitors. In 60 examples of ideal interior decoration and furnishings, the architects have packed the homes full of modern-day furniture, in which the Scandinavians set the pace and plenty of Braun appliances are on view. **Herbert Hirche**, himself a Braun designer and architect at *Interbau*, is the man behind this optimal form of marketing, which made Braun famous all over the world. – The model *KM 3* from Braun becomes the mother of all kitchen appliances. – Peter Raacke brings the new systematic approach to the world of office furniture with his *Zeitgewinn* (Time Gain) program. – The race to outer space is launched with the Russian *Sputnik*.

**1958** Egon Eiermann's glass pavilion at the World Exposition in Brussels is a showcase of the new dawn of German design. Just three decades after *Barcelona*, functional minimalism is once again the official style of the German state. – **Wilhelm Braun-Feldweg** is appointed Professor of Industrial Design in Berlin, which he transforms into a further hotbed of Neo-Functionalism. – Teenage frenzies following rock'n'roll films and concerts mark the beginning of the era of youthful rebellion in West Germany.

**1959** 120,000 copies of a completely revised version of *Die Schöne Wohnung* are sold by 1963 in four editions. Featured are numerous wall unit and shelf systems, but also an amazing variety of children's rooms. – Students at the Ulm Academy put the analytical curriculum into practice in their dissertations. While **Hans "Nick" Roericht** develops the first functional dishware, stackable of course, Herbert Lindinger intellectually dissects the radio. His "building block concept" ultimately engenders Braun's *studio 2*, the archetypical stereo system. – Peter Raacke's sleek, straight-lined silverware *mono-a* is tantamount to a manifesto against the contemporary wave of culinary overindulgence. – Unemployment is virtually unknown, and the phrase "standard of living" makes sense for the first time when applied to normal everyday consumers. The "motorized Biedermeier" populace surround themselves with furnishings in the weighty, ornately decorated style known as "Gelsenkirchener Barock". Ponderous historicizing "Stilmöbel" furniture dominates the catalogues of the big mail-order firms.

**1960** The Rosenthal Studio House in Nuremberg is a test run for the world's first designer chain store. – In Hamburg the magazine *Schöner Wohnen* comes out, the first journal devoted exclusively to the domestic environment, whose name, roughly translatable as "Better Homes", becomes part of the vernacular. Market researchers soon count over two million readers. One of the most popular columns is **Peter Maly's** *Skizzenbuch* (Sketchbook), in which the young interior designer solves readers' furnishing dilemmas. – The Bauhaus Archive is established on the Mathildenhöhe in Darmstadt. – Copenhagen is the unofficial design capital of the world.

**1961** Dieter Rams is named head of design at Braun. The company, along with the department under his charge and he himself will become legendary. Rams belongs to the generation of war children whose formative years took place during the second period of Modernism and who has left his mark on the image of German design up until the present day. This cohort also includes such prominent personalities as **Klaus Franck**, Peter Maly, **Ulf Moritz**, Peter Raacke, Hans "Nick" Roericht and mavericks like **Luigi Colani**. – The Berlin Wall is also something new to the world.

**1962** In Italy, Dino Gavina reissues Marcel Breuer's tubular steel chair *B 3* as *Wassily* and declares it a "classic". – Refrigerators and washing machines now take the form of straight-edged cubes. – Slick, smooth-lined cars such as the BMW *1500*, the compact Opel *Kadett* or the Mercedes-Benz *230 SL* the following year demonstrate that even this key industry is searching for the kind of "pure" form inaugurated in Ulm.

**1963** The chancellor's bungalow in Bonn, a glass box created by architect Sep Ruf, is furnished by **Herta-Maria Witzemann**. Just as was the case one year before when the Neue Nationalgalerie by Ludwig Mies van der Rohe opened in Berlin, the West German republic is once again cloaking itself in an immaculate modern image. Chancellors from Ludwig Erhard to Helmut Kohl make their homes in this purist ambience, which veritably compels forward-looking thinking. – The Auschwitz trials begin in Frankfurt. – The visit of US President John F. Kennedy to West Berlin is akin to a triumphal procession.

**1964** Among the much-admired innovations on display at the *Cologne Furniture Fair* are the **Bofinger Chair** and the combination sofa set **Conseta** from **COR**, a seating group of heretofore unimagined simplicity and variability. – The Ruhr University is built in Bochum, a concrete machine for learning and one of the biggest construction projects in West Germany. The libraries are outfitted with the brand-new modular shelving system *606* by Dieter Rams. – The song *I Want to Hold Your Hand* by the Beatles storms the US charts. The pop revolution goes global.

**1965** The exhibition *Good Form* in London, intended to boost exports, demonstrates the edge the West Germans have gained in the design realm. Some visitors, however, are struck by the strange contrast between the cultivated clarity of the exhibits and the wholly different look of the surrounding world. Their standards have once again started coming apart at the seams. From London, now the capital of pop, come new cultural role models.

ILLUSTRATIONS:
above: *Addiform* upholstered furniture system by Rolf Benz, 1964
below l.: *Ming* vase by Trude Petri for StPM Berlin, 1963
below r.: *Ssymmank* floor lamp by Günter Ssymmank for Mawa, 1959

# 1966 – 1979 Plastic conventions

**1966** Grandma's outmoded household goods are thrown away and the world is once again reinvented. Since progress is now expressed in plastics, all eyes turn toward the chemical industry of Cologne and the yearly *Furniture Fair* that takes place there. – Two major unconventional thinkers of German design bring Pop Art to the people before it can be seen in Germany in the form of art. **Peter Raacke** sells his *Papp* cardboard furniture system in poster-bright colours. **Ingo Maurer** makes his *Bulb* lamp into a cult object. – When seating specialist **Wilkhahn** hires progressive minds from Ulm, the company achieves the status of paragon of "good form". Others follow suit in the ensuing years, among them Lufthansa, **Erco** and **FSB**. – No one wants to make do any longer without a television, refrigerator and washing machine – and a white, Formica-fronted linear kitchen and modular stereo system are likewise musts for the modern home. – The miniskirt liberates the legs. – In the World Cup final at Wembley Stadium, the Germans prove that they can also be gracious losers.

**1967** Television is now in colour. The message *All You Need Is Love* goes around the world, live. The Beatles become harbingers of hippiedom and TV marketing. – Arno **Votteler** designs a container ship utilizing a modular, additive system. – **Hans "Nick" Roericht** founds an idea factory called Design Research in Ulm.

**1968** The last edition of *Die Schöne Wohnung* is bigger and more colourful than ever before, with 250 pages and over 600 illustrations. – An exhibition in Cologne shows Pop Art from the USA for the first time in Germany, a culture shock that forms the lively focus of *documenta 4*. Pop Art and pop music join forces. New styles now issue from the "underground". – Plastic furniture changes people's visual and sitting habits. There are sculptural pieces like Peter Ghyczy's *Gartenei* (Garden Egg) or the slick *TV-relax* by **Luigi Colani**, as well as ergonomically optimized sitting machines such as the *Floris* chairs designed by Günter Beltzig and *SM 400* by **Gerd Lange**. – Inflated visions are coupled with strict pragmatism. While **Rolf Heide** stacks sleeping surfaces on top of each other like industrial pallets in his *Stapelliege* (Stacked Lounger), **Habit** introduces the first stackable sofa: the *Wohnlandschaft* (Lounge Landscape). – Satellite housing developments start to spring up on green fields everywhere. Passing lanes are added to the motorways and pedestrian zones to city centres. Everything seems to fit into the neat grid projected by Ulm. – At the exhibition *50 Years of Bauhaus* in Stuttgart, Germany and the rest of the world discover a long-buried past. – The Academy of Design in Ulm closes.

**1969** Willy Brandt, the first Social Democrat to become Federal Chancellor, wants to venture "more democracy". – The new Bohemian lifestyle caught up in anti-Vietnam demonstrations and the loose mores of the sexual revolution is showcased in the fiction film *Rote Sonne* (Red Sun), whose protagonists loll about on mattresses on the floor, but entrust their Beat music records only to a cool record player from **Braun**. They are not only children of Marx and Afri-Cola, but also fuse the world of shag rugs and plastic furniture into a new kind of counter-culture backdrop. How this new scene can be made commercially profitable is soon demonstrated by stores **Magazin** and **Mawa**. The apartment of the film's female star is furnished with an ultramodern piece of furniture: the *Bofinger Chair*. – Systematic interior design makes its way into middle-class apartments. The combination cabinets with their roots in classical Modernism are developed further into room-encompassing programs and functional wall units, a process that still continues today, helped along by designers such as **Hans Gugelot, Herbert Hirche, Jürgen Lange** and **Peter Maly**. – **Burkhard Vogtherr** wins the new Bundespreis Gute Form (Federal Award for Good Design) for a new phonograph/TV combination in four cubes. – **Walter Gropius** and **Ludwig Mies van der Rohe** die in the USA.

**1970** At the *Cologne Furniture Fair*, **Poggenpohl** makes a splash with a spherical kitchen by Luigi Colani: the UFO version of the *Frankfurt Kitchen*.

Going even this kitchen one better is the total interior dubbed Visiona, a psychedelic environment created by Basel-based Danish designer Verner Panton for chemical giant Bayer in the belly of a steamship on the Rhine. – Peter Maly goes out on his own and is taken on board by Leo Lübke as freelance art director at **Interlübke**, becoming one of the first Germans in the furniture industry to attain international standing. – Maly is succeeded at *Schöner Wohnen* by Rolf Heide, who from this post quietly influences West German home design for over two decades through his carefully staged domestic settings. – The plastic door handle *111* opens up a new world of colour. – **Egon Eiermann** dies in Baden-Baden.

**1971** The gigantic *Wohnlandschaft* (Lounge Landscape) with which **Rolf Benz** makes its debut at the *Cologne Furniture Fair* is an invitation to sprawl and another innately German furniture innovation. – In a back courtyard in Stuttgart, a mixture of capitalist criticism and idealism gives birth to the business idea for the Magazin stores. – Molldesign by **Reiner Moll** is the first studio established in Schwäbisch Gmünd, today Germany's secret design capital in the midst of a region known as an incubator for innovation.

**1972** Luigi Colani relocates his studio to Harkotten Castle in eastern Westphalia, a stronghold of bathroom and furniture production. – With the *Olympic Games* in Munich, which for the first time open with a Party of Nations, Germany launches a campaign aimed at improving its image in the world's eyes so that it can once again be considered a welcome member of the international community. The campaign's impresario is **Otl Aicher**, who for the first time develops a homogeneous national image for this kind of large-scale event. The image campaign ranges from logo and pictograms for the various athletic disciplines, to guideposts and uniforms, all the way to functional furnishings for the accommodations in the Olympic Village, a hive-like monument to concrete building. Many of these elements are simply taken for granted in later, comparable events, as is the idea of an overall coherent design and the visual communication of a uniform identity – pioneering achievements that put a contemporary face on what **Peter Behrens** accomplished at the beginning of the century.

**1973** An Arab oil embargo sets off an "energy crisis" and makes plastic taboo. – The "organic food store" becomes another source of wholesome food products.

**1974** Swedish furniture maker Ikea opens its first store near Munich, soon followed by many more. The company, whose early expansion largely takes place in Germany, is in the right place at the right time with its inexpensive furniture range. It becomes the supplier of choice for young, unconventional shoppers, alongside *Schöner Wohnen* the most important arbiter of taste when it comes to home furnishings. – **Hansgrohe** comes out with a completely newfangled showerhead it dubs *Tribel*.

**1975** Herbert Ohl uses net material to create a new kind of chair in his *O-Line*. – Thanks to the *Avantgarde-Kollektion* of wallpapers from **Rasch**, everyone can now surround themselves in Pop Art. – **Flötotto's** all-encompassing *Profilsystem* renders other furniture superfluous.

**1977** **Siegfried Bensinger** is appointed interior design chief in the editorial team at *Schöner Wohnen*, which is still setting trends. The magazine sells its *Buch vom Wohnen* (Book of the Home) via the coffee store chain Tchibo. – The designer label Mawa comes into being in the back courtyards of Berlin-Kreuzberg. – Left-wing terrorism reaches a climax in the "Deutscher Herbst" (German Autumn).

**1978** Robert Venturi's *Learning from Las Vegas* heralds post-modernism. – **Stefan Wewerka** invents anti-functionalism and combines art with seating. He stubbornly refuses to include any right angles in his three-legged *B 1* chair and other equally contorted designs.

ILLUSTRATIONS:
above: Interior with *Polycor* chair by
Luigi Colani for COR, 1968
mid: *Alnoscan* kitchen by Alno, 1965
below: *N 02* easychair by Peter Ghyczy, 1970

# 1980 – 1989 Style rebellion

**1980** *From Bauhaus to Our House* is American writer Tom Wolfe's settling of accounts with the taste dictates of the domestic design ascetics. – The *FS-Linie* swivel chair animates the user to a more active form of sitting.

**1981** All is well apparently in the world of the new German objectivity. The wall clock *ABW 41* by Dietrich Lubs and the *Mono Classic* teapot by Tassilo von Grolmann fuse formal sophistication with technical elegance. – **Otl Aicher's** plea for a more communicative kitchen based on a professional standard is implemented the following year in *System b* from **Bulthaup**. – When the Memphis group in Milan shows wild and whimsical furniture, handmade objects and lamps at an exhibition, the post-modern counter-reformation gets off to a rollicking start. Similarly to what happened with Jugendstil a century earlier, the public, only stunned for a brief moment, reacts as if it had long been waiting for this kind of cheekiness. – **Marcel Breuer** dies in New York.

**1982** The exhibition *Möbel Perdu – Schöneres Wohnen* in Hamburg offers under its suggestive title a panorama of the delight in experimentation that is bubbling up from the underground and congealing into the "Neues Deutsches Design" (New German Design) movement. – **Richard Sapper's** model *9091* is the first "designer water kettle". – Apocalyptic punk or disco. Anything goes. In the 1980s a climate of hedonism reigns. Design, often merely another word for luxury, forms the perfect expression of this mood. What is chic, especially in terms of furniture, is now largely defined in Italy. Different yet co-existing lifestyles crystallize out: the rise of brands such as Bree, **Brühl** or **Rolf Benz** can be viewed against this backdrop, as can the rediscovery of the kitchen and the bathroom. – Frog is Germany's first internationally active design studio. Its Apple desktop computers ring in the PC age and become everyday requisites, joining the ranks of radios and television sets. – Hundreds of thousands demonstrate in vain against nuclear warheads.

**1983** The Möbel Perdu gallery in Hamburg becomes a home base for domestic design revolutionaries. In Germany, unease in the face of the seemingly nature-given hegemony of the Bauhaus paragons could at first find no adequate vent. When Punk and Memphis open the floodgates, there is nothing left to stop the rampages of the young and the restless. They incorporate kitsch and camp, garbage and pop, Bauhaus and the 50s, and last but not least their deep-seated queasiness at traditional German domesticity into their furniture parodies. Unlike the Italian trailblazers, the style rebels in these climes show a marked penchant for raw materials such as stone, steel or untreated wood, also utilizing half-finished goods such as cardboard or cellophane as well as ready-mades found in everyday life. The converted shopping cart **Consumer's Rest** from Stiletto becomes the emblem for the revolt. It is followed in the ensuing years by equally ambivalent caricatures such as the *Verspanntes Regal* (Tense Bookcase) by Wolfgang Laubersheimer, Heinz Landes' concrete cantilevered chair *Solid*, and the *Tabula Rasa* table-and-bench ensemble from Ginbande. – **Marianne Brandt** dies in Kirchberg near Chemnitz.

**1984** The *Zyklus* easychair by **Peter Maly** and the *YaYaHo* lighting system by **Ingo Maurer** represent ingenious syntheses of post-modern whimsy and Teutonic functionalism. – The *T-Line* seating system by **Burkhard Vogtherr** and *Tattomi* (1985) by **Jan Armgardt** boast a high level of innovative charisma and enduring visual impact. – A whole series of quite disparate firms, including **Thonet**, **Tecta**, **Tecnolumen** and **Vitra** as well as later **ClassiCon**, **Richard Lampert** and **sdr+**, develop a historically reflexive relationship to their products. Important milestones in German design for living find their way back into their catalogues. An exception is formed by the company **Anthologie Quartett**, which still today devotes its energies to reviving the bold spirit of the 1980s. – Those who wish to can decorate their homes with the brainchildren of star designers. Brands such as **Alfi**, **FSB** and **WMF** rediscover the designer-branded product once introduced by **Rosenthal**, working sometimes on individual products and sometimes on

an ongoing basis with the industry greats whose names promise quality design, an attractive image and healthy sales. – Let there be light: Following in the footsteps of **Erco**, Ingo Maurer, **Anta**, **Mawa** and **Serien**, **Tobias Grau** establishes yet another upscale brand for German lighting design.

**1985** Galerie Weinand in West Berlin becomes a showcase for "Neues Deutsches Design", or "NDD" for short, with exhibitions such as *Betonmöbel* (Concrete Furniture) or *Griff in den Staub* (Grab the Dust). Although the exciting home design ideas are not taken up by department stores, they do change taste standards thanks to their media presence. – For the first generation of high-speed trains, the *ICE*, Alexander Neumeister designs not only the sleek outer skin, but also the bold interiors. – Herbert H. Schultes is named head designer at Siemens, a corporate giant whose products are ubiquitous in German households. – **Ferdinand Kramer** dies in Frankfurt.

**1986** The Düsseldorf exhibition *Gefühlscollagen – Möbel von Sinnen* (Emotional Collages – Furniture Out of Its Senses) shows objects caught between art and scrap recycling.

**1987** Ironically enough, the style uprising of the 1980s is the work of the first generation of designers, who also studied this field. The deconstruction of cosy complacency they initiated remains however largely a sub-cultural happening. Although it attracts a significant media response, not a single model created in the name of "New German Design" goes into series production. More than a few of its academically trained protagonists return to the universities, such as **Andreas Brandolini** and **Uwe Fischer**, who henceforth form a guild of opinion-makers. The German furniture industry, by contrast, largely ignores the homemade "*Design Spring*". – At documenta 8, visitors recover from the exhibition's first design show by having a coffee at Café *Casino*, bizarrely decorated by the Pentagon group. This is also where users can access the Internet, a technology that is still plagued by connection problems. – **Performa** becomes a precursor of the young German firms committed to profound thought and unpretentious reserve. – The EU starts conferring its own *European Design Award*. – When someone says design, he now means Milan.

**1988** **Dieter Sieger** moves to Harkotten Castle and makes use of its strategic location at least as cleverly as **Luigi Colani** before him.

**1989** The **Spot** easychair by **Stefan Heiliger** and **Anita Schmidt's** sofa *322* are the very incarnation of "designer furniture". – *FNP* by **Axel Kufus** is the first in a long series of cleverly conceived shelf systems to spring from the singular convolutions of the German mind. – Authentics introduces semi-transparent plastic, a small aesthetic refinement that changes the look of the home. – Vitra founds a design museum. – The crumbling of the Berlin Wall comes as a surprise to everyone.

| 1980 | *FS-Line* Office Chair |
| | Tecnolumen founded |
| 1981 | *ABW 41* Wall Clock |
| | *Mono Classic* Teapot |
| 1982 | *Einschwinger* Chair |
| | *9091* Water Kettle |
| 1983 | *Consumer's Rest* Chair |
| | *Allegroh* Tap |
| | Seefelder Möbelwerkstätten founded |
| | Serien founded |
| 1984 | *Kitchen Tree* Kitchen Furniture |
| | *YaYaHo* Ceiling Lamp |
| | *T-Line* Easychair |
| | *Zyklus* Easychair |
| | *Verspanntes Regal* Shelf |
| | Anthologie Quartett founded |
| | Fischer Möbel founded |
| | Tobias Grau founded |
| 1985 | *Art 1* Television Set |
| | *Tattomi* Lounge Chair |
| 1986 | *Solid* Chair |
| | *Flying Carpet* Eayschair |
| | Bisterfeld + Weiss founded |
| 1987 | *Tabula Rasa* Table and Benches |
| | *Trio* Coat Rack |
| | Möller Design founded |
| | Performa founded |
| 1988 | *Lia* Textile Collection |
| 1989 | *WK 698 Spot* Easychair |
| | *Achat* Thermos |
| | *FNP* Shelf System |

ILLUSTRATIONS:
above: *Casino* interior by Gruppe Pentagon
at the *documenta 8*, 1987
mid: Interior with *Zyklus* arm chair and *Cirrus* sofa
by Peter Maly for COR
below: *One From The Heart* floor lamp
by Ingo Maurer, 1989

# 1990–2007 A different view of things

**1990** West Germany adopts the GDR. – The firms **Dedon** and **Zeitraum** take two different approaches to the same principle, revisiting an old material and making it modern. While Dedon ennobles artificial fibre, Zeitraum takes a fresh look at wooden furniture, dusting off an old German myth. – The computer goes mobile. The laptop takes shape.

**1991** **Konstantin Grcic** opens a studio in his hometown of Munich and becomes Germany's premier designer. He launches intense collaboration with the company **ClassiCon** founded one year earlier. – With the high-tech *Arco* tap from Phoenix Design and its retro counterpart *Tara* (1992) by **Sieger Design**, the bathroom becomes a new designer playground. Manufacturers successful on this terrain, such as **Dornbracht**, **Duravit**, **Hansgrohe**, **Keuco** and **Villeroy & Boch**, increasingly become full-service suppliers.

**1992** Swabian designer **Nils Holger Moormann** and Bavarian Hubert Matthias **Sanktjohanser** join forces to establish their own company and, in the process, their own domestic ethos. One century after the emergence of "room art", it is once again the outsiders who strive for an alternative to the pretentious bourgeois style. – Karl Friedrich Schinkel already realized back in the mid-19th century that the garden deserves its own brand of modern furniture. **Fischer Möbel** takes up this tradition anew.

**1993** **Carpet Concept** weaves ideas into its carpets. – The *Virage* washstand by **Reiner Moll** turns the sink into a co-ordinated room element.

**1994** *Endless Shelf* by **Werner Aisslinger** unites simplicity and systematic planning with the idea of infinity. The shelf system concept forms a canvas for the exercise of the typical German virtues. This is demonstrated in the years to come by designs such as *Plattenbau* from **Kaether & Weise**, *Freddy* from **Hertel & Klarhoefer**, *Mein_Back* from **Magazin** and *Screen* from **Performa**. – The office furniture system *Confair* from **Wilkhahn** is at least as flexible as the modern office worker. – When the old AEG is swallowed up by the Swedish Electrolux group, no one yet labels it globalization. – Peter Schreyer becomes head designer at Audi and gives the brand an edge through up-to-the-minute design. – Everybody soon knows what e-mail is.

**1996** The 1990s are founding years, in terms of design for living as in other matters. **e15**, the first German furniture manufacturer to get its start in the new design mecca of London, debuts with *Backenzahn* (Molar). It belongs to a group of young companies that have established themselves on the fringes of the industry and take a fresh view of design. But perfectionism still forms a common denominator. Perhaps, if a certain degree of unity can be achieved, the roots for a third wave of German domestic modernization can be found. Starting things off are brands such as **elmarflötotto**, Nils Holger Moormann, Performa, Sanktjohanser and Zeitraum. Other interesting projects soon join in, including **Jonas & Jonas**, Kaether & Weise, **Raumwerk** and **Leise**. – Stilwerk opens in Hamburg, Germany's first department store for design.

**1998** The fact that even a classical material like glass still harbours a great deal of design potential is demonstrated by no-frills designs like the ingenious pullout table *8950* by **Norbert Beck** and the *Screen* family of lamps by **Peter Maly**. – Two American students invent an invisible "engine" by the name of Google.

**2000** With its designer piano *Pure*, **Sauter** ventures into one of the last design-free zones. – **Extratapete** makes even wallpaper mobile, urging people to take a "different view of things".

**2001** In the light cube *EO* by **Wulf Schneider**, another variation on the theme of the wall unit system, high-tech sets a soothing mood. – *Schöner Wohnen* gets company. When a wave of new home furnishing magazines floods the market, the Hamburg doyenne is still the oldest, but no longer the only one. "Cocooning" is the buzzword of the day, a withdrawal back into the comforts of one's own four walls.

**2002** A steady progression of new, transformable "miracle sofas" come out of Germany. To name just two examples: *Lobby* by **Siegfried Bensinger** and *Scroll* by **Studio Vertijet**. – *Silver* by Hadi Teherani contradicts the general prejudice that swivel chairs can't be sexy.

**2004** The *Milanolight* chair by **Wolfgang C. R. Mezger** is a masterwork of laminated wood, another material that has long been known but whose history is by no means at an end. With seasoned command of his metier and new digital tools, the designer pushes the limits to new extremes.

**2005** **Reiner Moll** reacts to demographic change with *Aquamove*, the first hydraulic shower tap. – Kitchen maker **Alno** is the first furniture manufacturer to set up production in the Arab state of Dubai. Three quarters of a century after the invention of the *Frankfurt Kitchen*, innovative German kitchens are an international export hit. Key players are companies including **Bulthaup**, **Eggersmann** and **Poggenpohl**, as well as **Gaggenau** and **Miele**.

**2007** The claim that nothing really new is presented anymore at the *Cologne Furniture Fair* is put to rest by *Nuf*, the laterally sliding drawer system from Performa. – The Deutscher Werkbund celebrates the hundredth anniversary of its founding, when Germany succeeded in taking the lead, in particular in the key design discipline of home furnishing and decoration, producing a number of designers of international renown. The fact that this is also the case today is evident when we take a look at the wealth of design talent available. Seasoned industry figures such as **Jan Armgardt**, Siegfried Bensinger, Konstantin Grcic, **Gerd Lange**, Peter Maly, Ingo Maurer, Wolfgang C. R. Mezger, Reiner Moll, **Ulf Moritz**, **Anita Schmidt**, Dieter Sieger and **Burkhard Vogtherr** can always be relied on to create cutting-edge products. At the same time, the eminence grise of the second wave of Modernism, including designers like **Luigi Colani**, **Jürgen Lange**, **Peter Raacke**, **Dieter Rams**, **Hans "Nick" Roericht**, **Richard Sapper**, Arno **Votteler** and **Otto Zapf**, have no intention of disappearing into quiet retirement anytime soon. Finally, the eruptive 1980s gave rise to personalities with their own unmistakable signature. Among them are **Uwe Fischer**, **Stefan Heiliger**, **Axel Kufus** and **Christian Werner**. The technological paradigm change of the 1990s, during which the credo "Anything goes" was suddenly made possible by digital tools, engendered a disciplined, but by all means experiment-happy generation. Some talents have yet to impinge on the broad public consciousness, such as **Thomas Althaus**, **Martin Ballendat**, **Norbert Beck**, **Justus Kolberg** or the studios **Lepper Schmidt Sommerlade** and **Neunzig° Design**. Others have already made a name for themselves, including **Werner Aisslinger**, **Stefan Diez**, **Tobias Grau**, **Gioia Meller Markowicz**, **Torsten Neeland** and Studio Vertijet. The reinvention of our interior environment that was already initiated by the "room artists" at the century before last, and which made enormous progress in the first and second waves of Modernism, is still in full swing today. Comprehensive information on German design for living can be found at:

www.formguide.de.

| | |
|---|---|
| **1990** | ClassiCon, Dedon and Zeitraum founded |
| **1991** | *Arco* Tap, *Stitz* Leaning Aid<br>*Picado* Parmesan Knife |
| **1992** | *Tennis* Garden Furniture, *Tara* Tap<br>Nils Holger Moormann founded<br>Sanktjohanser founded |
| **1993** | *Take Five* Hanging Lamp, *Virage* Washstand<br>Carpet Concept founded |
| **1993** | Richard Lampert founded |
| **1994** | *Confair* Office Furniture System<br>*Endless* Shelf Shelf System |
| **1995** | *Eagle* Pullout Table, sdr+ founded |
| **1996** | *Wonder Boxes* Shelf, *Time Documents* Chair<br>*Spanoto* Table, *Menos* Cabinet System, *x-act*<br>Desk System, *Backenzahn* Stool, e15 founded |
| **1997** | *S 20* Kitchen System, *Zettel'z* Hanging Lamp<br>Conmoto founded, Jonas & Jonas founded |
| **1998** | *Happy D* Bathroom Series, *8950* Table<br>*Screen* Lamp, *Hats Off* Coat Rack<br>*Velvet* Silverware, Kaether & Weise founded |
| **1999** | *Sax* Table, *Soft Cell* Chair and Lounger |
| **2000** | *Soest* Stool, *Weaving* Felt Carpet, *Pure* Piano<br>*Soon* Table Lamp, *Design* Edition Carpet<br>Collection, *Fridtjof 1* Hanging Lamp<br>*Nudo* Standing Desk, Raumwerk founded<br>Studio Vertijet founded, |
| **2001** | *EO* Cabinet System, *Performa* Coat Rack<br>Extratapete founded |
| **2002** | *Scroll* Sofa System, *Diana* Occasional Table Series<br>*Lipse* Chair System, *Kant* Desk, *Lobby* Sofa<br>System, *Silver* Office Chair, Leise founded |
| **2003** | *Raindance* Shower, *Mimo* Television Set<br>*Janus* Folding Table, *Mars* Easychair,<br>*Baureihe e* Cabinet System |
| **2004** | *Balance* Fireplace, *Plattenbau* Shelf System<br>*Dono* Sofa System, *Freddy* Shelf System<br>*Milanolight* Chair, *Fusion* Room Divider |
| **2005** | *Mein_Back* Shelf System, *Sputnik* Office Chair<br>*Kollektion 3* Wallpaper, *Couch* Sofa |
| **2006** | *Socialbox* Universal Furniture,<br>*Form 2006* Porcelain Tableware |
| **2007** | *S 3500* Easychair, *Yin Yang* Garden Easychair<br>*Plupp a.p.* Functional Sofa, *Nuf* Cabinet System |

ILLUSTRATIONS: above: *Backenzahn* stool, *Chiba* basin
and *Nara* mirror by Philipp Mainzer for e15, 1996 / 2004
mid: *b3* kitchen by Herbert H. Schultes for Bulthaup, 2004
below: *Trick Stick* coat rack by Patrick Frey and Markus Boge
for Nils Holger Moormann, 2005

1830

# Milestones A Product Chronology

# 1830

## Garden Chair

Design:
**Karl Friedrich Schinkel**

Manufacturer:
Anthologie Quartett (re-edition)

Small photo:
Garden chair with armrests

# Schinkel

The victory over Napoleon in 1815 triggered a building boom in which Karl Friedrich Schinkel, the director of the Prussian construction authority and an architect who was open to every modern development, would play a central role. His projects included a number of royal palaces surrounded by parks. A whole series of park benches and chairs was needed to furnish these gardens. Schinkel invented a new type of furniture for this purpose, choosing cast iron, a material that would become immensely popular during the course of the 19th century. The characteristic element in his pieces is their basis in two identical side parts, each cast in one piece. Their double-T cross-section, which provided great stability, also minimized material requirements and thus weight. The connecting rods are set into drilled holes. This structure allowed benches of various lengths to be made from the same cast-iron mould. Schinkel decorated his very simple design with ornament in the French Empire style – ornament that was however still integral to the construction. The individual elements are easy to assemble. Schinkel's 1830 chair design was not only used for royal gardens, but also went into serial production at various Prussian ironworks. His designs thus represent an early example of rationally produced series furniture. Schinkel, co-editor of a series of publications called "Models for Manufacturers and Artisans" therefore exerted a considerable influence on the taste of his contemporaries.

# 1859

**Chair**

Design:
**Michael Thonet**

Manufacturer:
Thonet

Small photo:
Model *214 PF*

# No. 14

One of the first examples of industrial furniture, this chair became an archetype of modern design. Its popularity laid the foundations for the rise of the **Thonet** furniture company. Indeed, the simply built chair became one of the most successful industrial products of all time, ultimately produced in the millions. Yet it was originally developed from a rather traditional piece constructed in laminated wood. Only after a series of experiments in extreme wood bending was it possible to use solid wood for the "consumer chair", the armchair version that even representatives of classical Modernism like Le Corbusier came to regard as iconic. Michael Thonet's special bending technique, in which steam and high pressures are applied to beech rods, gave designers a freedom that was unmatched until the much later arrival of plastic furniture. At first, however, the design was rather controversial. Was Thonet's method teasing out the wood's hidden potential, or was it doing violence to the material? The chair's simplicity revolutionized furniture retailing, since it could be supplied as a kit for assembly. *No. 14* consisted of just six wooden parts, ten screws and two nuts. With shipping made so simple, the chair proved an ideal export product.

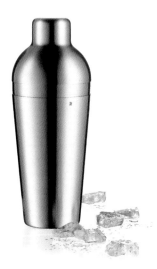

# 1891

**Cocktail Shaker**

Design:
**WMF** (original)

Manufacturer:
WMF

Small photo:
Lounge cocktail shaker
by James Irvine for WMF, 2002

# No. 1/2

If the concept of the "classic" makes any sense at all, then this is a perfect example. Originally made from a nickel silver alloy, this cocktail shaker is still in production today, now in a stainless steel version. Coming upon an article that has stood the test of time for over a century is already quite unusual. But finding one that doesn't even betray its venerable age is even more astonishing. The first cocktail shaker made by **WMF** – still referred to in the 1891 catalogue as an "Eisbecher" (ice cup) – is in many ways a phenomenon. It came in 0.3-, 0.5- and 0.7-litre sizes. The latter cost 10 Reichsmark and 50 Pfennige, roughly equivalent to the weekly take-home pay of the average worker. Amidst the otherwise as a rule elaborately decorated productions of that ornament-happy era, this elegant silver object seems like an immaculate being from another world. The shaker probably owes its smooth, well-proportioned form to a sculptor working in the design studio that WMF was already running at the time. How he managed to renounce every modicum of frippery and thus so convincingly anticipate the kind of functional sobriety that would gradually come to prevail only much, much later remains a mystery. The shape is ergonomically ideal since the tapering body permits a sure grip. The two conical sections are connected in a highly elegant fashion. Flattening above and below ensure a stable standing position. *No. 1/2*, which one can well imagine in the extravagant establishments of its day, created a type that the Bauhaus would call for a quarter of a century later.

# 1899

**Chair**

Design:
**Richard Riemerschmid**

Manufacturer:
formerly Dresdner Werkstätten
für Handwerkskunst

Small photo:
*Armlehnstuhl (Armchair)*
by Richard Riemerschmid, 1903

# Music-Room Chair

The now famous "music-room chair" originally formed part of a modern, sparsely decorated music room that was shown at the 1899 Dresden Art Exhibition and founded the reputation of its creator. **Richard Riemerschmid**, one of the leading figures in the reformist Werkstätten (workshops) movement and probably the most successful designer financially of the first generation of reformers, understood how to design soundly constructed furniture that is simple yet never looks ordinary. The strong diagonal supports, only hinting at armrests and giving the musician full freedom of movement, have been interpreted by some as the first step towards modern furniture. This element, with its gentle wave, forms sharp angles at the front leg and the oblique rear leg, thus creating a geometry that lends the chair a sculptural quality. And every detail contributes to the chair's structural strength. This integrity is another reason why the original chair, in bog oak, is considered a furniture masterpiece of Jugendstil. Originally made by the Associated Workshops with the designation Number *4059*, the design soon attracted international acclaim through an edition by Liberty's of London.

# 1899

**Porcelain Tableware**

Design:
**Hermann Gradl**

Manufacturer:
formerly Nymphenburg

# Fish Service

When the **Nymphenburg** Porcelain Factory received a gold medal at the World Exposition in Paris in 1900, it was a sign of an artistic turning point. After all, at previous international trade fairs, German products had only rarely shone as models of an exemplary aesthetic. This porcelain, which can easily be classified as typical of the heyday of Jugendstil, was very obviously recognized alone for its style and not its functional merits. The fact that its creator, painter Hermann Gradl, was not even 20 years old at the time he designed it is typical for the situation in those days. Young artists were galloping to the forefront in Germany, finding a place for themselves in porcelain manufacture as in other fields. Dining table accoutrements played an important role in bringing the new taste in decoration and art – known in French as "Art Nouveau" – into upper middle-class homes. Born in Bavaria, Gradl, who would later achieve dubious fame as Hitler's favourite painter, created a small yet complex composition made up of a shallow oval bowl sporting representational to slightly abstract motifs whose proportions correspond harmoniously with the outlines of the object. The artist cleverly made use of the vessel's profile to further enhance the liveliness of the flow of line. The stylized water plants contrast with the naturalistically depicted animals. Each dish naturally features a different motif. Gradl's service marks the end of the era of historical stylistic plagiarism in favour of inventive freedom of form.

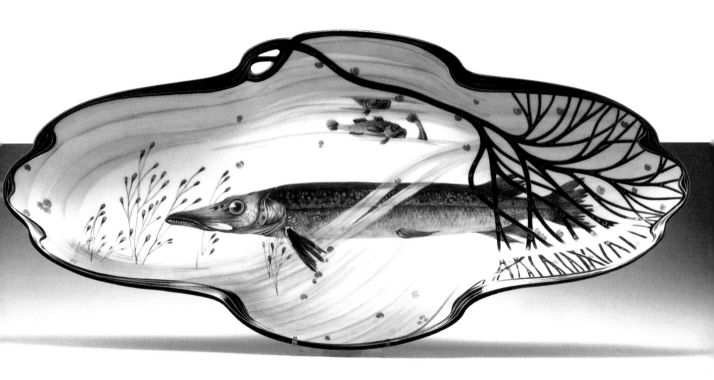

# 1901

## Chair

Design:
**Peter Behrens**

Manufacturer:
formerly Hofmöbelfabrik
J. D. Heymann

Small photo:
chair, table and bench for
*Behrens' House* by Peter Behrens,
1901

# Behrens' House

For German furniture design, the turn of the last century was a time of grand exhibitions and leaps of artistic achievement. In 1901 a colony of artists living and working on Darmstadt's Mathildenhöhe presented their latest work in an exhibition entitled "*A Document of German Art*". One of the exhibits was a whole home, designed by **Peter Behrens**. The graphic artist, architect and later product designer had conceived every detail of the interiors and furniture. Among the most remarkable creations on display were the graceful dining-room chairs, executed in poplar and painted white. These chairs, along with a bench, were to evolve into a classic furniture series. The chairs (with and without armrests) have a lightweight structure that features a narrow, ornamental backrest and a seat tapering in from the front. Its appearance seems to give an Art Nouveau twist to the English Windsor chair. There are echoes here of both **Henry van de Velde's** *Bloemenwerf* chair and Charles Rennie Mackintosh's high-backed chairs. White, the colour of purity, was the overall colour scheme of the room. For these reformers white meant brightness and hygiene. The seats were originally upholstered in red leather to match the ruby-red feet of a set of drinking glasses, another Behrens creation.

# 1903

**Porcelain Tableware**

Design:
**Richard Riemerschmid**

Manufacturer:
formerly
Porzellanmanufaktur Meissen

# Service with Leaf Decor

Strongly influenced by the rediscovered art of East Asia, ceramics and porcelain production boomed toward the end of the 19th century, especially in England and France, including a new flowering of Jugendstil ornament. It says volumes about **Richard Riemerschmid** that he simply ignored all the exoticism and elaborate decoration proliferating around him, as he did the torrent of useless knick-knacks flooding middle-class homes. Porcelain manufactories were veritably compelled to inaugurate a new style during this period in order to survive on the market. This was the case for the stoneware industry in the Westerwald region just as it was for the Meissen porcelain factory, for which **Peter Behrens** and **Henry van de Velde** had already worked. In comparison with the curvaceous elegance of Meissen Jugendstil objects exemplified by the work of van de Velde, Riemerschmid brought an almost crude component into play. His dishes are notable for their simple forms and reduced leaf, vine and fruit décor, which might well have been inspired by the uncomplicated folk patterns produced in Bunzlau, in what is today Poland. His later tableware designs for home and hotel likewise focused on functionalism and usability. Just as simple and virtually archetypical are his numerous beer steins, whose outstanding aesthetic quality can best be appreciated when compared with the ill-proportioned and kitsch-laden monstrosities widespread at the time – and still found everywhere today.

# 1909

**Water Kettle**

Design:
**Peter Behrens**

Manufacturer:
formerly AEG

Small photo:
Water Kettle (variations)
by Peter Behrens, ca. 1909

# Behrens

They came in three basic shapes (octagonal, squat oval and teardrop), three materials (brass, nickel-plated brass and copper-plated brass), with three surface textures (smooth, combed and mottled) and in three sizes (0.75, 1.25 and 1.75 litres). The combination of the parts and the various features yielded a total of 81 possible product variants, of which only 30 went into series production. The electrical connections and heating elements were the same for all three basic shapes, i.e. interchangeable. This modular standardization is one of the fundamental rules of the serial production that would come to prevail in particular in the USA by the end of the 19th century. What was new here was that the designer deliberately took advantage of these necessary structural and manufacturing features. With his building block system, **Peter Behrens** was putting into practice the kind of standardization he stood up for in the famous Werkbund debate. This concept was so innovative that one can justifiably regard it as the hour of birth of modern industrial design, with Behrens as its father. At the same time, it spelled the entrée of the factory aesthetic into the domestic environment, a process that would later recur several times, for example in the form of tubular steel furniture or the early phonographs from **Braun**. Behrens drew on traditional forms in the design of his kettle, but freed them from all extraneous ornament. The "honest", undisguised handling of materials was also important. The new kettle series anticipated the transition from luxury item to consumer object, while also heralding a revaluation, even an exaltation of the industrial form, which now took pride of place on the starched white tablecloth, an effect that would later be echoed in the products of **Alfi, Mono** or **Pott**. Priced from 18 to 26 marks, this was by no means a low-ticket item. The Behrens kettle remained in production for around 20 years – another indicator of its design value.

# 1920

**Easychair**

Design:
**Walter Gropius**

Manufacturer:
Tecta (re-edition)

Small photo:
*F 51-3* sofa with
*Oblique* nesting tables
Tecta, 2005

# F 51

The architect **Walter Gropius** designed this armchair and matching sofa in the early 1920s for his own director's office at the Bauhaus. Although not very well known, this furniture is programmatic. It is a part of the architecture while also demonstrating Bauhaus coherence as a design object in its own right. Its simple, rectangular interlocking blocks reflect the same constructivist principles found in the furniture of Gerrit Rietveld, **Marcel Breuer, Peter Keler** and others. The *F 51* as a whole, like its wooden frame, forms a cube from which the seating space is "cut out". This reproduced the theme of the cube-shaped reception room in which it once stood. Gropius' systematic approach follows the holistic idea of the "Gesamtkunstwerk", or total work of art, expounded by the Werkstätten movement and realized for the first time here in its minimalist mode. In fact Herbert Bayer formulated precisely the geometric relationships found here. The armchair's cantilever construction anticipates the later cantilevered models. The *F 51* appears self-contained, even solidly prestigious. The original had an ebonized wood frame in cherry and was upholstered in a lemon-coloured woollen fabric. This colour contrast gave stark emphasis to the shape.

# 1920

## Carpet Collection

**Design:**
**Gertrud Arndt,**
**Monica Bella-Bronner,**
**Kitty Fischer, Grete Reichardt,**
**Gunta Stölzl u.a.**

Manufacturer:
Vorwerk (re-edition)

Small photo:
left, centre: carpets by
Gunta Stölzl
right: Monica Bella-Bronner

# Bauhaus Carpets

Every bit as varied and disparate as the many directions represented at the Bauhaus are the products they brought forth. This also goes for carpets, a metier where artistic expression and mechanical fabrication meet and meld. The fact that primarily women were active in this field admittedly implies the persistence of patriarchal structures, and yet the Bauhaus – exemplary for the 1920s – was also a place in which libertarian women could find fulfilment. The "Women's Class" evolved into an efficient weaving workshop where tough, but fruitful, competition prevailed, inspiring students to experiment extensively. The conflict between free design and carpets that could actually be commercialized was always at issue in the workshop. Director Gunta Stölzl, the only female master at the Bauhaus, distanced herself from the "idea-heavy" designs of the early years. Industrial rug production – by contrast with wallpaper – was still in its infancy. Under the most difficult of conditions, artists such as Anni Albers, Gertrud Arndt, Monica Bella-Bronner, Kitty Fischer, Lilly Reich, Grete Reichardt and Gunta Stölzl created a number of designs that would only be realized as serial products seven decades later, by Vorwerk. The majority of the designs consist of clear geometric patterns in harmonious colour schemes. Echoes of the new abstract, cubist art currents of the era are unmistakable. With their regular patterns, these rugs not only form the perfect counterpart to the rational architecture and interior design aesthetic, but are also objects of beauty in their own right.

# 1922

**Door-handle**

Design:
**Walter Gropius**

Manufacturer:
S. A. Loevy (original)

Kleine Abbbildung:
*1102* door-handle and
*3432* window-handle
by Alessandro Mendini (re-design)
FSB, 1986

# Bauhaus Door-Handle

It is a "symbol of the connection between the architect and industrial production", wrote design historian Siegfried Giedion, almost euphorically. Created in the private Weimar studio of the founder of the Bauhaus, the door-handle is made up of two very simple basic forms, a cylindrical and a square rod. If one considers that this door-handle is nothing more than a mere rod, it is hard to imagine any further reduction. That the bent square rod forms the link to the lock plate and the handle is cylindrical to fit nicely in the hand also makes perfect sense. This version had a less elegant forerunner and was presumably first used in summer 1923 in the pilot house "Am Horn". The Berlin bronze foundry S.A. Loevy is named as manufacturer of the fittings for the "Am Horn" house. This tradition-steeped company already produced the fixtures for Gropius' factory at the Cologne Werkbund Exhibition in 1914 and was regarded as the manufacturer of choice in particular for Berlin architects. The later Dessau variant of the door-handle differed from the Weimar model in size and displayed a more pronounced break between the square rod and rounded grip. The minimalist fixture was produced throughout the 1920s and 30s and today takes its place – alongside the **Wagenfeld** lamp and **Breuer's** *Wassily* chair – amongst the early design icons created at the Bauhaus. It is often referred to simply as the "*Bauhaus Door-handle*". The design was so successful that it soon attracted imitators. The re-edition produced by **FSB** is the result of the work of Italian designer Alessandro Mendini, who came up with a variation on the Gropius design during a workshop by changing the material, harking back again to the original.

# 1924

**Table Lamp**

Design:
**Wilhelm Wagenfeld
Karl J. Jucker**

Manufacturer:
Tecnolumen (re-edition)

Small photo:
*WG 24* table lamp
with glass base

## WA 24

Marking the debut of its creator's career, this lamp was destined to remain a solitary highlight for him. The design for the lamp, probably the best-known product to issue from the famous Bauhaus Academy for Art and Design, represented the very first project of then 24-year-old **Wilhelm Wagenfeld**, which the Bauhaus neophyte undertook in conjunction with his colleague Karl J. Jucker for their teacher Lázló Moholy-Nagy in the metal workshop. The combination of metal and glass fit in perfectly with the ideal of cool restraint. According to the Bauhaus principles, designers should create industrial products that looked like such. In reality, however, the designs were produced by hand, as was also the case here. The licensed replica of the lamp, still successful today, is also made by hand. The table lamp with flat base and dome-like glass shade echoes pre-war designs by Vienna architects Adolf Loos and Josef Hoffmann. Wagenfeld and Jucker tightened the form, rid it of all embellishments and chose a small format measuring 18 centimetres in diameter and 36 centimetres tall. A special feature here is that the shade is pulled further downward to form a three-quarter globe, which reduces the opening at the bottom. The version with glass base and stand created a few months later seems even more original and high-tech, reflecting with its transparency the concept of open living. The lamp's ability to blend in neutrally in any milieu was important to Wagenfeld. But success at first came slowly. Only 50 lamps of this version were produced, mainly for architects. Today, the compact lamp is not only an icon of Modernism, but also functions as a status symbol demonstrating the good taste of the owner.

# 1924

**Teapot**

Design:
**Marianne Brandt**

Manufacturer:
Tecnolumen (re-edition)

Small photo:
ashtray
by Marianne Brandt, 1924
Alessi (re-edition)

# Tea-Extract-Pot

This teapot was part of a service of which only one complete set survives. It was created toward the end of **Marianne Brandt's** first year at the Bauhaus, when she was still an apprentice, and attests to her enormous talent as well as the courage to set off down radically new paths in the design of everyday objects. Unlike **Peter Behrens'** electric kettle, which was still being sold at the time and was oriented on traditional forms, Brandt created an entirely new type of object here. Similarly to her contemporaneous ashtray design, she replaced the conventional circular base with two crossbars in which the hemispherical pot nestles. The circular upper surface created by the bisection of the globe at its exact centre is left as a flat plane, as is the likewise circular top to the teapot. Since the wooden handle of the original was also a semi-circular disk, the whole takes on the look of an exercise straight out of a geometry textbook. The replica that is now once again in production (by **Tecnolumen**) has a bow-shaped handle that also forms a semi-circle. This pot in a way exemplifies the design principles prevailing at the metal workshop during that era: The individual forms are as simple as possible and arranged in clear opposition to one another. This additive constructional method also allowed the contrast between the various materials to be deftly utilized to great optical effect, with a number of different combinations having been tested. Innovative here was the use of different metals in the same object. Although the teapot was still made completely by hand, the metalworking process is no longer visible in the finished product. The object thus took on a machine-made character. The overall impression, despite pain-staking adherence to strict formal rules, is by no means artificial, but rather extremely harmonious.

# 1925

# Albers

Nesting tables were right in step with the functionalist furniture trend and were employed by Josef Hoffmann and **Marcel Breuer**, among others. This variation was part of an apartment that the artist **Josef Albers** – who like Breuer, **Peter Keler** and others worked in the Bauhaus carpentry workshop – furnished for the couple Fritz and Anna Moellenhof, psychoanalysts in Berlin. Its special charm can be attributed to the simple straight lines of its construction and the use of ash, which gives the furniture a much warmer feel, and even more so to the glass tabletops painted from below that are inserted into the wooden frame. In addition to white, Albers, who was asked by **Walter Gropius** to set up a workshop for glass painting, uses the popular basic colour palette of the Bauhaus (also seen in the work of Herbert Bayer and Peter Keler). Not only systematic but also suggestive, the importance of this colour scheme is often underappreciated, especially when it comes to furniture. Similar to what he did in his church windows and the "Homage to the Square" painting series that brought him world fame, Albers presents the colours in the nesting tables in such a way that they have equal impact alone or in combination. Glass provides him the ideal medium for this purpose.

# 1925

**Easychair**

Design:
**Marcel Breuer**

Manufacturer:
Knoll International (re-edition)

Small photo:
*B 4* folding chair, 1927
as *D 4* from Tecta (re-edition)

# B 3

It caught the eye of lecturers, students and visitors at the Bauhaus in Dessau when they came across this chair in the masters' quarters in the "Meistersiedlung". And as early as 1926, the year it went into production, the *B 3* was exhibited in the Dresden Kunsthalle and hailed as a masterpiece. **Marcel Breuer's** first tubular steel chair immediately attracted huge publicity. The *B 3* later became known worldwide as the "Club Chair" or the "Wassily". This international reach was a factor behind the emerging fascination with all things Bauhaus. And the *B 3* also triggered a global boom in tubular steel furniture, representing at the time the avant-garde application of industrial aesthetics to the private sphere. The contrast of black and silver was also new, at once evoking precious jewellery and modern machinery. With this combination Breuer created his "magic of precision", as one French critic wrote. Breuer approached furniture as an "apparatus of modern living". It should be light, open, inexpensive, easily dismantled, and hygienic. All these criteria were met by the *B 3*, which also came in a folding version. Breuer built it in his spare time with the help of a mechanic. His design concept took up some of the ideas already developed by Gerrit Rietveld and others. With the *B 3* Breuer did not, as he intended, create an object of everyday use but rather a new furniture paradigm and an "abstract-real sculpture" (Sigfried Giedion) that represents in its geometry the minimalism of the new inventors of form. It became the ultimate design icon and a central emblem of Modernism. Hardly surprisingly, the Club Chair was the first piece of furniture to be marketed as "a classic" in the 1960s.

# 1925

## Hanging Lamp

Design:
**Marianne Brandt
und Hans Przyrembel**

Manufacturer:
Tecnolumen (re-edition)

Small photo:
*DMB 26* hanging lamp
by Marianne Brandt, 1926

# HMB 25

In an extremely productive phase in 1926, 33-year-old **Marianne Brandt** – at the time still in Weimar – designed in the first six months alone a large variety of lighting solutions, usually hanging or ceiling lamps, as well as a whole series of objects of everyday use such as egg cups, dinnerware, bowls and containers. Together with Christian Dell and Poul Hennigsen from Denmark, Brandt also focused intensely on electric lamps, whose design had by no means yet reached maturity. As witnessed by the models she created, she and her above-mentioned colleagues embarked on a broad field of experimentation: from options for adjusting brightness and optimizing the direction of light, to various methods of light distribution and concessions to different environmental conditions such the dusty workshop, and on to the selection of various materials for different light dispersion effects. This explains why each model was executed in several different variations. The emphasis in Brandt's designs was not on playing with basic forms or striving for spectacular formal contrasts, but rather on creating proportions suitable for serial production. For example, she tried to shape the product body almost entirely out of a single form. Shades are made of aluminium, nickel silver or nickel-plated sheet copper. The latter metal is used in the replica being produced today by **Tecnolumen**. As simple as the design purportedly was, the lamp's areas of application were nonetheless manifold. It could be used in all conceivable areas: in living rooms, restaurants or workshops. If there is such a thing as an object that is "timeless", then this lamp is a serious candidate for this otherwise over-used honour. It formed the prototype for all future hanging lamps.

# 1926

## B 9

**Nesting Tables**

Design:
**Marcel Breuer**

Manufacturer:
Thonet, Knoll International
(re-edition)

Small photo:
*Laccio coffee* table
by Marcel Breuer, 1926
Knoll International (re-edition)

Having designed the skeletal *B 3* armchair, **Marcel Breuer** went on to apply his cool industrial aesthetic to other types of furniture. Nesting tables had already emerged as a furniture idea before the First World War, as seen in Josef Hoffmann's tables, but Breuer's design was intended as far more than an accessory. He is said to have taken the idea for the runners in tubular steel from the aircraft technicians at the nearby Junker Works at Dessau, who used sled-based stools for their work. The tubular runners, with their narrow surface contact, can slide easily while still providing stability. The four knee-high tabletops perform a variety of functions for a new style of "Liberated Living" (Sigfried Giedion), the interior counterpart to Neues Bauen, the new architecture of the Bauhaus. The tables are light, mobile and open. They reveal the principle of industrial line production and the rationalist concept of space. At that time the cube was considered the ideal shape. The modular nesting concept offers spatial economy, mobility and diversity through combination, again expressing the emancipatory trajectory of Modernism.

# 1926

**Kitchen**

Design:
**Margarete Schütte-Lihotzky**

Manufacturer:
formerly various trades
including
Georg Grumbach Cabinetmakers
Harrer Brothers
(metal storage drawers, taps, sink)
Prometheus
(gas and electric stove)

Small photo:
Storage drawers for the
Frankfurt Kitchen, 1926

# Frankfurt Kitchen

"The problem of rationalizing the work of the housewife is of equal importance in almost all strata of the population", wrote the young Viennese architect Margarete Schütte-Lihotzky, who had the job in the communal project "New Frankfurt" in the mid-1920s of simplifying kitchen work. The *Frankfurt Kitchen* that the staunch Socialist ultimately came up with as the result of her studies was a groundbreaking accomplishment, built into some 10,000 new apartments in the ensuing years. The compact design with closely placed cabinets and appliances reflected the small size of the apartments, which had no room for conventional kitchen furniture – an argument that is still valid today. The kitchen was built right into the apartment, something totally new at the time. It can thus be regarded as the prototype for the modern fitted kitchen. There were earlier examples, for example at the Bauhaus or by **Otto Haesler** in the Celle settlements, but never before was the task approached with such thoroughgoing consistency. The use of modern materials, such as aluminium for the storage drawers, was of course de rigueur. The basis for the *Frankfurt Kitchen* was formed by the idea of Taylorism that came out of the USA, a method for scientifically managing labour to yield greater productivity. All steps taken by the housewife in her kitchen work were measured with a stopwatch. The less time she needed to perform these regular duties, the more time she would have left over for her family – that was the guiding principle. In order to ensure that everything can be reached quickly, the kitchen is kept very compact: a narrow cooking laboratory with a row of cabinets and work surfaces on each side that set the trend for kitchens to come. All of today's fitted kitchens had their origin here. That the countermovement toward a new communicative style of kitchen, propagated for example by the **Bulthaup** company, would also arise in Germany, is only logical.

**Chair**

Design:
**Ferdinand Kramer**

Manufacturer:
formerly Thonet

# Kramer

Around 1928, **Ferdinand Kramer**, at the time manager of the progressive Frankfurt Building Authority, travelled through Austria and Czechoslovakia, including visits to the furniture works of the **Thonet** company. Fascinated by the mass production practiced there, which fit in so well with the Socialist concept of cheap apartments for all, the visionary wrote about his experiences shortly thereafter in an article titled "18,000 Chairs a Day" (published in 1929 in *Die Form*). As liaison to one of the most extensive communal apartment-building programs, he was of course of interest to Thonet and remained in contact with the company. The *Kramer chair* had been created shortly beforehand for the Vocational Education Institute of the City of Frankfurt, for which Kramer was in charge of selecting furnishings. The chair was produced in two versions, with or without armrests. It came in natural wood or painted black. Seat and backrest were made of plywood, the rest of bentwood. The magazine *Das Neue Frankfurt* featured the chair the year it was created on its title page, to publicize the exhibition "*The Chair*". It was regarded as a shining example of reform-minded pragmatic living. Notable is the relatively large, square-shaped and nearly flat seat as well as the original support structure. Front and back legs converge in a bent wood arch and receive further stability from four additional arches. Kramer's squat-looking design exudes the dry flair of the Frankfurt variant of the "New Objectivity".

# 1927

**Chair**

Design:
**Ludwig Mies van der Rohe**

Manufacturer:
formerly Berliner Metallgewerbe
Josef Müller (original)

Small photo:
*MR 20*, from Thonet
as *S 533/R/RF* (re-edition)

# MR 10

**Ludwig Mies van der Rohe's** world career began with a chair requiring no back legs: the cantilevered Freischwinger (also known as Kragstuhl). The new seating design was not without precedent. Mies van der Rohe had noticed Mart Stam's cantilevered chair while planning the Weissenhof housing project and a long-running legal dispute ensued over authorship. The design also included **Marcel Breuer's** idea (then just two years old) of using steel tubing instead of wood. Mies van der Rohe combined both innovations, but his synthesis makes the most of the cantilever principle by putting spring into the floating seat. This was achieved by means of two features: in material terms, by using seamless, specially drawn steel tubing; and in design terms by arcing the uprights from runners. These arcs give the chair its special elegance – clearly a hallmark of Mies van der Rohe's work – while exploiting the potential springiness of the tubular steel (in contrast to the right-angled designs by Stam and Breuer). This elasticity also improves seating comfort. The Freischwinger has been supplied from its very first version in various sling materials (leather, woven fabric or natural-coloured wicker) and with optional armrests. The armrests are attached smoothly to the back section but mounted more conspicuously onto the front legs. Its suspension principle and rational aesthetic have elevated the *MR 10* to the ranks of the most eminent 20th century furniture design. It has become an icon of Modernism, not least because, in contrast to other Bauhaus furniture, this model has been produced almost continuously to the present day.

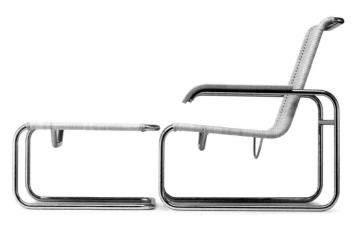

# 1928

**Easychair**

Design:
**Marcel Breuer**

Manufacturer:
Thonet

Small photo:
Armchair with *S35 RH* footstool
Footstool designed by
manufacturer, 1979

# B 35

When **Marcel Breuer** set up a furniture show of the products of the German Werkbund at Paris' Grand Palais in 1930 – the debut presentation of the German "Modern Movement" in France – the *B 35* chair he had designed in the years immediately previous was among the items on display – representing a further development of the cantilevered chair. Breuer had succeeded in incorporating all of the functions of a comfortable tubular steel armchair in a single continuous tube. This had the effect of enhancing the chair's springiness, since even the armrests, equipped with wooden overlays, are unsupported. The seated person thus maintains his "balance" through the double swing of body and arms. Even more importantly, the "club chair" on runners did not infringe on the copyright of cantilevered chair inventor Mart Stam. But it by no means consisted of a single tube. Two crossbars at the back and front ensure structural stability, along with an invisible tension rod under the seat. The connections between the three parts of the frame were concealed under the Eisengarn upholstery. This textile, a waxed cotton weave with a metallic sheen, was developed in the Bauhaus weaving workshop expressly for the Breuer chairs. The model shown at the Grand Palais was covered in leather, however, and wicker was also used in the early years.

# 1929

**Easychair**

Design:
**Ludwig Mies van der Rohe**

Manufacturer:
Knoll International (re-edition)

Small photo:
Barcelona lounger and
coffee table
Knoll International (re-edition)

# MR 90 / Barcelona

The seating designed in the late 1920s for the German pavilion at the World Exposition in Barcelona certainly deserves the epithet "classic". On the one hand, the furniture ensemble in the open, light and airy pavilion made the cool and sparse look – later established as the "international style" – world famous. On the other, the designs flirt with historical references to antiquity. Inspiration no doubt came from the Greek folding or scissors chairs that served as a throne for divine or earthly rulers. So the *MR 90* is a sort of modern-day throne (without the fold-away option). Indeed, it was originally intended for highly prestigious functions, which contradicted the social, or even socialist, goals advocated by many protagonists of the new architecture, *Neues Bauen*. For the World Exposition, **Ludwig Mies van der Rohe** used strip steel and leather upholstery in festive white. The *Barcelona* lounge chair was clearly a luxury item and hardly suited to mass production. The frame had to be painstakingly welded by hand, so it was not until an altered version emerged that manufacture began in 1948. Nevertheless, the Barcelona is a genuinely innovative design that has extended the modernist repertoire. The separate, detachable cushions for the seat and back are the same size and simply slip into the right position of their own accord. The chair has a visual fascination that derives not least from the contrast between the flowing line of the frame and the rather static impression of the leather slabs.

# 1929

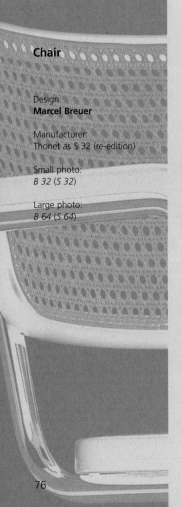

**Chair**

Design:
**Marcel Breuer**

Manufacturer:
Thonet as S 32 (re-edition)

Small photo:
*B 32 (S 32)*

Large photo:
*B 64 (S 64)*

# B 32

When, at the end of the 1920s, this chair went on the market under the name *B 32*, a legal dispute was raging over copyright. Rival claims on the cantilevered chair, or Freischwinger, were asserted by Mart Stam, **Ludwig Mies van der Rohe** and **Marcel Breuer**, along with the **Thonet** company. The chair's novelty lay in the fact that Breuer's design combined for the first time the two bendable materials, bent beechwood and steel tubing, which had played such a key role in modern furniture design. The design juxtaposes the cool hardness of the steel and the softness of the wooden frame, creating a new sense of comfort that is underlined by the use of filigree wickerwork as a traditional seating material. It is hardly surprising that this simple chair was to become Breuer's greatest commercial success. The functional style reflected a major trend, especially in the architecture of the late 1920s. Bauhaus became all the rage, and the liberally minded were especially keen to try out the latest furniture if, like the *B 32*, it did not look quite so radical. This model and the *B 64* (with armrests) were later to become an archetype of modernist furniture in the form of cheap copies produced for a mass market and as the first ever "re-edition". In 1962 the Italian company Gavina supplied the chair under the name of *Cesca* (after Breuer's daughter Francesca), marketing it as a "classic".

# 1930

**Wallpaper Collection**

Design:
**Students at the Bauhaus**

Manufacturer:
Rasch

# Bauhaus Wallpaper

This is the kind of project that seemed just perfect for the first academy that devoted itself to the design of industrially produced objects of daily use. But the Bauhaus director at the time, Hannes Meyer, a strictly anti-bourgeois Swiss socialist, first had to be persuaded of that fact. The idea of wallpaper smelled too much of fusty middle-class cosiness, which seemed irreconcilable with avant-garde aspirations. Finally, a competition was held among the students. Teachers like **Josef Albers** and Joost Schmidt selected the winners. Around 150 different wallpapers – 14 patterns in five to 15 colour schemes each – were chosen for series production. With their matte surfaces and fine lines, grids and spots, the Bauhaus wallpapers represented a new approach to the wall as neutral backdrop, in keeping with the sober interior style expressed in tubular steel furniture and functional lamps. Using new technologies, it was possible to achieve previously unimagined effects. For example, slight nuances in a pastel hue created a pattern that optically blurred once on the wall but gave the whole an appealing vibrancy. The practical advantage was that the patterns did not have to be matched, so the sheets could be glued without any waste. But when the Bauhaus wallpapers finally came onto the market, only three retailers were interested in ordering the new product range. Wallpaper manufacturer Emil **Rasch**, who had the initial idea for the project, reacted by placing ads in major newspapers, which finally led to the desired success. Later, Rasch was the only one who was still permitted to use the name of the ostracized school during the Nazi era. The Bauhaus wallpapers are the only industrial product of the famous art academy that has been in production without pause since its creation.

# 1930

Chair

Design:
**Ludwig Mies van der Rohe**

Manufacturer:
Knoll International (re-edition)

Small photo:
*MR 50* chair
version with tubular steel frame
Knoll International (re-edition)

# MR 50 / Brno

When furnishing the villa he built in Brünn (now Brno, in the once German-settled Czech region of Moravia) for the wealthy business family of Tugenhat, **Ludwig Mies van der Rohe** actually intended to put in the cantilevered *MR 10*, which he had designed three years earlier for the Weissenhof Estate in Stuttgart. But the chair took up too much space and, with its backward tilt, was unsuitable for the dining table. So he created a smaller, more compact chair. The L-shaped seat makes this model comfortable while encouraging an upright posture (possibly a reason why the MR 50 became a favourite studio chair for TV talk shows in Germany). The right-angled seat and backrest elements are mounted between two flexible steel arches. The joints are hardly visible. In the Brünn villa there were 24 examples, with versions in both tubular and flat steel, upholstered in white or red leather – optical exclamation marks punctuating the rooms. The chair was originally supplied in chrome-plated, nickel-plated and lacquered versions. This design creates a formal tension between the near right angle of the seat and backrest and the curve of the metal frame, making it one of the most elegant of all the cantilever chairs.

# 1930

## Light Switch

Design:
**Robert Berker**
**Hugo Berker**

Manufacturer:
Berker

Small photo:
*Serie 1930* light switch
(re-edition)

# 1930

Although we see and use it every day, the light switch is a part of our homes that hardly receives much attention. It might be due to its small size and the fact that it is built in and therefore regarded as a given that it took so long before architects gave it much notice as a design element. As a matter of fact, however, it is one of the few things that are present in every room and which thus subtly help to define the furnishing style. Light switches comprise only two visible elements, the switch itself and the switch plate concealing the actual mechanism. For this kind of minimal apparatus the general design rule applies that the simpler the object, the more any design faults catch the eye. Up to the second half of the 20th century, the turning switch was the standard version for this ancestor of all control buttons. At the end of the 1920s, by which time the "New Objectivity" proclaimed in art and architecture had made its way into the private sphere, the **Berker** company was producing this omnipresent item in easy-to-use and clearly articulated versions. The round plate dictated by the turning movement was available both with a central concavity determined by the size of the switch as well as with variously graduated edges. The attachment screw is visibly integrated into the switch, which tapers at both ends. Now this early turning switch has been re-issued as replica, further ennobled through its use in the renovation of the historic Bauhaus building in Dessau.

# 1930

**Desk Lamp**

Design:
**Christian Dell**

Manufacturer:
formerly Gebr. Kaiser & Co.

# 6632

His lamps were produced for over half a century, but have not yet been re-issued. Silversmith Christian Dell, a student of **Henry van de Velde**, worked at the Bauhaus as master craftsman in the metal workshop. The basic shape of his lamps stems from a model designed by the Austrian company Coranda in the mid-1920s. At the end of the 1920s, Dell went to Frankfurt to take up a post as director of the metal workshop at the Frankfurt Art Academy. He developed his lamps, for which the Kaiser company ultimately obtained a license, in collaboration with another ex-Bauhaus artist named Adolf Meyer, according to a progressive modular principle. Thus emerged the Idell series, one of the largest lamp families ever produced. Exemplary as well was their rational assembly out of just a few variable parts. The characteristic ball joint and the bulb socket are the same in all the table lamps. But there are a wide variety of different shade types as well as various arms and bases. Furthermore, the same shades were also used for hanging lamps and – equipped with a pivoting arm – for wall lamps as well. Overall, the systematic thinker designed some 500 lamps. The striking silhouettes of his usually black-and-silver light sources, which exude the prim charm of the "New Building" movement, not only made their mark on German offices, but were also licensed worldwide. The type *6632* with chrome-plated base, also known as the "President Lamp", could once be found on the desk of many a German executive. For their secretaries, the simpler model *6556* was chosen.

# 1931

**Porcelain Tableware**

Design:
**Trude Petri**

Manufacturer:
KPM

# Urbino

The "New Objectivity" had long since found its way into everyday German life, but in the case of dishes – next to silverware a key status symbol in any middle-class household – imitations of historical styles continued to predominate for many years. The fact that Modernism had nevertheless made inroads in the lifestyle of broad circles of society is demonstrated by the decision of a tradition-steeped manufacturer like the Berlin Porcelain Factory to hire an avant-gardist like Trude Petri as designer. With *Urbino*, her strictest design, which builds on the spherical segment as basic shape, she created a new type whose visual impact stems solely from the clear flow of line and which for the first time ventured a marked contrast to the dominant styles of bygone centuries. Inspired by the rimless *Urbino* plates of the Italian Renaissance and the elegance of East Asian porcelain, Petri succeeded in creating a service whose concave, rimless plates and bowls are derived from the spherical segment. Her contemporaries must have sensed that she had devised proportions that were decades ahead of their time, particularly in her tea and coffee pots. Her carefully calculated design was greeted with the highest international honours in the 1930s, for example at the *Triennale* in Milan and the World Exposition in Paris. Already in 1950, the beginning of the decade that would draw on her formal specifications, *Urbino* – along with the far more moderate service *1382* by Hermann Gretsch – was presented to the world at New York's Museum of Modern Art as an embodiment of "Good Design".

# 1931

**Chair**

Design:
**Hans und Wassili Luckardt**

Manufacturer:
Thonet (re-edition as *S 36*)

# ST 14

It looks very sleek and poised. The backrest snuggles into the rounded frame, and the thin plywood seat seems to float like undulating cloth in the wind, leaving the boldly arced frame visually dominant. The line of the frame lends this design its unusual dynamism. It seems to prefigure the era of streamlined shapes but is rooted in the expressionist past of the two architects. Like other chair designs of those years, the supporting structure consists of a continuous loop of tubular steel. But unlike **Marcel Breuer** or **Ludwig Mies van der Rohe**, who preferred an underlying geometry, the Luckardt brothers insisted on the freely drawn line of the artist. The backrest, a deeply curved crescent which almost seems to fly away, and the seat, S-shaped when seen from the side, are characteristic of this chair's radial diversity and spatial complexity. Backrest and seat form hollows, making the chair so comfortable to use. A folding version also made the *ST 14* suitable for row seating.

**Porcelain Tableware**

Design:
**Hermann Gretsch**

Manufacturer:
Arzberg

Small photo:
*Form 1382* service
in a current colour scheme

# Form 1382

Immediately following his hiring as artistic director at **Arzberg**, Hermann Gretsch designed this service, with which he inaugurated a new epoch on the dining table. It has been praised for its simplicity ever since first being introduced at the autumn trade fair in Leipzig, a quality that pleasantly set it apart from the historicizing and Art Deco tableware of the day. And not only its style was something special: *Form 1382* was a tea, coffee and dinner service in one, the first set of dishes that could be purchased individually. Five years after its launch, it was awarded the Gold Medal at the VIth Milan *Triennale* and was presented as a shining example in 1950 in the exhibition "*Good Design*" at the Museum of Modern Art in New York. Interior design magazines and glossies repeatedly used *1382* as background decoration (similar to what happened with **Richard Sapper's** *Tizio* lamp in the 1980s). With its moderately rounded forms, *1382* did not seem quite as constructivist as **Marianne Brandt's** tea service from 1924, or as minimalist as Trude Petri's *Urbino*. Modernism as plain fare. The teapot is especially well conceived, with a round body, spout and handle that meld into a harmonious whole. Its creator propagated the renunciation of ornament and frills. The businesslike name he gave his service – simply using the production number – was already programmatic for this approach. The undecorated cups, plates and terrines must have seemed like foreign bodies on the department store shelves of the day. But Gretsch had cleverly managed to straddle the worlds of the avant-garde and mass taste, as attested by the astonishing fact that this tableware has been produced without interruption ever since its creation.

**Shelf**

Design:
**Egon Eiermann**
**Fritz Jaenecke**

Manufacturer:
Richard Lampert (re-edition)

Small photo:
*Eiermann* shelf with cabinet

# Eiermann

Due to the disastrous economic crisis that started in 1929, the apartment program in the Weimar Republic, already oriented on the "minimum for survival", had to tighten its belt even further. But this cost pressure also had the effect of unleashing creative powers. Starting in 1930 a whole series of competitions and exhibitions were held that served to compile good ideas for small, inexpensive and self-built houses. Architect **Egon Eiermann**, at the time a young man in his late twenties, took part in one such show in Berlin in summer 1932, titled "Sun, Air and House for Everyone". One of the pieces he showed was a shelf that was as yet unprecedented in its construction. The basic elements are two tubes onto which boards with holes in them are "strung". The shelf unit can be fixed in place in two ways: It can either be screwed into the wall using pins, or clamped between ceiling and floor. The latter version was especially innovative, but this was on the whole an unusually light-weight, fully new kind of construction principle and structural engineering that surpassed the traditional shelf grid for the first time. This simple, unpretentious, even anti-bourgeois shelf unit did not go into series production at the time. It just didn't fit in with the rustic ideal that began to permeate Germany in the Nazi era after 1933. However, the shelves were custom built for a few of Eiermann's building commissions. Seven decades after its creation, Eiermann's archetype finally went into serial production at **Richard Lampert**.

# 1933

**Servierwagen**

Design:
**A. Bamberg**

Manufacturer:
Thonet (original)

Small photo:
Thonet (re-edition)

# S 179

One can well imagine it as a requisite prop for a metropolitan bar or a sophisticated film scene. The *S 179* trolley table has a simple yet cosmopolitan air. Like the furniture of **Ludwig Mies van der Rohe**, it is an early example of the adaptation of the New Objectivity to middle-class surroundings. Designing a trolley as a tubular steel construction was only logical once the Bauhaus had come into fashion, and the idea was first realized by **Marcel Breuer**, in a three-or four-wheeled version (1928/32), each with removable trays. The design here by Bamberg has some additional surprises in store. The dual functions of transport and stability when standing still are solved in a way that is as simple as it is functional, without the need to lock the wheels. This is done by limiting the wheels to the front of the cart so they come into play only when the handle of the trolley is lifted. This handle is located at the end of a pole that runs down the centre of the trolley, giving the structure stability and also connecting handle to wheels – an effortless and elegant solution. In the two or three identical shelves, industrial multiplication is exemplified the way it is in the parallel bands of floors in modern high rises, such as those seen for example in Erich Mendelsohn's department stores. With its rounded corners, the *S 179* recalls the Shell House in Berlin that was opened the year before.

# 1934

**Desk**

Design:
**Marcel Breuer**

Manufacturer:
Thonet

Small photo:
*B 117* nightstand
Thonet, manufacturer's design, 1934

# S 285

The Bauhaus saw itself as a laboratory for shapes and forms. Traditional designs were to be replaced by completely new "types": models of innovation that would almost inevitably have to challenge the prevailing ideas. This certainly applied to the *S 285* desk. When **Marcel Breuer** created this model he had actually left the Bauhaus and opened his own office in Berlin. While office desks had until then consisted of side cabinets supporting a worktop, Breuer sought here to escape the structural opposition between above and below. The individual elements fit into a holistic construction, linked – both aesthetically and technically – by the steel tubing. A single tube meanders around the drawers and work surface, embracing the three elements. This has two advantages: it enhances mobility by replacing legs with runners and it cleverly uses space. Both the worktop and the cabinets are raised, generating shelf space under the top and allowing us to look through a more open structure. The contrast between the serious black and the metallic creates the impression of quality and technical precision.

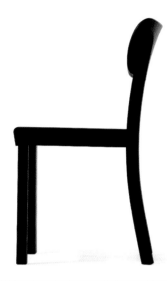

# 1936

**Chair**

Design:
**Anonym**

Manufacturer:
Magazin
(re-edition as *Frankfurt chair*)

# 2200 / Olympic

It stood, and still stands, in the backrooms of post offices, railway stations (supplied to German Rail right up to 1987) and many other official premises. It was so ubiquitous it was largely taken for granted. Yet the 2200 was an interesting design achievement. As a mass-produced piece of furniture reduced to its most essential parts, its quality lies in its unpretentious simplicity. This bentwood chair is built using the **Thonet** method. In the 1920s numerous manufacturers made similar models, mainly as kitchen chairs, in the course of the New Objectivity movement. In the mid-1930s the Frankenberg-based firm Bombenstabil (today Stoelcker) developed a chair in laminated beech to allow for a much simpler production method. For instance, the height of the seat frame was increased in order to dispense with the bracing elements. Front legs and front seat support and the curved back legs were glued as a single step in the production process. Model *2200*, which came onto the market in 1936, was chosen to equip all the team accommodations at the Berlin Olympic Games that year. This "people's chair" later became a standard item in numerous public authorities. Rooted in the 1920s, the *2200* is, like the "people's car", the Volkswagen, an example of the amazing continuity of modernist design in Germany. This no-frills "anonymous" chair is now produced by **Magazin**, fitting perfectly into this supplier's concept.

# 1948

## Basket Chair

Design:
**Egon Eiermann**

Manufacturer:
Richard Lampert (re-edition)

Small photo:
with *E 14* footstool

# E 10

Four years after the end of World War Two, a furniture exhibition was held in Stuttgart that attracted considerable interest. Its title was a question that inevitably preoccupied many Germans at the time: *Wie wohnen?* – How to live at home? The centrepiece of the fair was a fully furnished four-room home designed by the architect **Egon Eiermann**. He chose furniture in wood, steel tubing, plywood and other materials, placing them casually about the place. These pieces included a number of his own creations, among them the basket chair *E 10*. With its central trunk foot and deep hollow seat opening out like a flower, this lounge chair served as an international prototype for many similar designs that followed (especially well-known is Isamu Kenmochi's easychair from 1961). Comfortable yet aesthetically rigorous and attractive, this chair is one of the masterpieces of the prolific architect/designer, although it has not achieved anything like the popularity of some other Eiermann furniture. It is a piece of seating sculpture which demonstrates Eiermann's fascination with organic shapes and can only be made by hand. A skilled basket-weaver needs around 25 hours. Only rattan is used. The flexible canes are stiffened through the weave and become very strong. Internal bracing in the base gives the design further stability. It is immediately apparent that the shaft, seat, armrests and back form an organic whole.

# 1949

**Chair**

Design:
**Egon Eiermann**

Manufacturer:
Wilde + Spieth (original)

Small photo:
Wilde + Spieth (re-edition)

# SE 42

This is the chair people often confused in its early days with the *DCW (Dining Chair Wood)* created five years earlier by Ray and Charles Eames, although the *SE 42* would never achieve the international fame of its American counterpart. The design of both chairs does in fact display a few common features: organically shaped seat and backrest panels made of compression-moulded plywood, resting on as few points as possible on a frame of bent, assembled plywood strips. The visible screws in the seat and backrest panels are a characteristic and distinguishing feature of Eiermann's chair and reveal a telling detail of the construction. In the *SE 42* the screws go through both plywood parts and an additional rubber shock mount, while in the Eames model they are screwed only into the frame and otherwise glued. A further structural difference: **Egon Eiermann** only seemingly cast doubt on the stability of the chair by omitting the fourth leg. In fact, this reduction actually works to make the structure shine through more clearly. The idea of the three-legged chair was repeated two years later by the Danes Arne Jacobsen (*Ant* chair) and Poul Kjaerholm (*PK0* chair). Where the *S 42* showed true daring was in taking the material properties to the extreme. The tight bending radius of the front section of the only nine-millimetre-thin seat put the plywood to a real test. Overall, the flow of line is quite complex, giving a lively impression.

# 1950

## Chair

Design:
**Egon Eiermann**

Manufacturer:
Wilde + Spieth

Small photo:
with *S 38 S* footstool

# SE 68

A grace period of a few years normally intervened before developments in America began to spread in Europe as well. The designer couple Ray and Charles Eames, who lived in California toward the end of the Second World War, had created the prototypical 1950s seating with their chairs made of plywood bent in three dimensions resting on thin tubular steel frames. This lightweight, comfortable and therefore practical combination inspired imitators in many countries. **Egon Eiermann** was among the first to apply the new body design on this side of the Atlantic (two years before Arne Jacobsen's *Ant*). In his pure plywood chair two years before, the *SE 42*, the modernist and conceptualist had already oriented his design on the transatlantic model. In this case he developed out of this forerunner a slightly reduced, more stringent and thus probably more typically German variant. His delicate model *SE 68* with four legs is a true multipurpose wonder. Its stackability predestines the chair for furnishing school, seminar and other lecture rooms. Generations of students have taken notes on the optional foldout desk section. Since the light and easy piece of furniture soon became a symbol for the new awakening in design, it became a popular item for the modern-minded. Seat and backrest are made of multiple laminated real wood veneer strips. Characteristic distinguishing features for Eiermann are the visible screws on the front side, a structural detail that also underscores the chair's high degree of rigidity and durability.

# 1950

○

**Cabinet System**

Design:
**Hans Gugelot**

Manufacturer:
formerly Bofinger (original)

Small photo:
version with shelves
and sideboard

# M 125

Now it was possible to "build walls whose main characteristic is to be containers", remarked **Hans Gugelot**. For three years the reformer played around with his "wall unit", which he planned to use to divide large rooms, until it was presented for the first time in 1953 at the Basel Mustermesse (samples fair). It would take another three years, though, until one of the first and most consistently variable cabinet systems made up of standardized individual parts would go into production at **Bofinger** (until 1988). The models on which it was based included the German Typenmöbel and Anbaumöbel modes of modular furniture (pioneered by **Richard Riemerschmid** and **Marcel Breuer**) as well as American concepts such as the *Storagewall* by George Nelson. The new type of furniture, which countered the single cabinet with a variable set of combinable units, was the result of an empirical process. Gugelot had measured a number of items ranging from ring binders to record albums and calculated the average eye, grab and operating levels. From these studies, he derived a measurement unit of 125 millimetres. The principle was to use boards as the smallest units, linking them to form fixed cubes, a revisable process that at the same time made industrial production possible. The plastic surfaces, at first designed in Mondrian colours, were later kept light-coloured to reflect a maximum of light. The universally deployable *M 125* with its characteristic round recessed grips was sold both as furnishing for the private home and as comprehensive office furniture program that could be stacked to dizzying heights.

# 1952

## Door-handle

Design:
**Johannes Potente**

Manufacturer:
FSB

Small photo:
*1932* doorknob

# 1034

Johannes Potente, who was born in 1908 in Brakel in Westfalen and died in the same town almost eight decades later, was a trained chaser, toolmaker and a real stroke of luck for the local furnishings company **FSB**. Long before the company spearheaded the reinvention of design, the craftsman Potente had taken the solid principles to heart in this product that would later be formulated eloquently by design master **Otl Aicher**. The *1034* door-handle, which in addition to its ergonomic advantages also expresses the formal vocabulary of the 1950s in an appealingly unobtrusive manner, was the first major effort of the great design talent, and it would be followed by many others. Created in the early years of Germany's "Economic Miracle", this seminal prototype was copied and marketed a million times over across the globe after the patent expired. The *1034* did not have a simple geometry, but rather curving lines that are pleasant to grasp. The oblique linear cut-off at the end of the handle contrasts with the dominant curves, lending the design the kind of additional dynamic that was much prized in that optimistic era. Johannes Potente, who surely knew more about opening doors than many an expert today, is supposed to have been quite surprised when, shortly before his death, he was told that he was considered a "designer".

# 1953

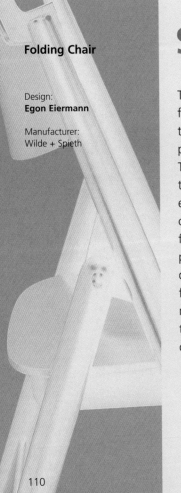

**Folding Chair**

Design:
**Egon Eiermann**

Manufacturer:
Wilde + Spieth

# SE 18

This practical folding chair from the early 1950s clearly followed with its rounded wooden frame and the organic curves of seat and backrest a formal ideal that had crystallized during the previous decade in particular in Denmark (this is made even more evident by a version in pricey teak). The same can be said of this chair as of the other models by **Egon Eiermann**: The special achievement of this architect and designer lies in the happy symbiosis between technology and a formal design that seems effortlessly natural. An open construction and economy of materials, the principles that the neo-functionalists adopted as if from the catechism of classic Modernism, were only one side of the coin. A lively, suspense-creating flow of line, as could be derived from a study of the Scandinavians, was the other. Every part of the chair – he later experimented with such things as plastic backrests – is designed down to the last detail. Eiermann tailored the model especially for furnishing large rooms, for **Wilde + Spieth**. And it would remain unrivalled in this field for some time to come. It is nonetheless astonishing that the *SE 18* was part of the furnishings of the Academy of Design that would soon open in Ulm, seeing as in that city a straight-edged sobriety was more the order of the day.

# 1953

**Easychair**

Design:
**Herbert Hirche**

Manufacturer:
Richard Lampert

# Deep Easychair with Footstool

By the 1950s, the showy salon style of domesticity had made way for a collection of furnishings that responded to the desire for a more free-flowing sociability and also fit into the more limited living space. **Herbert Hirche's** *Deep Easychair* is the veritable embodiment of the new culture of living, one that was oriented on the American way of life and on Scandinavian models. Hirche had originally designed the chair and footstool for his own home in Stuttgart. Other designers had already done away with a high backrest and armrests and reduced the cushions to flattened cubes. But Hirche's version takes this paring-down to extremes. Atop a tubular steel frame bent to form runners and frame, the seat and backrest are screwed on at right angles. It would be hard to picture an easychair with less mass. The minimal frame meant that the flat cushions had to float beyond it. The shiny chrome tubing and the striving for the greatest possible formal rigour attest to Hirche's training at the Bauhaus. But the gracefulness of this chair, its extremely low seating height and the humbleness of the materials – foam cushions upholstered in a simple wool fabric – at the same time stamp it clearly as a child of its times.

# 1953

**Salt and Pepper Shakers**

Design:
**Wilhelm Wagenfeld**

Manufacturer:
WMF

Small photo:
Eggcup and butter dish
by Wilhelm Wagenfeld for WMF

# Max and Moritz

That it is possible to lend a quite unprepossessing object which in terms of dining etiquette lags far behind dishes, glasses and silverware a high design value is something that **Wilhelm Wagenfeld** proved convincingly here. The North German designer, who appreciated the little things in life and drew inspiration from the Bauhaus, gave humble salt and pepper shakers the consecration of fine design. In the early 1950s, when the dawn of the German "Economic Miracle" was making itself felt in a new culture of living and dining, he designed a completely new prototype for these small, but frequently used containers. The combination of glass and metal was already an innovation – one that emerged effortlessly from Wagenfeld's own works biography, but which is by no means coincidental. While up to that time the difference between the pepper and salt shaker had to be labelled on the outside (for example, by holes forming the letters "S" and "P"), this was no longer necessary here due to the transparency of the glass. The two shakers are in fact identical, differing only in the colour of their contents. Finally, the design harbours a technical innovation as well: the tops are not screwed but stuck on, holding tight through the tension of the metal alone. The duo – whose names, taken from Wilhelm Busch's renowned children's book, lend them an added touch of personality – attracted attention in particular with their wasp-waisted shapes, an organic form typical for both their creator and for the times, which here also fulfils its purpose well. Their waists make *Max and Moritz* easy and comfortable to hold while also preventing the salt and pepper from clumping together. The theatrical component is underscored by putting the two into their own little "ship", also making them easier to transport.

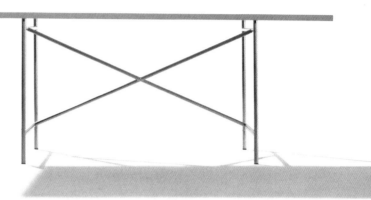

# 1953

**Table**

Design:
**Egon Eiermann**

Manufacturer:
Richard Lampert (re-edition)

# Table Base with Cross-Bracing

Among **Egon Eiermann's** furniture designs, tables play more of a minor role. But one construction idea that is typical of his way of thinking is this table base made of two tubular steel side frames welded to diagonal crossbars holding them together. With a drawing board as tabletop (an unmistakable reference to the origins of this design), this "architect's table" formed the workspace for generations of Karlsruhe architecture students. The same type of chrome-plated tubular steel frame in slightly modified dimensions carried a clavichord at the 1954 Milan *Triennale*. In the 1960s the table was also available in a version with vertical crossbars set either in the middle or towards the rear – the *Eiermann 2*. Although this idea came from an assistant, the table, suitable e.g. for dining, is still known as the "Eiermann base" since it was derived from the *Eiermann 1*. Both versions are today once again being produced, by **Richard Lampert**. The original base now also comes in a version that can be dismantled for transport. As far as the tabletop is concerned, Eiermann did not prescribe anything specific. He himself worked on a solid limewood surface, and many of his students on a door panel.

# 1954

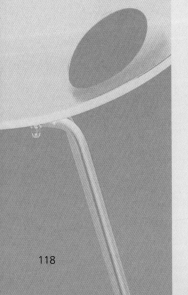

**Chair**

Design:
**Eddie Harlis**

Manufacturer:
Thonet

# S 664

Whoever was up on the latest trends had one in their living room. The shell chair was an achievement of the 1940s (with early designs contributed by Eero Saarinen and Ray and Charles Eames). But only in the ensuing years would it rise to the status of icon. In the S 664 the seat and backrest are made out of a single piece of plywood, a material that could be used, like concrete in architecture, to create a whole world of organic, often dynamic and as yet unimagined forms. The freedom of its lines displayed what today sometimes seems like the naïve optimism of the era. The combination of wood and a base of thin tubular steel likewise draws on the aforementioned models, although a strict geometric arrangement of the bars lends the design its own special appeal. Despite its bold curvature, the seat shell seems simple and straightforward. Viewed from the front, it forms a circle; from the side, a triangle. But it is the tension-charged fusion of constructedness and expressiveness that elevates the *S 664* above the average chair. The real eye-catcher is doubtless the inclusion of two openings in the lower backrest. Naturally, they look like eyes – of an animal or perhaps an alien. But they are by no means simply a deft aesthetic touch; they actually fulfil various purposes. They were necessary on the one hand to make the extreme deformation of the plywood shell possible in the first place, and on the other hand they provide ventilation and can be used as handle.

# 1955

**Stool**

Design:
**Max Bill**
**Hans Gugelot**
**Paul Hilbinger**

Manufacturer:
Ulm Academy of Design (original)

Small photo:
re-editions from Zanotta

# Ulm Stool

The multifunctional box created the year the Academy of Design was founded in Ulm is inextricably tied up with this legendary institution, which saw itself as the successor to the Bauhaus and even exceeded it in loyalty to a fixed set of principles. The construction of the box is simple as can be: three rectangular pine boards, connected at right angles by box joints, plus a round beechwood rod that penetrates the sideboards close to the ground and provides stability while forming a convenient handle. This concept, strict and ascetic, was regarded as a manifesto. After all, the rectangular form and its combination in a grid system was the ideal of the Ulm reformers, who thought in rationalist, straightforward terms and for whom every bit of ornament, every symbol and every instance of "dishonesty" were anathema. And in fact this practical minimum in design is an extremely versatile piece of furniture: for sitting on at two heights, as a side table for working or eating breakfast, as footstool, as transport box, as tray, as pedestal for speakers and – in groups – as bench, presentation surface and book table. But the spartan design also reflected another fact: due to the constant lack of funds at the oh-so-famous design school, more elaborate furnishings were out of the question.

# 1956

**Phono Combination**

Design:
**Hans Gugelot**
**Dieter Rams**
**Wilhelm Wagenfeld**

Manufacturer:
formerly Braun

Small photo:
*L 1* speaker

# SK 4 / Phonosuper

Radio-plus-record-player combinations were for a long time the industry's top product, usually in the form of corpulent "music chests". The *SK 4* provided a striking alternative, using materials that were utterly out of place in the middle-class living room: the metal housing and Plexiglas cover that would become standard over the next few decades. It was one of the first phonographs that did not try to hide its purpose by pretending to be a normal piece of furniture, but instead highlighted it. Further breaks with tradition can be found in its compact boxy form and a minimalism that was tantamount to culture shock. The application of the Bauhaus principles to a modern industrial product celebrates its premiere in this design. The same dissolution into constituent parts to which chairs were subjected in the early 20th century was now transposed onto a phonograph. The scale typography used followed **Otl Aicher's** specifications. The record player itself with its somewhat softer forms came from the drawing board of **Wilhelm Wagenfeld**. **Hans Gugelot** had the idea of using a U-shaped piece of metal for the housing. This product was therefore a joint effort. The structurally necessary contrast between the white apparatus block and the side panels of reddish elmwood was perceived at the time as giving the whole a desirable Scandinavian look. The ventilation slits likewise came out of Gugelot's stock of forms, reminiscent of rows of windows. Since they were almost identical in the front and back, the device did not have an unsightly rear view that had to be hidden. The *Phonosuper* thus fulfilled another criterion for modern furnishing concepts as an object that could be placed in the middle of a room and enjoyed from all sides. It's no surprise that this item soon became one of the architects' favourite props, perfectly corresponding as it does with its sober straight lines with those blocks of stone, steel and glass that the post-war master builders were just in the process of erecting on the bombed-out plots of German cities.

# 1956

**Easychair**

Design:
**anonymous**

Manufacturer:
Walter Knoll

## 369

The shell chair rose to become the symbol par excellence of Modernism at the latest when American designer Eero Saarinen managed to transfer its three-dimensional organic lines into an upholstered version he called *Womb* at the end of the 1940s. Not only the graceful flow of line (and thus the almost complete absence of straight edges) represented here a complete departure from the traditional easychair, but above all the fusion of all elements of the chair into a coherent whole – just as its functionalist version was in the process of being broken down into its constituent parts. One glance at the 1959 edition of the standard reference work *Die schöne Wohnung* shows that the model apartments illustrated were not furnished only with Saarinen's original, but also with a range of variations on the theme. By the mid-50s, the shell chair was a standard feature everywhere. A particularly successful variation on this new type in formal terms is the relatively small model *369*. The circular opening of the seat shell and the triangular side silhouette lend it a calm, formally balanced appearance. This equanimity is further underscored by the lateral placement of the tubular steel legs. One slides comfortably into the inclined seat, but it is still short enough to be able to climb out easily again.

# 1956

**Bed**

Design:
**Hans Gugelot**

Manufacturer:
Habit Wohnformen (re-edition)

# GB 1085

A bed is a bed is a bed. **Hans Gugelot**, one of those independent thinkers at the Ulm Academy of Design, knew how to get to the bottom of things, in both his product and furniture designs. The Dutchman, who grew up in Switzerland, had already delivered one furniture item for the new, rational style of modern living before his Ulm period: the grid-patterned *M 125* wall unit (1950). Now, with the phonographs manufactured by Braun, especially the compact box-shaped *SK 4* of 1956, known the world over as "Snow White's Coffin", a new era in product design had begun. That same year witnessed the creation of *GB 1085*, the minimal version of the bed. Here as well, Gugelot pays tribute to the "pure" rectangular shape, the key to classic Modernism. It stands for the kind of reason that does away with anything extraneous – most especially with pathos. *GB 1085* has a frame of black-painted metal, like **Herbert Hirche's** *Bar Trolley* of the same year, and is constructed just as simply. The bed consists of a metal base with an inward-bent L-profile that holds a slatted frame and mattress. The thin tubular feet complement the ascetic, if not even existentialist, flair: I sleep, therefore I am.

# 1956

# Bar Trolley

A piece of furniture made of iron, glass and rubber. The choice of these industrial materials alone could hardly be more programmatic. Added to this is a minimalism that is already defined in the design's outside edges, which at the same time form the object's main physical substrate. The trolley gives the impression of a geometric drawing transposed into three dimensions. A composition of abstract surfaces and straight lines becomes a theoretical object. The demands for visual openness made by "Liberated Living" have been consistently realized here. The contrast to the usual built-in, closed bar cabinets of the day could not be greater. This almost "immaterial" serving cart, which nonetheless serves quite earthbound needs, is a room manifesto on wheels. With its radical design, it goes beyond even anything ventured by its classic modernist predecessors (see *S 179* by A. Bamberg from 1933).
**Herbert Hirche**, who had already designed several domestic furniture programs for the Christian Holzäpfel company, came up with his *DHS 30* office furniture ensemble the same year, in which he also used rectangular steel tubing in black – a solution that would set an important precedent. This steel tubing formed the bar trolley's welded angle profile, in which industrial glass plates could be laid (Hirche's acquaintance **Hans Gugelot** used the same principle in his *GB 1085* bed). The hybrid table/shelf had four rubber wheels for mobility.

**Television Set**

Design:
**Herbert Hirche**

Manufacturer:
formerly Braun

Small photo:
with furniture by Herbert Hirche

# HF 1

**Braun** succeeded at realizing what the Bauhaus had demanded yet never truly accomplished, namely to develop prototypes that could stand for an entire genre. An outstanding and yet nearly forgotten example is the model *HF 1*. This stunningly clear design constituted a caesura in the development of TV sets. Where two years before designers had bid farewell to heavy audio chests with the *SK 4*, here a major step was taken away from the television set as furniture. The most prominent feature of the design is its box-like form, which with a slight delay would prove a formative influence on televisions to come. Its formal self-containment was underscored further by its monochromatic restraint. This TV set – which at the time must have seemed as eerily strange as an alien from a science fiction film – still looks astoundingly modern half a century later. **Herbert Hirche's** grey TV cube was the first such device without any visible wood. Conspicuous also is the strict symmetry, highlighted by the prominent pattern of lines formed by the loudspeaker slits. The chromatic and formal rigour resulted in a neutral appearance, making it easier to concentrate on the picture itself, a principle that has long since become standard. Controls that are not in constant use are concealed behind a flap on top – a groundbreaking innovation. By banishing less important functions, the central power button takes pride of place as the sole visual control, a purism that cannot be surpassed. Finally, the thin-legged steel base turns the whole thing into a minimalist statue.

# 1959

**Porcelain Tableware**

Design:
**Hans Theo Baumann**

Manufacturer:
formerly Rosenthal

# Berlin

**Hans Theo Baumann** himself was most certainly not out to cause a sensation. In his opinion, objects of daily use should blend into the background. But it was precisely the way he conceived his designs so consistently and how seriously he took the battle against unnecessary frills that brought about just the opposite. Contemporaries who found *Berlin* too simple took offence at the nakedness of the form. Quite restrained compared to the usual porcelain of the day, his coffee and tea service, the first sketches for which he did as early as three years before, did in fact cause a stir. The 35-year-old was far ahead of his time with his abstractive method (just like Trude Petri with her *Urbino* service a quarter-century earlier). Like **Hans Gugelot** with his *SK 4* phonograph (for **Braun**) and **Peter Raacke** with his *mono-a* (for **Mono**) – both similarly shocking in their simplicity – Baumann had carried clean-lined design to its logical extremes, thus anticipating a linearity that would not really come into its own until the 1960s. All of the pot-bellied charm that had so long shaped the history of tableware gave way here to an almost architectonic severity, which was underscored even further by the graphic decor. Eye-catching in the design is the slightly outward-bending upper edge of the pots, cups and jars. This standing collar makes drinking easier and ensures secure placement of the lid. But it also gives the design its own special character and acts as a visual element uniting the various pieces. Baumann, who designed a total of 20 services, achieved his masterpiece here. Glasses were later designed to match, along with sleek flatware of the same name.

# 1959

**Upholstered Furniture System**

Design:
**Michael Bayer**

Manufacturer:
formerly COR

# Quinta

Square, cube, rectangle. From the aspect of pure form alone, *Quinta* represented the kind of antithesis to cosy romanticizing imitation that was perfectly in step with the times. The 1950s brought proof that the visual language of the new objectivity could also be realized in the soft material of upholstery. The historic references are impossible to overlook. What had begun around 1955 in the field of industrial design and in particular in the collaboration of the **Braun** company and the Ulm Academy of Design now arrived in living rooms everywhere. The direction dictated by pioneers like **Hans Gugelot** and **Herbert Hirche** was expanded here into an entire program. *Quinta* was the first upholstery scheme to follow the lead of the modular cabinet units. The seating group consisted of five elements – hence the name "Quinta" – and allowed for a completely new, flexible style of furnishing. Easychair, sofa, folding lounge chair, table and cabinet were supplied in various matching variations. The chairs came either with or without armrests. Just like the pictures on the wall that once stayed in place "forever", furniture up to this point had consisted of heavy, quasi "immovable" objects. Now this established order was gradually dissolved. Whether in an I-, L- or U-shaped-pattern, the seating elements could be grouped differently at will and moved again anytime. A systematic concept and light weight were the features distinguishing this group both from contemporary furniture and from historic predecessors.

# 1959

**Silverware**

Design:
**Peter Raacke**

Manufacturer:
Mono

## mono-a

It was its very objectivity that summoned such emotion. As with **Hans Gugelot's** *SK 4* phonograph (for **Braun**) a few years previous and **Hans Theo Baumann's** nearly contemporary sleek *Berlin* service, the reactions to this flatware program were extreme. Furious rejection from some quarters came up face-to-face with enthusiastic open arms from others. The rupture between restoration of historical models and modernity that tore through the republic was now laid out for all to see on the crisp white tablecloth. The successful sales of *mono-a* showed that the avant-garde most definitely had its devotees. Revolutionary here was not only the spartan form but also the high quality of the flatware, which with its material-saving method of fabrication, which produced little waste, also anticipated ecological concerns. **Peter Raacke**, in his early 30s at the time and a vehement defender of rational product design, created here – if we may be allowed to invoke an often overused term – a design icon. *mono-a* set a new standard, making its predecessors look simply clumsy by comparison. The form- and material-conscious designer reduced the handles to an absolutely straight, flat, "chopped off" band that segues harmoniously, particularly in the fork and spoon, into the rounded sections. Raacke likewise left his mark on the corporate image. At first, the knife was punched out of a single piece of stainless steel, a so-called monoblock. And thus was born the new name of both product and brand.

# 1959

**Hi-Fi System**

Design:
**Dieter Rams**

Manufacturer:
formerly Braun

Small photo:
*LE 1* standing speaker

## studio 2

"Two speakers are needed for stereo playback." The phono combination *studio 2* introduced in 1959 was so new that the basics of stereophonics had to be explained in the brochure. The "stereo system", as people would later call it, spelled the final departure from the classic radio apparatus. The transition from "audio furniture" to phono system proceeded by separating out the radio as a discrete unit. The *CE 11* "receiver" – the tuner – was the first building block. The principle of separate functions that Ulm student Herbert Lindinger, a student of **Hans Gugelot**, had developed in his dissertation constituted a landmark. The co-ordinated components could be developed independently according to the respective device requirements and placed atop or next to one another depending on the user's needs. The option for the user to put the devices together to create a custom system was already inherent in the design. The amplifier, still combined with the record player in the *CS 11*, emancipated itself two years later (in the *CSV 13*). *studio 2* already anticipated many of the features that would characterize hi-fi systems over the decades to come. This included the silver colour and a format consisting of flat shoebox-like elements with instrument panels on the front that was known at the time from other technical devices. Industrial coolness also set the tone for the controls, the rational arrangement of which conveyed an impression of scientific precision. Surely only crystal-clear sounds could issue from such a clean-lined design. The hi-fi system advanced to a cult object of the Beatles generation.

# 1959

**Stacking Tableware**

Design:
**Hans »Nick« Roericht**

Manufacturer:
formerly Rosenthal / Thomas

# TC 100

"The demonstration model submitted as product proposal concludes this dissertation",
**Hans "Nick" Roericht** wrote at the end of a student paper for the Ulm Academy of Design.
The set of dishes in question would lead in the history of tableware to similarly radical
changes as for instance the *Frankfurt Kitchen*. Before the systematic Roericht even addressed
the form of the porcelain objects in his thesis, however, he first delved into all the issues of
marketing, material and production techniques. This procedure, by which the form emerges
from the analysis, corresponded to the Ulm doctrines. The rationally designed service,
naturally in white, was based on tightly co-ordinated double cylinder shapes that allowed for
almost artistic stacking. One key detail was that separate lids were not necessary; the bowls
could do double duty as covers. Designed for commercial kitchens, this innovative service,
which with its stunning simplicity and stringency was also welcomed by innumerable private
enthusiasts on the design scene, was snapped up almost immediately by the Museum of
Modern Art in New York, where it was displayed in a glass case as well as being put to use
in the museum cafeteria. In 1961 the highly functional design, which celebrated the aesthetic
of the masses, was launched on the market by **Rosenthal** subsidiary Thomas as *Thomas
Compact 100* and henceforward led a niche existence. Since the design was not developed
further, production of the first, but at some point outmoded, compact service was discon-
tinued almost half a century later.

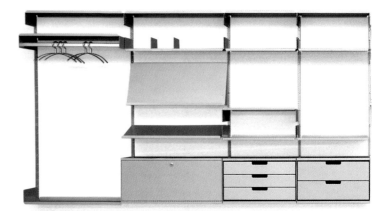

# 1960

**Shelf System**

Design:
**Dieter Rams**

Manufacturer:
sdr+ (re-edition)

# 606

**Dieter Rams**, who had been working since the mid-1950s with Ulm university lecturer **Hans Gugelot** on new phonographs for **Braun**, presented his first modular furniture with the *RZ 57* shelving. His concept consisted of nothing other than a continuation of the path he had embarked upon at Braun. As in the radios and phonographs, the transition from wood to metal represented another important step in the subsequent *RZ 60* shelving (known today as *606*). Robustness and stability were increased, surely not an insignificant aspect for a piece of furniture designed to carry loads. But the industrial impetus that turned this shelf unit into scaffolding elevated it above the average furniture of its day. This signified a change in paradigms that can be compared to the growing use of steel in the 1920s. The reserved grey as well, a fundamental colour in the new German matter-of-factness, made the same references to Dessau and Ulm – and therefore also picked up the principle of neutrality as espoused by Braun. Finally, in the early 1970s, the wall-mounted shelves expanded into a whole "room system". The basic structural element remained the perforated aluminium E-profile that carries and connects the various elements. The versatile system can be expanded to create a workplace or used as a wardrobe. With the additional option of a freestanding version, the variations increase exponentially. Customers today can put together a system precisely tailored to their own needs using an Internet configurator.

# 1962

**Easychair**

Design:
**Dieter Rams**

Manufacturer:
sdr+
as *620* program (re-edition)

Small photo:
with footstool, headrest
and occasional table

# RZ 62

In the early 1960s, the *RZ 62* (and *RZ 60*) easychairs were taken up in the furniture program offered by the Vitsoe company. The program was put together by **Dieter Rams**, who at the time had just been promoted to design chief at **Braun** and who was also the author of the *606* shelving system (today **sdr+**). A stable wooden frame with a spring core formed the basis for the chair's construction. This is covered by a shell of dust-resistant plastic that functions as backrest and outward-bending armrests. The shell surrounds a cosy enclosed seating area (a concept that, for example, Rams' student **Christian Werner** would take up in his *6900* sofa). All elements including the side and back shells are easy to remove and thus replaceable. The armchairs can easily be converted into two-seater or larger sofas. Later, the system was extended to include side tables, connecting panels (to line up elements) as well as "sector elements" allowing for a circular arrangement. Additional accessories included wooden boxes in light grey or matte black. In terms of form and material, Rams oriented his design on American models such as George Nelson's *Modular Seating System*. *RZ 62* gains its aesthetic independence through its neutral appearance, for its creator believed in unobtrusiveness in the living space, with furniture that displayed a timeless attitude.

# 1962

**Wall Lamp**

Design:
**Wilhelm Braun-Feldweg**

Manufacturer:
Mawa (re-edition)

# Britz

That **Wilhelm Braun-Feldweg**, pioneer of modern product design and spurner of everything fashionable, who had been working since the end of the 1950s as designer, artist and university teacher in the western part of divided Berlin, would name a lighting series after his newly adopted homeland, can presumably also be taken as a gesture of appreciation for the erstwhile centre of classical Modernism. Now the **Mawa** company has reissued these designs from the second German Modern period – designs that explicitly draw on the first one. The *Britz* wall lamp – named after the district in the south of Berlin in which Bruno Taut's famed horseshoe settlement was founded – is a telling example of this provenance. Its brass housing sports a matte nickel coating, brushed and painted white inside. This forms a mono-chromatic rectangle at the front, which functions as lampshade. Around the lamp a wreath of light emerges that changes according to the position. The side parts are triangles whose apex is attached to the wall so that the lamp can be tipped upward or downward on a hinge. Pushed all the way down, the light is cast up toward the ceiling, and in the other direction, toward the floor. Several variations in between are also possible, with various amounts of light shining up or down. Reminiscent of a rocker switch, this mechanism, immediately comprehensible, generates a lovely indirect light with very little technical effort. All it takes is a touch to completely transform the mood.

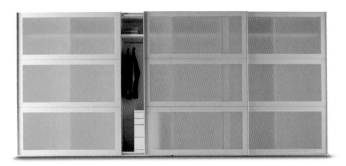

# 1963

**Closet System**

Design:
**Team Form AG**

Manufacturer:
Interlübke

Small photo l.:
*SL* closet in the revised
version by Rolf Heide

# SL

The fact that the company eventually adopted for itself the name given this piece of furniture says all we need to know about its unique significance. The *Interlübke* wall unit (today known as *SL*) was the initial spark to which the Westphalian firm owes its rise and its prominent profile today. The design actually arrived at the company as an unsolicited idea and almost landed in the waste bin. Walter Müller of Team Form, a Swiss design studio that still works with **Interlübke** today, had sent a newsletter to German furniture makers in which he proposed a new, unprecedented closet system. The interesting aspect for Leo Lübke was that the unit could be put together out of very few parts, as the crown and base were identical. Turning the closet around 180 degrees thus makes no difference. Units could be placed side-by-side to form an endless floor-to-ceiling wall unit. The wall-to-wall surface all in white was a major departure from the traditional solitary wardrobe, as well as from the modular wall unit made up of small parts such as the *M 125* system by **Hans Gugelot** (1950). The aesthetically appealing additive principle, significant for its doors opening in the same direction, concealed a highly variable interior arrangement including diverse shelves, baskets and drawers, and even a foldout bed.

# 1964

**Children's Chair**

Design:
**Richard Sapper**
**Marco Zanuso**

Manufacturer:
formerly Kartell

# K 4999

The children's chair that **Richard Sapper** developed in his adopted homeland of Italy with Marco Zanuso was a pioneering achievement, although the project took unusually long to complete. There were preliminary versions in various materials such as wood, metal or fibreglass. Then the design was completely reconceived when, in the early 1960s, the patents for thermoplastics expired and the almost infinitely malleable material became affordable, replacing plywood as furniture designers' favourite medium. In the latter half of the 1960s, innovative applications multiplied, such as the Bofinger Chair *BA 1175* (1966) and the *Garden Egg* (1968). Sapper and his partners were among the first to use the new miracle material for a chair. The injection-moulded polyethylene they chose has various advantages: It is extremely durable, lightweight, not too hard and allows colours to be used that appeal to children. The rounded corners and edges reduce the risk of injury. An eye-catching detail is the ribbed seat. One of the most important design specifications was that the chair be stackable. When the designers opted for thick, cylindrical legs, they came upon the playful idea of clamping these behind the backrest for storage. The chair thus became a kind of toy, with children able to mix and match the colours of the components to suit their fancy.

# 1964

**Sofa System**

Design:
**Friedrich Wilhelm Möller**

Manufacturer:
COR

Small photo:
individual sofa with runners

## Conseta

Comparing the current *Conseta* range with the originals from the 1960s, one has to look very closely to discern any correspondences. Like a car model that changes from generation to generation, this upholstered furniture group, which has remained on the market for over four decades, has been adapted to fit the respective aesthetic. The most striking detail that has survived are the metal runners that serve as legs, just one of seven available variations. What has also remained is the strict rechtilinearity that makes the upholstered parts seem like components in a construction kit. This was not the first modular sofa system. Rather, it was modelled on earlier examples, such as the *Modular Seating System* by American designer George Nelson in 1955, the basic idea of which **COR** was the first to adopt, with *Quinta* in 1959. *Conseta* offered an even wider variety of options. Five chair units, combined into two- and three-seater sofas, result in widths ranging from 60 to 240 centimetres. The corner units and connection system that allow the sofa to fit almost any room have today long become standard. This concept was nothing less than the invention of the corner sofa, which, in symbiosis with the television set, would henceforth form the focal point of the living room (a new development that **Rolf Benz** picked up on the same year with its *Addiform* program). Over half a million elements have been sold of this Volkswagen among sofas.

# 1966

**Chair**

Design:
**Helmut Bätzner**

Manufacturer:
formerly Bofinger

Small photo:
table to match "Bofinger Chair"

# Bofinger

When the first plastic chair formed from a single piece was introduced at the Cologne Furniture Fair in 1966, it was once again a case of a happy marriage between an inspired designer and a like-minded entrepreneur. Architect Helmut Bätzner had developed a seating system for the reconstruction of the state theatre in Karlsruhe. Looking as if a skin had been stretched over an imaginary frame, the chair is marked by a complex system of grooves and angles. The practical advantages are obvious: Although it weighs only four kilograms, the polyester chair is stable, weather-resistant and can be stacked to extreme heights. The **Bofinger** furniture company was excited about Bätzner's design, found the right plastics expert and commissioned the 10-tonne press needed for fabrication. The Bofingerstuhl was available in eight bright colours and, with 120,000 sold, became one of the most widespread Pop-Art-inspired objects anywhere. At the same time, it holds its own as a true industrial prototype. The *BA 1171* (aka *Bofinger Chair*) served as model for a whole new type of chair (one year later, Vico Magistretti designed the polyester chair *Selene* for Artemide), a mass phenomenon similar to the bentwood chairs *No. 14* (1859) and *2200* (1936). Repeated attempts by the **Habit** company to reissue the chair did not meet with success, but it can nonetheless be found in gardens and street cafés the world over in a panoply of less aesthetically demanding adaptations.

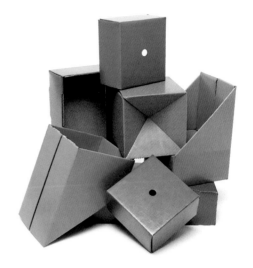

# 1966

**Furniture System**

Design:
**Peter Raacke**

Manufacturer:
formerly Papp-Faltmöbel

Small photo:
*7 Sachen* children's
cardboard furniture

# Papp

In the 1960s, **Peter Raacke** was working as lecturer at the Academy of Design in Ulm. And the first furniture series made of cardboard definitely speaks the conceptual vernacular we are familiar with from those circles. It is not only pure systematics, but also a critique translated into form, colour and material of the merchandise aesthetic that had become part of the standard student repertoire at the universities during those years. Aspects important to Raacke were simple, effortless production using primitive technologies, a low price and a new and unconventional domestic aesthetic. Lightweight and changeable furniture was still a highly subversive concept at the time: It was perfectly clear to Raacke that *Papp* would hardly find its way into living rooms, but did have a chance to be accepted for children's rooms, party rooms and student apartments. The project in fact began with children's furniture, which proved so successful that it was soon followed by versions for adults – a rare transfer in the history of design. The fact that these cardboard pieces were meant to be self-built – they came in pre-punched cardboard sheets – was part of the emancipatory concept. The program included stools, sofas, tables, a shelf and various chairs, including the stackable *Papp-Otto* (→ p.**518**) that would later become so famous. The cardboard furniture came in pink, red, violet and white. As a manifesto against the absolutist conviction that objects had to be created for eternity, the relatively short service life of this instant furniture in addition demonstrated the new throwaway principle.

# 1966

**Lamp**

Design:
**Ingo Maurer**

Manufacturer:
formerly Design M

Small photo:
*Lucellino* wall lamp
by Ingo Maurer, 1992

# Bulb

The bulb in the bulb was his first product: a pop object in the form of an oversized light bulb in the manner of Claes Oldenburg. The master of the meta-level would create several variations on this ambiguous design. It comes in both clear glass (→ p.**464**) and milky white plastic, the latter version a new type of lamp that no longer stood or was hung up, but rather could be laid down anywhere. This of course fit in perfectly with the casual lifestyle of that non-conformist era. The theme of the light bulb never lost its fascination for Ingo Maurer, who lived for a time in the land of Thomas Edison. Where others tried to hide the traditional light source, he highlighted and thus exalted it. The model *Wo bist Du, Edison, ...?* (*Where Are You, Edision?*) from the late 1990s consists of a 360-degree hologram of a light bulb surrounded by a cylindrical shade, so to speak a high-tech variant of his first design. In between came the chandelier *Birds Birds Birds*, with winged bulbs that begin to glow when connected by means of touch with the earth (an innovation at the time). The option of changing the position and direction of the individual flexibly attached light sources would also set a precedent. The design gleans its particular charm from the virtuoso dramatic contrast between the naturalistically rendered wings and the open construction consisting of standard light bulb and bent glass. These same quotes are repeated in *Lucellino*, the solo version of the wall lamp. In this flying light bulb with its goose-feather wings, the designer-cum-artist has condensed his playful and symbolic handling of lighting technology into a single memorable visual metaphor.

# 1967

**Chair**

Design:
**Günter Beltzig**

Manufacturer:
formerly Gebrüder Beltzig

Small photo:
table and low version of
*Floris* chair

# Floris

With all our enthusiasm for the wave of utopian designs made possible by the first flowering of thermoplastics in the late 1960s, we often fail to recognize that good design is not a case of a random recourse to science fiction. Thus, the young designer Günter Beltzig was not interested in creating a spectacular figure, an "eye-catcher", but rather in sounding out the possibilities inherent in such an extremely malleable material. His aim was to create an optimized device for sitting. The basic idea behind his *Floris* chair was that it should snuggle up to the body like a second skin and in particular provide support for the back, a theme that is still of great pertinence today. The biomorphic shape of the three-legged chair – one that even now still takes some getting used to with its neck support reminiscent of the head of an alien – was a prime example of ergonomy. It was not a case here – as with **Luigi Colani** for example, who is often mentioned in the same breath as Belzig – of a "sculptural" formal concept, but rather of a problem whose solution takes the form of numerous step-by-step compromises. Elasticity and stability are finely balanced. The unpleasant sweating that can come from sitting on closed plastic shells is prevented by ventilation channels. The stackable *Floris* was produced in an edition of 100 by the company Belziger had founded the year before with his two brothers (in the late 1980s there was a re-edition in a similar quantity). The chairs were manufactured in the "shocking colours" of orange, red and yellow, and some in white as well for painting in other colours. The originals were semi-matte, and the new edition glossy. A 1960s original went for around 17,000 euros in a recent auction.

# 1967

# Sinus

"Between the inherent necessity of the object and the freedom of form there exists a curious scope for choice", explained theorist Walter Zeischegg. Apart from **Otl Aicher**, he was the only Ulm Academy of Design teacher who was on the faculty all the way from the planning phase to the closing of the institution. Abstract, sculptural thinking and the new scientific approach met and melded in the sculptor Zeischegg. He occupied himself with geometric structures, but also, for example, with the use of magnets, and he owned a whole series of patents. In addition to his work at the academy, Zeischegg was in charge of designing **Helit's** line of office supplies starting in the late 1960s. The systematic thinker had designed over 70 products for the Westphalian company by 1983. One of the first was the plastic ashtray *Sinus*, which is available in a whole palette of intense colours – atypical for Ulm but right in step with the Pop Art era. The colour effects are in fact one of the strengths of this design. What is perhaps the best known, but at any rate the most-awarded ashtray in history emerged from studies Zeischegg performed on the geometry of the sine curve. His research focused on the abstracting analysis of form. Applying the results of this analysis was at first viewed as being only of secondary interest. But the assignment of a purpose after the fact worked to perfection in the case of *Sinus*. The sine waves created not only the object's feet and the indentations for holding cigarettes, but also made the ashtray optimally stackable. With its combination of formal rigour and playful whimsy, this ashtray is even suitable for non-smokers: as a fun-to-look-at small plastic sculpture adorning the desk.

# 1968

**Garden Easychair**

Design:
**Peter Ghyczy**

Manufacturer:
Ghyczy Novo (re-edition)

# Garden Egg

The chair and stool were reinvented in the 1960s, not least due to the advent of the new plastics. The contribution made by Hungarian designer Peter Ghyczy to this development was a piece of garden furniture totally unlike anything seen before. The closed, round shape, an ellipse both from above and from the side, happily does without all the features of a standard chair. The so-called *Gartenei* (*Garden Egg*), a lightweight at about 70 centimetres diameter and 14 kilograms, probably reminded its contemporaries as much of a space capsule as the egg that gave the chair its nickname. It resembled another futuristic chair that had come out a year before: *Pastilli* by Eero Aarnio of Finland (today made by Adelta). Ghyczy's ingenious idea was the integrated cover that acts as backrest when flipped open and, when closed, protects the cushion. Ghyczy himself began producing the comfortable, 45-centi-metre-low garden chair again in a limited edition a few years ago, with better sealing around the edges and extras such as a 360-degree swivel disc. The high-gloss version can be made in practically any colour.

# 1968

**Bed**

Design:
**Rolf Heide**

Manufacturer:
Müller Möbelwerkstätten

# Stacking Lounger

Back in the days when hitchhiking was in vogue and the improvised mattress camp was regarded as "progressive", the idea that furnishings should be just as variable as the modern peripatetic lifestyle couldn't be far off. In the mid-1960s, **Rolf Heide** designed the first bed whose position wasn't permanently defined – something that is still the rule even today. The principle of mobility was joined by the concept of multiple uses. The result was a bed that can be used as a sofa by day without having to incorporate any special mechanism. The basic idea is already betrayed by the name: the bed frames are made to be stacked atop one another. This allows an extra bed to be stowed away in a space-saving, "invisible" manner. The uncovered screws emphasize the "low-tech" character of the solution and the many practical applications for this unconventional, unpretentious piece of furniture. Other advantages of this bed alternative are easy assembly and disassembly, along with easy transport. Today the *Stapelliege* (*Stacking Lounger*) is offered as part of a furniture program called *modular* (**Müller Möbelwerkstätten**), in which new editions are being issued of early Heide designs.

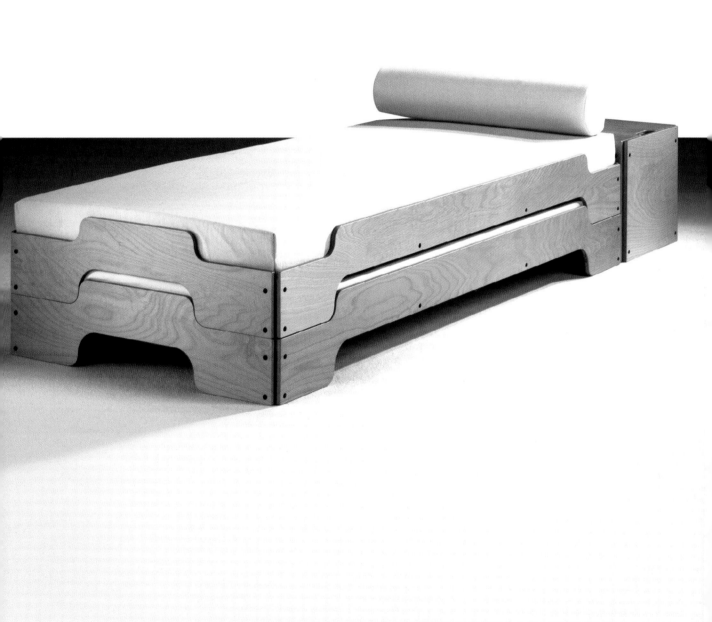

# 1968

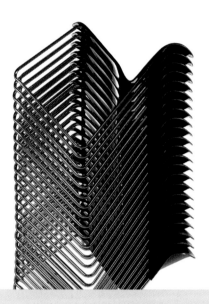

**Chair**

Design:
**Gerd Lange**

Manufacturer:
Drabert

# SM 400

In the "swinging sixties", chairs became pop objects, brightly coloured gems that at the same time exploited the form-giving advantages of the new plastics. One of this era's most successful chairs was the fully plastic model *BA 1171* from **Bofinger**. It was quickly followed by the *SM 400*, likewise stackable, but substantially lighter. This is due to a clever construction concept in which a plastic shell and tubular steel frame lend each other stability. Even this combination was innovative, giving birth to a whole new chair type. The identical steel tubes at each side function as horizontal supports under the seat, form runners along the ground and then disappear vertically into the backrest. In yet another rendition of the shell chair, backrest and seat fuse into a single sculptural object. A notable detail is the pronounced depression between the two. *SM 400* is an organic design with an unusually curvy surface whose complexity exceeded all that had gone before – a chair that still looks astoundingly modern even today. The soft transitions were naturally also adapted to fit the curves of the body, an ongoing concern of the **Drabert** company. The strong recess formed by the backrest and a seat that flares up slightly at the sides, along with the "tongue" at the front, are visible comfort factors.

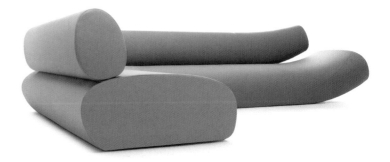

# 1968

**Upholstered
Furniture System**

Design:
**Tata Ronkholz-Tölle**

Manufacturer:
formerly Habit

Small photo:
*Lava* sofa elements by
Studio Vertijet for COR, 2007

# Landscape For Living

It was sofa, easychair, lounger and stool all wrapped up in one. Since the traditional furniture terms no longer fit, a new one had to be invented. The **Habit** company lays claim to presenting the first "begehbare Wohnlandschaft", or "walk-through landscape for living", at the end of the turbulent 1960s at the Cologne Furniture Fair. The sources behind this German innovation, one that would add a new and enriching dimension to the cultural history of sitting, are obvious. It was for one thing a further development of the systematic, modular way of thinking that was already widespread in the country. Like the building blocks of the stereo system created by **Braun**, the seating elements are stacked one on top of the other, a brand new idea as removable cushions had up until then only been available individually. By combining these in both vertical and horizontal directions, a "landscape" can be laid out featuring a variety of heights. The arrangement could be changed at will in this interactive furnishing scheme, making it suitable for multiple purposes, i.e. multifunctional. The imposition of an official formal placement was passé. The distinction between sitting and reclining was abolished here just as that between space and furniture. The Wohnlandschaft, which even does without a frame, is one with the floor. Mattress camps and sit-ins were of course an integral part of the youth protest culture of that era, without which the emergence of this variable relaxation area would have been unthinkable. Almost every furniture maker was soon busy developing its own landscape type, such as **Otto Zapf** with his *Pillorama*. Now this earthbound furniture scheme is experiencing a late revival in current designs like *Lava* from **Studio Vertijet**.

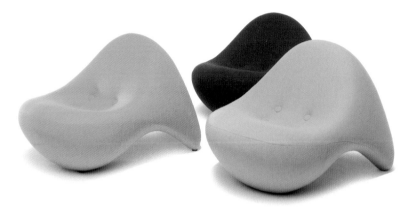

# 1968

**Lounge Chair**

Design:
**Luigi Colani**

Manufacturer:
Kusch + Co (re-edition)

Small photo:
*TV-Relax* easychair (re-edition)

# TV-relax

It's hard to believe that this strange object could offer a relaxing perch. The practicality of **Luigi Colani's** late-1960s lounge chair is already called into question by the object itself with its strange and striking looks. Can such a "free-flowing" form really be functional? It doesn't have any corners or straight edges, but instead features fluid transitions and surfaces from which nothing projects. In purely physical terms, the design consists only of two main elements: the inner, evidently mouldable mass and its fabric skin. In fact it is a foamed form, a technique that had up to then been used primarily in the automotive industry and was applied to furniture here for the first time. Two feet "grow" out of the backrest at the rear of the chair. This construction, which also comes in a smaller version as easychair, rests on a central base. The customary elements of a chair have been dissolved and melted into a single overall shape. This transforms the lounge chair into an object in space that can readily be compared to a Henry Moore sculpture. But isn't it also a piece of Pop Art, the art form that turned everyday objects into art and vice-versa? Despite its unusual proportions, Colani meant this chair to be an object of everyday use. The moulded seat is obviously designed to fit the line of the human body, while the elongated point recalls instead the nose of an airplane. The year of its creation, 1968, a date that has long since taken on mythical proportions in Germany, marked the high point of a cultural rebellion. 40 years old, Colani delivered a whole inventory to match the mood of the times, creating futuristic pieces whose emblematic power still resonates today. This curvaceous divan was recently put up for auction at Sotheby's in New York and went for a six-figure price. The sale was a signal that it was high time to re-issue the sixties brainchild, and now it can be enjoyed again in over 60 colours.

172

**Tea Service**

Design:
**Walter Gropius**

Manufacturer:
Rosenthal

# TAC 1

After emigrating to the USA in the late 1930s, Bauhaus founder **Walter Gropius** worked as an architect and had reached the ripe age of 85 when he launched his tea service *TAC 1* on the market – making this a late work. He named it after his famous architecture office, The Architects Collaborative, which he founded in 1945 in Cambridge, Massachusetts, and where a handful of architects worked with him on his designs. By enlisting Gropius, the **Rosenthal** company, for whom the old master designed a porcelain factory in Selb and a glass works in Amberg starting in 1963, completed the arc to classical Modernism of German provenance. What resulted in the case of the tea service is a tribute to the circle that is distinguished by finely calibrated proportions and interesting radial transitions between curved and flat zones. The service was obviously inspired by the traditional Chinese tea bowl, a form dating back thousands of years. This model dictated not only the voluminous form of the cups, but also, stood on its head, the wide-bodied teapot, creamer and sugar bowl. As the central element of the ensemble, the teapot derives its harmonious effect from the closed hemispherical form into which the lid is integrated (comparable to Trude Petri's *Urbino* from 1931 and the exact opposite of the teapot designed by **Marianne Brandt** in 1924). Functional and well-thought-out details include the flat and relatively wide double handle, which allows the lid to be held on while the tea sieve is removed, the long, upward projection of the spout and the tapering base. The overall impression yielded by the interplay of curve and anti-curve lends the design a signature silhouette, particularly in the black version that was Gropius' favourite.

# 1969

Design:
**Luigi Colani**

Manufacturer:
formerly COR

# Orbis

A wide-open chair surface that invites casual lounging, *Orbis* epitomizes the anti-authoritarian spirit of the 1960s, a longing for freedom that was even reflected in looser sitting manners. New furniture came onto the scene to fit the trend, often making use of the new, mouldable plastics. This particular solution may be less radical than the work of some contemporary colleagues such as Verner Panton or **Otto Zapf**, who designed entire sofa landscapes. Yet it represents nothing less than the reversal of the traditional concept of an armchair supported by an interior frame. **Luigi Colani** brought the frame to the outside, as had Le Corbusier in his *Grand Confort* (1928), where the cushions are put in a cage. Foam then became super-fluous. The body of the *Orbis chair*, formed of one piece and holding a loose cushion in its hollow, rests in a shallow shell made of polyurethane – a construction resembling that of the *RZ 62* chair by **Dieter Rams** (1962). In *Orbis*, the sides remain free. The black or white shell forms a stark contrast with the brightly coloured upholstery in the original. The chairs can be connected via snaps to form a sofa. The fact that these monuments to sitting are also set atop casters for mobility was tantamount to a renunciation of the rigid furniture hierarchy of the forefathers.

# 1969

**Wall Storage Unit**

Design:
**Dorothee Maurer-Becker**

Manufacturer:
Vitra Design Museum (re-edition)

Small photo:
1970 version

# Uten.Silo

The idea of not trying to hide the smaller objects of daily use, but instead presenting them proudly on the wall in a fitting setting, perfectly exemplifies the mood of the artistically inspired 1960s. While hatching a concept for a toy in which children could stick geometric forms into a wall panel, Dorothee Maurer-Becker, at the time married to **Ingo Maurer**, came up with the idea for a three-dimensional bulletin board. Small utensils and paraphernalia could be stowed in containers of varying sizes and shapes. Thus emerged a universal organizational system that could be used in the office, the kitchen, the bathroom, or in children's or student's rooms. After presenting a prototype at the Frankfurt Fair in spring 1969, the decision was made to manufacture a metal injection mould for the piece, a tool that weighed over three tonnes and cost a quarter of a million marks – an amazing sum for the time, seeing as a mid-class car could still be purchased for well under 10,000 marks. The investment paid off. The odds and ends display – available today in red, black, white and chrome – was right in step with the spirit of the times and soon became a cult object. The possibilities offered by plastic as material were exploited thoroughly here in what amounted to a Pop object for everyman. Its charm lies in part in the contradiction between industrial precision and whimsical freedom, as well as between logical arrangement and the original, random choices of which objects to stow, which made every *Uten.Silo* a one-of-a-kind personal "artwork".

# 1969

**Chair**

Design:
**Herbert Hirche**

Manufacturer:
Richard Lampert (re-edition)

# Santa Lucia

The frame consists of two U-shaped bent and diagonally angled tubes. Conspicuous here is the concave chair back, the front edge of which forms a single unbroken line with the back legs – a detail that gives the design a certain severity, and at the same time a stable construction in which the sitter's back is enclosed but his arms are still free to move. Back in the early 1950s, **Herbert Hirche** had already designed his first stackable wicker chair, with the tubular steel frame typical for the times as well as other formal similarities to later models. Back and seat were connected, the back legs slanted. On the quest for greater freedom and mobility, he developed over the course of the next two decades a whole series of these lightweight, sturdy work chairs: a classic example of careful variation on a theme (he used a version on runners as his own desk chair). In 1957 he was commissioned to furnish the Italian restaurant Santa Lucia in Stuttgart. The result was an even lighter wicker chair, in which modernity melds with nostalgic echoes of "Bella Italia". No less a figure than **Walter Gropius** used this chair that very same year in his model flat at the Berlin *Interbau* architecture exhibition. A good decade later, when the restaurant was expanded, Hirche created his last wicker chair – and also his most elegant, for the flow of line is particularly harmonious here.

**Door-handle**

Design:
**Rudolf Wilke**

Manufacturer:
Hewi

Small photo:
*111* door-handle in aluminium

# Series 111

Industrialist and engineer Rudolf Wilke developed a door-handle that echoes some of the features of **Walter Gropius'** design from the early 1920s, but differs in some key aspects that make it at least as important an innovation as its famous model. Similarities include the cylindrical shape of the handle and the corresponding round forms of the plate and lock. These logical formal decisions account for the clear-cut overall impression made by both designs. A decisive extra, however, is the extension of the model *111* to form a "U" (with a straight mid-section and two 90-degree arcs), a modification that avoids at least two disadvantages of conventional handles: the slipping off of the hand and the involuntary hooking of things onto the handle when walking past. What ultimately raised Wilke's design to the status of trendsetter was the use of plastic. A polyamide was chosen from the class of thermoplastics, a relatively hard, heat- and weather-resistant material that possesses high formal stability. Other advantages offered by plastic are obvious: In addition to its malleability and surfaces that are somewhat softer and warmer to the touch than metal, door-handles could suddenly be supplied in different colours. This multiplied the design potential exponentially: handles could serve as an orientation aid through the use of various colour schemes, for example, or be deployed to create artistic effects in the interior. *111*, the nucleus of an entire product family, thus became the favourite of architects and one of the most copied products ever.

# 1971

# Container

Only an adaptable piece of furniture can accompany its user move after move. Grid, module, program: these are the catchwords designers use to describe flexible solutions that aspire to this kind of longevity. Among the German furniture designers who succeed at this aim time and again is **Rolf Heide**. One of the systematic thinker's specialties is "case furniture". He gave his first foray into the field the laconically descriptive name *Container*. The system consisted of cabinet and shelf elements of varying depths and heights, set on casters for mobility – an innovation at the time. The option of arranging the storage units in multiple ways in relation to one another and to the room gave the system a never-before-seen flexibility. This led to a revival of the moveable closet units, the series' original form, in the latter half of the 20th century, when they took on a whole new dimension. Under the name *Modular*, Heide's program was reissued by **Müller Möbelwerkstätten** in a highly modified version.

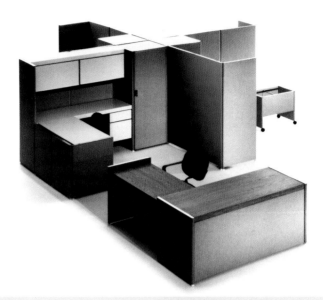

# 1971

**Cabinet System**

Design:
**Otto Zapf**

Manufacturer:
formerly Zapf

Small photo:
*Zapf Office System* for
Knoll International

# Softline

**Otto Zapf**, who worked with Niels Vitsoe and others to set up a production and sales company for the furniture designed by **Dieter Rams**, also created many of his own ground-breaking designs, which he also produced largely on his own. Among them is the modular *Softline* program from the year 1970. Flexible materials and their connection by snaps were the characteristics of this furniture series, which comprised shelves, cabinets, tables, chairs and beds. Dedicated to the modular concept and to humanitarian ideals, the furniture reformer was asked to develop an office system for the US company Knoll International at the beginning of the 1970s, and this is where he started. The incredibly successful furniture program, originally named after its designer, is grounded in the basic concept of the "human touch". Within a single year, Zapf had developed stable, replaceable parts out of which an open office could be laid out and rearranged at any time. The main elements were fabric-covered wall panels in various sizes, which swallowed sound and softened the overall ambience. This impression was enhanced even further by the rounded corners. The dividing walls created shielded work cubicles: an office within the office. Concentration-promoting visual calm was achieved by renouncing handles. The combination of simplicity, a high degree of functionalism and high-grade materials proved to be a strong incentive to buy for capital-rich clientele. This became Knoll's entrée into the world of modular furniture.

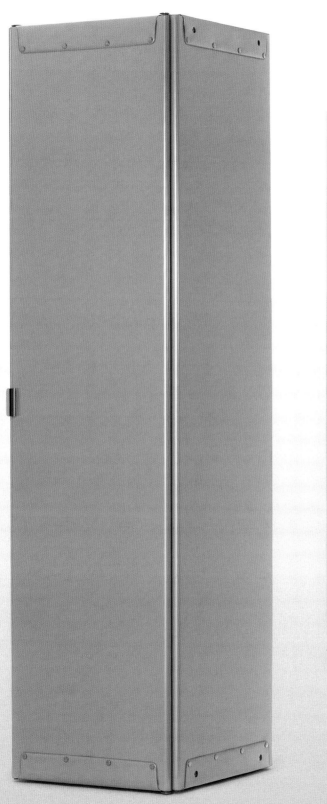

# 1972

**Table Lamp**

Design:
**Richard Sapper**

Manufacturer:
Artemide

# Tizio

It was a commission from Artemide. **Richard Sapper** took up the challenge, and then realized that he himself didn't even have the perfect desk lamp. His mission was to try to square the circle like so many designers before him: the desideratum was the greatest radius of action in the smallest amount of space. *Tizio*, named after a giant in Greek mythology, was one of the early lamps created for the tiny new halogen bulbs that had been invented a good decade before and were finally becoming widespread. This was a fortunate coincidence, because the Milan-based designer wanted to create a lamp that would cast light only where it was needed, a task for which a small reflector is ideal. The low weight of the light source was also advantageous for the construction of the lamp, which works like a mobile. The mechanical parts consist of two parallel arms that swing like a gymnast around the high bar. In the first prototype Sapper used jam jars as weights, which he filled with water until the weight was right; in the second one he used metal disks threaded onto the arms. A relatively small, pot-like foot on which the user can rotate *Tizio* like a building crane provides sufficient stability. This makes the lamp extremely variable and lets it be moved into innumerable different positions. Sometimes it is folded together and looks like it's ducking, and at other times it stretches up straight and high. A light touch is enough to change the lamp's position. The design is free of all decorative elements. The lamp head, which can be tipped, takes the form of a parallelogram, echoing the construction principle. Until the early 1990s, *Tizio* was put together by hand, although it had been designed for industrial series production. Sapper fought for a long time for a reduction in price, since his original intention was to design an economical lamp.

**Coffee Maker**

Design:
**Florian Seiffert**

Manufacturer:
formerly Braun

# KF 20

Once upon a time, the comforting gurgling sound of the coffee machine was as yet unknown in kitchens and offices. Although automatic coffee making did look back on a long history and was even a topic of discussion at the Bauhaus, it would take half a century for an electric coffee machine based on the German filter to become a universal appliance. Gradually, coffee drinking – which had always been something of a festive, ritualized act – became part of the everyday routine. Industrial designer Florian Seiffert, who at the time belonged to the young guard at **Braun** and later started his own business as a specialist in this metier, succeeded at creating a model that from the very outset was regarded as one of those milestones that define an entire product genre. In fact, an apparatus for brewing the roasted brown beans actually leaves plenty of scope for creative design. A wide range of constellations is conceivable. Seiffert chose a structure oriented around the hierarchical principle of the water tower: on top is the tank, in the middle the snap-in filter and at the base a glass pot standing on a hotplate. A circular vertical section was the obvious choice due to the round shape of both pot and filter. From these premises emerged a stately column some 40 centimetres high, available for a time in a range of bright colours. The two pipes conducted along the exterior underscore the mechanical character of the coffee-making process. In practice, *KF 20* rationalized this process considerably, not least due to extremely easy operation from the front via a solitary rocker switch with a clearly visible on-off lamp for the forgetful. But the story did not end there: The new Braun model *KF 400* also comes from Seiffert's drawing board.

**Sitting Device**

Design:
**Luigi Colani**

Manufacturer:
formerly
Top System Burkhard Lübke

Small photo:
1978 children's chair

# Zocker

With the availability of the new mouldable plastics, furniture conventions also became more fluid. Together with colleagues such as Helmut Bätzner (*Bofinger Chair BA 1171*, 1966) or Peter Ghyczy ("*Garden Egg*" 1968), **Luigi Colani** was one of the pioneers who consistently sounded out the possibilities offered by the malleable mass. The *Zocker* chair, developed for children, and the somewhat larger, formally identical *Colani* chair he later added for adults, are multifunctional pieces whose desk-like "backrest" can be used as a perch for a variety of items, such as a glass, writing implements or toys, or even just an elbow. The chairs them–selves can be used for work or play. Their smooth edges and the seamless transition between the functional parts minimize any risk of a child's getting injured. Lightweight and sturdy, the chairs are stackable as well as impact- and scratch-resistant. They are more like an artistic masterstroke than a planned construct – a biomorphic, imaginative sculpture for everyday enjoyment. Finally, this anti-authoritarian experimental furniture is also a telling barometer of changing lifestyles. The neon colours act like an invitation to step right up and give them a try.

# 1973

**Nesting Tables**

Design:
**Peter Draenert**

Manufacturer:
Draenert

# Nurglas

An utterly simple table in a single piece, which is transparent and thus maximally preserves the feeling of open space while also illustrating other principles of classical Modernism. This neutral accessory, which visually negates itself, also has practical advantages, e.g. stability, secure footing and an easy-to-clean surface. Club table, side table and nesting tables are made of float glass bent at a temperature of 800 degrees Celsius – a highly complex process. Under this enormous heat, the purity of the glass is put to the test, with the risk of it developing a "dimpled skin" or rainbow effects. Since glass bending is a demanding manual task that must be performed on each piece individually, no table turns out like any other, which in essence completely contradicts the anonymity of this design. On the other hand, it is precisely its minimalist concept that dictates the compulsion to exactitude; any excessive deviation would be immediately noticeable. Of late, *Nurglas* has become available in coloured versions as well (practically any RAL colour is possible). Whether transparent or opaque, the harmonious and eye-catching U-shape is what comes to the fore.

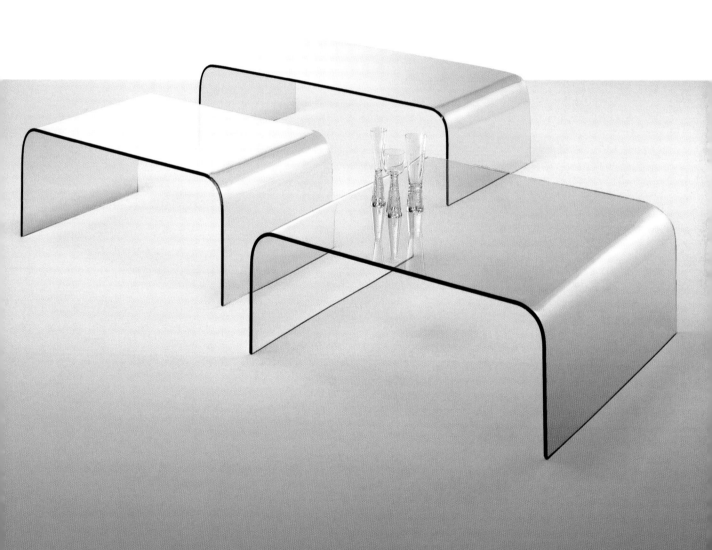

# 1975

## Easychair

Design:
**Herbert Ohl**
**Jutta Ohl**

Manufacturer:
Arflex (original)

Small photo:
*Nuvola* easychair
for Wilkhahn, 1982

# O-Line

A lightweight helicopter seat and a baggage net out of nylon webbing came together here in the idea to design a chair with low volume, low weight and a transparent look. The relationship of the *O-Line* concept that emerged with the classical Modernist designs of the 1920s is more than skin deep. It represents the continuation of the principle of "open living" propagated back then, translated by way of the latest technical advances. Ohl's net concept was realized for the first time in the 1970s by the Italian company Arflex as a flat, comfortable easychair made of two identical parts. The designer himself drove forward the further development of the concept by visiting workshop after workshop in Milan and even building the machine to produce the chair himself, until finally the renowned office furniture manufacturer **Wilkhahn** decided to collaborate on the project already underway. This second-generation chair owes its striking silhouette to the two spherically curving aluminium rings that form the frame, onto which the elastic material is tightly stretched. The tubular frame continues into a likewise idiosyncratic metal base made up of closely linked concentric circles. Unusual in many aspects, the design set the stage for the net backrests that are so prevalent today in office chairs, whereas this innovation is now largely absent from the domestic realm. With *Nuvola* (Wilkhahn 1982), Ohl and his wife later came up with a lighter variant: a stackable cantilevered chair, the armchair version of which embraces the sitter with a large, wing-like backrest.

# 1975

**Cabinet System**

Design:
**Manufacturer's design**

Manufacturer:
Flötotto

Small photo:
closet

# Profile System

In the mid-1970s **Flötotto** developed a furniture system designed to be extremely simple, practical and variable. The Ulm Academy of Design no longer existed, but its schematic spirit lived on, finally making its way into the German everyday routine with the *Profilsystem*. The heart of the system was the patented corner connector, enabling pieces to be assembled out of just a few different standardized parts without any need for glue or pegs. These connectors in conjunction with the wood profiles that gave the system its name formed the framework for this universal case furniture, into which coloured panels of either glass or plastic could be inserted. This created containers that could be stacked or lined up at will, forming the basis for wall units, towers, room dividers, shelves or vitrines – practically a complete furniture program which could be used to furnish not only homes, but even offices. Since the *Profile System* is not only flexible, but exceptionally robust as well, it lends itself to use in schools, kindergartens and children's bedrooms. The container concept dovetails perfectly with the constant need for rearranging furniture entailed by the dynamics of groups of children. The brightly coloured building block furniture itself becomes a kind of toy, a challenge to creativity. In addition, special furniture items, such as a changing table, can be created as needed. Another decisive advantage is that damaged components can simply be exchanged for new ones.

# 1975

**Spotlight**

Design:
**Manufacturer's design**

Manufacturer:
Erco

Small photo:
2006 version

# TM

Measuring only 20 centimetres and able to pivot in any direction, this lamp, launched on the market in the mid-1970s, is the ultimate spotlight. The "spot", as these lamps are known for short, had come into use a decade before, making it possible for the first time to systematically illuminate tightly defined areas from a great distance. Applications range from exhibitions, concerts and trade fairs to the private sphere. The islands of light that were now possible could be used to create never-before-imagined accents, for designing lighting schemes that went beyond setting light/dark contrasts to encompass much more finely differentiated and original effects. This was one of the first new lighting media to be added to the classic light bulb. *TM* is an effective "light machine" whose housing and handle of high-grade cast aluminium openly convey their functions. Accessories such as glare shields, wall floodlights, lenses or coloured filters can be slid into the guide rails at the sides or directly attached to the housing. *TM* is a tube whose cylindrical form acts as reflector for the light source. There is nothing extraneous in this almost banal form, surely one of the reasons it has stood the test of time. *TM* is available in white, black or silver – neutral colours that underscore its lasting value. Finally, the minimalist model is also a good example of the way reduced design can resist changes entailed by advances in technology. Maintaining the same proportions, the lighting series was merely supplemented with smaller formats for halogen, PAR, low-voltage halogen and metal halide lamps.

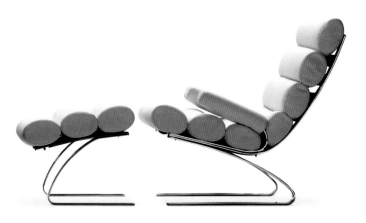

# 1976

**Easychair**

Design:
**Reinhold Adolf
Hans-Jürgen Schröpfer**

Manufacturer:
COR

# Sinus

It was out of production for years, sharing the fate of much more famous furniture classics. This space-dominating chair derives its strong visual impact from the interplay of several unique features. These include its graceful silhouette, seeming less like a mathematically calculated angle than the bold stroke of an artist's hand, as well as the parade of identical cushion elements. Historical references include **Ludwig Mies van der Rohe's** chaise longue of 1931 and the chair Eileen Gray created one year later, *Pirelli*, which already used the hard/soft contrast between metal and cushions that is seen here. What's special about *Sinus* is the frame made up of a broad metal band that stands on steel runners of equal width, which give way like a flat spring, contributing not insignificantly to the chair's comfort. Belts are woven around the frame and the cushions snapped onto them. In its basic conception, Sinus appears to be a synthesis of Mies van der Rohe's *Barcelona chair* and his cantilevered chair. However, the cantilever principle has been reversed here, with the runners opening at the front instead of behind. The opposing lines increase the optical tension. When the matching footrest is added and the ensemble viewed from the side, the opening in front is closed and a new and incisive graphic image created.

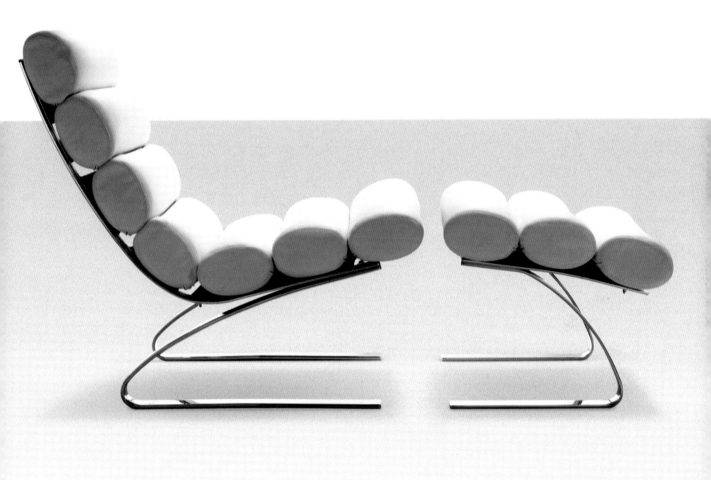

# 1976

**Silverware**

Design:
**Carl Pott**

Manufacturer:
Pott

Small photo:
from left to right: cheese knife,
salad servers, fish servers

# Model 33

In a field where it seemed that everything that could be done had been done, this new series caused quite a sensation in professional circles. Carl **Pott** had in effect reinvented the fork. The entrepreneur and designer made this tool of European dining culture, a finger substitute we use to safely conduct cut-up food to our mouths, even more foolproof. This was achieved by broadening the head of the fork. The more generous surface was intended to make it easier to scoop up sauces and vegetables. Food stays on the fork and even the notorious peas can't escape quite so easily. But how could the designer accommodate this larger width without making the tines unnecessarily broad or the intervals between them so wide as to defeat the purpose? The solution was to make five tines instead of four: an absolute innovation in the several-hundred-year history of this tool of civilization. Overall, this is a harmoniously articulated flatware set, in which the widened fork corresponds with the generous proportions of the spoons. The designer lent *Model 33* – which comprises a total of 31 different implements including a bouillon spoon, cheese knife and a fish serving set – an original graphic accent in the form of a fine line inscribed horizontally at the end of the rounded handles. This striking marking is an unmistakable signature that underscores the clear language spoken by the form. One of Carl Pott's last designs, *Model 33* is still today one of his most successful, part of the collections of numerous museums of applied art and design.

# 1980

**Office Chair**

Design:
**Klaus Franck**
**Werner Sauer**

Manufacturer:
Wilkhahn

# FS-Line

Office chairs – half furniture, half office equipment – are hybrid creatures. They have their own long tradition, but have seldom ascended to the Mount Olympus of design icons. One exception is model *FS* from **Wilkhahn**. It heralded nothing more and nothing less than a paradigm change. Those who accomplished this and gave the chair its name epitomize classic German, innovation-oriented and functional industrial design. While the office chairs that went before had offered a steadily growing range of adjustment options, particularly in the ergonomics-obsessed 1970s, *FS* was the first chair to practically adjust itself. Its main structural and at the same time design-dictated feature are the lateral pivoting arms. In connection with the flexible mid-zone of the seat and the chair's frontal rotation axis, they ensure that seat and backrest are tilted toward one another at the most favourable angle. Whether the sitter bends forward over his work or leans back to relax, his body is always supported. Many test models had to be made before this could be achieved, in order to study the behaviour of the torsion fields and to perfect the pronounced curve of the seat back. By "pervading the product system with uniformly designed, visible functional elements" a high degree of brand recognition was achieved. Three million *FS* chairs are in use all over the world today.

**Wall Clock**

Design:
**Dietrich Lubs**

Manufacturer:
Braun

Small photo:
*ABK 30* from 1982

# ABW 41

This clock shows us nothing more than the time. It is a pure dial freed of all superfluous detail. The setting button as well – which has been brought to the front to make it possible to set the time without taking the clock off the wall – disappears in its position as central point (onto which the hands are also attached). The time disk is thus a purely geometrical, graphical object that seems to "float" before the wall, its hands confirming in their steady progress the wisdom of the principle that "form follows function". While Dietrich Lubs kept to the familiar visual and typographical purity people had come to expect from wall clocks, he also added a third dimension of depth to his model *ABW 41*. The dial step-backs on three levels were something new, lending the clock a spatial texture. This small intervention had significant consequences: the *ABW 41* was the flattest clock in the world. The three-dimensional tiers of the body also created rings of shadow and gave the hands an extra visual guide. Both increase readability, especially from a distance, which is of course the very essence of wall-mounted clocks. Although this clock series can be deemed a prime example of applied minimalism, it comes in an astounding array of variations. The same year the Memphis studio in Milan was calling into question all commonly accepted design truths, and garish decoration was once again rising from the ashes, **Braun** provided a renewed demonstration of how formal restraint and consistent functionalism can be combined in a fresh-looking product.

# 1981

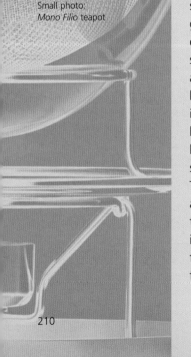

**Teapot**

Design:
**Tassilo von Grolmann**

Manufacturer:
Mono

Small photo:
*Mono Filio* teapot

# Mono Classic

He certainly succeeded at his aim of creating a new aesthetic for the enjoyment of tea. And his teapot had some impressive forerunners in this endeavour, including **Marianne Brandt** (1924), Trude Petri (1931) and **Walter Gropius** (1969), but it was nonetheless unprecedented. Not even **Wilhelm Wagenfeld's** glass teapot from the 1930s (for Jenaer Glas) in what was still a conventional shape served as role model. What distinguishes Tassilo von Grolmann's glass and metal design from all the rest is its modular structure. While **Braun** had broken down the radio into its constituent parts back in 1960, now it was the teapot's turn. Pot, stand, lid, sieve, tray, warmer – every element is discrete, can be taken off, cleaned separately and put back again. The structural concept is based on a stand made of thin stainless steel bars, a principle that recalls early tubular steel furniture. The teapot, open at the top, is hung in this stand. The tea strainer, which corresponds in shape and size with the pot, is then hung inside the pot. The strainer is designed with generous proportions to give the tea leaves plenty of room for steeping. When the hot water is poured in, what happens in the strainer and pot can be observed from outside. Tea preparation becomes a sensory experience. The lid is a shiny round metal disc with a large cutout in front for pouring and a smaller one at the back to let in air. It is balanced in such a way that it can't fall off even when the pot is tilted at an extreme angle. The individual parts of the various types of warmers are not fixed in place either but rather simply laid atop one another. The weight of the pot itself lends them the necessary stability. This very high-tech-looking design, which does without any form of ornament, exudes a feeling of calm and harmony just right for drinking tea.

# 1982

**Chair**

Design:
**Stefan Wewerka**

Manufacturer:
Tecta

# Einschwinger

Furniture as food for thought. The concepts hatched by artist/designer **Stefan Wewerka** are made to shake up our viewing and usage habits. And his sinuous *Einschwinger* can be seen as the very epitome of his anything-but-straightforward thought process and the manifold layers of meaning he incorporates in his designs. The name is already a play on words based on the august *Freischwinger*, or cantilevered chair. Even though this is not exactly the first one-legged cantilevered chair – predecessors include the *Snake Chair* by Danish designer Poul Henningsen (1932) and the *Gru* chair designed by Silvio Coppola of Italy (1970) – Wewerka managed to create an extremely coherent design within this special discipline, on that moreover went into production and stayed there. His tubular steel chair consists of a single tube over three metres in length, which is bent by machine into seven equal radii. This zigzag line looks almost like a geometric model. Not only the main material harks back to classical Modernism, but also the minimalist concept, which includes the elimination of the backrest, whose support function is taken on by a stuck-on cushion. This cushion's sausage-like form follows the curvature of the steel tube and, together with the coloured seat, lends the whole a Pop Art feel. But Wewerka's ominous-looking object also turns out to be great to sit on: whoever dares a try will experience a double swing – to the side and back and forth – a nice surprise for first-time sitters.

# 1982

**Water Kettle**

Design:
**Richard Sapper**

Manufacturer:
Alessi

# 9091

He was annoyed by the ear-splitting tone water kettles usually emit when they have done their duty. "Why not create a musically appealing acoustic instead?" thought **Richard Sapper** to himself. And while the product reformer was at it, he went ahead and rethought the water kettle from the ground up. He did in fact start by reinventing the whistle emitted when the water boils, which should now sound more like a pitch pipe. In the course of systematic research, he dug up an artisan in the Black Forest who had spent his whole life perfecting these instruments and was thus able to create the desired triad. Sapper decided to forego the usual lid, which always falls off anyway. This led to a domed form, which substantially contributes to the kettle's imposing appearance. The chrome-plated surface reflects its surroundings, with the resulting unavoidable distortion of reflected faces a side effect that was by all means desired. Water is poured into the kettle via the throat, which can be opened with one hand using a mechanism in the handle. The plastic handle – Sapper would have preferred metal – recalls a cockscomb, just as the entire design resembles not so much a water kettle as an exercise open to wide-ranging associations. Sapper thus provides here a textbook model for how to elevate an object of daily use above the ordinary. One year after Memphis, the world's first "designer kettle" ushered in a new era in which metaphors and symbolism triumphantly return to the domestic stage.

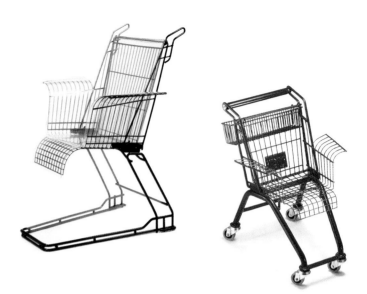

# 1983

**Chair**

Design:
**Stiletto**

Manufacturer:
formerly Stiletto Studios

Small Photos:
left: version without wheels
right: *Short Rest*
children's chair from 1990

# Consumer's Rest

The easychair as metal cage. It is probably meant to be understood as a commentary on our consumer society in which anything and everything, including the human being, is turned into merchandise and as a logical consequence winds up in the shopping basket. In the early 1980s, when the marriage of punk and postmodern gave rise to an anti-aesthetic, young designers in Germany were likewise rising up in rebellion against design conventions. One widespread approach was the ready-made, popular ever since Dada, in which everyday objects were alienated, recycled or assigned a new function. In this case an object was employed that everyone knows, which probably contributed to the popularity of this design. Made to convey goods through the supermarket, but always used as a child seat as well, the shopping cart is here opened up at the front. This makes room for an adult to sit, although this object is surely more of a message-bearer than a genuine piece of useful furniture. *Consumer's Rest* came either with or without wheels. A sofa, a table and a children's version diverged from the format of the original. Bent sides serve as armrests and a transparent plastic cover affords a modicum of seating comfort. The English name contains an allusion to the global character of the design, as global as its origins. And, as a matter of fact, the ironic object did manage to make its way into the world's design collections, joining the *Verspanntes Regal* (1984) and the *Solid* easychair (1986) as icon of "New German Design".

216

# 1983

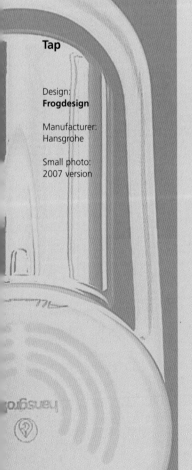

**Tap**

Design:
**Frogdesign**

Manufacturer:
Hansgrohe

Small photo:
2007 version

# Allegroh

From the purpose-built sanitary facility to personal sanctuary, from profane object to professionally designed accessory, from individual product to decorating scheme: the Allegroh tap is
one of the earliest and best examples of the changing concept of the bathroom, a development that is still in progress today. Just as the leading makes of car lost their sharp edges
during the 1980s and became finely polished status symbols, the curving lines of this single-
lever tap signalize the reappraisal of a living area that was long neglected or relegated to
mere pragmatic hygienic functionalism. *Allegroh* by Frogdesign, a studio dedicated to the
emotionalization of form, is angled forward. It thus bows down before its users. The spout
from which the water issues is also somewhat inclined. These slanting contours lend the
water tap a dynamism, a symbolism that harmonizes well with its essential function: to
conduct a stream of water. The tap is operated by means of a pronounced, ring-shaped
lever, which is easy to grasp and in its vertical section, direction and dimensions corresponds
to the exit spout. The complex surface texture of *Allegroh* with its many diverse radii and
gentle transitions stands for the integration of the bathroom into the overall domestic realm.
The limousine of single-lever taps comes fittingly adorned with a logo in sterling silver.

# 1984

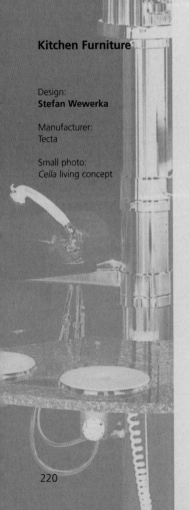

**Kitchen Furniture**

Design:
**Stefan Wewerka**

Manufacturer:
Tecta

Small photo:
*Cella* living concept

# Kitchen Tree

A solid iron pole – a tree trunk, so to speak – forms the foundation for this construction. It can be rotated and adjusted in height and can thus adapt itself to both the space at hand and the user's needs. The chrome-plated pipe acts as water supply pipe and conduit for electric cables as well as holding the various functional elements. These fan out from the centre, a form that **Stefan Wewerka** also favours in his tables, viewing it as "democratic". Among the functional elements that can be mixed or matched along the pipe are a range, a sink, a wooden countertop and a towel holder. Artist/designer Wewerka, who rose to fame with furniture designs notable for their highly unusual fusion of construction and deconstruction, devised this apparatus as part of his *Cella* concept, a domestic landscape in which furniture stops clinging to the walls and comes out into the middle of the room. This idea harks back to "New Building" movement's desire to replace the block building style with a centralized building plan, revealing Wewerka's affinity to the Bauhaus. The pioneer of paradigm changes delivered here an early alternative to the seemingly inevitable kitchen-as-row-of-cabinets. What's more, his "trees" also lend themselves to other uses: snack station, standing desk or wardrobe.

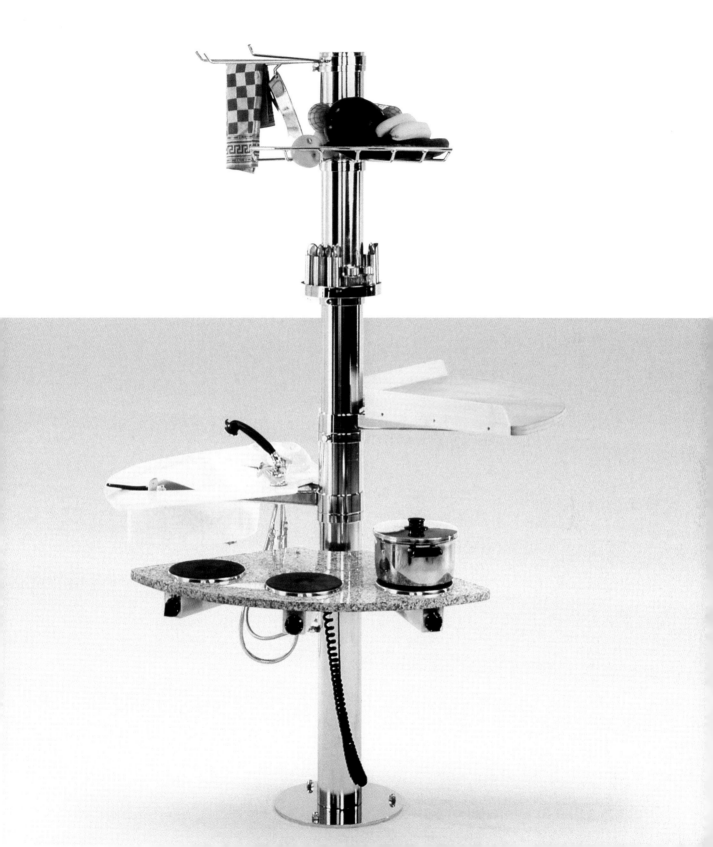

# 1984

**Ceiling Lamp**

Design:
**Ingo Maurer**

Manufacturer:
Ingo Maurer

# YaYaHo

Glass, ceramic, plastic and porcelain can be used, among other materials. In the 1980s technical refinement and industrial materials came to the fore in **Ingo Maurer's** designs, without detracting from their experimental character. He hit the jackpot with his oft-copied low-voltage halogen lighting system *YaYaHo*, a quantum leap in lighting design and a global success on a par with **Richard Sapper's** pivoting *Tizio* lamp. From thread-like ropes and cables that run across the room from wall to wall are strung lamps that are reduced to points of light. Since the elements can be moved horizontally and in some cases vertically as well, the design possibilities are virtually endless. It is an almost immaterial-seeming lighting system, similarly abstract to the "Light Module" from Bega, but just as consistently functional as the spotlights produced by **Erco** and as modular as the Ulm Academy could ever have imagined. The large distance between the ropes gives it an airy appeal, while the technical details add whimsy and the overall look exudes sophistication. Still avant-garde looking even two decades later, this system is not only popular with businesses and culture centres, including the Centre Pompidou in Paris, Villa Medici in Florence and the Louisiana Art Museum in Denmark, but has also made its way into countless homes. The set of lights comes with a construction manual that turns the purchaser into his own lighting director. But it is also possible to buy a plug-and-play complete set. Ingo Maurer succeeded here in creating a whole new paradigm. The almost incorporeal and ever-changeable YaYaHo is the perfect counterpart to the world of digital networks.

# 1984

**Easychair**

Design:
**Burkhard Vogtherr**

Manufacturer:
Arflex

Small photo:
two-seater

# T-Line

When **Burkhard Vogtherr** joined the *T-Line* project, which would give birth to a new type of easychair, he was on a quest for the most versatile kind of seating possible. That's why he tried out a series of different versions, varying the height of the backrest and other parameters. The result is a mixture of the formal clarity of a chair and the comfort of an armchair that boasts a striking graphic flow of line to boot. This design spelled the breakthrough of the German-born Frenchman-by-choice in Italy. What is innovative about the *T-Line* concept is essentially the reduction of the chair to two pancake-flat rectangles set at an almost 90-degree angle to one another. The silhouette thus created suggested a good name for the design. The curved armrests with their generous diameter and base runners that might have come straight out of a comic book help to create a surprise effect in those who see the chair for the first time. The armchair is space-saving, comfortable and easy to assemble, consisting only of a steel frame hidden by upholstery. The springs are reinforced by elastic bands. The fact that *T-Line* can also be combined well with other pieces makes it ideal for use in a variety of spaces, whether at home, in waiting rooms or in TV talk shows.

# 1984

**Easychair**

Design:
**Peter Maly**

Manufacturer:
COR

Small photo:
with footstool

# Zyklus

Already in the year of its launch, when it was granted a starring role in the German comedy film "Men", this easychair ascended to the status of cult object. But what was probably the most famous piece of German furniture in the design-infused 1980s has even more stories to tell. It owed its very existence to the fortunate coincidence that designer and manufacturer happened to be on the same wavelength. Helmut Lübke, at the time managing director of **COR**, wanted to demonstrate his commitment to avant-gardism, realizing that the time was ripe for new forms. The curious point of departure for this successful product was an old doll's chair from the 1930s, which appealed to Lübke and which he warmly recommended to designer **Peter Maly** as model. The latter, somewhat irritated by this challenge, abstracted the toy further and further, basing his efforts on a strict nine-centimetre grid. All radii are likewise a factor of nine. There thus emerged a meticulously calculated, harmonious design in which formal rigour is coupled with a playful air. The press was thrilled – not least because Lübke and Maly proceeded to present their showpiece all over Europe. It was no accident either that *Zyklus* found its way into Doris Dörrie's film.

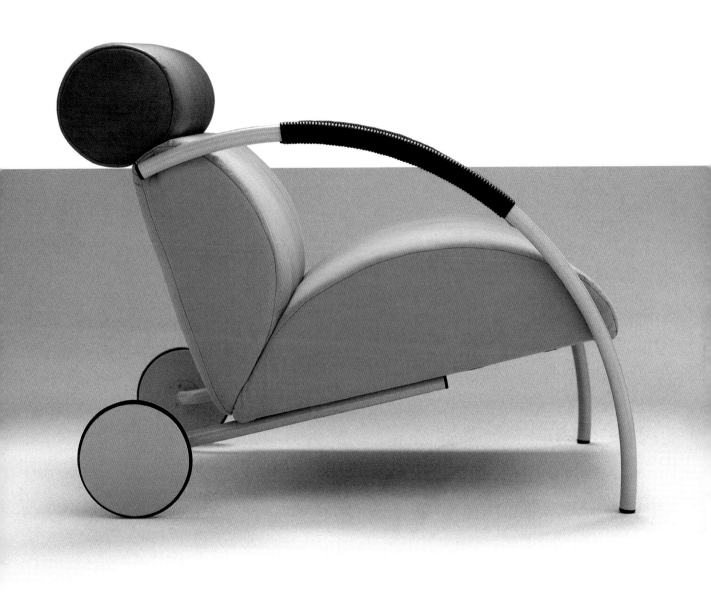

# 1984

**Shelf**

Design:
**Wolfgang Laubersheimer**

Manufacturer:
Nils Holger Moormann (re-edition)

# Tense Bookcase

Two parallel side panels of sheet steel are connected via permanently welded shelves of the same material set at equal intervals (30 centimetres). A steel cable stretches along one side, creating a slight bend from the vertical. This cable is not merely a decorative or formal gag; instead, the tension it creates (which gives the piece its name *Verspanntes Regal*, in English Tense Bookcase) is what gives the slim construction the inner stability indispensable to a shelving unit. The critical disadvantage of sheet steel for building shelves is thus compensated by means of a simple, patent-protected trick. A tense equilibrium is created that echoes the principle of the cantilevered chair. The stiffening through the cable corrects the material's natural wobbliness (similar to what happens in a half-timbered building), in fact making the shelf unusually steady, capable of holding up to three tonnes of readable or non-readable material without losing its footing. Wolfgang Laubersheimer, who has always been interested in reducing design to its fundamentals, delivered here, alongside Stiletto's *Consumer's Rest*, one of the few pieces of furniture of the "New German Design" era that went into series production. With its inherent functionality, it's no wonder that the bookcase is still in production today. One can easily read into it a subtle attack on the right angle that was so sacrosanct to classical functionalism.

# 1985

**Television Set**

Design:
**Manufacturer's design**

Manufacturer:
formerly Loewe

Small photo:
*Art Vision*
by Alexander Neumeister, 1992

# Art 1

It's just part of the logic of trailblazing designs that they set a new standard and therefore seem perfectly natural when looking back with the privileged gaze of the present. What is so extraordinary about the design, what contemporaries once found so amazing, is difficult to imagine after so many imitators have intervened with their variations on the original model. This is exactly what happened in the case of the television set with the programmatic name *Art 1*, the first model completely equipped with digital technology, one that would inaugurate a new calendar in its field and would rise to become a universal status symbol. Those were the days when Japanese electronics manufacturers seemed to have such an immense technological edge on their German rivals that it would be impossible to ever catch up. Even the **Braun** brand, once such an uncontested leader in this industry, which with **Herbert Hirche's** *HF 1* had introduced the first modern television set, had already begun to retreat from this difficult market. **Loewe** decided instead to go into the offensive and developed a device whose outstanding technical advances were clothed in a form that perfectly expressed this superiority. They first entrusted their own in-house designers with this task. But the line was eventually put under the charge of Alexander Neumeister, a graduate of the Academy of Design in Ulm whose studio designed the *Transrapid* magnetic monorail system, and who had worked in Japan and was busy at the time conceiving the first generation of the *ICE* trains. The problem posed by the hefty and clumsy-looking 72" picture tube was solved by immersing it in a black monolith. The housing was shaped in the back as a stepped pyramid. The front was transformed into a flat rectangular surface. This was accented by a band of touch controls that replaced the usual buttons. The actual television set perches on an integrated substructure out of which the hi-fi sound issues.

# 1985

**Lounge Chair**

Design:
**Jan Armgardt**
**Ingo Maurer**

Manufacturer:
Mobilia Collection

# Tattomi

With a backrest that can be adjusted into four positions and a seat offering three different options, *Tattomi* can be used as a chair, lounger or guest bed. This early and endlessly copied multifunctional piece of furniture, which is in production again today, allows for a dozen different sitting and reclining options. In the early 1980s, **Jan Armgardt** set out to study all the possibilities for rotating or folding furniture parts. In discussions with furniture-maker Werner Dechand of **Mobilia Collection**, the idea emerged of developing an easychair that could be folded out to make a lounger. Or, vice-versa: a mattress that turns into a chair. The aim was to create a practical piece of furniture for unconventional people living in small apartments. The prototype, introduced at the 1985 Cologne Furniture Fair, met with great enthusiasm – not least on account of its sensational simplicity. One of those who took note was light designer **Ingo Maurer**, who spontaneously put the designer in contact with Milanese manufacturer DePadova and also contributed the name *Tattomi*. This started Dechand thinking again, and he came up with the final "relaxing crease". This meant that the second joint could be set at various angles so that even if the backrest were leaning far back, the sitter could put his feet up to read or watch TV.

# 1986

**Chair**

Design:
**Heinz Landes**

Manufacturer:
formerly Heinz Landes

Small photo:
left: *Nussknacker* (Nutcracker)
right: *Betonsessel* (Concrete Chair)
Heinz Landes, 1986

# Solid

Seven bent iron bars inserted in a concrete base offer plenty of fodder for interpretation. Of course, this version of the cantilevered chair almost verges on blasphemy. Weighing in at up to two hundred pounds, *Solid* is in terms of weight as well the antipode to the chairs that designers **Marcel Breuer** or **Ludwig Mies van der Rohe** tried to make as lightweight as possible. With *Solid* – which can be compared to Stiletto's ready-made chair *Consumer's Rest* (1983) and the *Tense Bookcase* by Wolfgang Laubersheimer (1984) – design satirist and furniture experimentalist Heinz Landes created one of the last icons of "Neues Deutsches Design". Upon closer examination, however, the concrete chair does possess some qualities that one would not expect to find in such a brute. The structure itself already displays a certain logic. The concrete block vouches for steadiness and tilt resistance. The iron reinforcement rods, which serve to create stability-lending tension in their original architectural use, are likewise appropriate as a material for this application. The seat really does swing as called for by the German word for cantilevered chair "Freischwinger" (literally: "free swinger"), and does so, unlike its "role models" even under extreme loads. Furthermore, this unique object, which is still available today and was once just one part of a whole concrete furniture collection, is of course a monument: to strong ideas and against the harmlessness of design.

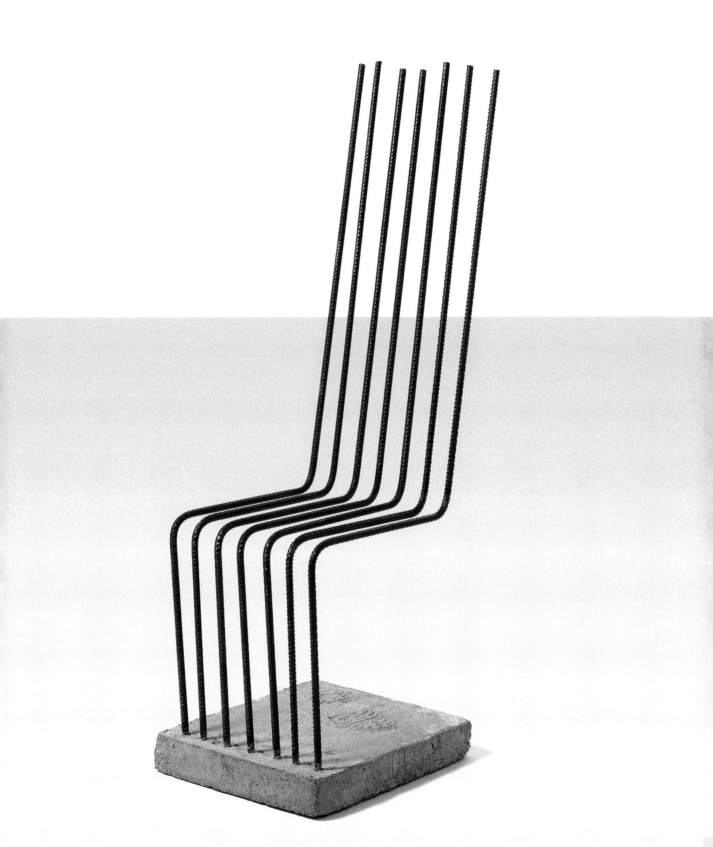

# 1986

# Flying Carpet

Its flightiness is already apparent at first glance. Designer Simon Desanta, who made a name for himself in the industry with numerous furniture patents, created a sculpture for sitting whose form comes from the idea evoked in its name. The easychair consists of a single rectangular surface that is creased twice to become a chair. Turned so that one corner of the rectangle rests on the floor, actually on a base plate, the chair gives the impression of flying. The design is one of those whose charm lies in its astounding simplicity, which can't help but raise the question of why no one thought of it sooner. After all, the springy construction is actually the renewed, but highly original, continuation of the seemingly endless story of a single German furniture innovation: the "Freischwinger", or cantilevered chair. The triangular backrest allows the arms plenty of freedom of movement. Its unorthodox form, which enters into an exciting dialogue with various – of course removable – covers, virtually begs for the sitter to have some fun. A stiff, formal sitting position would seem completely out of place here – the chair is an invitation to loll about. All of this makes *Flying Carpet*, which is not as well known as it could be, a phenomenon worthy of admiration, combining entertainment value with highly practical qualities.

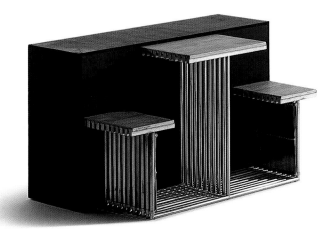

# 1987

**Table and Benches**

Design:
**Uwe Fischer**
**Klaus-Achim Heine**

Manufacturer:
Vitra

# Tabula Rasa

A real table is heavy and immovable. The concept that furniture is static is probably anchored nowhere as firmly as in our idea of what a tabletop and four legs should be like. **Uwe Fischer** and Klaus-Achim Heine, who established a creative workshop for "Neues Deutsches Design" that they christened Studio Ginbande, set out to abolish this convention. Their table-and-bench combination can not only be adapted in length to fit a number of people, but can also be reduced again to free up space in the room. *Tabula Rasa* thus fluctuates between less than one metre to about five metres in length. In order to achieve this kind of flexibility, the design duo developed a structure made of a folding grille and roller blind mechanisms, with birch-wood panels cut into segments for the benches and tabletop. Pushed together, this adaptable dining table fits into the wooden box attached at the side. It's like a magic trick that the long table can actually disappear into such a small container. *Tabula Rasa*, a design whose function also encompasses a social dimension, is far more than just the product of conceptual deliberations – it is also a piece that is surprisingly easy to use.

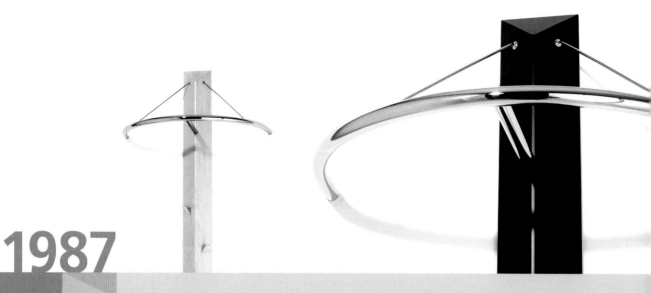

# 1987

**Coat Rack**

Design:
**Jürgen Lange**

Manufacturer:
Schönbuch

# Trio

When **Jürgen Lange** came to the Cologne Furniture Fair in 1987 to present his new design, he had a small surprise in store for visitors. Next to his new product he displayed a large-format portrait photo of himself, a nice gesture that is anything but common even today. Lange, who still works for **Schönbuch**, had decided to take a common furniture type back to the basics. *Trio* is regarded as one of the first thoroughly functional coat stands. Considering the fact that most entrance halls don't have much space, but that space is just what's needed for putting on coats and jackets, the idea was to find the most space-saving solution. The coat stand itself would also have to be economical, i.e. consist of as few parts as possible. Lange finally seized on the idea of cutting the usual freestanding coat rack pole in half and attaching it permanently to the wall, which also eliminates the problem of stability. The main element is a wooden profile pole available in various colours (harking back to the wood-working origins of the manufacturer). The hooks attached to the pole at various heights offer spots low enough to be reached by children. Above them, a semicircular steel tube provides space for hanging things on hangers. The tube structure with its two struts forms a triangle that vaguely recalls a hanging bridge. *Trio* is not only a reduced and therefore highly practical design, but also an example of how a design can evolve out of the relationship between space and furnishings.

# 1988

**Textile Collection**

Design:
**Heinz Röntgen**
**Designteam Nya Nordiska**

Manufacturer:
Nya Nordiska

# Lia

A polyamide weave managed to shape company history for two decades, receiving design awards along the way and thus demonstrating aesthetic longevity in the midst of the ephemeral. How can something like this come about? When Heinz Röntgen attached the first sample to the wall himself at the Frankfurt Home Textiles Fair, measuring just one square metre – no goods were yet in the warehouse – it didn't take long for the first reactions to take place. That was the auspicious start of the extraordinary career of this fabric with its structure reminiscent of Japanese paper. The decorative material was developed to series maturity in 18 variations and produced as basic goods in more than 50 colours. By now, over two-and-a-half million metres of *Lia* fabric have been sold. Using a new type of embroidery machine, Röntgen had succeeded in setting fine dots in a free-form arrangement and without an even rapport into the basic weave, which had until then only been possible with hand stitching. *Lia-Saki*, with a design made up of square seams, and *Lia-Quinto*, with a triangle-covered surface, received several awards. The embroidered points in *Lia-Pong* and *Lia-Gibson* soon attracted many industry imitators. In the variation *Lia-Daisy*, the basic fabric was dotted with appliqué flowers: haute couture for the window. *Lia-Ciao* – the product name says it all – was to ring in the end of the *Lia* embroideries, but further variations were still to come.

# 1989

**Easychair**

Design:
**Stefan Heiliger**

Manufacturer:
WK Wohnen

# WK 698 Spot

Even a layperson can immediately tell that this easychair can do something special. The springboard for the project was formed by the idea of using flat aluminium profiles, the making of which is not exactly simple. They are pressed through a stencil at around 400 degrees Celsius. The profiles have two grooves each on the left and right, which prompted Stefan Heiliger to come up with a new idea. He wanted to construct a functional easychair in which the seat and armrests move along these grooves. The result was one of the most adjustable of armchairs: a well-thought-out sitting machine with the kind of flexibility familiar only from office chairs. A special advantage is that the chair seat can be pulled forward as much or little as desired. Like a car seat, the back can be tilted with a lever. The movability of the parts is eloquently expressed in the swing of the lines. Technology, function and form create an almost symbiotic unity which permeates the whole design down to the last, but by no means insignificant, detail. For example, thanks to a recess in the upper edge of the backrest, the head pillow can't slip. Decisive for the great success of this model was the possibility to glide into such a wide variety of sitting positions. *Spot* is – just like its offspring *Flex* and *Solo* – the ideal TV chair, but is just as inviting for reading or dozing.

# 1989

# Achat

The everyday thermos was either a simple canister or was modelled after a porcelain tea or coffee pot, such as in the case of Alfi best-seller *Juwel*. But then designer Tassilo von Grolmann, a specialist in dining culture who had already interpreted the teapot in a highly modern way a few years earlier with his modular version (for **Mono**) ventured to depart from the formal conventions of the metier. The inventor of forms lent the one-litre insulated container a new and striking silhouette. His model *Achat* is a steeply angled cone, the most eye-catching version of which is grooved with parallel rings in fingernail intervals. They gave the product its name: *Achat* (Agate) is a gemstone with streaky markings. It is known for its hardness and resistance to chemicals, qualities that surely also played a role in its choice as name. While the handle, arranged parallel to the body of the thermos, is a circular bar that displays a geometry as simple as that of the thermos itself, the one-handed hinged lid and spout are distinguished by flirtatious curves that form an appealing contrast. Whether smooth or fluted, the thermos is available in ten different variations and in aluminium, chrome or copper, the latter with a wicker cover. Grolmann, who designed half a dozen thermos containers for **Alfi**, succeeded in creating an eye-catcher with an elegant look that makes an attractive gift demonstrating the good taste of both giver and recipient. *Achat* is a welcome guest on any coffee table.

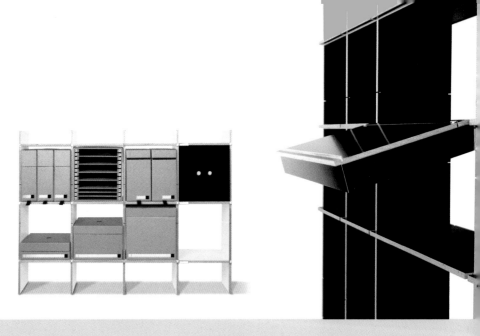

# 1989

## FNP

**Shelf System**

Design:
**Axel Kufus**

Manufacturer:
Nils Holger Moormann

Small photo:
left: with boxes
right: with standing desk

"The question is always: How can I make something even simpler?" explains **Axel Kufus**, describing a goal that is difficult to achieve. In this modular shelf system, one of his early designs, he succeeded in this endeavour in an exemplary fashion. As a pure grid, the system is reduced to shelves and sides, which are connected by way of aluminium rails to create a transparent design. Thanks to its simple yet intelligent construction, the system can be adapted to virtually any room situation. Today there is even a configuration program available on the Internet. In the freestanding versions, tension rods provide additional stability. *FNP*, which set new standards in easily dismantled shelving, can be assembled without any tools whatsoever. Precise fabrication ensures that the elements can be put together to create an exceptionally stable structure. Despite this robustness, however, the shelf maintains a graceful air. The fact that there is a story behind this utterly transparent product is indicated by the ironic name, borrowed from city planning bureaucracy along the lines of "Neues Deutsches Design". Kufus pursued still another idea as well by keeping construction simple: he wanted to have the shelving unit produced decentrally by regional manufacturers.

# 1991

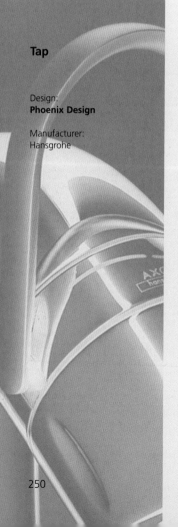

**Tap**

Design:
**Phoenix Design**

Manufacturer:
Hansgrohe

# Arco

This is the kind of innovation that takes place in an invisible area and thus goes undiscovered if no one bothers to explain it. The amazingly simple form of a bent pipe, which recalls basic pre-industrial water pipes, has an aesthetic value in and of itself and made this tap a favourite object amongst architects. But there is more to it than that: in fact, this was the first single-lever tap to mirror in its outer form the route taken by the water. While in comparable taps the water first flows upward and then, after cold and hot have been mixed, runs back down again, in *Arco* the water exactly follows the path of the pipe. In order to achieve this, a new kind of cartridge had to be developed. As a practical extra, the front part of the pipe can be rotated 180 degrees so that the water bubbles upward like a small fountain. One could say that *Arco* is the apotheosis of the single-lever tap. Its primeval form is hard to reduce any further. The integration of the lever, which has the same radius as the pipe and can be operated with just one finger, is a glowing exemplar for the design textbooks. During a period when other products have rapidly showed their age in visual terms, this tap has demonstrated striking longevity. What's more, *Arco* is an ideal reflection of how a long-term manufacturer/designer relationship can yield lasting value.

# 1991

## Stitz

**Leaning Aid**

Design:
**Hans »Nick« Roericht**

Manufacturer:
Wilkhahn

"The healthy chair is a fiction", claims **Wilkhahn**, an unquestioned authority when it comes to the ergonomics of sitting. People with desk jobs would actually do well to stand up and move around as frequently as possible if they are to survive the long hours of sitting. *Stitz* was invented to make such interruptions superfluous – but not by the Wilkhahn company, who at first wanted nothing to do with the strange hybrid creation. As the "Trimm dich" fitness wave swept through Germany in the 1970s, **Hans "Nick" Roericht** began to think about how a piece of furniture could enable a healthy alternation between sitting, standing and leaning. What resulted is a completely new type of chair. His standing/sitting hybrid, the first prototype of which he built himself and christened *Stitz 1* (and which is still being made today by **Ingo Maurer** in a back courtyard), motivates the sitter to assume a more erect posture and challenges him to constantly engage in playful changes in position. In the later model, *Stitz 2*, with technical specifications more conducive to mass production (now produced by Wilkhahn after all), the height is infinitely adjustable using a disc with all-round access under the seat. A leaning aid, the chair relieves physical strain during the performance of various activities, but the sitter himself must maintain his balance. As a positive side effect, this constant movement trains muscles and tendons and stimulates circulation.

# 1991

**Parmesan Knife**

Design:
**Ralph Krämer**

Manufacturer:
Pott

Small photo:
*42* silverware from 2003

# Picado

When young designer Ralph Krämer, who had just decided to go out on his own, introduced himself to the famous **Pott** company at the Frankfurt Trade Fair in 1984, there was no way of foreseeing that this would lead to one of the most productive partnerships in the industry. It would still take a few years until the first design breakthrough. It went by the name of *Picado*. The cheese knife has two features that ushered in turning points in flatware design: it was one of the first knives to boast a stainless steel handle, which – apart from the technical difficulties involved in its fabrication – lent the whole a much higher degree of visual and haptic homogeneity. Secondly – and even more important – it was one of the extremely rare examples of the successful realization of an asymmetrical form in this product realm. Everyone knows that the human hand is not symmetrical, but the logical consequence took a long time to gain acceptance on the market and, what's more, posed a very demanding task for the designer. "Free-hand" forms can easily appear clumsy. At the beginning of the process of conceiving this flatware, 20 extremely diverse basic designs were drawn, four of which were made into models. One of these was the prototype for *Picado*, which then after several months finally took on its final shape. The asymmetry gave rise as well to the organic quality of the form, which was technically tricky to realize. Since it has no edges, polishing is much more difficult. The successful knife later gave birth to the children's silverware *Bonito* and – in response to overwhelming customer demand – to the adult version *Bondia*, or *42*. This progression is also quite unique in the market.

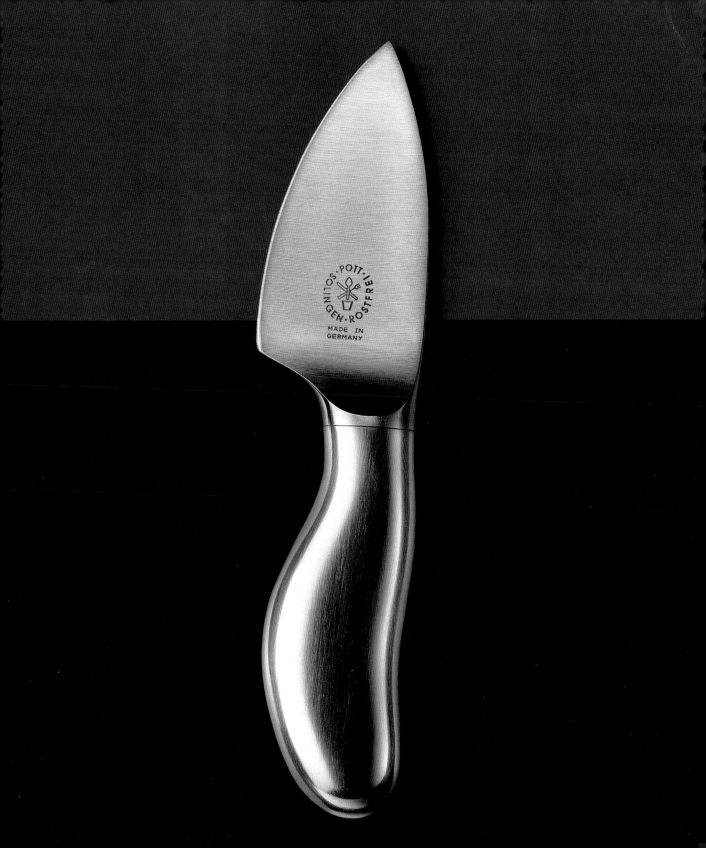

# 1992

Design:
**Kurt Ranger**

Manufacturer:
Fischer Möbel

Small photo:
chair and serving trolley

# Tennis

The wooden easychair as central design of a furniture series. A chair that does not try to deny its origins in the classical lounge chair, deriving its formal stringency from the consistent, slightly curved line described by the wooden bar that forms both backrest and front legs. Robust, yet elegant, this chair can be adjusted into three different positions using the integrated metal fittings made of stainless steel tubing, as well as folded up to save space. Suitable for both dining and relaxing, the chair is coupled with a height-adjustable footstool. This is one of the early examples of garden furniture that displayed its own idiosyncratic design, going beyond the conventional models to encompass an entire outdoor furnishing line. This succeeded not least due to the original material combination of wood, steel and plastic webbing, the transparency of which lends the chair its feeling of lightness. Three tables in different shapes and sizes can be folded out and back together again to adapt to various situations. A practical detail is the integration of heatproof stainless steel inserts for resting hot saucepans on the tabletop. Particularly successful are the lounge chair and serving trolley – simple, rectilinear structures reduced to their essentials, whose most conspicuous hallmark are two mobility-lending disc-shaped wooden wheels.

# 1992

**Tap**

Design:
**Sieger Design**

Manufacturer:
Dornbracht

## Tara

The Western faith in progress also rules the design realm. For the concept of the bathroom, this means that the process of washing is continually optimized through enhanced technology. The single-lever tap, which this same year found its formal culmination in the model *Arcor*, perfectly typifies this striving. If **Sieger Design** now apparently took a step backward and deliberately used the ostensibly outdated original two-lever solution, this should not be construed as an expression of cultural scepticism or a renunciation of high technical standards, but rather as a critique of the one-dimensionality of creative thinking. Just as **Otl Aicher** initiated the move to overcome the purely functional kitchen, the *Tara* tap symbolizes the attempt to add a new dimension to the idea of the bathroom, one that goes beyond mere speed and efficiency and makes room for the kind of sensuality that can be found in Eastern bathing cultures. In formal terms, Studio Sieger takes advantage of the symmetry that is already inherent in the dual-lever system. The levers, reduced to simple round tubes, form cross shapes – telling symbols that resonate deeply in individual and collective memory. The water pipe with its sweeping semi-circular radius likewise has an iconographic character. Doesn't it also convey to us that slowness has its own special value? The retro tap won numerous design awards worldwide and was copied at least as often.

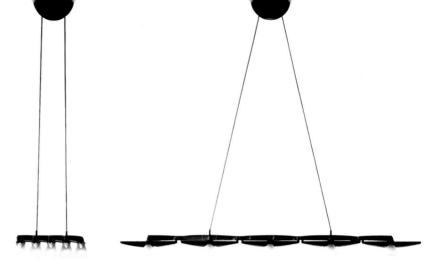

# 1993

**Hanging Lamp**

Design:
**Uwe Fischer**
**Klaus-Achim Heine**

Manufacturer:
Serien

# Take Five

The expandable lamp that grows with the table. A folding grille – like the one design duo Klaus-Achim Heine and **Uwe Fischer** used a few years previous in their *Tabula Rasa* table – lets *Take Five* be expanded in a single motion from its original 36 centimetres to a maximum of one-and-a-half metres to fit the respective space or table length. This for example offers the perfect lighting solution for pullout dining tables. The original comes with five incandescent lamps that continue to form a straight row when the lamp is pulled out. Today the hanging lamp made of polycarbonate, available in five colours, also comes in a flatter halogen version for a different take on lighting the table. While in the incandescent lamps glare is eliminated through the use of opalized glass, the halogen bulbs shed light at a 60-degree angle directly downwards. A dimmer can be integrated in both cases. In addition to the functional advantage of the variable areas that can be illuminated thanks to the application of a simple, familiar technology, the serial scissoring principle of the design also lends the lamp an original, unmistakable look.

# 1993

# Virage

**Reiner Moll** had already worked for several years as freelance in-house designer for the upmarket bathroom brand Villeroy & Boch when he came up with this product, in which he integrated the sink into the washstand. *Virage* is one of the key moments in the reinvention of the bathroom that began in the 1990s and is still going on today. The design derives its significance and formal rigour from the combination of circle and rectangle. The imaginary line formed by continuing the front edge of the washstand would bisect the circle of the sink straight through the middle. This creates not only harmonious proportions, but also frees up a generous projecting half-circle of sink space. The user has more leeway to move and two can even stand at the sink simultaneously. *Virage* is part of the new generation of ceramic washstands that can be cut to size to fit the given space situation in the bathroom. In both the single- and double-sink versions, the user can choose between a symmetrical and asymmetrical arrangement. One of the special features of the ensemble is the curving line inside the sink – an aesthetic extra in a double sense. It not only lends the overall design a complex tension; the spiral curling into the sink also makes it possible to shift the overflow hole to an invisible spot so that the dirt that unavoidably gathers there is hidden from view.

# 1994

Office Furniture System

Design:
**Fritz Frenkler**
**Justus Kolberg**
**Andreas Störiko**
**Wiege**

Manufacturer:
Wilkhahn

# Confair

Studies and field research have revealed that information exchange in the office takes place today above all in two ways – in formal meetings and in small teams. In order to switch back and forth quickly between these two situations, a new kind of furniture is needed that is easy to convert, can be combined with other pieces, and can be stored in a minimum of space when not in use. In short: furniture that is movable and adaptable. The first office furniture program to fully fulfil these criteria was *Confair*. It consists in part of old familiar products that have been optimized, and for the rest features newly developed components such as mobile desks that can be stacked. There are seven elements in all in the system, including two types of table, room dividers that can be used as pinboards or blackboards, a three-tiered serving trolley – the Server – and a mobile lectern. One of the central designs is a conference table on wheels by Andreas Störiko, with a divided tabletop that comes in a version that can be folded together like the wings of an insect. The recessed trays built into the tabletop are nothing less than magic: even when the table is folded up, the pens and pencils stowed there don't fall out. Dynamic, team- and process-oriented, self-organizing, detailed and mobile. The attributes of *Confair* might well have been taken straight out of the textbook on modern office communication, making the furniture family a product every bit as innovative as the *FS* line a decade before.

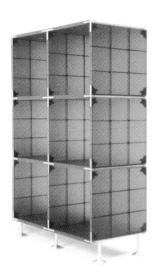

# 1994

**Shelf System**

Design:
**Werner Aisslinger**

Manufacturer:
Porro

Small photo:
*Endless Plastic* from 1998

# Endless Shelf

*Endless Shelf* seems to be an endless success story. The first product designed by **Werner Aisslinger** has probably won more awards than any other shelf system in recent history, and is one of the most commercially successful to boot. It can be found not only in living rooms, offices and boutiques, but also in various design collections around the world. The principle is easy to explain: its "secret" is in the aluminium crosspiece that elegantly connects the panels and gives the furniture a striking, graphic face. Similar to the *FNP* shelf by **Axel Kufus** (1989), the system is absolutely modular, meaning it can be endlessly added on to, expanded and modified. Produced in Italy, this assembly wonder is like a minimalist version of the construction kit concept that has been a recurring motif in German furniture design for over a century. In the late 1990s, the MDF panels (with veneers in birch or cherry) were joined by the option of using semi-transparent plastic panels in various colours, in whose structure the chequerboard pattern is echoed in miniature format.

# 1995

**Pullout Table**

Design:
**Peter Draenert**
**Georg Appeltshauser**

Manufacturer:
Draenert

# Eagle

Nero Assoluto or Imperial White granite, Statuario marble or Roman travertine limestone – the choice of stone sounds exquisite, but it's not what distinguishes *Adler*, in English *Eagle*, from all the others. What's unique is that even the swivelling extra leaf in the centre is made of one of these precious and extremely heavy types of stone and not, as is customary, of wood. A cleverly engineered mechanism was called for to make this engineering feat work easily and smoothly. This entails the two sides of the tabletop gliding apart on rails. They gave the table its name, which alludes to their enormous "wing span" of almost four metres and the ability to extend and retract these wings. In order to synchronize both movements, the panels are connected via a chain frame. The central leaf then swivels 90° and is at the same time raised by means of a spring-loaded pivotal lift mechanism. The patented machinery – a well-kept company secret – is hidden in the central pedestal. The pedestal also contains casters onto which the table can be lifted using a lever. This makes the table, which weighs up to 300 kilograms, much easier to move.

# 1996

**Shelf**

Design:
**Anette Ponholzer**

Manufacturer:
Freiraum

# Wonder Boxes

There had probably never before been a piece of furniture that faces in different directions at the same time. *Wunderkisten* (Wonder Boxes) are six variously sized wooden boxes stacked on top of each other, connected by an aluminium pole fixed to a base plate. This seemingly simple arrangement conveys both cohesiveness and flexibility. Thanks to the simple mechanism and pyramid-like construction, the elements can be pivoted and interchanged at will. They can even be turned on their sides. The holes into which the pole is inserted do double duty as outlets for cables, and casters are available to make the whole structure mobile. The fan principle applied here can also be seen in the *Küchenbaum* (**Stefan Wewerka**, 1984), for example. The shelf/cabinet hybrid produced by Freiraum seems however to renounce all technical ambition, recalling with its understatement similarly tricky wooden constructions by **Konstantin Grcic**, for example the wardrobe *Hut ab* (**Nils Holger Moormann**, 1998). *Wunderkisten* can perhaps be regarded as essential or even existential minimalism, taking its place in the long tradition of case and modular furniture that goes back to forebears like the Bauhaus or late-1960s orange crates.

# 1996

**Chair**

Design:
**Beata Bär**
**Gerhard Bär**
**Hartmut Knell**

Manufacturer:
Bär + Knell

# Time Documents

It all started with a feeling of frustration that nothing was being made out of the accumulating mountains of plastic waste other than boring drainage pipes and flowerpots. Three young creative talents then came up with the idea of producing furniture from PET bottles and plastic bags. In the recycled products, the colours and familiar logos of the packaging used would remain recognizable, only slightly distorted by the production process. Each object is thus unique, a document of everyday life at a certain point in history. This is furniture that, layer for layer, tells the story of the living habits of modern industrial society and its world of things. Behind this idea is the urge to experiment, the quest for technical procedures able to salvage plastic refuse with its singular composition and give it a new lease on life. A stretched Aldi bag drapes itself across the seat, demonstrating that the widely publicized *Zeitdokumente* chair was given this name for good reason: it represents a snapshot of the current state of capitalism, an allusion to changing consumer predilections, trends and fashions. Recycling with artistic profundity. The furniture produced by Bär + Knell has something of the Ready-Mades, of Pop Art, recalling the works of the French decollagistes, but also the spontaneous drip paintings of Jackson Pollock. This is coupled with an explicit reference to design: *Zeitdokumente* borrows its basic shape from the "Bofinger Chair" *BA 1171* (1966). Later, Bär + Knell also transported the classic *SE 68* chair by **Egon Eiermann** into the here and now using recycled materials that generate a speckled pattern.

**Table**

Design:
**Jakob Gebert**

Manufacturer:
Nils Holger Moormann

# Spanoto

What more could anyone want from a table? *Spanoto* combines lightness with a high degree of stability and strength. The tabletop of beech plywood only six millimetres thick is flexible and therefore doesn't wobble, even if the table is placed on an uneven surface. The table surface can be covered in linoleum if desired. The legs, made from two flat boards that are screwed together near the floor, diverge toward the top to form a "V". They come as individual units that can be mounted with an assembly aid in the side aprons in any position desired, and changed at will. When the assembly aid is removed, the legs are braced within the guide rails and remain fixed in position. They are just as easy to remove again and can be slid underneath the tabletop along with the assembly aid for flat transport. A variety of accessories is available, such as a board that can be slid into one side, corner connectors and a drawer system. *Spanoto* is a prime example of the laconic functionalism one has come to expect from **Nils Holger Moormann**, who is following in the large footsteps of classical Modernism with such pleasantly modest reserve.

# 1996

**Cabinet System**

Design:
**Peter Maly**

Manufacturer:
Behr International

# Menos

Keeping up with the fortunes of his various products and continuing to support them over the years is important to designer **Peter Maly**, which is why he found the task of expanding and refining his *Menos* cabinet system a good decade after its conception particularly compelling. The point of departure for the system, which freely acknowledges its status as "case furniture", was a square chest of drawers. The division of the front into 16 equal-sized squares emphasizes the serial and modular character of the piece. Details like the mitred, finely rounded corners and corner connectors underscore the overall feeling of elegance, recalling the sleek finish commonly found in contemporary automotive design. Small, likewise square, aluminium handles punctuate the surface, arranged as graphic highlights in various patterns. This cabinet program represents a further instalment in a long line of modular furniture, such as the "growing home" of the 1920s and wall units such as the *M125* (**Hans Gugelot**, 1960) or *BMZ* (**Behr International**, 1955). It reflects the rationalist imperative of the Bauhaus, in effect harking back to the Enlightenment tradition. This grounding in intellectual history is condensed in the symbolic value of the square, perhaps explaining why *Menos* is one of the most extensive and variable furniture systems anywhere, with elements ranging from cabinet to coffee table.

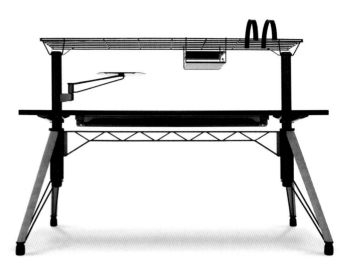

**Desk System**

Design:
**Klaus Franck**
**Werner Sauer**

Manufacturer:
Planmöbel

# x-act

The central design element of *x-act* is made up of two-footed telescope tubes onto which modular lattice frames are attached – optical exclamation points that immediately draw attention to the uniqueness of the concept. Their peculiar, tripod-like structure allows for tabletops in virtually any format to be used and to be infinitely adjusted in height. The tubes that jut through the tabletop can be used to equip the workplace with additional shelves and practical accessories such as telephones or book clamps. Another unusual feature is the option of attaching a lattice bridge lengthwise across the table at eye level, which can be used as a shelf or to hang things from: trays, lights or even a talisman. On behalf of Planmöbel, the well-known team of **Klaus Franck** and Werner Sauer has designed a formally and aesthetically independent system whose charm lies in its high level of flexibility. This allows, for example, each staff member in a company to modify his own workspace to suit his needs, an aspect that should not be underestimated in terms of worker motivation.

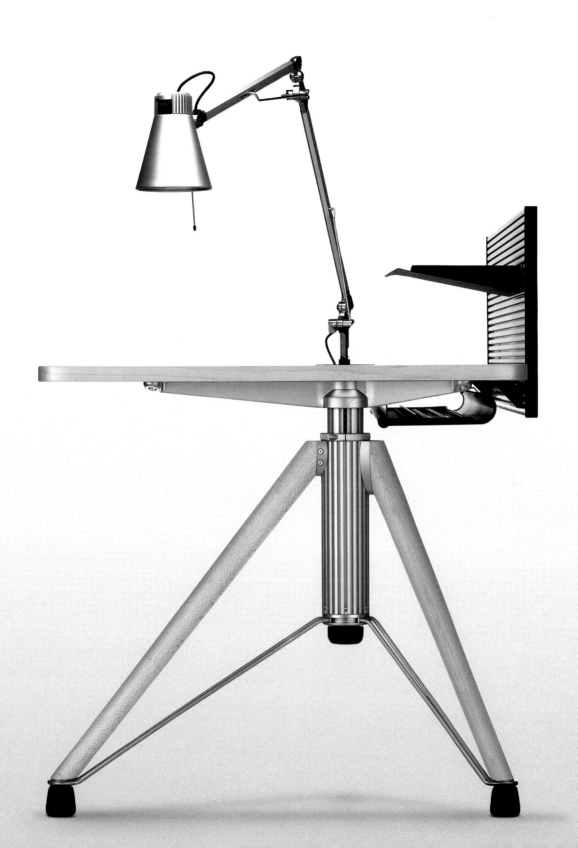

# 1996

Design:
**Philipp Mainzer**

Manufacturer:
e15

Small photo:
*Bigfoot* table and *Taro* bench
by Philipp Mainzer
and Florian Asche, 1994

# Molar

The study of design teaches us that the highest level of quality is always achieved when form and function are effortlessly intertwined. This is exactly what the *Backenzahn* (Molar) stool achieves, and what's more, it does so in a way that was hardly to be expected shortly before the end of the 20th century. The small, blockish construction is put together solely from four identical tapering heartwood legs. The doubly symmetrical arrangement derives its appeal from the tension between the astoundingly simple geometry and the rustic, rough-hewn aesthetic, which also entails a certain irregularity of lines and surfaces. The magic of the design is underscored further by the apt onomatopoetic name. A deliberate roughness and central depression serve to ensure secure seating. This places *Molar* in the company of other comparably simple German stool designs, such as model *B 9* (1927, by **Marcel Breuer**), which came off the assembly line, and the *Ulm Stool* (**Hans Gugelot**, 1950), which was conceived for the Denkfabrik. The fact that the age-old material of wood is still in step with the times was demonstrated by **e15** with its massive, collapsible *Bigfoot* table, in which the fissures in the wood form part of the design.

**Kitchen System**

Design:
**Herbert H. Schultes**

Manufacturer:
Bulthaup

Small photo:
cabinet element, sink element

# S 20

"This is where I like to sit, if possible for several hours, and to enjoy spending time with friends and family", said designer Herbert H. Schultes. For one-and-a-half decades, the former design head at Siemens has been creating kitchen concepts for **Bulthaup**. *B 3* (2004) was the third in a series of systems that all share the same tenor: the kitchen must function smoothly, but should also serve as a full-fledged living space alongside the dining and living rooms. An innovation introduced by the *S 20* was the patented system of supporting pylons made of an aluminium alloy. The term "industrial design" is taken to its logical conclusion here, exemplifying the workbench character that helped define a new kitchen type in the late 1980s. Another industrial touch is the dominance of metal, signifying mechanical precision. Further highlighting the technical dimension are the striking parallel grooves in the side walls, which underscore the sturdiness of the construction (and vaguely recall the *Ju 52*, probably Germany's most famous aircraft). The concept of freestanding modules would be developed further, with the individual elements not permanently stationed in one place, legs hidden behind a panel, as had become the custom, but instead given visible feet or casters for easy moving. "We liberated the kitchen", Gerd Bulthaup rejoiced when the *S 20* was introduced.

# 1998

**Bathroom Series**

Design:
**Sieger Design**

Manufacturer:
Duravit

Small photo:
*Happy D* bathtub

# Happy D

D for Design. The **Sieger Design** studio drew inspiration from the traditional form of the sink and accentuated the letters of the alphabet sometimes evoked by it through graphical simplification. Just like at the beginning of the decade with the *Tara* tap (for **Dornbracht**), the designers from Westphalia took recourse to historical domestic icons and used them to devise an up-to-the-minute, clean-lined formal vocabulary. The new wave in bathroom design, in which they played no small part, thus remained connected to collective memory through quotations of familiar schemata. In *Happy D*, which has in the meantime become one of the most comprehensive bathroom series including sinks, bathtubs, furnishings and accessories, the striking letter is put through its paces in a diverse set of designs, resulting in a formal stringency that has earned the line several German and international design prizes. The wide variety of washstand solutions – which is after all the place people spend most time in the bathroom – carries the whole program.

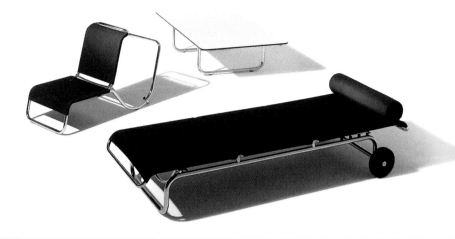

# 1998

# Dia

At the end of the 1990s, it was quite surprising that a manufacturer with an upscale design profile would come out with a series of garden furniture, a theme that did not play much of a role on the design scene. The *Dia* program, which includes a chair, a lounge chair and two tables of different heights, offered the kind of versatility that invited a variety of uses (not only outdoors, but also inside). With a single flip, the chair turns into a low lounge seat (the two levels corresponding to the different table heights), and, what's more, can be stacked in groups of eight. The lounge chair has casters and many different adjustment options at both head and foot ends, allowing for varying reclining positions. A round cushion for the head provides additional comfort. The polished stainless steel frame with fabric stretched between is an unmistakeable reference to the tubular steel pioneers of the 1920s. Nowhere is the choice of durable materials so important to function as in furniture designated for outdoor use. Carefully conceived, elegant, robust: **Gioia Meller-Marcovicz** recommends her garden ensemble as an "investment for life".

# 1998

**Table**

Design:
**Norbert Beck**

Manufacturer:
Rolf Benz

# 8950

In the second half of the 1990s, expandable glass tables were still a technical novelty for which hardly any prefabricated components were available. This meant that the rails and sliding parts had to be developed from scratch. Existing drawer slides were too weak to carry the heavy glass plates, while ball bearings were rejected as being too complex. The goal was to come up with the simplest possible solution: a divided glass plate that could be pulled apart so that a wooden panel lying underneath could be flipped up in the middle. Table specialist **Norbert Beck** achieved this aim by using two long steel profiles as rails. The end points also consist of profiles. The cross-connection is formed by transverse steel bars that seem to rest freely on the independent wooden legs (but which are in fact anchored by means of invisible steel pins). The appeal of this design lies in its transparency, in both senses of the word. The use of glass makes the table literally see-through – a joy to look at thanks to its logical construction. And, unlike some elaborate, complicated pullout systems, here the mechanics of how the table works are immediately transparent to the user without any instructions. No levers are necessary. The table can be pulled out in three moves and changed back just as easily. As Beck is the first to admit, this oft-copied technology possesses the kind of clarity that even for him would be difficult to repeat.

# 1998

**Lamp**

Design:
**Peter Maly**

Manufacturer:
Anta

# Screen

A penchant for high-grade yet soft-spoken materials, sensitively finished and combined. The urge to eliminate all extraneous details. Finally, the striving for harmonious proportions. Here, manufacturer and designer are quite obviously on the same wavelength. But then again, it's not really that simple. For one thing, the road to the minimized and therefore so logical-seeming design probably presented a few more bends than the product itself. Secondly, it's always the case that the more reduced the design, the more precisely all the elements have to fit together. The *Screen* lamp is an outstanding example of this truism. Greater reduction is hard to imagine. The well-ventilated light source is sandwiched between two identical glass plates. The result is clean, diffused light. At the same time, the square light source exudes an emblematic presence in the room. The uncomplicated, easy-to-comprehend structure includes two parallel lines that "frame" the shade at the upper and lower edges. In the base as well, which is the same width as the shade, the square returns in a horizontal position. With this lamp, system developer **Peter Maly**, otherwise known for designing a number of modern wall unit programs, transferred the same kind of logical thinking onto a new product field. The fact that *Screen* also functions as a product family, in which all that varies is the length of its twin legs, makes the whole thing simply perfect.

# 1998

**Coat Rack**

Design:
**Konstantin Grcic**

Manufacturer:
Nils Holger Moormann

# Hats Off

Munich designer **Konstantin Grcic** takes a fresh look here at the traditional coat stand. Six thin poles of raw ashwood are connected via three joints, creating a simple scissoring mechanism. Hooks plus protrusions at the end of the poles provide a variety of hanging options: from simply throwing a jacket over a hook to more orderly arrangement on hangers. The bend between the long and short bars provides room for handbags. When the coat stand is not in use, it can simply be folded together quickly for space-saving storage. Over the years, Grcic has invented a whole series of small useful items for **Nils Holger Moormann** that never existed before, such as the step stool *Step* and the permanently slanted shelf unit *Es*. All of them have one thing or another in common with *Hut ab* (Hats Off). They are all simple, the opposite of high-tech, and they are not rigid, but nonetheless stable. The construction is designed in such a way that their own weight keeps them in balance. Finally, Grcic's occasional furniture pieces constitute small irritations, reminders that not everything can simply be taken for granted. We can't trust our eyes, start doubting the natural laws and are sometimes sceptical if the product can really work. *Hut ab* does.

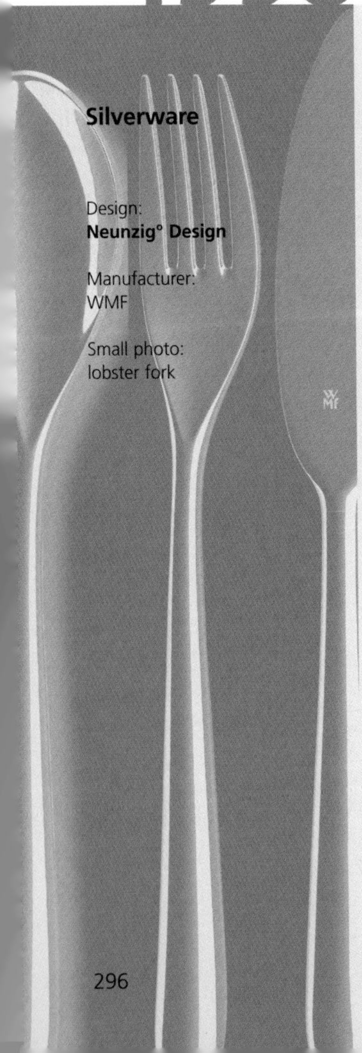

**Silverware**

Design:
**Neunzig° Design**

Manufacturer:
WMF

Small photo:
lobster fork

# Velvet

In this product field, where a single millimetre can make a big difference, and a great deal of sensitivity and experience is called for in mastering the intractable material, beginners are the exception. That makes it all the more remarkable that the first serial product brought out by the studio **Neunzig° Design** was silverware of all things – the ultimate challenge amongst metal objects. Designers Barbara Funck and Rainer Weckenmann presented their design to **WMF** in the mid-1990s – with success, because this flatware showed a brand new approach. It was no longer all about the geometric minimalism customary in this metier, but instead about formal frugality borrowed from nature herself. This fact is not immediately apparent when looking at *Velvet*, because the critical difference is on the reverse side, which features a hollow groove. This is the kind of structure found for instance in a blade of grass, which as we know achieves great stability with little material. The same principle used in car chassis is applied here to flatware handles, making them lighter in weight, considerably deeper and better to grip, and lending them a plumpness that feels pleasant in the hand. The organic approach is underscored by the overall pliant flow of line. That a great deal of creative and technical fine-tuning went into achieving this balance is demonstrated by the long development time of over a year until *Velvet* was finally launched on the market. The customers didn't fail to pick up on the bionic message. The durable silverware, made in Germany, has now been expanded to a line of 26 different pieces, including such exotic implements as a special serving spoon for potatoes.

# 1999

**Table**

Design:
**Christoph Böninger**

Manufacturer:
ClassiCon

# Sax

It's a table, the rectangular panel tells us. But already at second glance, we realize that we can't really classify this object so easily. Occasional table or serving trolley? It's both. And that's what makes it so special. Mobile forerunners include **Herbert Hirche's** *Bar Trolley* (1956) or **Glen Oliver Löw's** folding table *Battista* (1991), although these are limited to only one height. The theme of the height-adjustable table suddenly took on new meaning with **Christoph Böninger's** *Sax*. This masterpiece of engineering bears similarity to Ginbande's *Tabula Rasa* (1987), as both of them work with a folding grille mechanism, revealing their cleverly conceived substructure for all to see. In *Sax*, the table legs attached to the mobile elements can be moved back and forth along the underside of the table edge. Depending on the height, this changes the angle between the elements, lending the base a different geometry each time. The server changes in stature. Sometimes he stands up straight and tall, sometimes he takes a bow.

# 1999

**Chair and Lounger**

Design:
**Werner Aisslinger**

Manufacturer:
Cappellini

Small photo:
lounger for Zanotta

# Soft Cell

In 1996 **Werner Aisslinger** visited the *Mutant Materials* design exhibition at the New York Museum of Modern Art, which for the first time spotlighted innovative uses for materials. The most fascinating exhibit for him was the gel an American manufacturer used to cushion a bicycle seat. From then on, he found himself wondering how to apply this technology to the world of furniture. He researched companies that made the gel, finally coming upon an Italian business that had purchased a license from Bayer. This was the first gel without plasticizer, meaning it would retain its properties over many years. In *Soft Cell*, two units are put together to form a gel "sandwich" and mounted on a chrome-plated linear metal frame. The "sandwich" is made up of a supporting nylon lattice between two layers of gel. Organic design is carried on down to the micro level here. The gel surface is smooth and has a texture like human skin. The transparent minimalist structure of tubular steel furniture meets up here with the elasticity and sitting comfort of an upholstered chair. The organic grid pattern shows through the translucent surfaces like the veins of a leaf. As the gel's colour changes with the fall of light, the furniture's appearance undergoes a continual metamorphosis.

# 1997

**Hanging Lamp**

Design:
**Ingo Maurer**

Manufacturer:
Ingo Maurer

# Zettel'z

In the pre-digital age the note jotted down on a slip of paper was the universal mnemonic device. The note box ("Zettelkasten" in German) rose to fame in particular through German writer Arno Schmidt, from whose pen came the novel *"Zettel's Traum"* (Zettel's Dream).
**Ingo Maurer's** one-of-a-kind lamp is also a reminiscence on the past and on linguistic culture as well as his most direct attempt to combine design poetry with the literary kind. One might view it as a hybrid of pinboard and hanging lamp, or as an avant-garde chandelier for stimulating communication and contemplation. The lamp comes with 31 printed slips of paper and 49 sheets of unprinted Japan paper in DIN A5 format for the owner to use as he wishes. Of course, there are no limits to the kind of paper that can be used and what can be written or drawn on it. The freedom with which each individual can make this lamp his own is part of the liberating concept behind the design. Not only communication is encouraged, but also interaction with the designer. The body of the lamp is made of stainless steel, with a heat-resistant glass plate as diffuser. The light cast is suitable for illuminating large rooms and tables, with both a dispersion lamp and spots directed downward. This paper chase showcase, although a bit difficult to assemble and hang, is a best-seller amongst the designer lamps.

# 2000

## New Designs Living in the 21st Century

# 2000

**Stool**

Design:
**Christoph Böninger**

Manufacturer:
formerly Mabeg

# Soest Stool

Stools form a secondary line of progression in the history of German furniture design, but one with regularly recurring reinterpretations. Whether as tubular steel construction (**Marcel Breuer**, 1926), *Ulm* Stool (**Hans Gugelot**, 1950), or *Backenzahn* made of heartwood (Philip Mainzer, 1996), this simplest of all chairs has sometimes inspired designers to come up with astonishing solutions. A high-tech version was contributed by **Christoph Böninger**. The Munich-based designer has long followed the latest innovations in material technology, and began in the late 1990s to experiment with aluminium sheeting, which he wanted to shape into a chair. The result was the *Soester Hocker* (Soest Stool), industrial furniture at its purest. At 43 centimetres high and 45 centimetres wide and deep, it is nearly a cube, but only nearly. In contrast to the famous *Ulm* Stool, whose naming concept it followed (Soest is the location of the Mabeg company, which also manufactures things like bus stops), its surface is characterized by flowing forms. Soft transitions and hard metal form sensual antipodes. Lateral indentations that look like the folds of a curtain serve to increase stability. Slipping is prevented by a circular hollow in the seat. The carefully orchestrated wavelike structure resembles the exterior of a modern automobile. Also impressive is the load-bearing capacity of this small stool: although it weighs in at a little over one kilogram, it is able to support three hundred pounds.

# 2000

**Felt Carpet**

Design:
**Bernadette Ehmanns**

Manufacturer:
Hey-Sign

# Weaving

As a cultural technique, weaving has a tradition that goes far back to the earliest days of human history. Using industrial felt for a carpet, however, is a complete novelty, continually revealing fresh angles, such as is often the case with the less spectacular innovations. Graphically, the surface of the rug *Geflecht* (Weaving), which comes in various sizes ranging up to a three-and-a-half-metre square, is made up of smaller squares. Since it is now available in almost 40 colours, the possibilities for adding accents to a room are manifold. The interweaving of the individual five-centimetre-wide felt strips lends the rug its unique three-dimensional structure, which is exact but nevertheless not entirely uniform. This is because the felt is woven by hand. This leads to slight bulges and edges that create a pattern of shadow, which also dictates the tactile properties. Walking on the weave barefoot is a very pleasant experience – with the interplay of texture and pliancy feeling almost like a massage. It's no surprise that the sensuous felt pad, which is made of pure wool, is often used as a yoga mat.

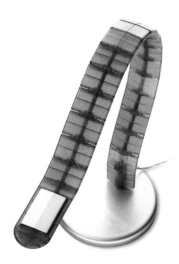

# 2000

**Table Lamp**

Design:
**Tobias Grau**

Manufacturer:
Tobias Grau

# Soon

The same principle as in the spinal column: a number of identical bodies and joints are strung together flexibly to form a band, which segues seamlessly into a lamp head of equal width. The backbone of *Soon* is formed by a double flat steel band inside that fulfils several purposes. Electricity is conducted through the metal strip and it also lends the whole the necessary stability. The use of translucent plastic makes this inner structure visible. The appeal of the design, and not only in aesthetic terms, but also from the standpoint of practicality, lies in its simple, self-contained and easily comprehensible form. Thanks to the elimination of any outer mechanisms (such as are virtually celebrated in **Richard Sapper's** *Tizio* for example) as well as the lack of a shade, this graceful lamp takes up little room. It bends snakelike over the narrowly confined space that is lighted, leaving the surrounding work area free. The transformer is integrated into the plug so as not to disrupt the slim line. With a length of about half a metre, the lithe helper has a sizeable radius. *Soon* is almost a textbook example of the melding of structural, functional and semantic aspects. While the white version has a technical look, the orange one seems almost venomous. Finally, *Soon* is yet another example of how **Tobias Grau** uses high-precision tools to create clickable and snap-together parts that allow for extremely minimal solutions.

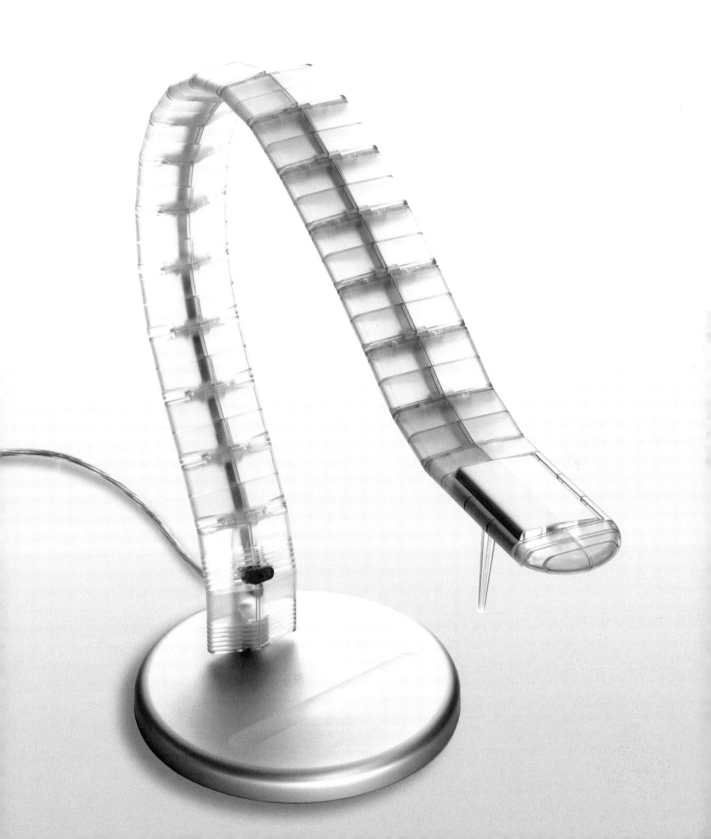

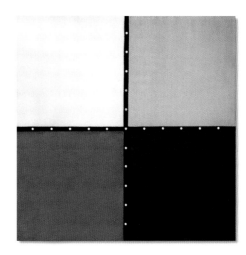

# 2000

**Carpet Collection**

Design:
**Rodolfo Dordoni**
**Konstantin Grcic**
**Ross Lovegrove**
**Peter Maly**
**Pascal Morgue**
**Michal Shalev**
**Studio Vertijet**
**Christian Werner**
**Atelier JAB Teppiche**

Manufacturer:
JAB Anstoetz

Small photo:
carpets by Peter Maly

Photo on page 311:
carpets by Studio Vertijet

# Design Edition

The idea of launching a modern carpet collection by five designers from four European countries – Rodolfo Dordoni, **Konstantin Grcic**, Ross Lovegrove, **Peter Maly** and Pascal Morgue – was in and of itself an innovation. Maly took charge of the co-ordination and contributed an extensive series of rugs. The serial, square motifs look like abstract pictures in an exhibition, but they can still be walked on. Despite all the purism of his designs, the master of industrial minimalist art declared that his goal was to lend these rugs "a third dimension". He therefore varied the height of the pile as one graphic element. What intrigued Grcic about this assignment was its connection to architecture. His carpet was not to be an accessory, but rather a constitutive element of the building. The second edition came out in 2004, featuring exclusively German designers: **Studio Vertijet**, **Christian Werner**, the in-house team from the JAB Teppiche studio and Maly again. This time, there were prescribed themes. In the case of Studio Vertijet, the focus was Mediterranean country house style. The resulting rugs are handmade of pure wool, supplemented by elements in silk, metal and leather. The rich nuances are meant to reflect the intense colours and the light of the South. Plans are to add further chapters to the authors' carpet series.

# 2000

**Piano**

Design:
**Peter Maly**

Manufacturer:
Sauter

# Pure

It's one of those objects that are so simple, they raise the question of where the design factor comes in. And at the same time it is the model with which the tradition-steeped Swabian piano maker Sauter firmly established its design line. **Peter Maly** was asked to conceive an instrument that fits in well with a modern living environment while also harmonizing with contemporary art. He indubitably succeeded at this task – by creating a piano body of smooth rectangular surfaces in which straight lines dominate. Metal bands emphasize the most important lines, giving the work a clear articulation, particularly in the black version. This reduction makes *Pure*, which also comes in red and white, look at once compact and generously dimensioned. This is what a Bauhaus piano might have looked like if the masters of classical Modernism had come upon the idea of redesigning the furniture piece amongst the music instruments. But they neglected to do so. And thus pianos still looked as if they had come out of the previous century. *Pure* is the logical counter-design: a well-proportioned double block with every bit of frippery polished away. The handle on the keyboard cover melds into the archetypal image as a small straight line of metal. Although the formal solution takes centre stage here, it is hardly an end in itself. By omitting all distractions, the concentration is focused on what counts: the music.

# 2000

**Hanging Lamp**

Design:
**Martin Wallroth**

Manufacturer:
Mawa

# Fridtjof 1

The name of this lamp is a bow to the Berlin modernist Fridtjof Schliephacke, an architect, designer, professor and friend of **Ludwig Mies van der Rohe** who was virtually unknown outside his hometown. Following in his footsteps, company founder Martin Wallroth designed a highly sober, technically and aesthetically high-scale lamp series perfectly exemplified by the model *Fridtjof*. Optically, the infinitely adjustable hanging lamp, whose grey colour comes from the silver-anodized aluminium of the housing, describes three parallel lines in space. The cables are extremely thin thanks to the low voltage used. The simple bar form is high-tech, reserved and goes well with both professional and private surroundings. The lighting element itself, enclosed by two corner profiles, was chosen for the desired light effect. Thanks to the variable height and the light that radiates laterally from both ends, an area more than double the length of the lamp itself can be illuminated. Special glass makes the light softer and warmer, affording by means of a slightly stepped-back bulb level an almost glare-free light despite the streamlined, reduced form. The joint in the aluminium body lets a bit of light stream upward as well. All in all, the result is a surprisingly complex, but pleasantly measured lighting situation.

# 2000

Design:
**Bernd Benninghoff**
**Karsten Weigel**

Manufacturer:
Jonas & Jonas

# Nudo

Even in these rapidly changing times, there are some things we assume will continue to look the same, because they have always looked that way: for example the box-like lectern. But now, even this old standard has been given a fresh new appearance. The reduced, three-legged stand developed for **Jonas & Jonas** looks more like a camera tripod than anything else. Like a tripod, it is reduced in form and adjustable. The tubular stainless steel legs come together at a junction that is equipped with a Bakelite knob for adjusting the height and angle of the tray. Elastic bands or a wooden rail set into the work surface prevent papers from sliding off. *Nudo*, just as health-promoting as the *Stitz* leaning aid (**Hans "Nick" Roericht**, 1991) because standing eases the burden on the spine, offers versatile options for use – as an improvised breakfast table, an easel for quick sketches, a telephone shelf, music stand, projector table or – why not? – a lectern. After all, the lack of a barrier to the audience means that the speaker is visible from head to toe, making the situation that much more democratic.

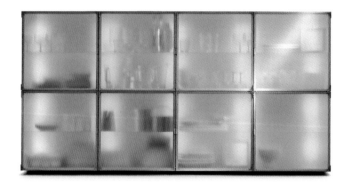

# 2001

**Cabinet System**

Design:
**Wulf Schneider**

Manufacturer:
Interlübke

# EO

At the end of the 1990s, **Interlübke** was looking for a new direction when Helmut Lübke took the rudder again and put the company back on a design-oriented course. The key product proclaiming a new start was **Wulf Schneider's** cabinet program *EO*, a global first that created a huge buzz at the major furniture shows. Based on a square grid and outfitted with glass doors, the system is lit from within and can change colour at the touch of a button. This makes it the first piece of furniture that cannot only be altered according to mood but can itself create various ambiences. The combination of colour and music further enhances this effect. The psychedelic trend of the 1960s had now arrived by way of cutting-edge technology in the contemporary living room. *EO* directly fuses the functional with the emotional. The basic idea behind this avant-garde furniture concept is additive colour mixing. Inside are red, green and blue LED lamps operated via remote control. Virtually every conceivable colour can be achieved by changing the proportions of the primary colours. Five favourite colours can be saved. Available with either doors or drawers, hanging on the wall or standing on the floor, the therapeutic lighted cabinet is extremely adaptable and can also be used as a room divider – with or without light diodes.

**Coat Rack**

Design:
**Martin Kleinhans**

Manufacturer:
Performa

# Performa

The springboard for this design was a client who was looking for a place for her entire family to hang their coats. In response, Martin Kleinhans developed a coat rack meant to grow with the needs of the family, exhibiting the utmost in simplicity in both looks and functionality. The basic concept was to provide parallel slits into which various hooks and shelves could be slid and held firmly in place through their own tension. Children would use the bottom slits, adults the upper ones. So much for the obvious uses of what is in principle a classic wall-hung coat rack. But the two-centimetre interval between the block and wall already indicates that this is not only a mundane object of everyday use, but also a monochromatic sculpture. The square-shaped hook holder is elevated above the ordinary by its pristine surface, which turns it into a perfect body in space. Compounding this impression of hermetic closure is the soft skin of linoleum or rubber. Incidentally, not only clothes can be hung on the **Performa** *Garderobe*; it can also form the basis for a personal installation of photos or other private objects.

# 2002

**Sofa System**

Design:
**Studio Vertijet**

Manufacturer:
COR

# Scroll

Kirsten Antje Hoppert and Steffen Kroll, who founded their company **Studio Vertijet** in order to have the freedom to "dream", added a sofa to the **COR** product range that was designed to expand awareness of sitting and reclining. Their concept earned kudos from all sides. This time out, their imaginations led them to envision a lounging island: the *Scroll* sofa, which – similar to *Lobby* (**Siegfried Bensinger**, 2003) – can be used in several different ways. Departing from frontal two-dimensionality, the upholstered piece is transformed into a communication medium, redefining the relationship between space and the seating group. The program comprises a single chair, a narrow two-seater, a chaise longue and a sofa. The basic form consists of flat, low-lying upholstered elements whose rounded corners give them a striking, graphic presence. The backrests can be adjusted to four different inclinations. Its outsize width lets *Scroll* transform itself from an ordinary frontal sofa to a chaise longue with room for two. When several modules are combined, lively upholstered landscapes can be created to match the current activity or mood.

# 2002

**Chair System**

Design:
**Wolfgang C. R. Mezger**

Manufacturer:
Davis
License: Walter Knoll

# Lipse

It comes as a stackable four-legged chair or on a pedestal base, or lined up along tandem beams as a multi-seat unit. *Lipse* is one of those chairs that are suitable for universal application, and it is also one of the most interesting to look at. The basic idea was to put together two differently shaped wooden shells to form an organic hollow that is reminiscent of the concave double surface of two hands (and which incidentally is not possible to realize with a single plywood part). The aluminium rod that holds the two parts together also functions as an optical hallmark, both providing a graphic dividing line and creating a contrast between cold metal and warm wood. The chair thus becomes a symbol of unity and separation.

*Lipse*, a play on the words "lip" and "ellipse", is a sculpture whose harmonious proportions **Wolfgang C. R. Mezger** worked out step-by-step by hand using a single block of styrofoam as scale model. The result looks good from every angle. This becomes evident for example when several swivelling double shells are lined up along a tandem beam. The chairs even look harmonious when placed at random, a property that not only speaks for their aesthetic quality, but also opens up a choice of communication options – whether turning toward the others or turning away.

**Desk**

Design:
**Patrick Frey**
**Markus Boge**

Manufacturer:
Nils Holger Moormann

Small photo:
with drawers
and computer compartment

# Kant

It's the simple and therefore most obvious improvements that are sometimes the most difficult for our minds to conceive of, according to Gestalt psychologists. A tabletop with a bend is presumably one of those phenomena that in principle anyone could come up with, but which runs so contrary to the tropes we take for granted in our everyday experience that our thinking first has to overcome this hurdle. But the fact is that this simple intervention, which Patrick **Frey** and Markus **Boge** ventured to make after all, harbours several positive effects. Order is finally brought to the desktop when books and other odds and ends can be stowed out of the way along the back edge. These items are even held in place by their own weight – further heightening the organizational utility. Finally, this neatness bonus also brings structural advantages, as the double bend significantly increases the desk's stability. Additional reinforcement is provided by the crisscross legs that continue the line formed by the rear panel. The proclamatory name of *Kant*, which diverges somewhat from the reserve otherwise demonstrated here, is presumably an appeal addressed to those doing the work of the mind to think outside of the box now and then. **Nils Holger Moormann**, who chose the upper Bavarian countryside as location for his firm, might be reminded when contemplating this fold of a well-ploughed furrow.

## Sofa System

Design:
**Siegfried Bensinger**

Manufacturer:
Brühl

# Lobby

Here, the concept of the combi-sofa takes on a whole new meaning. *Lobby* is a simple construction of three cubes: a flat main body on which two backrests of varying length are asymmetrically arranged. Because the main backrest is set in the middle, there is seating space all around. The effect is to create a seating island similar to the *Scroll* sofa (**Studio Vertijet**, 2002). This unusual design opens up seating for a large number of people. On what other sofa can one sit back-to-back? When multiple pieces are combined, infinite constellations are possible, like on a chequerboard. Soft throw pillows optically mitigate the architectonic severity. As already seen in the work of **Herbert Hirche** and other neomodern pioneers, clear lines are coupled here with a high degree of freedom. Finally, *Lobby* offers a very special extra: for use as a bed, the backrest and armrest are simply sunk into the main body by pulling a cord and pressing down lightly to create a large flat surface. "By day, it doesn't look like a sofa bed", assures **Siegfried Bensinger**, who had the new, flatscreen TVs in mind when conceiving his design. Television manufacturer **Loewe** is a neighbour of the **Brühl** company.

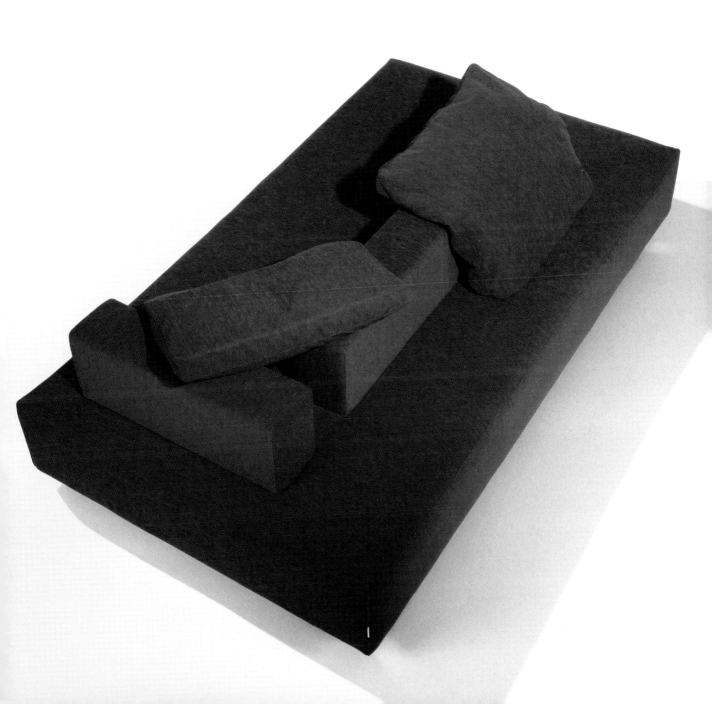

# 2002

## Office Chair

Design:
**Hadi Teherani
Hans-Ulrich Bitsch
Ulrich Nether**

Manufacturer:
Interstuhl

# Silver

Office furniture is a lot like cars these days. Since all of the leading manufacturers already fulfil every possible technical and functional demand, the salient factor has become innovative design. This is why the **Interstuhl** company approached Hamburg star architect Hadi Teherani, who aspires to design things that convey emotions. The aim was to conceive a high-quality swivel chair that would overcome the usual style conventions. A mental dimension was to be superimposed over the aesthetic one in what had to date been quite emotionless terrain. It took about a year until the idea for *Silver* took shape. In the meantime, several workshops were held in Hamburg and Messstetten. The market launch sparked a public sensation seldom seen in Germany in reaction to a mere office chair. The reasons are obvious. What distinguishes *Silver* from other products in its class are its structure and appearance. It is made up of shells that form a smooth, flat skin reminiscent of Eames's *Lounge Chair* and which one might also construe as a chassis, an impression that is underscored by the fine joints. The name-giving metallic colour makes the association with an expensive sedan complete. *Silver* is a prestige object, a consciously dramatized myth. Its modularity forms the basis for a full product family with high recognition and identification value. The resounding media echo raised the status of the brand itself. Now Teherani has taken the concept a step further. The next level of emotionalization is the introduction of handmade originals with deluxe surfaces in lacquer, wood, velvet or silk to further enhance that S-Class feeling.

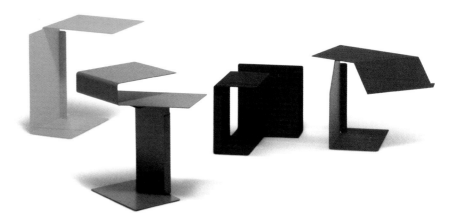

# Diana

Coffee table, lectern, stool, reference library, magazine stand, TV or notebook table.
**Konstantin Grcic's** metal table series is open to a wide variety of uses and interpretations.
The appeal of these cut and folded objects lies in the contrast between the hard, industrial material and the almost playful forms, whose folds look as effortless as if made out of paper. The small, powder-coated metal sculptures are available e.g. in deep black, oxide red or cream (special colours can be ordered as well). They give the impression of a kind of puzzle made out of colours and spatial geometries, steel origami with displaced surfaces. The recourse to straight lines and mostly right angles quotes classical Modernism, but is far more complex here than in **Herbert Hirche's** 1950s *Bar Trolley*. In fact, the shelf elements remind one a bit of the utopian sculptures of the Russian constructivists from the 1920s. But perhaps they also allude to the burnished metal skin of the car parked in front of our house. Just as we form and invent words out of letters, the *Diana* tables can be grouped in various ways. Using this three-dimensional alphabet, new readings can continually be created for the same room.

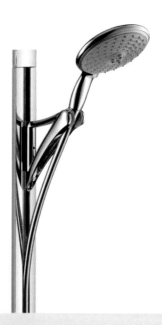

# 2003

**Shower**

Design:
**Phoenix Design**

Manufacturer:
Hansgrohe

# Raindance

Not only the experts are aware that the size of a showerhead influences the shower experience. With a larger showerhead, the water spray covers the whole body, which is perceived by most as a pleasant sensation. In order to achieve this effect in conventional shower systems that are not permanently fixed in place, it was necessary to combine the generous stream of a rain-type showerhead with the flexibility of a handheld shower. This is why *Raindance* has a large-diameter head on a relatively small handle, which was shortened substantially in order to make it more manoeuvrable. The reversal of the customary pro-portions not only created a new product type; it also made it possible to experience the above-mentioned relaxation effect even in smaller showers. The *Raindance* showerhead comes in a rounded and a flatter discus version. *Raindance* is inserted into the *Allrounder* pivoting shower pole right at the head and not at the handle as in conventional systems, so that showerhead and pole form a single unit that can be moved with just one hand and infinitely adjusted into any position. In the *Air* system that is today integrated into all *Raindance* showerheads, some 100 litres of air are drawn in per minute and mixed in with the water. The softer water droplets that result rain down onto the body out of 180 openings.

# 2003

**Television Set**

Design:
**Phoenix Design**

Manufacturer:
Loewe

# Mimo

Characteristic of the *Mimo* family of flatscreen televisions, which come in four screen sizes, are the rounded corners and the neutral white colour. Both features set them apart from the majority of the usually black, sharp-edged TV sets of the competitors, making these exceptional devices seem not hard and technical but rather lightweight and unobtrusive. These are not "apparatus" dominating the room – instead, they offer an unusual degree of flexibility in room arrangement. They come in a three-footed tabletop version, as a wall-hung screen, with a freestanding and movable tripod, or with a small cubic cabinet in matching style for hiding a DVD player. An *iPod* would also look good there. Thanks to its light weight, this is a television set that can really be carried around with no problem. One version even has a recessed grip on the back. For lovers of variety, the colour can be changed by means of exchangeable covers, like in a mobile phone. The sacred telly is thus transformed into a playful domestic highlight. *Mimo*, made to stand alone anywhere in the room, is inimical to any and every kind of elaborate and needlessly ponderous media furniture set-up. It would be hard not to notice how the device series with its basic, streamlined form picks up seamlessly on forerunners such as **Herbert Hirche's** *HF 1* (for **Braun**). The parallels extend even to the single, centrally placed control button and the perforated field over the integrated speakers, which is today however less conspicuous.

# 2003

## Folding table

Design:
**Luzius Huber, Florian Steiger**

Manufacturer:
Seefelder

# Janus

Variable and imposing: the two faces of *Janus*. Its surface area can be doubled – or cut in half. The table from **Seefelder**, a firm that is better known for its high-end upholstered furniture, can be transformed at a touch from a space-saving black table for four to a long red dining or worktable – and back again. And the way it accomplishes this anything-but-ordinary feat is a marvel to behold. Instead of the two table halves simply sliding apart as in most of its kin, *Janus* unfolds as spectacularly as a drawbridge. The patented mechanism behind this metamorphosis is the brainchild of Swiss designers Luzius Huber and Florian Steiger, who came up with the design for the firm of Seefelder, based near Munich. To switch from one face of *Janus* to the other, the two shorter table edges are first removed. Then the latch on the underside of the table is released. Now the tabletop can be swung out with minimal force. The table is manufactured under the Seefelder credo, which places the small southern German producer squarely in the great German tradition of holistic thinking. This includes not only the clever dual functionality but also clear divisions between products and the option of replacing parts.

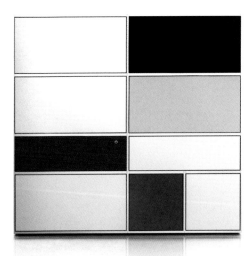

# 2003

**Cabinet System**

Design:
**Gert Wessel**

Manufacturer:
Weko

# Baureihe e

After demonstrating its commitment to the grid with its streamlined *Baureihe M* in the mid-1990s, thus veering away from the phalanx of indistinguishable competitors, **Weko** of Cologne found itself wondering: "Can purism be taken even further?" *Baureihe e* answers this question with a resounding "Yes!". A few rather unspectacular features are what make the difference here in terms of quality. For example, the doors come down so low that they cover the bottom board. All of the visible horizontals are therefore upper boards. When two units are placed side by side, the 10-millimetre-thick side panels add up to a width of 20 millimetres, the exact thickness of the horizontal boards. This results in an even grid. Both sleights of hand together ensure that the whole always yields a uniform block, no matter how many units are combined. The homogeneous look is further reinforced by the lack of handles. "A few years ago, this would have been inconceivable", explains company owner Gert Wessel, pointing out the narrow vertical edges. This kind of extreme reduction was only made possible by new production processes. The "pure" form as envisioned by the pioneers of classical Modernism can hence be approximated even more closely today thanks to advances in technology. At the same time, the impression made by this minimal furniture is just as contradictory as that of its famous role models: it exudes both a stylish reserve and an imposing presence as magical monolith.

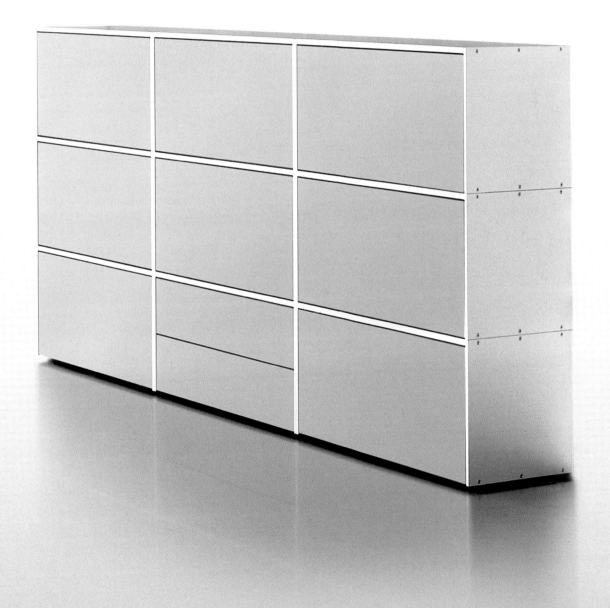

# 2003

## Easychair

Design:
**Konstantin Grcic**

Manufacturer:
ClassiCon

Small photo:
*Pallas* table

# Mars

*Mars* is an in-between thing: a chair judging by its height, but also an upholstered easychair. The synthetic resign body is covered in fabric or leather – an out-of-the-ordinary solution that makes the chair look as though it were dressed. Largely lacking in right angles, *Mars* has a surface structure full of oblique lines. Its figure is defined in particular by the projecting, slightly tapered seat and the quite massive base that widens towards the floor. These elements are joined by a surface compiled like a collage out of basic geometric forms and defined by its edges. The pattern here is made up of rectangles and triangles. Conspicuous is a crease that runs down the middle from top to bottom. All of this lends *Mars* its unconventional proportions and a silhouette that, as already seen in **Konstantin Grcic's** *Diana* and *Pallas* tables, recalls the works of the Russian Constructivists. When covered in rich red or black fabric, this association comes even more strongly to the fore. *Mars* not only looks unusual; its moulded seat, lower in the middle and inclined slightly backward, also makes it exceptionally comfortable.

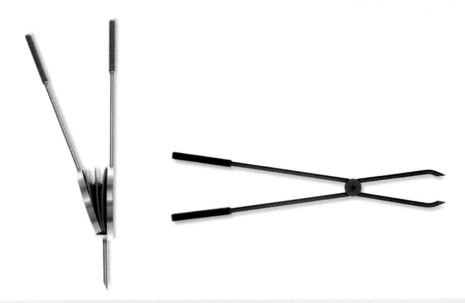

# 2004

## Fireplace

Design:
**Peter Maly**

Manufacturer:
Conmoto

Small photo:
fireplace implements
for Conmoto, 1997

# Balance

When the idea of developing new fireplace implements began to grow popular in the late 1990s, manufacturers and designers found themselves venturing onto as yet largely design-free terrain, a situation that was not really new for **Peter Maly**. He was faced here with the enticing task of reinventing a product type. And he succeeded in this endeavour by applying his well-known double strategy. It goes without saying that in the process he optimized all the tools involved – from bellows to andiron to ash shovel to poker – but at the same time he also lent the old familiar implements a whole new sense of style. They now seem modern and up-to-date, not least due to the unusual choice of materials – but they also exude a feeling as archaic as a discarded sword. After reforming the accessories, it was only logical that he would go on to rethink the fireplace itself. Who could have been better suited to this challenge than systematic thinker Maly, a specialist in wall unit programs? The outcome is the first additive oven in which fireplace and wood storage form co-ordinated modules. The solitary fireplace has been overcome and now the elements can be freely adapted to fit the respective living situation. A bench can also be integrated on the same level. Very elegant: the leg-free version in which *balance* is exemplified by a horizontal line.

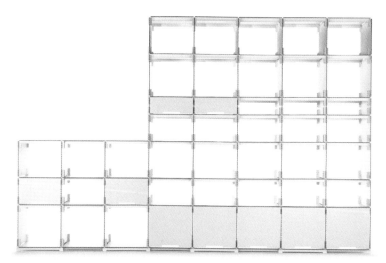

# 2004

# Plattenbau

Unlike many other shelf systems that hide their construction secrets, these are in plain view in *Plattenbau* (German for "prefabricated building") from **Kaether & Weise**. The shelf modules are equipped with a visible peg system that allows them to be assembled without tools. Since all elements - i.e. both horizontal and vertical panels – are made of a high-pressure laminate, they can be milled using CNC technology. This guarantees absolute consistency. Florian Petri's design derives its elegance not least from the use of panels that are only four millimetres thick. The Berlin designer made this leanness possible by basing the construction principle on a T-beam. Horizontal and vertical bracing ribs increase the load-bearing capacity many times over, allowing both for extreme heights and for shipping in conveniently small packages. A six-shelf unit fits in a briefcase. Lightness, stability and weight-bearing capacity thus enter into a happy liaison. Finally, various panel heights, depths and widths as well as hanging doors and back walls make the minimal shelf system extremely variable.

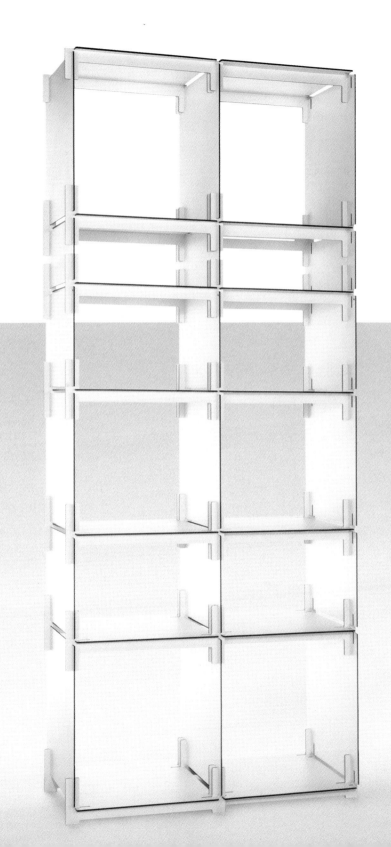

# 2004

# Dono

The sofa developed to celebrate the fortieth anniversary of the **Rolf Benz** company was originally planned as a new version of *Addiform*, the product that captured the spirit of the 1960s so well that it put the firm on the road to success. But **Christian Werner** refused to do a mere redesign job. Instead, he translated the design triumph of yesteryear into something more in step with the present: a sofa to fit today's lifestyle. After all, the function of the sofa has changed in many ways. Like the living room, it has increasingly lost its formal character and become part of a personal, almost intimate space in which a wide variety of activities are carried out with the most diverse paraphernalia and in just as many different positions. Therefore, *Dono* was to be above all versatile, an aspiration that Werner fulfilled using amazingly simple means. The main body is a rectangular slab with a large, open area for reclining. Replacing the otherwise expected backrest is a shelf onto which two cushions can be fixed in any position desired. *Dono* can thus be transformed into a bed with lightning speed, paired to form a corner sofa or - with the addition of cushions doing double duty as armrests – can play the part of a classic two-seater.

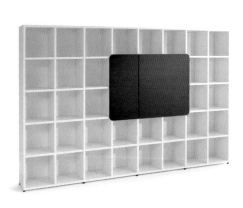

# 2004

# Freddy

We will probably never know whether the *Freddy* bookshelf is named after Frederik, the son of company owner Elmar Flötotto, or after the singer and record millionaire. What we do know, though, is that the idea hatched by design studio **Hertel & Klarhoefer** to create alternatives to the traditional bookshelf based on horizontal boards flanked by vertical sides was a successful one. The innovative Berlin architecture and design duo already patented their idea in the 1990s (executed for the first time in 1999 for **Zeitraum**). In the wake of systems such as *FNP* (from **Axel Kufus**), *Endless Shelf* (**Werner Aisslinger**) and *Plattenbau* (Florian Petri for **Kaether & Weise**), they made yet another flexible shelving solution available, which differs from the others in one important point. Instead of being stacked, the elements are interlocked like Lego bricks. The advantages include variability, theoretically unlimited height, the small size of the individual elements as well as the uniform thickness of their walls, which gives the whole a consistent optical homogeneity. Freddy (designed for **elmarflötotto**) is sold in packages. If a customer wants to add on to his bookshelf, he simply purchases another package. "People often only understand the principle once they have assembled their shelf", explains Sebastian Klarhoefer.

# 2004

**Chair**

Design:
**Wolfgang C. R. Mezger**

Manufacturer:
Brunner

Small photo:
*Milanolight* table

# Milanolight

Viewed from the side, the laminated wood describes a thin, neat stroke, underscoring the special quality of this design. For all those who appreciate a self-contained form, this chair was a revelation. Going its predecessor *Milano* one better, *Milanolight* incorporated the same aesthetic serenity and enhanced it by connecting seat and backrest. The unique touch here is the L-shaped transition, which looks almost like a fold and whose narrow radius had never before been realized in laminated wood. The sharp 90-degree bend in the nine-millimetre-thick shell was achieved in collaboration with specialist firm Becker after months of experimentation using prototype moulds. The minimal radius was ultimately only made possible by reducing the veneer. This idea was proposed by **Wolfgang C. R. Mezger**, who wanted to give his "architect's chair" even more streamlined, logical lines. The close-fitting frame, which is not bent but instead welded together with mitred corners, further contributes to this impression. A fine tribute to the right angle.

# 2004

**Room Divider**

Design:
**Harry & Camila**

Manufacturer:
Koziol

Small photo:
left: *Fusion* lamp
right: *Fusion* room divider

# Fusion

This hybrid of curtain and screen is a lightweight, hanging surface whose modularity lends itself to a variety of uses. It adapts to the situation at hand and leaves plenty of room for creativity. The idea comes from designer duo Harry & Camila from Barcelona. *Fusion* is made of partially transparent plastic squares that are hung together to create very unusual-looking walls of colour. The lively, irregular thread-like structure is vaguely reminiscent of the Abstract Expressionist drip paintings of Jackson Pollock. Rooms can be divided without completely blocking out the light, and sight contact is also preserved. Since the size is unlimited, *Fusion* can be used in extremely high rooms such as trade fair halls, museums or lobbies. *Fusion* also functions as a coloured area on the wall that, depending on which of the eleven hues is chosen, can influence the mood of the room or mark off certain zones using colour coding. Since the size of the panels is standardized at 27 centimetres, *Fusion* can be combined with elements from other series in a variety of patterns. Assembly is quick and easy: the squares are interhung using hooks, i.e. not fixed permanently, which means it's possible to redecorate at any time. What's more, *Fusion* can also be used as individual element for small areas, for example to decorate a window, as an eye-catcher or a partition in the home. **Koziol** itself has discovered yet another option: The transparent material is also available in the form of a square lamp.

# 2005

## Shelf System

Design:
**Hannes Bäuerle**
**Claudia Miller**
**Alexander Seifried**

Manufacturer:
Magazin

# Mein_Back

One look at the grey latticework crates is enough to summon the aroma of freshly baked bread and rolls, because these lightweight yet stable containers are used everywhere in bakeries (and restaurants) to deliver baked goods. Turned 90 degrees, this commonplace transport container becomes the basic element in an inexpensive shelving system. Used in this new way, the humble crate suddenly exhibits amazing qualities in terms of stability and quick assembly. *Mein_Back* can be put together without tools. To connect the crates a profile is simply clamped on, which also functions as a flat shelf surface. At the sides, U-shaped clips connect additional crates onto the vertical unit. If desired, *Mein_Back* can be placed on casters or even bent into a curve. The ready-made bookshelf, which also resonates with faint echoes of the orange-crate fad of the refractory 1960s, proves wonderfully suitable for transport and moves – which is hardly surprising given its origins. It can also be used as a room divider and, because it is weather-resistant, as an outdoor balcony shelf. Once installed, the modular system hardly betrays its pedestrian background, especially in its "frosted white" translucent version.

# 2005

**Office Chair**

Design:
**Votteler & Votteler**

Manufacturer:
Interstuhl

# Sputnik

Nearly half a century after designing his first swivel chair and a good two decades after his last, Arno **Votteler**, working together with his son Matthias, succeeded at creating a design for **Interstuhl** that could very well presage a new generation of office chairs. The task at hand involved one of the key questions in industrial design: Is it possible to design a product that can be produced inexpensively and at the same time offers top design quality and exceptional comfort? A competition was held and Votteler Senior and Junior prevailed against high-calibre international competition by squaring the circle and trimming the price. *Sputnik* is composed almost exclusively of machine-made plastic parts. This enables an exacting fabrication and also benefits the customer since the chair can be put together in just a few minutes using a simple connector system. A fresh design detail is the way the armrests are integrated into the seat, an eye-catching simplification that serves to give the chair greater stability. Another advantage that could set a precedent is the height adjuster located on the upper edge of the seat, which can be operated blindly. The rapid and successful development of the *Sputnik* was in great part based on the beneficial exchange between company management, engineers and the external designers.

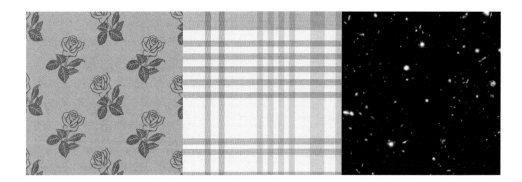

# 2005

## Wallpaper

Design:
**Kathrin Kreitmeyer**
**Matthias Gerber**

Manufacturer:
Extratapete

# Kollektion 3

The wallpaper picture, which results from an extreme enlargement of the page of an atlas, shows a small island somewhere in the ocean. The patterns are formed by elements familiar from geography: the network of meridians, the topographic lines, the printed names as well as the colour nuances between brown and blue. When we get closer, we notice that the matrix dots have begun to break up at this level of magnification. Although references to art – especially Pop Art – are conspicuous here, this is not the decisive point. Extratapete develops small, clearly defined collections that each follows a unifying principle. The aim is to achieve a different, innovative treatment of the graphical possibilities offered by wallpaper. In the case of *Kollektion 3*, the motifs are taken from found graphics spontaneously collected by Kathrin Kreitmeyer and Matthias Gerber. This might be a map, a piece of fabric or wrapping paper, or perhaps an excerpt from a picture on the television screen or a photo downloaded from the Internet. Enlargement breaks open the finer structure. Patterns emerge that are not artificial and which are virtually unparalleled in their vitality. Subsequent processing then enhances the wallpaper character. Through the use of hardly identifiable, but nonetheless real original objects, the dimension of content is added. When for example in *Pedro* (→ p.**439**) a postcard misprint shows only the outlines of a beach resort, the myths of the South come into play. The new wall decoration hence not only offers interesting fodder for our perceptual faculties, but also, through its sometimes ironic handling of meanings, becomes a playful kind of cultural medium.

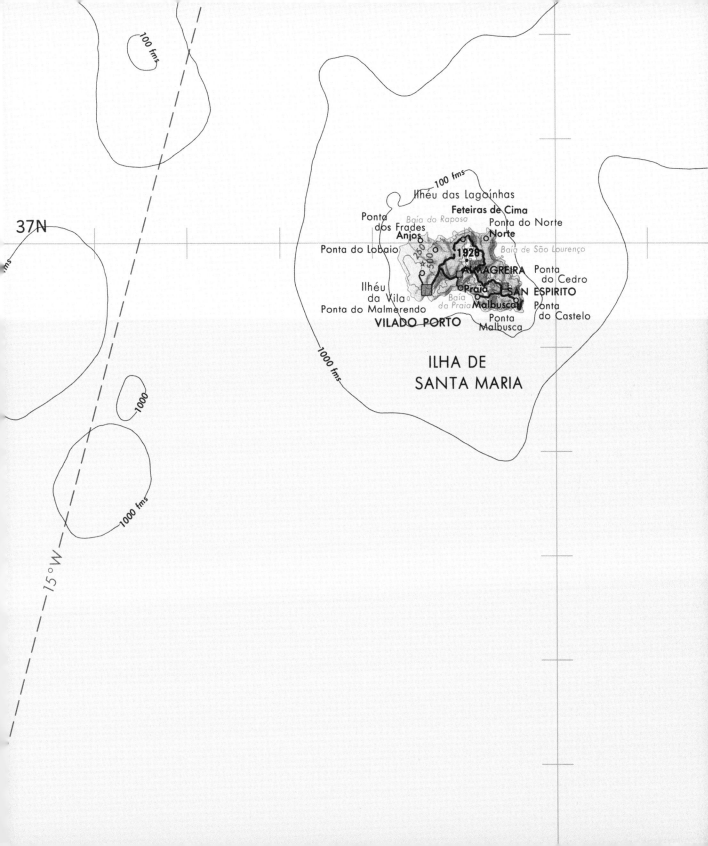

100 fms

37N

15°W

1000

1000 fms

1000 fms

100 fms

Ilhéu das Lagoínhas

Feteiras de Cima

Ponta
dos Frades      Ponta do Norte
Anjos        Norte

*Baía do Raposa*

Ponta do Lobaio          *Baía de São Lourenço*

250        1926

300      A MAGREIRA

Ilhéu          Ponta
da Vila    Praia      do Cedro

*Baía*      SAN ESPIRITO

Ponta do Malmerendo   *da Praia* Malbusca

VILA DO PORTO    Ponta    Ponta
Malbusca   do Castelo

ILHA DE
SANTA MARIA

# 2005

Design:
**Stefan Diez**

Manufacturer:
elmarflötotto

# Couch

A "couch" is casual and comfortable and isn't necessarily out to impress anyone. The product name already reveals its aim: a cosy and robust piece of upholstered furniture for daily use. Munich designer **Stefan Diez** discovered a new kind of construction to achieve this end. A canvas interior structure is filled with foam and ergofill beads, which not only create stability but also lend the whole an eye-catching form. Put together out of squares (even the seat formed by equally high armrests and backrest forms a square) the simple form recalls in its simplicity designs from the 1920s, such as the *Bauhaus-Kubus* from **Peter Keler** (today made by **Tecta**). Diez derives the rules governing the series from simple geometry. Minimal variations lead to an easychair, footstool and bench. The pieces come in neutral colours like grey or white, but also in shrill yellow, light blue or light green. The washable outer cover is extremely durable (although not when it comes to rain!). This footless furniture is made in China, but only filled after transport to save on costs. The interior sack is divided into various chambers using drawstrings and then the filling is blown in using a kind of reverse vacuum cleaner. Then the outer sack is pulled over the whole. The end points of the inner cords are visible as points punctuating the exterior. This "quilted" structure makes for lively surfaces reminiscent of the club chairs of the olden days.

# 2006

# Socialbox

He delivers one example after the other for the new minimalism in German design for living. And now a **Sanktjohanser** brainchild that was originally planned for a New York art fair has evolved into a brand new type of multifunctional furniture: *Socialbox*, a mixture of bench, cabinet and shelf. If the term "cabinet furniture" is ever appropriate, then it is here, where the right angle has an unchallenged monopoly. The structure consists of four permanently attached elements made of MDF panels. Three of them are composed of three cubes and the other of two. Stood on end they form an approximately shoulder-height shelf open on all sides. Two of the elements can be tilted down to the side to make a bench or corner bench (which can of course also be used for storage). The adaptability of *Socialbox* is dictated by the arrangement of the hinges. It is not an expandable system, but rather a changeable single piece of furniture which lends itself to versatile applications. It can serve as corner seating, lectern, secretary and much, much more. The combination of MDF and aluminium makes it very sturdy, while at the same time exuding understated, upscale simplicity.

# 2006

# Form 2006

Famed for his sleek yet exquisite perfume flacons, as well as occasional excursions into the theatre world, Peter Schmidt has now turned his gaze, as always attuned to essentials, toward the field of porcelain. Over the decades, exceptional designs have emerged in Germany again and again on this terrain, including Trude Petri's *Urbino* service and *TAC 1* by **Walter Gropius**, to name but two examples. Schmidt as well, a master of simplicity, bases his service – how could it be otherwise? – on geometric shapes. The interesting thing about it, though, is how he puts these graphic building blocks together: namely with relatively large "soft" radii as well as an ambivalent relationship of circle and rectangle. While the cups and pots have a cylindrical form, the saucières, bowls and sugar and jam jars are flat cubes with strongly rounded corners. A striking element because it's so unusual is that in the plates and platters Schmidt has set a rectangle inside a circle. This creates edges of varying widths, which makes the design complex and lively despite a clearly ordered structure. As is often the case in tableware, the pots are at the heart of the design. In this case, the pot ascends to the status of tabletop monolith. The fact that the choice of geometric figures is not mere random formal play is shown by the base of the bowls, which fit into the recesses in the plates. This results in diverse combination options.

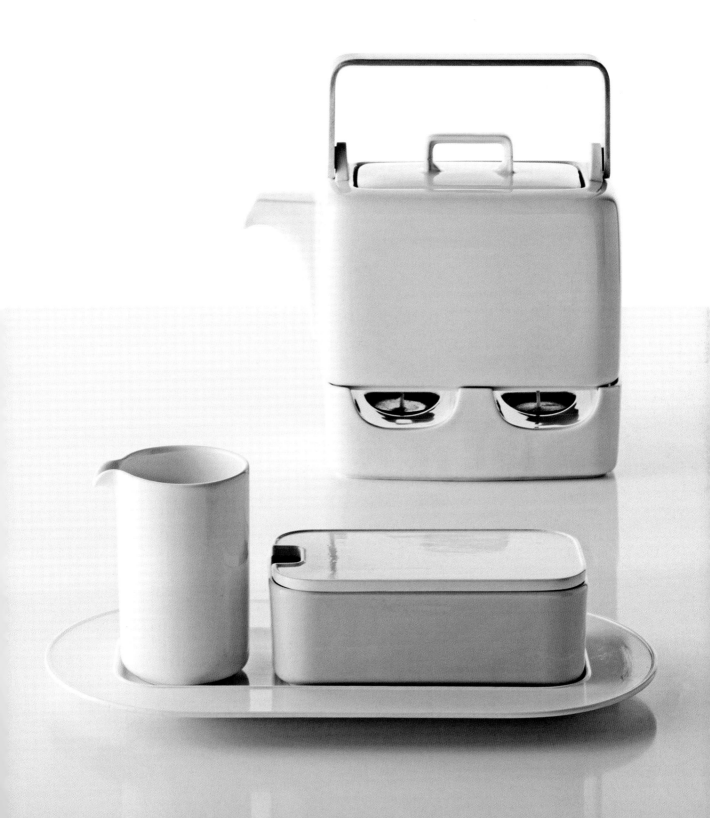

**Lounge chair**

Design:
**Wulf Schneider**

Manufacturer:
Thonet

Small photo:
left: *S 3501 easychair*
right: *S 3502 two-seater sofa*

Large photo:
*S 3501 easychair*
with *B 97* nesting table
Thonet, 1933

# S 3500

A serene form that directly and unmistakably recalls classical Modernism, but with a technical twist that provides dual functionality in a way that is simply ingenious. In his S *3500* upholstered furniture **Wulf Schneider** demonstrates how it's still possible to achieve some surprising effects using the old familiar rational tools of the German domestic designer's trade. The result is a line of easychairs and sofas that are of course right at home at **Thonet**. That an easychair, which also comes as a two-seater sofa, can be transformed into a lounge chair using a pullout mechanism is in itself nothing special. What's new about it is the intelligence of this clear-cut solution. The seat cushion doesn't have to be bent or hidden away somewhere, but rather simply slides underneath the back cushion and back out again on easy-slide rails: back to sit upright, and forward to put your legs up. It could hardly be easier. Everything is above-board, the functionality plain to see – just like the design forefathers once decreed. The base and frame are both of chrome-plated tubular steel, that eternal symbol of the Bauhaus and its holistic approach. With details like solid wood armrests, Schneider deliberately makes reference to this legacy. Thanks to its reserved, minimalist design and a practically unlimited choice of seat covers, this new seating furniture fits into a wide variety of environments.

# 2007

Design:
**Nicolas Thomkins**

Manufacturer:
Dedon

# Yin Yang

The hallmark of this design is the harmonious relationship between concave and convex surfaces that glide into one another and which mirror in their flowing lines the likewise anything but angular human form. Pushed together, the easychairs form a unit with a circular ground plan. This creates a cosy tête-à-tête situation for two. In order to find just the right position, designer Nicolas Thomkins set dummies into his prototype. Thomkins' sculpture studies undoubtedly aided him in developing these complex objects. The double *Yin Yang* chairs are reminiscent of the abstract sculptures of the 1950s, or perhaps of sand dunes or of Ice-Age boulders. And the material used can in fact withstand extreme climates: it is tearproof, colourfast, weather- and UV-resistant and naturally just as washable as the cushions placed on top. Like all other **Dedon** furniture, *Yin Yang* is woven by hand in East Asia. Made of artificial fibres measuring some four kilometres in length, this nearly two-metre-long and 30-kilogram-heavy seating element comes in matte brown and grey. The deluxe shimmering surfaces and organic proportions fit well in a variety of contexts, whether in nature or against the backdrop of modern minimalist architecture.

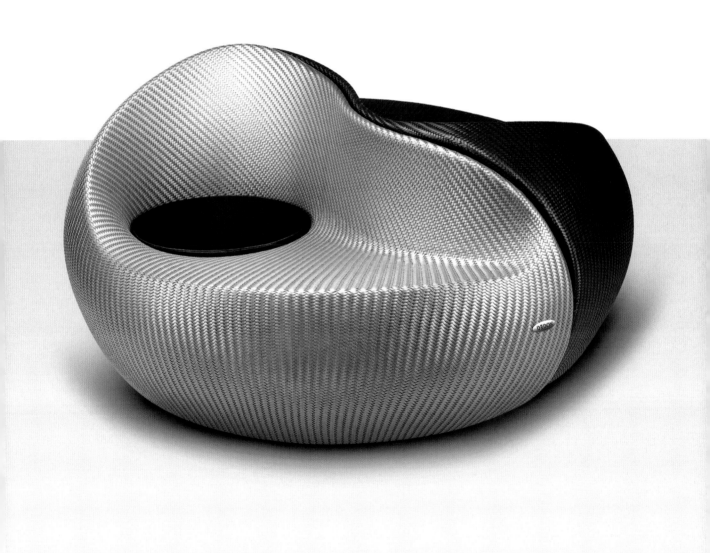

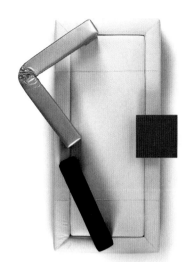

# 2007

**Functional sofa**

Design:
**Kati Meyer-Brühl**

Manufacturer:
Brühl

# Plupp a. p.

The sofa with the informal, onomatopoetic name is among the most variable of its genus. The model before it, likewise the brainchild of Kati Meyer-Brühl, already stemmed from one of those incredibly simple ideas that it is hard to believe no one ever came up with before. The designer has combined an upholstered body on lightweight metal runners with padded tubular backrest sections and a table element that can be inserted into holes in a variety of positions. With so many holes dotting the sofa's edge, the possible combination and usage options are manifold. By adding or subtracting one or more backrest and table modules, the lounger becomes a reading corner, the cosy couch a workplace, or a face-to-face situation becomes a back-to-back one. Plupp can also serve as a full-fledged bed. This modular furniture system is thus a top performer when it comes to rapidly adjusting to any circumstance. In the new version the tubular stick-in backrests have been replaced with square-edged ones whose simple geometry recalls earlier functionalist designs such as **Walter Gropius'** *F 51* armchair. The body comprises a rectangular middle section and a surrounding "frame", which allows for an additional colour accent. The holes for the backrest and table modules are hidden in the gap in between. In this more severe variation, the functional modular sofa attains a high graphical quality that lends it the look of a modern sculpture. And then all of a sudden – Plupp! – echoes of classical Modernism leap into view.

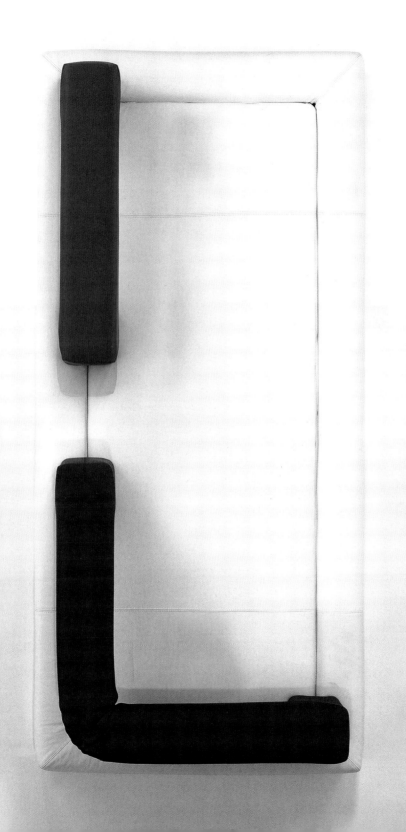

**Cabinet System**

Design:
**beyonddesign**

Manufacturer:
Performa

# Nuf

Cabinet, chest of drawers or sideboard? When conventional terms fail, we simply call it a container and, as we all know, these are mobile. The various elements in this highly unusual storage furniture are not permanently connected as is otherwise customary. The highlight here is that they can not only be stacked freely, but also easily and silently shifted across one another. The Swabian manufacturer is renowned for its immaculate linoleum and rubber surfaces, with which it sparked a renaissance for these almost forgotten materials, even in the most demanding design circles. With its new program, **Performa** has once again pushed the edges of processing technology. Based on a design by the Stuttgart studio beyonddesign, a concept emerged that is already highly interesting to look at and is bristling with astounding refinements to boot, such as lightweight, hingeless front flaps. As a matter of fact, *Nuf* is nothing more nor less than a new furniture type. The wave on the upper and lower sides is the key. These recesses are the nucleus of the design, both aesthetically and functionally. 1The individual containers of varying sizes slide in this groove as precisely as a train car on rails, so that this flexible cabinet system can be adapted to various room widths and usage ideas with the least effort imaginable. *Nuf*, which comprises six different container formats and comes in many colours, is a highly variable sculpture in space. This is the most creative storage design since the invention of the chest.

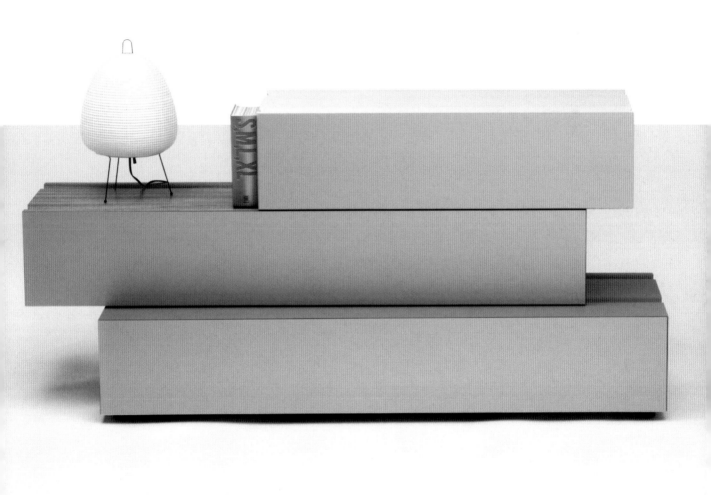

# **Lexicon** of Designers and Manufacturers

AB

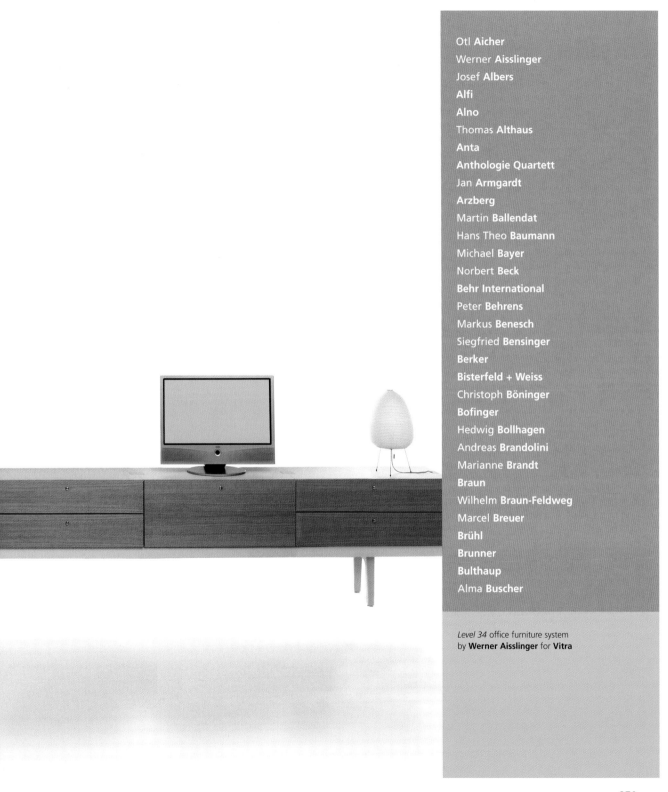

Otl **Aicher**
Werner **Aisslinger**
Josef **Albers**
**Alfi**
**Alno**
Thomas **Althaus**
**Anta**
**Anthologie Quartett**
Jan **Armgardt**
**Arzberg**
Martin **Ballendat**
Hans Theo **Baumann**
Michael **Bayer**
Norbert **Beck**
**Behr International**
Peter **Behrens**
Markus **Benesch**
Siegfried **Bensinger**
**Berker**
**Bisterfeld + Weiss**
Christoph **Böninger**
**Bofinger**
Hedwig **Bollhagen**
Andreas **Brandolini**
Marianne **Brandt**
**Braun**
Wilhelm **Braun-Feldweg**
Marcel **Breuer**
**Brühl**
**Brunner**
**Bulthaup**
Alma **Buscher**

*Level 34* office furniture system
by **Werner Aisslinger** for **Vitra**

379

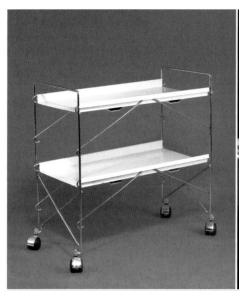

# Otl **Aicher**

graphic artist, born 1922, died 1991

He had made trips to Greenland and the Sahara. There, he said, the light was "clear and sharp". This penchant for extreme landscapes is no coincidence. Aicher's way of thinking was regarded as elementary and uncompromising. A member of the resistance and a deserter during the Nazi era, he was a co-founder of the Hochschule für Gestaltung (Academy of Design) in Ulm after the war. He made formal asceticism obligatory for generations to come. The resemblance of his work to that of representatives of classical Modernism such as **Josef Albers** can be attributed not only to his concentration on essentials, but also his endeavour to meld separate areas of reality in an overarching synthesis. He thus almost inevitably became a protagonist of two long-lived themes in German design: minimalism and systemization. As an opponent of everything superficial and decorative, he perhaps changed the world around us more than any other German designer. Starting in 1954, he taught "Visual Communication" in Ulm, as rationalized graphic design has been called ever since. **Braun** is where he – like **Peter Behrens** before him at AEG – first became initiator of a coherent and confidence-building corporate strategy in which product design played a major role. Clients including **Bulthaup**, Dresdner Bank, **Erco**, **FSB**, Lufthansa and television station ZDF followed. He achieved his ultimate breakthrough with the Olympic Games in Munich. The creative team he led was not only in charge of all graphics – from logo to posters to the pictograms used for guidance – but also designed the uniforms and the building interiors. This all-encompassing design of a major event was a completely new concept, and one that brought Aicher's radical approach acclaim far and wide. In 1980 he designed an office furniture series made of chrome-plated tubular steel, including a stool with wheels, shelves, lattice bridges and a trolley for hanging files (today made by Manufactum). Furniture was reduced here to a skeleton. Getting to the bottom of things – that was his method. He used this approach to help kitchen-maker Bulthaup move beyond the linear kitchen in the early 1980s. His modular *System b*, which was based on an astute study, ushered in a far-reaching paradigm change.

PHOTOS: l.: File trolley for Siegel, r.: Trade fair stand for Braun

# Werner **Aisslinger**

furniture designer, born 1964, studio in Berlin, **www.aisslinger.de**

"While metal, stone or glass exude coolness, plastic can give a warmer, softer effect", says Werner Aisslinger, explaining why he likes to use a mixture of natural materials and acrylic polymer for surfaces. For Aisslinger, who was an assistant in Jasper Morrison's London studio in 1990 – like **Konstantin Grcic**, with whom he is almost coeval – dealing with new materials is a fundamental working principle. Only when design reacts to rapid technical advances and taps all the possibilities these offer can it be truly innovative, might be the Berlin-based designer's credo. As a case in point, his chaise longue *Soft* (→ p.**300**) was the world's first serially produced furniture to use a kind of gel that was originally developed for medical purposes. The reformer based his grid chair **Soft Cell** on the same material. Similarly, a striking grid structure in the backrest and seat gives the plastic chair Nic – an updated version of the cantilevered chair – its characteristic look. The use of the gas injection technique ensured increased stability coupled with weight reduction. Aisslinger's design-world ascent began in the mid-1990s. His very first product, the additive shelving system **Endless Shelf**, was already a best-seller and launched a career that has made the designer – alongside Grcic – one of the leading figures of a new generation in German furniture design. This soon became evident when Italian manu-facturers began taking up his designs as part of their own

programs. In the German showcase discipline of cabinet furniture he followed in the footsteps of German modernists like **Herbert Hirche** and **Peter Maly**, designing systems for companies including **Behr** and **Interlübke**. In his *Level 34* system (2005 for **Vitra**), the idea of freestanding modular furniture was applied to the office. Another focus – along with store furnishings and exhibition architecture – is chair design. Here as well he managed to make a spectacular debut. The *Juli* chair of 1996 was not only notable for its feminine lines – with marked echoes of the 1950s – but also because of the synthetic foam used. Aisslinger's domestic visions go beyond individual furniture pieces, however. His project *Loftcube*, a flexible room unit that can be hoisted onto the flat roofs of city buildings, is geared toward the nomadic lifestyle of today's metropolitan residents.

PHOTOS: l.: *Juli* chair for Cappellini
r.: *Level 34* modular furniture collection for Vitra

MILESTONES: **Endless Shelf** shelf system → Page **266** | **Soft Cell** chair and lounge chair → Page **300**

# Josef **Albers**

artist, furniture and glass designer, born 1888, died 1976, **www.albersfoundation.com**

Although he was the only designer to shape the Bauhaus through nearly the entire course of its existence and in almost all of its facets, Josef Albers is usually identified today more with his later work: the abstract painting of the 1950s and 60s. After growing up in the coal and steel landscape of the Ruhr Valley that was just emerging at the time, where he worked as an elementary school teacher, he was so inspired by early encounters with modern painting that he decided to make a career in art. Following stations in Munich and Berlin, where he did art studies and already worked as a freelance artist, the 32-year-old registered as a student at the Bauhaus in Weimar. He taught a preparatory course there and did glass paintings oriented on the style of Paul Klee. One of his early objects was a flat, cylindrical bowl made of glass, metal and wood that he designed in 1923. A *Tea Glass* (1924) of similarly reduced form with a removable metal band and offset wooden handles went into series production. In the same period, he also designed the furnishings for the anteroom of the university's administrative offices. The suite included a bookshelf, a glass case, a table and folding chairs. In his large, two-tone painted oak table, he followed in the tracks of constructivist Gerrit Rietveld. Although Albers directed the Bauhaus furniture workshop from 1928-29, he – like **Erich Dieckmann** for example – never used the tubular steel that had

been inaugurated there. His furniture was instead made of various kinds of wood, giving it a less high-tech look. The combination of wood with coloured glass surfaces – such as in his ***Nesting Tables*** – is a special feature of his designs, presaging his later painting style. A bed and sofa from 1927 are reduced to cubes. By contrast, the lightweight easychairs he created in the ensuing years, such as his serially produced laminated model *Ti 244*, display the acute angles and large radii that would later be typical features of Scandinavian chairs. Albers was among the creative pioneers, such as **Marianne Brandt**, **Marcel Breuer** or **Alma Buscher**, who delivered the blueprints for a new domestic inventory. Never one to separate art from life, he was one of the most radical advocates of a tabula rasa in furnishing conventions – in his private life as well. With his like-minded wife, Anni, whom he met at the Bauhaus working in the weaving mill, he was one of the first Bauhaus members to emigrate to the USA, in 1933, where he enjoyed a successful academic and artistic career.

PHOTOS: l.: Easychair, 1929, r.: Fruit bowl, 1923

MILESTONE: *Albers* nesting tables → Page **58**

# Alfi

manufacturer of vacuum jugs, Wertheim / Bavaria, founded 1914, **www.alfi.de**

Whether hot or cold, Alfi products keep their temperature. The tradition-steeped Thuringian firm has been making vacuum jugs ever since its founding, experiencing its first boom during the First World War, at the end of which it employed 75. The "Aluminium-warenfabrik Fischbach" – origin of the name Alfi – entered the export business as early as the 1920s. By 1960, following an interval when the family owners had been forced to surrender the company to the state in East Germany and the plant was relocated to the Main River, the workforce had doubled (to about 200 today). At the time, the maker of vacuum jugs could boast 50 models in some 300 variations, available in over 60 countries. The most successful jug is still *Juwel*, a design stemming from the company's early days, when it received a contract to outfit the dining cars for a US railroad. This classic, sold today in a total of 16 versions, cut a fine figure on the white tablecloth and became the prototype for the whole genre. With a silhouette reminiscent of a classic coffee pot, *Juwel* combines elegance with robustness – an impression that is further underlined by its easy-to-use and reliable stopper. The 1980s brought a conceptual turning point, when the company appealed to star designers for fresh inspiration – at nearly the same time as pioneers like Alessi or **FSB**. International greats such as Philippe Starck from France, Ross Lovegrove from Great Britain

and Makio Hasuike from Japan have since supplied designs for the manufacturer in Wertheim, lending its product, once associated with lunchboxes and camping, a new dignity. The breakthrough for the new strategy came in 1986 with the *Kugel* jug designed by Ole Palsby of Denmark. The jug's striking clean-lined geometry formed a counterpoint to the more traditional styles that had gone before. Three years later, to mark its 75th anniversary, the company unveiled ***Achat*** by **Tassilo von Grolman**, a cone with haptically intriguing grooves. Trendy materials such as translucent plastic, along with whimsical curvy forms, have since given the brand, which is today part of **WMF**, a younger touch. Like FSB in its realm, the company has thus plumbed the many dimensions of its core product.

PHOTOS: l.: *La Ola* vacuum jug, m.: *D.I.N.K.* silverware series
r.: *Juwel* vacuum jug

MILESTONE: *Achat* thermos → Page **246**

# Alno

kitchen manufacturer, Pfullendorf / Baden-Wurttemberg, founded 1927, **www.alno.de**

In one model the stove is fixed to the side of a solid wood table as a glass panel, in another a metal table and a large workspace can be joined together in varying ways. In co-operation with students at Muthesius University in Kiel, five new kinds of cooking stations were recently developed as prototypes for the kitchen of tomorrow. Alno – the brand comes from the name of the founder, Albert Nothdurft – was one the few German furniture companies to ascend on the wings of the Economic Miracle in the 1950s. Sales for what is now the second-largest kitchen-maker in the world have gone from the equivalent of 2.5 million euros in 1960 to around 613 million in 2005. The number of employees – 2,700 – is also far above the industry average. In 2005 Alno set up a plant in Dubai, making it the first European kitchen manufacturer to start production in the Middle East. Headed by a manager who is not part of the founding family since the beginning of the new millennium, a company first, Alno has always set its sights on quality and is therefore a prime example of why "Made in Germany" is a label to be proud of. Based near the Lake of Constance, the manufacturer relies on the indisputable strengths of the German kitchen industry and has in particular added a steady stream of new variations to the functional kitchen that was first developed in this country. The wide-ranging product line is dominated by the upper segment made up of "lifestyle kitchens" displaying streamlined forms. These series are named *Alnoart, Alnosign* and *Alnotec*. Original solutions for small details and the tendency to depart from the classic linear kitchen are among the newer concepts. The *Liberio* program, which responds to the growing need for a combined kitchen and living space, represents a reaction to changing lifestyles, as does the *Teatro* concept developed for apartments and small offices, in which the kitchen is hidden behind double doors. The Linzgau-based firm weathered the sales crisis of a few years ago with a strategy that incorporated both savings measures and an overhaul of its product range. The aim was to counter the "growing uniformity" of kitchens with innovations and a heightened awareness of trends. One result was the *Picture Line*, a patented process for printing images on cabinet fronts and other surfaces. Alno managed here to achieve a unique selling point that has proven popular, for example, for printing wood grains resembling exotic woods such as teak, olive and palisander. The process produces its own unique surface aesthetic while avoiding the depletion of natural resources.

PHOTOS: l.: *Alnotop* kitchen program, r.: *Alnosign* kitchen program

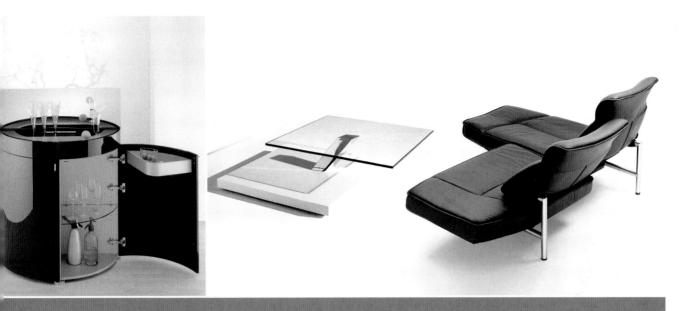

# Thomas **Althaus**

furniture designer, born 1957, office in Düsseldorf / North Rhine-Westphalia

*Stretch* is a new kind of sideboard that can be pulled apart like a slipcase and then pushed together again as needed. This example of case furniture can also be used as a room divider. Thomas Althaus designed the piece for **Die Collection**, a German manufacturer specializing in adaptable furniture. In fact, the Rhineland designer came up with a whole series of ingenious ideas for the brand, among them the *Fox* easychair, a seating cube that cleverly disguises the fact that it can be pulled out in just a few moves to make a bed. Althaus does not think much of putting abstract ideas into practice. An interior designer by training, he always keeps the actual application in mind when conceiving his pieces. As a specialist in multifunctional living, he strives for solutions that exude a discreet reserve but nonetheless offer their users a high degree of individual freedom. The furniture he has designed for **WK Wohnen** likewise reflects this dual principle. For example, the oblique occasional table *WK 838* not only boasts hidden wheels, but also a glass top that can be swivelled 360 degrees, putting for instance eating utensils or reading materials within easy reach. This kind of pragmatism, coupled with a laconic and clear formal canon, puts him right in line with the classical functionalism of German provenance that has been striving since the early 20th century to improve the potential of furniture by applying combinatory and mechanical strategies. Contemporary designers who pursue similar

approaches include **Jan Armgardt**, **Norbert Beck** and **Christian Werner**. Word of the capabilities of the "humane designer" Althaus, who shares a design office with his wife, has long since made its way to neighbouring countries such as France (Treca), Italy (Tonon) and the Netherlands (Royal Auping). Experience with a large number of prominent firms, including in Germany **Interlübke**, **Renz** and **Rosenthal** Einrichtung, has made him a constant in German domestic design. At the same time, Althaus has by no means done work only in the luxury segment. He is much more interested in the "minimalism of the budget", i.e. in making a lot out of a little.

PHOTOS : l.: *Roto* bar for Schönbuch
r.: *WK 838* table for WK Wohnen and *DS 450* sofa for DeSede

# Anta

lamp manufacturer, Hamburg, founded 1971, **www.anta.de**

The upscale, but still quite small Hamburg manufacturer is proud of its expertise in fabrication, ranging all the way to precision mechanics, as this provides a way to demonstrate its conceptual and qualitative aspirations. High priority is placed on selecting materials with beautiful surfaces that harmonize with the overall design. There are usually no briefings held at Anta. This is not necessary, because new designs arrive anyway almost daily: from designers who have worked for years for this premier lamp brand, and from those who would like to join them. Company founder Gertrud Kracht sees to it that the mixture is just right. Trained in advertising, she began in the 1970s with Chinese vases which she found in Copenhagen antique stores and fitted with lampshades. It was still a long road from the small workshop, which was soon working for **Christine Kröncke**, to a lamp-maker represented in the best design stores. At the heart of the product strategy is the designer lamp. The current product range comprises some 40 products, encompassing all lamp types and created by over 20 exclusively German designers. A total of eleven designs come from the drawing board of **Rolf Heide**. His Tuba standing lamp features a minimalist tube-shaped shade. One of the younger generation of designers is Carsten Gollnick, whose table lamp *Minami* evokes associations with Japanese culture. London-based designer **Torsten Neeland** supplied with

his *Cut* (→ p.**507**) a current best-seller in which the extreme contrast between the small shade and high stand creates intriguing visual tension. The height-adjustable standing lamp *Lee* by Jürgen Zeitler looks like a fine, curving line in space. Old master **Peter Maly** has put his stamp on the collection from the very beginning. Among his first products were the reading lamps *My* and *Bibo*. They were followed by the hanging lamp *Beam*, and finally the dramatic and ceremonious wall lamp *Ludwigsburg* as well as **Screen**, the only lamp family in the catalogue. "We do not tailor anything to the market" is the credo espoused by Gertrud Kracht. She has always simply "believed in good design" remarks Maly, explaining a recipe for success that is as stunningly straightforward as most of the lamps.

PHOTOS: l.: *Tuba* lamp collection by Rolf Heide
m.: *Drop* lamp by Fiedeler & Raasch
r.: *Belle* lamp by Klaus Nolting and Andreas Ostwald

MILESTONE: *Screen* lamp → Page **292**

# Anthologie Quartett

furniture and lamp manufacturer, Bad Essen / Lower Saxony, founded 1984, **www.anthologiequartett.de**

Based in Westphalia, a traditional furniture region, this company does not fit at all into its down-to-earth surroundings. Its only standard line is "no line", is how owners Rainer Krause and Michael von Jakubowski describe their unconventional strategy. As a matter of fact, the manufacturer with the somewhat academic-sounding double name has its roots in a time when the principle of negation was triumphant. With origins in the gallery milieu, situated somewhere between design, art, architecture and fashion, Anthologie Quartett was engendered by the spirit of insubordination that prevailed in the 1980s, when the protagonists of Memphis and "New German Design" stood the rules of design on their head. Today, what is perhaps the most unusual line of products in the industry encompasses an extensive collection of lamps and individual pieces as well as furniture systems, jewellery, porcelain and additional home accessories. Production is carried out by a network of small to medium-sized crafts enterprises sprinkled across Europe, in which the kind of highly prized expertise can still be found that threatens to be lost. On the company's impressive list of past designers are more than 150 names, over one hundred of which are still represented in the collection. The history of German design is reflected by personalities such as Karl Friedrich Schinkel, **Richard Riemerschmid** and **Marcel Breuer**. Overall, however, a marked inter-

national profile is conspicuous: from old-time great Ettore Sottsass, whose series Indian Memories is to be reissued for his 90th birthday, to the fragile furniture of Czech designer Bohuslav Horak. New in the line-up is historical grotto furniture, a romantic fad of the 19th century that the firm dared to revive recently without any audible protest from the ranks of the critics. Headquarters of the company with its 25 employees is Hünnefeld Castle, a popular tourist destination in the Teutoburg Forest, in the granary of which a brand new showroom has been built. The castle setting might sound elitist, but the company is by no means divorced from reality. The fact that "by relying on one's own style and not orienting oneself toward the mass market", in Jakubowski's words, "it's possible to do good business," has been proven by Anthologie Quartett once and for all. And this is demonstrated not only by *Cellula*, a modern iconic chandelier and perhaps the most-copied lamp in recent years.

PHOTOS: l.: Cellula chandelier by Nunzia Carbone and Tiziano Vudafieri
r.: Tray by Richard Riemerschmid

MILESTONE: *Schinkel* garden chair → Page **32**

# Jan **Armgardt**

interior and furniture designer, born 1947, office in Schondorf am Ammersee / Bavaria

For him, the home is where we can "withdraw from the hectic pace of the times". Cosy security and self-determination are the anchoring ideas behind his design concept. In short, furniture must "have a soul". The man who is not put off by this apparently old-fashioned dictum and thus pays tribute to the "Gemüt", or disposition, that untranslatable quality of the soul, is one of the busiest members of his guild. But although Jan Armgardt is undoubtedly one of the most productive designers, his work as well as his name are a well-kept secret amongst industry experts. He counts international furniture companies as clients, along with numerous German manufacturers including **Egoform**, **Müller Möbelwerkstätten**, **Nils Holger Moormann**, **Seefelder Möbelwerkstätten** and **WK Wohnen**. The trained cabinet-maker is regarded as being both traditional and unconventional. In fact, he is one of the few who, alongside series products, still occupies himself now and again with freely designed individual pieces. The environmentally aware designer has attracted attention with a project for woven furniture as well as with paper furniture, a theme that he also explored experimentally – 40 years after **Peter Raacke**. The career of the Bavarian-based Armgardt has likewise been rather unorthodox, including a stint as photographer. Following studies in interior design and experience working as a locksmith, an upholsterer

and in furniture stores, he designed his first piece of furniture in 1970: the foam blocks he dubbed *Quadrat*. Armgardt subsequently founded various furniture companies, until he finally decided to work as a freelance designer. Since then, he has hardly left a furniture genre untouched. Designs exhibiting an understated, familiar formal vocabulary such as the upholstered furniture programs *Rio* and *Jolly* (2003 and 2006, for Wittmann) are juxtaposed with highly expressive models such as the easychair *Gänsefüsschen* (1991 for Proseda), a bit of whimsy on runners. The shelf units *Vision Street* (1991 for WK Wohnen) and *1543* (2000 for Nils Holger Moormann) likewise diverge starkly in their irritating irregularity from what we are accustomed to. The quality of many of his designs is demonstrated by the fact that they have in some cases remained in production for decades. One of these long-lived hits is the folding easychair *Tattomi* (1985 for **Mobilia**). Armgardt began using intelligent mechanical elements early on – and not only in his many sofa beds. His oeuvre is every bit as diverse as furniture design itself.

PHOTOS: l.: *Rio* sofa for Wittmann
m.: *1543* shelf for Nils Holger Moormann
r.: *Farfalle* easychair for Unikat

MILESTONE: *Tattomi* lounge chair → Page **232**

# Arzberg

porcelain manufacturer, Schirnding / Bavaria, founded 1887, **www.arzberg-porzellan.de**

Only after the company had been in business for almost half a century did it first cause a stir, and did so with something utterly inconspicuous: the service *Form 1382*. Although there was nothing exciting about it, this tableware represented a turning point in the company history and, with its decor-free white surfaces, a milestone in domestic design. The tea, coffee and tableware service was designed by Hermann Gretsch in 1931, at the high point of "Neue Sachlichkeit" and has been in production without interruption ever since. Gretsch, an architect and Werkbund chairman, designed a further six services for Arzberg, without however being able to surpass his own initial success. After his death, Heinrich Löffelhardt took over as artistic director in the early 1950s. Löffelhardt, a friend of **Wilhelm Wagenfeld** and, like him, a champion of "good form", shaped the product range until 1971 with a total of 13 coffee and tea services. Of these icons of the West German "Economic Miracle", the model 2075 became a best-seller. *Form 2000*, like Gretsch's 1382 a gold-prize winner at the Milan Triennale, achieved comparably lasting formal quality and was elevated to an exemplary product of the young republic as the standard service in German embassies. In the 1970s, Arzberg was caught up in the general crisis in the porcelain industry. Ownership changed hands many times, until the company became part of the SKV Group in 2000, a union of small to medium-sized German porcelain manufacturers in which it takes a prominent position as well-known designer brand. Today, Arzberg, like **Kahla** and **Rosenthal** as well as **KPM** and **Nymphenburg** is a household name in modern German porcelain. The company carried on its policy of contemporary form, since the 1970s in conjunction with external creative talents such as artist **Hans Theo Baumann** or Italian architect Mattheo Thun. In the mid-1990s the company once again placed its trust in formal stringency and a renunciation of colour with Dieter Sieger's ambitious service *Cult*. The current designs as well, such as the combinable service *Profi* by house designer Heike Philipp Prechtl, exude the dual spirit of severity and versatility. Even more concentrated is the appearance of the *Form 2006* service. Peter Schmidt, known for his straightforward designs, has raised the circle and square here to a design principle.

PHOTOS: l.: *Form 2000 Collection* service by Heinrich Löffelhardt
r.: *Profi* service by Heike Philipp Prechtl

MILESTONES: *Form 1382* porcelain tableware → Page **90** | *Form 2006* porcelain tableware → Seite **370**

# Martin **Ballendat**

product and furniture designer, born 1958, office in Simbach am Inn / Bavaria, **www.ballendat.de**

"Design in the villa" is his slogan, which is meant to refer not to the pleasant working atmosphere in the Wilhelminian house he renovated, but to the fact that everything belonging to modern design is brought together here under one roof. Ballendat has expanded the studio, which is within walking distance of the Austrian border, into a complete development office, similar to **Reiner Moll** or ITO-Design. Many of his clients do in fact come from Austria, but also from the USA, Great Britain and Switzerland, joined by such diverse German manufacturers as **Brunner**, Dauphin, Hülsta and **Interstuhl**. Ballendat, who sees himself as a "problem-solver", employs a staff of ten, three of whom are occupied solely with building models. The industrial designer, who, following studies at the Folkwang School in Essen, worked for over ten years for various office furniture manufacturers, is among today's up-and-coming designers. One reason for his success is the full range of services he offers: from the idea sketch, to detailed models, to marketing. "We wrestle with every design down to the last detail" explains the perfectionist. Another decisive factor is of course building a good relationship with the corporate management, which must by all means play a role in the process. A specialty are swivelling office chairs. Ballendat always manages to find new refinements for these sitting machines, such as the innovative telescopic frame made

of aluminium and plastic parts in the model *Xenium* (for Grahl). This premium chair has a webbing backrest, in Ballendat's view a user-friendly element that lends transparency and lightness. Lightweight construction is a favourite theme of his, from the wooden *M.O.D.* stacking chair to the office cabinet system *Float* with its thin, transparent polycarbonate panels (both for Wiesner Hager). In addition to technical innovation, original form is also important to him, such as in his *Loungesessel* (Lounge Chair) for **WK Wohnen** in which the delicate metal legs, round seat and sweeping backrest of knitted net fabric display unusual proportions. Designs for pleasant living in the office and elsewhere include the easychair *L@p* (for Rossin), with an "enveloping" backrest that forms a practical shelf, as well as the *Tempus* executive chair (for Brunner) in which visual lightness is coupled with cantilevered comfort.

PHOTOS: l.: *L@p* easychair for Rossin, m.: *Xenium* office chair for Grahl
r.: *Shells* easychair for Tonon

# Hans Theo **Baumann**

artist, furniture and product designer, born 1924

"The essential part of a design", he once wrote, "does not come from formulas; it is alone the result of human capabilities", thus coming down on the side of **Henry van de Velde** in the eternal dispute between industry and art. For Hans Theo Baumann, the creative process is the decisive factor in design. His goal has always been not the geometricization of the world, but rather a humanization of technology. One of his very first furniture designs, an organically formed plexiglass chair, was a world premiere and the first chair produced by **Vitra** – at the time still called Fehlbaum. The co-founder of the *Verband Deutscher Industrie-Designer* (Association of German Industrial Designers) was one of the figures, along with **Egon Eiermann**, **Hans Gugelot** and **Herbert Hirche**, who shaped post-war German design, establishing a second wave of German Modernism. The initial spark was ignited by an encounter with the architect Eiermann, who put his young colleague in contact with other influential figures. He rose to fame with projects such as pioneering work for porcelain maker **Rosenthal**, including the cylindrical service **Berlin** (1959), which was followed in the next decade by perfectly shaped silverware of the same name. With his minimalist drinking glasses (for Gral-Glas) and lamps (for Vitra) he strode off down new paths, as was also the case with his services made of plastic and metal. Baumann's astounding productivity stems from a subjective, yet explicit concept of beauty, complemented by a strict practical orientation. Born in Switzerland, he studied sculpture in Basel and then led a double life as artist and product designer. The results of his work were correspondingly divergent: soft shapes alternate with angular ones. In his product design, however, whether organic or linear, he is committed throughout to a radical simplicity, as can be seen for example in his successful tableware systems. Starting in the mid-1950s the prolific creative talent developed items including a series of office chairs (for **Sedus Stoll**), practical folding chairs (for **Wilde + Spieth**) and angular easychairs (for **Walter Knoll**) in which square and triangle communicate. All of these designs made a profoundly avant-garde impression, but in a pleasantly effortless way.

PHOTOS: l.: *56* office chair for Sedus Stoll, r.; Vase collection for Thomas

MILESTONE: *Berlin* porcelain tableware → page **132**

# Michael **Bayer**

interior designer, graphic artist and furniture designer, born 1916, lives in Detmold

Bayer notes that two events during the 1930s determined his career path: a single conversation with charismatic architect **Ludwig Mies van der Rohe**, who implanted in his brain the idea of "open living", as well as his encounter with advertising and brand luminary Hans Domizlaff, whom he got to know at Siemens. His first design was for a swivelling sofa bed in 1947 – a best-seller in the days of post-war devastation. Bayer went out on his own and soon opened a studio near Munich in which he designed advertisements for the furniture and interior design industry. Through his book "Wir richten eine Wohnung ein" ("Let's Furnish a Home", 1954) about the Germans' favourite pastime in those days, he came into close contact with the furniture industry. The modernist, who had no direct contact with the Ulm Academy, was then able to put his design ideas into practice during the 1950s. By that time, the designer, a native of Bohemia, was living in Detmold, where he taught interior design at the new University of Applied Science to students including **Peter Maly**. For the **Interlübke** company (at that time called Gebrüder Lübke), only one hour away by car, he designed modern advertising campaigns and a new logo. Finally, in the late 1950s he was the first to develop an alternative to the conventional bedroom suite, calling his concept "An- und Aufbausysteme" (build up and onto systems). In order to educate people about the new lifestyle, the Westphalian company ultimately established its own domestic consulting service. The message: It is possible to furnish an entire apartment with a single modular furniture program. As in **Hans Gugelot's** *M 125* (→ p.**106**), all elements were co-ordinated according to a certain grid measure, in this case 55 centimetres. With the introduction of his comprehensive *Interlübke* system in 1962, not only a new company name was born. This step also represented the transformation of a medium-sized furniture factory into a design brand. The *Quinta* program that Bayer designed for Interlübke affiliate **COR** is considered the first thoroughly variable upholstered furniture system. Later, Bayer summed up his ideas in a *"Farbige Wohnfibel"* ("Domestic Colour Primer"), which he realized in conjunction with leading furniture-makers. This manifesto of modern German interior design was issued ten times in the 1960s and 70s, reaching a readership of one million, and was even translated into Japanese. The life of domestic reformer Michael Bayer mirrors the century of modern German furniture.

PHOTOS: l.: Dining room for Interlübke, r.: Children's room for Interlübke

MILESTONE: *Quinta* upholstered furniture system → page **134**

# Norbert **Beck**

furniture designer, born 1959, studio in Markdorf / Baden-Wurttemberg

When working with a company like **Rolf Benz**, for which he has designed no less than eight tables, he appreciates the thorough and targeted development work. This resulted recently in a functional sofa that can be transformed into a full-fledged bed. The trick: The backrest, whose firm rear side makes a good sleep surface, tilts forward like the back seat of a car when the sofa is pulled out. This is a remarkable example of an important detail in an invisible area – one of the strengths of German design, in which inconspicuousness has always been an aim. This also happens to be one of the strengths Norbert Beck is known for. His clients include Hülsta, Seetal Swiss, **Tecta**, **WK Wohnen** and Zumsteg. When asked to describe his work, he uses words like "quality", "long life", "sophisticated technology" and "precision". The demands he places on his products correspond one-to-one with the virtues that have long been considered the leitmotifs of German furniture design. The fact that this is not just so much talk is demonstrated most impressively by the fact that some of his designs have been in production for over ten years now – almost as long as his design studio near the Lake of Constance has been in existence. After starting out his career as an art teacher, Beck, who describes himself as an autodidact, began designing tables and chairs. He developed into a quiet industry maverick, who makes just as little fuss about himself as he does about his furniture, not least his carefully conceived pullout tables, e.g. the wooden *Doppio* (2005 for Zeitraum) with a bilateral pullout mechanism using a guide groove, and the first glass pullout table **8950** (1998 for Rolf Benz). But Beck has also designed cabinets, beds and upholstered furniture. His luxury sofa *540* (2006 for Rolf Benz) can be put together in myriad ways according to present needs, like a puzzle. However, the designer from Baden still remains true to his favourite theme: The new table and chair program *620* (2007 for Rolf Benz, → p. **526**) is his most comprehensive ensemble to date, in a way a crowning achievement of his design work, which incidentally heralds a modern revival of the traditional German bench.

PHOTOS: l.: Garden table for Zumsteg, r.: *540* sofa for Rolf Benz

MILESTONE: *8950* table → page **290**

# Behr International

furniture manufacturer, Osnabrück / Lower Saxony, founded 1912, **www.behr-international.de**

Case furniture – a somewhat awkward term for something the layperson would call a wall unit – is a major theme in German furniture design. Important chapters in its history were written by Behr. Company founder Erwin Behr was an entrepreneur with a vision. Convinced that serial production was the wave of the future even before the First World War, he built his furniture factory on the railway line between Stuttgart and Tübingen. His ideas, which he shared with other reformers, were to deliver quality at a low price, and to unite the worlds of industry and art. The fact that he was inspired by the reform movement of the day is demonstrated by the founding of the purchasing collective with the programmatic name "Deutsche Werkstätten für Wohnkunst" (German Workshops for Domestic Art), today **WK Wohnen**, for which Behr was for years the main producer. It is therefore no surprise that the company hired architects as freelance designers and already sought contact with the Bauhaus in 1923. This led to a groundbreaking world premiere, the "Aufbauprogramm" of furniture conceived by Franz Schuster, a combinable collection of pieces incorporating basic forms and stemming from similar concepts to Bruno Paul's "growing home" (for **Deutsche Werkstätten**). Along these same systematic lines, the post-war years witnessed the development of the legendary wall unit construction kit BMZ (Behr Mobel

Zerlegbar, 1955 by Johan A. Bus), in addition to designs such as the M 125 (→ p.**106**) by **Hans Gugelot** and the In-Wand by **Herbert Hirche**, one of the early German add-on shelf classics, which was produced for three decades and changed the look of the wall unit forever. Another milestone was the system 1600 (by **Jürgen Lange**) with its 32-millimetre grid. Headline, a program by the same designer which came out in 1983, featured a "functional column" that likewise caused a sensation. This was the period when Behr began collaborating with **Peter Maly**, a working relationship that still continues today. Maly soon took on the post of art director and produced a whole series of extensive wall unit systems including Metrix, **Menos**, Alas and Mundus. The Menos cabinet series pays homage to the cube with an enhanced formal rigour. In the late 1990s, Behr was taken over by new owners and product development began to stagnate. After another change in ownership and relocation to Lower Saxony, the company managed to make a fresh start, assisted by both Maly and **Werner Aisslinger**, whose cabinet system Pure does without handles and displays a new kind of balance between horizontals and verticals.

PHOTOS: l.: Pure sideboard by Werner Aisslinger
r.: Menos cabinet system by Peter Maly

MILESTONE: *Menos* cabinet system → page **276**

# Peter **Behrens**

artist, architect, product and furniture designer, born 1868, died 1940

He was a member of the "Munich Secession", the first German artists' group to take its leave of the established arts scene, in 1892. Around 1900 he switched his focus to applied arts and, straddling the worlds of avant-garde and industry, became a key figure in the emergence of modern design. He designed several tableware services, silverware, glasses, lamps, wallpaper and furniture, at the beginning still under the influence of Jugendstil. In 1901, the self-taught designer was hired for the project on Darmstadt's Mathildenhöhe. The house he built there, a total work of art, is among his most acclaimed achievements. The concept of a union of art and life was demonstrated here in part by allusions to Friedrich Nietzsche's *Zarathustra*, the bible of the "lifestyle reformers". In 1903 Behrens designed a dining room for the exhibition of the Dresdner and later **Deutsche Werkstätten** (German Workshops). As director of the Kunstgewerbeschule (School of Arts & Crafts) in Düsseldorf, he met Dutchman Mathieu Lauweriks, under whose influence his style grew more geometric. Behrens' career, highly successful despite recurring criticism that he was too modern, reflects a Germany in the days of the Kaiser that was torn between progress and reactionary conservatism. His office in Potsdam, where before the First World War **Walter Gropius**, Le Corbusier and **Ludwig Mies van der Rohe** worked, was a germ cell of Modernism. The reformer was one of the first to join the Deutscher Werkbund, founded in 1907. At the same time, he took up the newly invented post of "artistic adviser" at the AEG electric company in Berlin, whose corporate and product design he completely overhauled. From logo to products to architecture – everything was given a new look. This is regarded as the world's first comprehensive corporate identity program. Behrens' teapot and lamps, beautiful and yet designed for the requirements of series production, were groundbreaking achievements. Although he would later concentrate on architecture – famous late works include the Weissenhof housing development in Stuttgart and Berlin's Alexanderplatz – he was also a pioneer in practical, inexpensive type-based furniture, which came about e.g. in the context of early projects for workers' housing. In 1913 he once again designed furnishing ensembles for the Deutsche Werkstätten, becoming, alongside Bruno Paul, **Richard Riemerschmid** and others, one of the pioneers of industrial series furniture.

PHOTOS: l.: Radiant heater for AEG, m.: Chair for the Wertheim House r.: White wine glasses for Benedikt von Poschinger

MILESTONE: *Behrens House* chair → page **42** I *Behrens Kettle* → page **46**

# Markus **Benesch**

furniture and product designer, born 1969, offices in Milan / Italy and Munich / Bavaria, **www.markusbenesch.com**

If one doesn't know how to categorize a designer, this itself might already reveal an instance of true innovation. Markus Benesch's designs are situated somewhere between furniture design and wallpaper graphics – with strong echoes of the Pop and Op Art eras. In *Colorflage*, large-surface wallpapers and wall panels with which rooms can be articulated or simply attractively decorated, overall patterns optically change the proportions of the space. By applying this alienation effect – which remotely recalls the *Picture Line* kitchen series from **Alno**, as well as exhibiting parallels to the total works of art of the Jugendstil days, such as those executed by **Peter Behrens** – Benesch casts doubt on the traditional separation of room and furnishings. To this end, he makes use of striking surface finishes for tables, cabinet furniture, lamps and walls. *Foomy*, on the other hand, a series of seating elements made of foam, consists of discrete pieces of furniture. The lightweight objects are not only remark-able for their colourful stripes, but also due to their versatility. Whether it takes the form of a six-sided screw or a Y-shaped chair, each piece still functions as a seat even when turned on its head. The same kind geometry-based versatility can be found in the turned stool *Scaboo*. Benesch, a commuter between Munich and Milan, has designed interiors and trade fair stands and has worked for design-oriented companies such as wallpaper-maker

**Rasch** and the Italian lamination specialist Abet Laminati. For Memphis in Milan he recently conceived a comprehensive interior decor program called *La Casa di Alice*. Included are not only lamps, wallpaper, carpets and matching clothes, but also furniture, such as a rotating column-shaped chest of drawers with mirrors inside called *Torre di Alice*, which is available either with a monumental pattern of intertwining strands of colour or with "dancing points". Further variety is offered by the cabinet series *Strip'n'Tease*, which comes with nine self-adhesive patterns; when the user gets tired of one, he can simply switch to another look.

PHOTOS: l.: *Foomy* chair for Colorflage
m.: *L-Type* cabinet for Colorflage, r.: *Scaboo* stool for Memphis

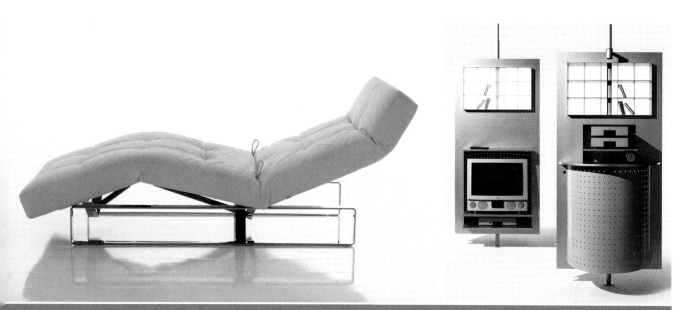

# Siegfried **Bensinger**

interior and furniture designer, born 1943, office in Buchholz / Lower Saxony

Many of Bensinger's furniture designs stemmed from projects he had conceived for private homes. His designs still benefit today from this direct connection to everyday use. Bensinger is a multi-talent. During his training as cabinet-maker and studies at the *Werkkunstschule* (School of Arts & Crafts) in Darmstadt, he also began playing saxophone in professional bands. He worked as interior designer in various furniture stores and then became product manager at the **Deutsche Werkstätten** in Munich (which was taken over during that period by **WK Wohnen**). All the while, he was also active as a freelance designer. His first design, with which he entered the fray in one of the prime disciplines of German furniture design, already caused a sensation: The *Container* cabinet system of 1972 (for WK Wohnen) was the first case furniture with plastic fronts. The highlight was a whole interior life – similar to a refrigerator door – integrated behind the curving facades. An important formative period was 1977 to 1988, when he was the executive interior designer in the editorial department of *Schöner Wohnen*, a trendsetting magazine at the time for which **Peter Maly** and **Rolf Heide** also worked. The *Scaletta* shelf system he designed in the mid-1980s, which needs no screws, was totally attuned to today's domestic requirements. This ingeniously simple take-along furniture ensemble was quite successful in Japan, the land of

small apartments. The shelf is one of Bensinger's typical concepts, offering high user value and, due to its uncomplicated structure, a long aesthetic half-life. This also goes for the sofa bed *Diwan* (1977 for Strässle) with its reduced forms and cover of finger-thick textured natural butt leather. He once again succeeded at creating a sofa bed that doesn't look like one with **Lobby** (2002 for **Brühl**). Similar freedom is offered by the sofa *Space* and the bed system *Tatami* (both 1987, for Strässle, respectively **Inter-lübke**), two additional contributions to the theme of mobile furniture. *Space* swivels on a floor plate and can thus be turned as needed, e.g. either to look out the window or at the television. In *Tatami* the distance between the beds can be varied. Now the system specialist has designed two programs that work anywhere in the home: *Artena* and *Cintura* (both for WK Wohnen). In *Artena* all of the cables disappear behind an indirectly lit wall panel. Cleverly calculated structural engineering makes the system look as if, instead of bearing weight, it were floating on thin air.

PHOTOS: l.: *Orbit* lounge chair for Brühl, r.: *Center* TV furniture for Interlübke

MILESTONE: *Lobby* sofa system → page **328**

# Berker

switch manufacturer, Schalksmühle / North Rhine-Westphalia, founded 1919, **www.berker.de**

Light switches are one of those nondescript everyday items that neither attract much attention nor are commonly associated with design. The people at Berker see things differently. Similar to the door-handle manufacturer **FSB**, the tradition-rich company from the Sauerland region does everything it can to overcome the curse of the ordinary in a product that is only simplistic on the surface. The fact that these efforts are oriented strongly on classical Bauhaus Modernism surely has something to do with the company's having been founded the same year as the famous design university in Weimar. Berker's ascent took place in parallel to the spread of electric light in the 1920s. The turning switch common at the time was an early example of functional design for industrial products. The firm picked up again on this pioneering phase of good design at the end of the century with its retro series *1930*. Looking back through the models of the interceding years, it suddenly becomes evident how these control elements that we touch so many times a day have engraved themselves in our visual memory. Berker became a design-oriented brand in the 1960s. At that time, the IF jury recognized the latest rocker switch as an example of "good form" and **Egon Eiermann**, master builder of the high-rise for the House of Representatives in Bonn, chose the model *Modul* for his building. During the ensuing decade, a collaboration with the Lengyel design studio

began that still continues today. This resulted not only in important contemporary product lines such as the popular *S.1* program and the award-winning series *B.1*; it was also the origin of the kind of organically developing design culture à la **Braun** and **Wilkhahn** that encompasses all elements of an enterprise. Innovative switch solutions would emerge in the process, such as the *TS* system by Tom Schlotfeldt, a completely new product type that has already taken on cult status. For the age of the digitized home, where all electric elements can long since be operated via central panels – but in which we still search in the dark for the good old light switch – Berker has concepts such as the minimalist interface *B.IQ* at the ready. In cooperative projects with **Rosenthal** and Swarowski, special applications using the materials of porcelain and crystal have been conceived.

PHOTOS: l.: Light switch, 1965, m.: *Modul* light switch, r.: *B.IQ* light switch

MILESTONE: *1930* Light switch → page **82**

# Bisterfeld + Weiss

furniture manufacturer, Eschborn / Hesse, founded 198, **www.bisterfeldundweiss.de**

The company's very first product, the *S 90* chair (1987) by Arno **Votteler**, was already a resounding success. It was the "founding chair" that not only established the brand, but also inaugurated a long working relationship with Votteler. The *S 90* is still in the program today, along with *Arno*, another brainchild of the Swabian designer. *Arno* has a special shell construction at the transition between seat and backrest. In this area there are fewer veneer layers than in the other parts of the seat shell. This results in a high degree of elasticity, which supports the sitter's back. Bisterfeld + Weiss was established in the mid-1980s with the aim of bringing more domestic comfort to the world of objects. For demographic reasons that are amply familiar by now, the firm devoted its energies early on to the increasingly important, but even today still not really popular, theme of the "old-age lifestyle". The objective of uniting solid wood construction with modern furniture design succeeded in the programs *Serie 80* and *Serie 90* by Votteler and was consistently driven forward up to the models *S 11* and *S 12* (2003 by Urs Greutmann and Carmen Greutmann-Bolzern). Another common thread running through the product history of Bisterfeld + Weiss is exemplified by the intelligent multifunctional tables, such as model *M* (1991) by **Reiner Moll**. With this and further designs, including the folding wonder-table *Adebar*, Moll introduced a more conceptual formal vocabulary. In 2003 the table system *P 1* was added, by Swiss designer Greutmann, for which the company registered its first patent. With his clean-lined style and a whole series of new products, he is now shaping the face of the brand. One of Bolzern's latest designs is the *S 20* chair (2005), a lean, simple and straightforward object for sitting made of wood and metal that is conspicuous by virtue of its very inconspicuousness, as well as due to high-quality design details that only become evident upon closer inspection.

PHOTOS: l.: *S 90* chair by Arno Votteler
m.: *Adebar* table by Reiner Moll, r.: *S 20* chair by Greutmann Bolzern

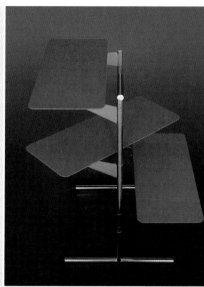

# Christoph **Böninger**

design manager and furniture designer, born 1957, lives in Munich / Bavaria

He did his studies in Munich and Los Angeles. For his dissertation as industrial designer in the early 1980s, Böninger designed the first laptop, a model that can be viewed today in Munich's *Pinakothek der Moderne* museum. Following his studies, he first worked for Schlagheck und Schultes in Munich, one of the premier addresses for German product design. Thereafter he went to Siemens, where at the end of the 1990s he organized the spin-off of the Siemens design department together with Herbert H. Schultes. This was the beginning of Designaffairs, with over 100 employees one of Europe's leading design studios, with Böninger as managing director starting in 1997. In addition to his main function as design manager, he also designed furniture under the label "Auerberg Sunday Morning Design". In the late 1990s he began to experiment with warping aluminium sheets. His initial design, first issued in a small series and quite well-known amongst insiders, is the **Soester Hocker** (Soest Stool, 2000 for Mabeg), a featherweight with remarkable capabilities. Weighing in at little more than a kilogram, the stool is able to support up to three hundred pounds. A more recent Böninger piece is the Buga rocking chair, a commission for the National Garden Show in Munich in 2005. This construction of rectangular steel tubing and sailcloth evokes double associations with the classic director's chair and the cantilevered chair of the

1920s, two chair types that stand in different ways for mobility. In other designs as well, such as the tables **Sax** and *Acca* (1999 and 2005, both for ClassiCon), Böninger refers back to the original meaning of the word *Möbel* (German for furniture), in Latin *mobilis*, i.e. mobile. In the meantime, the Munich designer has left Designaffairs and become senior partner of brain4design, an agency for design management. He is now applying his experience in material technology to new designs, such as the occasional table *#24* (for Articolo), once again a very lightweight marvel of stability, which is sold via the Internet. This is a product he conceived expressly for mail order: Thanks to its geometric features, which support the packing box precisely at the most vulnerable corners, *#24* requires extremely little packaging material.

PHOTOS: l.: *#24* occasional table for Articolo
m.: *Buga* chair for the National Garden Show in Munich
r.: *Acca* occasional table for ClassiCon

MILESTONES: *Sax* table → page **298** | *Soest Stool* → page **304**

# Bofinger

furniture manufacturer, founded 1879, formerly Stuttgart / Baden-Wurttemberg

Furniture should be smaller, lighter and, if possible, easy to take apart, was the opinion of Rudolf Baresel-Bofinger when he took over his father's cabinetry shop at the beginning of the 1950s. The first furniture in the new collection was licensed by clients. In his quest for the modular furniture of the future, he finally met Ulm pioneer **Hans Gugelot** and developed with him a product to series maturity that would enjoy a worldwide career: *M 125*, the first comprehensive cabinet and closet system. The visionary Bofinger – an aesthete first, and only then a business-man – had a passion for India and was in other respects as well an exception to the rule. The unorthodox thinker, alongside pioneers such as Christian Holzäpfel and **Otto Zapf**, played a key role in the early days of West German furniture design similar to that played by the Braun company in industrial design, whose owner, Erwin Braun, he knew personally. Both entre-preneurs were inspired by the Academy of Design in Ulm, where Gugelot taught. "What do we want?" a brochure from the 1960s asks: "Furniture that goes beyond every fashion trend". This is a credo right in tune with classic functionalism, which was now to be developed further using modern means. For the perfected *M 125* a new factory was erected in 1960 in Ilsfeld. Craftsmanship became high-precision industrial fabrication. Collaboration with the genius Gugelot continued until his death

in 1965. Tables, beds and chairs were created – all of them easily dismantled – along with a concept for a new kind of wall unit that could stand on its own and whose folding doors did not swing out into the room. Bofinger worked with additional free-lance designers such as the architect Helmut Bätzner, Swiss artist Andreas Christen and American entrepreneurial couple Estelle and Erwine Laverne. The collection includes both the first stack-able bed-couch made of polyester resin and the first serially produced compression-moulded plastic chair, Bätzner's famous *Bofingerstuhl* (Bofinger Chair). An unusual highlight was the Farmer program by **Gerd Lange**, snap-together furniture made of wood and sailcloth that could be stored so efficiently that furnishings for an entire room fit in a car boot. In the 1970s furniture-industry crisis, the company was bought by **König + Neurath**, which maintained the brand name for a long time.

PHOTOS: l.: *BA 1171* stool, r.: *M 125* closet by Hans Gugelot

MILESTONES: *M 125* cabinet system → page **106** | *Bofinger Chair* → page **154**

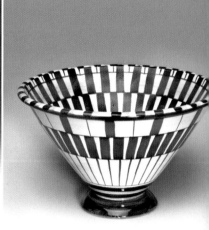

# Hedwig **Bollhagen**

ceramicist and entrepreneur, born 1907, died 2001, **www.hedwig-bollhagen.de**

Even Walter Ulbricht, the top dog in East Germany, felt compelled to point the cultural-political finger. According to the Social Realist way of thinking, Bollhagen's *558* mocha service was – being black and cylindrical – much too "formalist" and "cosmopolitan". The ideological verdict could hardly have been more damning. The popularity of the service mattered just as little as the reputation of Hedwig Bollhagen, who had already long been regarded as one of Germany's leading ceramicists. She learned her trade at 18 at a professional school in the Westerwald region, and in her subsequent "journeyman years" worked in various companies, including for the stoneware manufacturer Velten in the late 1920s. Its owner was open to new ideas and hired some Bauhaus ceramicists, who exercised a strong influence on the young Bollhagen. In 1934 she founded her own factory in Marwitz near Berlin. From the very start HB, as her fans call her, created simple, practical ceramic ware for serial production. The Brandenburg-based artist favoured basic shapes, striped decor – usually blue-and-white but also black-and-green – or geometric patterns. Over the decades, Bollhagen developed a range of sophisticated techniques allowing her to apply even complex patterns to her pieces using simple means. Her point of departure is often formed by black stripes which are then scored or distorted by turning the piece on a small potter's wheel and

then overpainting them with a different-coloured glaze. She also produced ceramics in naked white, but the clientele for such products was limited. To those who insisted on seeing her work as art, she liked to reply "They're just pots". Bollhagen was able to go on directing her operation as private owner for a while in the GDR before it was nationalized in the early 1970s. She remained artistic director, however. Following reunification she got her company back, and, at 85, became an entrepreneur again for a decade. Her successor was Heidi Manthey, a student of Charles Crode, with whom Hedwig Bollhagen had collaborated ever since founding her company.

PHOTOS: l.: Jug for HB-Werkstätten Hanover
m.: Pen rest for Velten-Vordamm, r.: Bowl for Velten-Vordamm

# Andreas **Brandolini**

architect, artist and furniture designer, born 1951, office in Saarbrücken

Three decades left their mark on him: the 1950s, when his childhood coincided with that of the German Federal Republic; the 1970s, when he was indoctrinated into functionalism during his architecture studies; and the 1980s, the halcyon days of the German design underground, the Berlin version of which Andreas Brandolini decisively influenced. It is to this latter era – he became one of the leading figures of "New German Design" – that his penchant for experimentation can be traced. The avant-gardist first rose to fame with his contribution to *documenta 8*, the first art show to focus on design. Brandolini exhibited a "German living room" there, an institution that he tried to come to terms with through irony: for example with a couch suite grouped around a sausage-shaped table under which a fire blazed – a pastiche of the petty bourgeois domestic idyll. Objects function here as "signifiers", an approach with artistic elements evoking a critique of the times, something Brandolini devoted himself to intensely. A table with metal-profile legs that come to a point where they touch the floor, a chair whose legs bend at their most fragile point, a book ladder that also functions as a newspaper basket: These designs, although relatively simply built, display irritating aspects, or even alienating factors, such as those familiar from the work of **Stefan Wewerka**. Such intellectual constructs calling into

question the concept of functionality were hardly suitable for series production. As counter-program, Brandolini founded a project called Utilism Collective in the 1980s. Joining him were **Axel Kufus** and Jasper Morrison, two protagonists of practical minimalism. As an ex-rebel, Brandolini has been professor of design in Saarbrücken for two decades, while working as architect and exhibit organizer as well as international mouthpiece for a somewhat different take on German design. Now he has presented a furniture ensemble that speaks a formal language just as fundamental as its inventory: bed, chair, table and bench of solid wood (for a.g. mandelbach). Designed for a school's country field centre, the ecologically impeccable furniture is strongly reminiscent of the "rural" homeland preservation style of the early 20th century.

PHOTOS: l.: *Little Sisters* bench, chair and stool for Zeus
m.: *Book Ladder/Basket* for Cappellini, r.: *IPT 01* table for Vereinigte Saarschreiner

# Marianne **Brandt**

artist, product and lamp designer, born 1893, died 1983

More than a few men at the Bauhaus were convinced that the metal workshop was no place for a woman. But Brandt managed to gain the support of the workshop's director, László Moholy-Nagy. In the small workshop, bursting at the seams with creativity, she met up with other talents, such as Christian Dell and **Wilhelm Wagenfeld**. The highly gifted designer was extremely productive. She created almost 70 products in Weimar and Dessau, including tableware such as creamers, sugar bowls, ashtrays and the ***Tee-Extrakt-Kännchen*** (Tea-Extract-Pot) that gained her posthumous fame. About half of her designs are for lamps, a metier in which she – along with Poul Henningsen from Denmark – set important trends. Her ***HMB 25*** hanging lamp with pull cord (a collaboration with Hans Przyrembel, made today by **Tecnolumen**) became the prototype for many dining room lamps. Brandt came up with the idea of mobile wall lamps on rails, a principle that would become standard half a century later. Another novelty were her ceiling lamps with aluminium reflectors – which she had to paint over in order to find buyers. When Marianne Brandt herself became master of the metal workshop, she turned it into the most commercially successful department in the Bauhaus. For lamp manufacturer Kandem she designed (with Hin Bredendieck) the *756* desk lamp and *702* nightstand lamp. Both models were produced in large quantities in the 1930s, the only mass products to issue

from the Bauhaus other than wallpaper. In the art field, Brandt made a name for herself with her collages and photographs. But the life of this successful designer did not always go smoothly. When she first came to the Bauhaus as the daughter of a high judicial officer, she was already 30 years old, a late bloomer like, for example, **Josef Albers**. Previously she had destroyed all the pictures she had executed thus far, in one radical gesture. She had studied art in Dresden and travelled to France and Norway. After leaving the Bauhaus at the end of 1929, she directed the design department at a metal goods plant in Gotha. But after only three years, her marriage having failed, she returned to her parents' home in Chemnitz and lived a withdrawn life there as a painter. It was not until after the Second World War that she was summoned to the Dresden Academy of Art by Mart Stam, a lecturer there. In 1952 she moved to East Berlin, which was now the capital of the GDR, and designed objects of daily use at the "Institute for Industrial Design", including a stackable canteen service as well as shoes, handbags and wallpaper. After this three-year guest stint, Marianne Brandt, the most famous female German designer, finally turned her back in 1954 on a design world now firmly under the sway of the reigning political party.

PHOTOS: l.: *702* table lamp for Kandem
m.: *656* ceiling lamp for Kandem, r.: Table lamp for Körting & Mathiesen

MILESTONES: *Tea-Extract-Pot* → page **56** I *HMB 25* hanging lamp → page **62**

# Braun

electric appliance manufacturer, Kronberg / Hesse, founded 1921, **www.braun.de**

Whether one thinks of phonographs, kitchen appliances or razors – since the 1950s Braun has been developing innovative devices that often became the prototypes for whole product groups. But even insiders sometimes have no idea of how closely the ascent of Braun design was tied to the ideas of what the modern domestic lifestyle should look like. Following the death of company founder Max Braun in 1951, his sons Artur and Erwin took the helm at the family company, which had been producing its own radios since the 1930s. The new FM device was the first national symbol of German prosperity. But these bulky pieces of "music furniture" also stood for the spirit of historical restoration. An early opinion survey revealed that the desire for a more contemporary lifestyle reached all the way down to the middle class, whereupon Braun set out to deliver the kind of modern devices that would go with the new furniture of the times, thereby tapping an as yet unoccupied market niche. Close collaboration with companies such as **Bofinger**, Knoll International and **Rosenthal** reflected this new commercial approach, as did co-operations with progressive furniture designers including **Hans Gugelot** and **Herbert Hirche**. Connections were also forged to the Academy of Design in Ulm, which by way of Braun first put its program into industrial practice. Ulm and Braun represented a one-of-a-kind

convergence in the history of design that was capable of engendering the kind of radical new ideas that were at the time presumably only conceivable in Germany. Under the aegis of **Otl Aicher** and the new advertising head Wolfgang Schmittel, consistent, reason-guided functionalism now dictated the face of the company and its products, whose homogeneous rigour was emulated the world over. Under the direction of **Dieter Rams** the "Department of Formal Design", as it was long called, maintained its high ranking in the company hierarchy. The interlocking of company image and product aesthetic is – after **Peter Behrens**' overhaul of AEG and the example of Olivetti in Italy – the most famous example of a thoroughly rationalized corporate identity. Braun would go on to become a total work of art, one that conveyed an enlightened view of life. The company executives exemplified this goal with their angular white homes. At some point, though, the rapid pace of innovation overwhelmed the resources of what was still a relatively small business. The result was a take-over by the US Gillette Group. The company has since departed from some product sectors, including the hi-fi system production that used to be its core business.

PHOTOS: l.: *Atelier* hi-fi system, r.: *RT 20* table radio

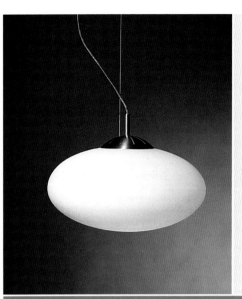
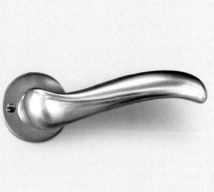

# Wilhelm **Braun-Feldweg**

painter, author and product designer, born 1908, died 1998

He first came to design after World War II. The newcomer, already 40 years old, then proceeded to design a whole range of diverse products, from silverware to bottles, from lamps to door-handles. Wilhelm Braun-Feldweg was a many-sided talent. He worked as steel engraver, vocational school teacher, painter, art historian, book author and finally as designer. A cabinet-maker's son, furniture is one field he left out, because wood, he categorically claimed, was something he "detested". But he liked glass very much, creating entire product families out of it that were always remarkable for styling that, although in step with the times, was still out of the ordinary. He thus decisively extended the canon of modern design for living, in a similar way to his contemporaries **Hans Theo Baumann**, **Hans Gugelot** and **Herbert Hirche**. Braun-Feldweg was at the same time a direct rival of the somewhat older **Wilhelm Wagenfeld**. By contrast to the latter designer, he repeatedly felt the urge to apply a single form to several different objects and applications. The *Tokio* hanging lamp, for example, looks just like an upside-down version of one of his vases – in keeping with the ideas of reduction and multiple uses. Whether in his products or his books, the Swabian designer was regarded as a perfectionist. He often executed over 20 models until he finally found a form that pleased him. Nor did he like to leave the layout of his books to

others. The multi-talent almost took a post as professor at the Academy of Design in Ulm, but, as father of five children, found the salary too low. At the end of the 1950s, he finally accepted an appointment to fill the newly created chair for "Industrial Form Design" at the Academy of the Arts in West Berlin. From this perch, he drove forward the professionalization of his trade, becoming the mentor of West German Modernism as well as a pioneer in the field of design literature. He likewise forged ties with classical Modernism through a lighting series that included the model *Britz*. His fundamental writings on the material of metal set new standards. The theorist and moralist railed against "fashion that was only skin-deep", criticizing the cult of star designers. He himself had brought out certain of his silverware series anonymously for this very reason. Although his products by all means followed the rationalist Ulm line, the doctrine of pure predictability was much too one-sided for him. He had the same problem with the radical student movement of the late 1960s. The old-school patriarch ultimately found that these developments had spoiled his profession for him. A prize for critical design texts has been awarded in his name since 2003.

PHOTOS: l.: *Mondello* hanging lamp for Mawa
m.: ZS 8962 door-handle for Dorma, r.: Vases and bowl for Marina

MILESTONE: *Britz* wall lamp → page **146**

# Marcel **Breuer**

furniture designer and architect, born 1902, died 1981, **www.marcelbreuer.org**

The Hungarian native came to the Bauhaus in 1920 at only 18, following a short course of art studies in Vienna. He began working there as an apprentice in the cabinetry shop, of which he ultimately became director. His colleagues included artists with similarly idealistic views, among them **Josef Albers**, **Alma Buscher**, **Erich Dieckmann** and **Peter Keler**. He started creating his first furniture designs in 1921, such as an expressionistic/folkloristic so-called "African Chair", tables and chairs for children, a vanity table and a cabinet with integrated vitrine. A leather easychair put together out of cubes stemming from these early days looks just as constructivist as a series of slatted chairs which reveal a close kinship with the work of Gerrit Rietveld. Breuer viewed his later furniture as "apparatus for today's way of life". The pieces had to be practical, lightweight, easy to dismantle, hygienic and affordable; a brusque refusal of any longing for mere cosy comfort. The **B 3** tubular steel easy-chair of 1925 – later known as the *Club Chair* or *Wassily* – fulfilled all these criteria. Although it did not constitute the object of daily use that he had hoped to create, it did set a precedent for a furniture type with which the industrial aesthetic could gain a foothold in the living room. *B 3* was – like jazz and neon – an emblem of Modernism, later going on to become the mother of all design classics and setting off a wave of tubular

steel furniture worldwide. Breuer himself also continued to explore the limits of this new paradigm with follow-up designs including stools, folding chairs, cantilevered chairs, tables, nesting tables, desks and a lounge on wheels (made today by **Tecta**). People tended to lose sight of the fact that the experiment-happy designer was also ahead of his time in other fields. In fact, he was also responsible for modular "add-on cabinets" (with units measuring 33 cm), an idea that would first be developed further by **Hans Gugelot** in the 1950s. Furthermore, he also occupied himself with architectural concepts such as the "slab high-rise". As a Hungarian Jew, Breuer had no future in Germany after 1933. Emigration took him via Switzerland to London, where he designed a series of interesting furniture pieces of laminated wood for Isokon, his last designs in this metier. His endless battle for the copyright to his chairs may have played a role in the cessation of his design efforts. Finally, Breuer followed his mentor **Walter Gropius** to the USA, where he managed in a brief space of time to inspire a whole generation of design students at Harvard, among them Philip Johnson, Florence Knoll and Eliot Noyes. After the Second World War, he became one of the first star architects.

PHOTOS: l.: *Slatted Chair*, m.: *D40* chair (re-edition by Tecta)
r.: *Dining Chair* for Isokon

MILESTONES: *B 3* chair → page **60** | *B 9* nesting tables → page **64** | *B 35* easychair → page **72** | *B 32* chair → page **76** | *S 285* desk → page **96**

# Brühl

upholstered furniture manufacturer, Bad Steben / Bavaria, founded 1948, **www.bruehl.com**

The Brühl brand stands for upholstered furniture with clean lines and clear concepts. Both are in many cases to the credit of managing director Roland Meyer-Brühl. The tradition is now being carried forward by his daughter Kati Meyer-Brühl, who studied industrial design in London and New York. With advertising campaigns conceived in-house, the corporate image is just as consistent as the product range. Both are notable for the renunciation of any exaggerated attitude, perhaps the most basic of all maxims of modern German furniture design. The cube easychair *Carrée* is a good example of this tradition, but by no means the only one. The product line comprises sofa beds and sofa ensembles that often have some surprises in store with their ingenious functionality. Examples are the sofa group *Chillin'* (by Kati Meyer-Brühl) with three relax positions, and the *Moule* sofa (Roland Meyer-Brühl), an adaptable additive system with a large choice of covers. The company has dedicated itself to offering an all-encompassing furnishings concept focusing on long product life and the use of high-quality, low-pollutant materials. With 170 staff members, the family-owned enterprise is not one of the largest, but can boast special expertise as a design-oriented manufacturer. Exquisite leather craftsmanship, with thicknesses up to five millimetres, can be found, for example, in the model *Visavis*. The origins of the firm go back to the

Saxony region, starting with a mattress factory built around the turn of the last century. In the late 1940s, the company moved out of the Soviet-occupied zone to Franconia in the West – once right on the border between the two Germanys, but today in the heart of Europe. The decisive creative reorientation already took place in the 1970s. Thereafter, the company steadily gained in prominence. One in eight people in Germany know this brand – a sizable number for a medium-sized furniture manufacturer with design aspirations. The collection includes pieces by external designers including Germans **Siegfried Bensinger** (with the quick-change sofa *Lobby*), Volker Laprell, Danes Johannes Foersom and Peter Hiort-Lorenzen, as well as London-based Shin and Tomoko Azumi. The latter stake their claim to the avant-garde with *Big Arm* and yet at the same time represent the kind of casual modernity one has come to expect from Brühl and which makes it so easy to integrate the furniture into any surroundings.

PHOTOS: l.: *Roro* upholstered furniture collection by Roland Meyer-Brühl
r.: *Chillin'* easychair by Kati Meyer-Brühl

MILESTONE: *Lobby* sofa system → page **328** I *Plupp a.p.* functional sofa → page **372**

# Brunner

furniture manufacturer, Rheingau / Baden-Wurttemberg, founded 1977, **www.brunner-stuehle.de**

"The product range encompasses waiting-room furniture for the lobbies of administration buildings, chairs and tables for seminar and conference rooms, swivelling office chairs, furnishings for cafeterias and canteens, auditorium seating as well as furniture for senior citizens' homes and hospitals." The fields of activity defined here sound precise and business-like, but, although quite wide-ranging, hardly inspire one to expect exciting design solutions. As insiders are well aware, however, the company based on the French border in the Baden region has repeatedly managed in the last few years to draw attention to itself with trade fair highlights. A medium-sized operation managed by its founders Helena and Rolf Brunner, around average size for the industry with its 300 or so employees, Brunner has departed further and further from the grey zone of ordinary everyday mass goods. This is only fitting in its Black Forest setting, Germany's paradise for tinkerers and technicians, which is also home to such diverse furniture designers as **Draenert** and **Rolf Benz**. In order to convey its corporate philosophy even more effectively, the firm recently erected a new, architecturally ambitious communications centre. The declared aim is to conceive innovations "that make people's lives more pleasant": a plausible, almost banal credo that is more demanding than it sounds. It might have been voiced by **Wolfgang C. R. Mezger**, the designer who played a decisive part in the new course Brunner has embarked upon, and who is strongly represented in the company's current collection, from the *Spira.sit* cantilevered chair to the modular and extremely adaptable waiting room seating program *Take*. Despite the existence of an internal development team that regularly contributes products to the range, such as the plywood chair series *Birdie*, *Eagle* and *Fox*, close collaboration with external designers has also become a key business principle. Other notable idea suppliers working for Brunner are Matteo Thun with his office system *MT.02* and **Martin Ballendat** with various chairs, for example Clear, a minimalist design in natural wood that is quite atypical for both maker and brand. Amongst the many innovations in recent years were surprises such as the graceful chair **Milanolight** by Mezger and a table that can be folded out at a touch, *Sleight* by **Lepper Schmidt Sommerlade**, a team that likewise goes way back at Brunner.

PHOTOS: l.: *Taceo* easychair by Martin Ballendat
m.: *Sleight* table by Lepper Schmidt Sommerlade
r.: *Milanolight* chair by Wolfgang C. R. Mezger

MILESTONE: *Milanolight* chair → page **352**

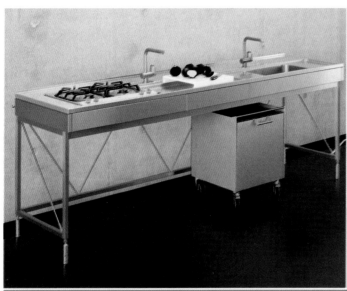

# Bulthaup

kitchen manufacturer, Aich / Bavaria, founded 1949, **www.bulthaup.de**

Using a proprietary laser welding technique, the gas stovetop is integrated seamlessly into the kitchen work surface. The first linear, unbroken connection between range and sink is a prerequisite for perfect kitchen work. Through ongoing innovation, the manufacturer from Lower Bavaria has continually redefined the home kitchen and established itself – according to a study by the magazine *Wirtschaftswoche* – as one of Germany's five leading luxury kitchen brands. In the olden days, the kitchen was a place of warmth, pleasant smells and congeniality. In the 20th century, under the influence of the Bauhaus movement, it evolved into an efficient, space-saving production site. Bulthaup was one of those producing "additive" linear kitchens, until in the early 1980s the "end of the architecture doctrine" was proclaimed. Graphic artist and unconventional thinker **Otl Aicher** had done some deep thinking on behalf of the firm and in the process rediscovered an existential activity. The springboard for his deliberations was by no means grandma's cosy old kitchen nook, but instead the kind of ergonomics and flexibility Aicher observed at the workplaces of modern professional chefs. The concept was first put into practice in 1982 with *System b* – a paradigm change that gave Bulthaup its unique selling point. At the heart of the new kitchen is a central work island. Instead of staring at the wall, the cook now has an unhindered view into

space. Later this workspace was varied, taking the form of a "kitchen workbench" (1988) made of stainless steel, a further milestone. The new way of using the kitchen called for a different type of furniture, e.g. ceiling-mounted cabinets, a shelf for ingredients from which spoons and saucepans can also be hung within easy reach. Along with its new furnishings concept, Bulthaup also brought out a range of high-grade saucepans and kitchen tools. Later on, tables and chairs were added with the series *Duktus* and *Korpus*. The systems designed by Herbert H. Schultes, *S 25* and ***S 20*** (1992 and 1997) are today regarded as standard, featuring counter heights that are easy on the back, rolling shutters replacing cabinet doors, and kitchen containers on wheels. Finally, Schultes developed the *b3* system (2004), which is no longer fixed in place according to a particular floor plan, but can be moved along a stable steel skeleton for a variety of different wall designs.

PHOTOS: l.: *Pur* kitchen workbench (manufacturer's design)
r.: *b3* kitchen system by Herbert H. Schultes

MILESTONE: *S 20* kitchen system → page **282**

# Alma **Buscher**

artist, furniture and product designer, born 1899, died 1944

When the Bauhaus was preparing its model home "Am Horn" in Weimar in 1923, a children's room was part of the plan. Entrusted with its conception and furnishings was student Alma Buscher, a designer whose career directly reflects the interconnection between the reform movement before the First World War and the Bauhaus. After completing her secondary school degree and attending a "women's school", she began in 1917 a three-year program of studies at the Reimann Art Academy in Berlin, an institute founded on the principle of reform education which also co-operated with the Deutscher Werkbund. The fact that, after another two-year course at the Berlin *Kunstgewerbe-museum* (Museum of Applied Arts), Buscher then took up yet another study program at the Bauhaus can only be explained by the institute's extraordinary magnetism, to which the impassioned arts enthusiast was only too susceptible. Here she found the vocation that would dominate her short life. Although there had already been individual instances of modern design in children's rooms and furniture during the *Werkstätten* movement, e.g. by Josef Hoffmann, Buscher's concept represented the first radical attempt to develop entirely new, child-friendly furniture types. Her changing table, the child's bed based on a connector system, the rolling ladder chair and the toy cabinet created a "prepared environment" for creative play as advocated for example by the

Montessori schools. The design was also innovative in its overall coherence. In the toy cabinet, which included shelves, a puppet theatre, a mobile toy chest and stackable cube-shaped boxes, the idea of a modular furniture program – something that **Marcel Breuer** was also working on at the time – was already immanent. One of her basic ideas was that all furniture should be movable and conceived for both building and playing. Buscher also developed toys, including cut-out sheets, building block systems, an abstract puppet theatre and so-called "throwing dolls" (dolls with unbreakable heads), for which she registered a patent. Her pieces were among the few commercial products of the Bauhaus, even though the revenues were quite modest. After she left the Bauhaus, her ideas were not pursued further there. She herself was only able to work sporadically due to the changing engagements of her husband, a dancer and actor. Shortly before the end of the Second World War, Alma Buscher lost her life in a bombing attack.

PHOTO: *Bauhaus Bauspiel* (building game, re-edition by Naef)

*Hemisphere* garden furniture collection by Richard Frinier for **Dedon**

# Carpet Concept

carpeting manufacturer, Bielefeld / North Rhine-Westphalia, founded 1993, **www.carpet-concept.de**

As there was no money in the budget for hiring designers, company founder Thomas Trenkamp simply designed the first collection himself. From his experience as sales director in a commercial carpeting firm, he knew his industry from the ground up and thought he could do things better. For example, he revived old weaving techniques and combined them with up-to-the-minute concepts such as metal inserts. The original craft of weaving is thus tied together with modern fabrication technology. The result is extraordinary carpeting that exudes the charm of old-time craftsmanship but with a high-tech finish. One of the main goals is – and the use of the vocabulary of classical Modernism is no coincidence – to create honest products that display their woven structure. The prerequisite for doing so is the existence of a lively design culture. The entrepreneur from the Westphalia region is committed to lasting quality, guaranteeing the continued availability of his products for 15 years. Companies like **FSB**, which stand for integrity and intensive communication with their designers, are explicit role models. Design is a top management priority. One of the difficulties in this mission, according to Trenkamp, is that both industrial and furniture designers always think in three dimensions. A surface that must subordinate itself to other things now and then is therefore alien to them at first. In the meantime, however, designers such as

**Konstantin Grcic** of Munich and the Hamburg-based Hadi Teherani and **Peter Maly** as well as Berliner Carsten Gollnick are represented in the catalogue. A larger dose of German avant-gardism is hard to imagine. This is demonstrated by the company's over 60 design awards, for products including *Tec Wave* and *Tec Pearl*. These novel woven carpets are all about the parity of nap and ground. The metal thread penetrates the coloured ground in waves. The designs arise out of the alteration between squares and stripes, with the metallic effects resting atop it all like a veil. Year after year, the *Lyn* collection by Maly and Gollnick has played a key role in anchoring the young brand's popularity, especially amongst architects. Carpet Concept products can thus be found in such prestigious surroundings as the Helmut Newton Museum in Berlin or the new Bayern Stadium in Munich, to name just two examples of many.

PHOTOS: l.: Carpet (*SQR* collection) by Peter Maly and Carsten Gollnick
m.: Carpet (*SQR* collection) by Peter Maly and Carsten Gollnick
r.: *Lyn* carpet by Peter Maly

# Christine Kröncke

furniture manufacturer, Munich / Bavaria, founded 1974, **www.christinekroencke.net**

Today the Munich company, which in its early days was known as Reim Interline after a southern German furniture store, bears the name of its founder instead, one of the country's pre-eminent interior designers. Originally captivated by the Bauhaus, Christine Kröncke nowadays views herself as a trend expert who harmonizes elements of Modernism with essential needs. A pronounced feminine touch and the suppression of too much cold slipperiness are deliberate. "An interior should have small mistakes" is one of her credos, involving putting the human being at the centre and turning away from the over-exaggerated tyranny of design. Her longstanding house designer is Andreas Weber, who with his penchant for hard materials like metal and glass stands more for the masculine element. He is responsible for example for the *Calisto* shelf system and the *Stratus* steel table. But collaboration with **Peter Maly** over the decades has also left its stamp on the company. The common denominator between the entrepreneur with her sure sense of style and the Hamburg designer is a striving for visual harmony. Maly felt drawn by Kröncke's classical side. Their first joint products already exhibited a clear structure, such as the versatile *Taxus* individual cabinet and the *Basis* adaptable cabinet system. The *Quadrat* cabinet program from the early 1980s, which is based on *Taxus*, carries on this product idea. It represents a game with the basic

geometric forms that Maly has played variations on over and over again. The best-selling piece is still being manufactured today, thus providing another example of a collection policy geared toward lasting value. Toward the end of the same decade came Maly's *Facades*, a showy series of individual cabinets with ornamental sliding doors. Also part of the program, alongside cabinets, sofas, armchairs and tables, are carpets, mirrors, vases and lamps. Christine Kröncke, who acts as publisher of furnishing collections, orients her efforts toward upscale retailers, not the department-store sector. Her aim is to create an all-encompassing domestic ambience in a style all her own.

PHOTOS: l.: *Zenitha* lamp, m.: *Shibu* shelf, r.: *Quadrat* cabinet by Peter Maly

# ClassiCon

furniture and lamp manufacturer, Munich / Bavaria, founded 1990, **www.classicon.com**

The company's name says it all. The product range offered by German furniture and lamp maker ClassiCon unites the classical legacy of the early 20th century with the contemporary avant-garde. A successor to the *Vereinigte Werkstätten* in Munich, the producer succeeded in the 1990s in developing a distinct profile that derives its fascination from the dialogue between re-editions of classical modernist pieces and up-to-the-minute designs. A leading role in the collection of re-editions is played by one of the few women to ascend to the design firmament, Eileen Gray of Ireland. Many of the best-known designs by the Paris-based talent are now being produced in Germany and sold worldwide. Also featured at ClassiCon is the work of US designer Norman Cherner, who made important contributions to 1950s furniture styles. This historical focus is complemented by a few pieces by Otto Blümel, the former director of the drawing school at the *Vereinigte Werkstätten*, as well as objects that Eckart Muthesius conceived for the Maharaja's palace in Indore. Some of the most delightful objects of the 1930s were created for this exotic project, moulded by the patrician taste of the client, who prized clear contours. In the contemporary department, the **Dia** tubular steel garden furniture series by onetime Munich resident **Gioia Meller Marcovicz** builds a bridge to classical Modernism. From Munich-based **Christoph Böninger** come the **Sax** folding table

and the *Acca* shelf. One of the newer pieces is the *Satyr* easy-chair, designed by the Austrian studio ForUse, in which retro and contemporary aesthetics meet and meld. Last but not least, the longstanding collaboration with **Konstantin Grcic**, likewise based in Munich, gives the ClassiCon program its present-day relevance. His slanting geometric furniture series *Chaos*, **Mars** and **Diana**, standouts in the company's Contempora collection from contemporary designers, reflect the bravado of both their designer and the manufacturer. These products go beyond a mere facile desire to please, exhibiting with their echoes of the functionalism and matter-of-fact forms realized by designers such as Herbert H. Schultes or Swiss studio N2 the company's ambitious stance. This dedication has brought ClassiCon to the fore as one of Germany's premier design-oriented brands.

PHOTOS: l.: *Satyr* easychair by ForUse, m.: *Odin* sofa by Konstantin Grcic r.: *Mandu* valet stand by Eckart Muthesius

MILESTONES: *Dia* garden furniture collection → page 288 | *Sax* table → page 298 | *Diana* occasional table series → page 332 | *Mars* easychair → page 342

# Luigi **Colani**

product and furniture designer, born 1928, office in Karlsruhe / Baden-Wurttemberg, **www.colani.de**

In various eras, the name Colani has been synonymous with design in Germany. From car to camera, from fountain pen to teapot, the designer left hardly a stone unturned, even designing his own person. Following brief art studies in Berlin, he matriculated at the Sorbonne in Paris, where he delved into aerodynamics. He received numerous contracts in the 1960s, particularly from the furniture industry, which allowed Germany's first star designer to set up his studio in the early 1970s as befit his rank in a country castle: one of the nation's first design agencies. Harkotten Castle is located in Westphalia, where Colani had important clients. The renegade anti-linearity crusader designed his spherical kitchen for **Poggenpohl** in1968 – a bit of practical science fiction that, although never produced, brought him overnight fame. His material of choice was plastic. What he shaped out of this malleable mass could by all means stand up to comparison to the designs of Scandinavian and Italian creative talents such as Eero Aarnio or Joe Colombo. Colani took the trend that had been set off by the *Bofinger Chair* in 1966 to its conceptual limits. In the foam lounge chair **TV-relax**, reissued by **Kusch + Co**, structural elements such as seat, backrest and legs dissolve into an overall shape reminiscent of a jet aeroplane, but also of a sculpture by Henry Moore. That Colani's soft, organic style has ergonomic advantages, especially when it comes to

sitting, is obvious. For **COR** the inspired moulder of form designed innovative products around 1970 including the racy one-legged shell chair *Polycor* (→ p.**25**) and the upholstery series **Orbis**. Probably his most well-known seating furniture is **Zocker**, a legless plastic chair that came in a blocky children's version and a more streamlined model for adults. In the field of children's furniture he was likewise a pioneer. It hardly comes as a surprise that this man with his many slogans and contradictions at some point turned his back on Germany, where his effulgent style simply couldn't squeeze itself into the prevailing rationalist grid. A stint in Japan was particularly triumphant. Now he has come home again and is celebrating a comeback along with the biomorphic forms he once spearheaded. The master of curves is finally recognized today for what he always knew himself to be: one of the true greats.

PHOTOS: l.: Garden chair for Essmann, m.: *Drop* service for Rosenthal r.: *Chair with Floating Armrest* for Kusch

MILESTONES: *TV-relax* lounge chair → page **172** | *Orbis* easychair → page **176** | *Zocker* sitting device → page **192**

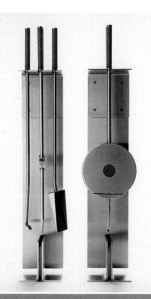

# Conmoto

fireplace and garden furniture manufacturer, Rheda-Wiedenbrück / North Rhine-Westphalia, founded 1997, **www.conmoto.com**

Young entrepreneur Johannes Wagner had plenty of experience in the industry from working in his father's fireplace company and knew that innovative ideas were in short supply there. Furniture-maker and design missionary Helmut Lübke, a seasoned adviser and distant relative of Wagner's, finally gave him the crucial tip: Hamburg designer **Peter Maly** was just the right man to take up the banner of reform in this tradition-mired terrain. The first product of their collaboration, a set of fireplace tools made of unusual materials which was as streamlined as it was practical, already set new standards. For example, a new name had to be invented for the "Holzlege", a stage-like place to stack logs, since no such thing had existed until then. Maly not only inaugurated a whole new type and catapulted one of the last untouched product areas into the contemporary design empyrean; he also became the conceptual mentor of a successful start-up. Encouraged by this triumph, the company set out to rethink the fireplace itself. What resulted was a fireplace system dubbed **Balance**, with which the Bauhaus finally arrived at the hearth-side. Since the orientation toward design was throwing up so many sparks, Wagner proceeded to seek the co-operation of additional external designers, such as Carsten Gollnick and Michael **Sieger**. The latter conceived the *Plaza* series, closed, block-shaped fireplaces without chimney connections that can

be positioned anywhere. From Fried Ulber came additional useful and remarkable fireplace utensils made of stainless steel, such as the *Z-Tisch*, a table that can be transformed at a touch into a newspaper stand or log shelf. The company has launched a new product line of late – garden furniture, once again enlisting Maly's assistance in the birthing process. This range is to be carried forward with the strongly Bauhaus-inspired series *Spring-time* by Matthias Demacker.

PHOTOS: l.: *Lucifer firebug* by Sieger Design,
m. *Peter Maly* fire implements by Peter Maly, r.: *Peter Maly* lounge chair by Peter Maly

MILESTONE: *Balance* fireplace → page **344**

# COR

furniture manufacturer, Rheda-Wiedenbrück / North Rhine-Westphalia, founded 1954, **www.cor.de**

The three letters are synonymous with intelligent upholstered furniture, the company from Westphalia being one of the few German manufacturers confident enough to stand up to the great Italian brands. This can be attributed among other things to COR's having managed to maintain good relationships with "its" designers over the decades and through diverse crises. Leo Lübke jun., who took over the business in 1994 from Helmut Lübke, has also kept up this important custom ever since. COR already started working with freelance designers in the late 1950s, one of the first in the industry to do so. Initial hits were the sofa systems *Quinta* (1959 by **Michael Bayer**) and *Conseta* (1964 by Friedrich Wilhelm Möller), two archetypes that ushered rational and functional aspects into the culture of seating furniture and, with them, the spirit of the Ulm Academy of Design. In the heady 1960s **Luigi Colani** designed futuristic models for the firm such as the one-legged shell chair *Polycor* (→ p.**25**), as well as the practical rolling shell chair *Orbis*. Inextricably bound up with the fortunes of COR is the name **Peter Maly**, who debuted there in 1967 with his *Trinom* easychair (→ p.**494**). With *Zyklus* he succeeded in creating a 1980s classic, whose geometric stringency he managed to match in the later model *Circo* in 1998 (→ p.**494**). Typical of COR are seating arrangements made up of various functional elements that can be freely combined.

**Wulf Schneider** took up this idea in his cube-shaped *Clou*, a contemporary reappraisal of the *Conseta* principle. Less familiar names can also be found in the collection, but their consistently German origin tells us something about their way of thinking. Whether in the model *Corian* by Peter Ulbrich and Oliver Zaiser (Designfriends Studio), *Ala* by Gabriele Assmann and Alfred Kleene, or *Trinus* by Jonas Kressel and Ivo Schelle, every design offers its own surprising, and useful, multifunctionality. An elegant and yet compact variation of this type is Maly's *Cirrus* (1992). The quick-change artist *Scroll* by **Studio Vertijet** as well, both a lounge chair and a sofa, likewise joins these ranks. To mark its fiftieth anniversary the company made itself and its customers the gift of a reissue of the cantilevered easychair *Sinus* by Reinhold Adolf and Hans-Jürgen Schröpfer, an elegant chain of cylindrical cushions arranged atop steel runners whose form is completed by a footstool docked on at the end. Here, the echoes of classical Modernism can't be missed – a fitting emblem for the clear line followed by the entire program.

PHOTOS: l.: *Clou* upholstered furniture collection by Wulf Schneider
m.: *Onda* lounge chair by Jonas Kressel, r.: *Fino* chair by Holger Janke

MILESTONES: *Quinta* upholstered furniture system → page **134** | *Conseta* sofa system → page **152** | *Orbis* easychair → page **176** | *Sinus* easychair → page **202** | *Zyklus* easychair → page **226** | *Scroll* sofa system → page **322**

# Dedon

garden furniture manufacturer, founded 1990, Lüneburg / Lower Saxony, **www.dedon.de**

When a serious injury put an end to the career of professional football goalkeeper Bobby Dekeyser of Belgium in the German Bundesliga in 1990, it didn't take him long to find a new one. Fresh out of the hospital, the 26-year-old founded a company he called Dedon, which first sold hand-painted skis. In an astonishingly short time, the transition was made to producer of exclusive hand-woven furniture, with around 3,000 employees and 60 million euros in turnover (2005). One key to the happy end was Dekeyser's parents, a family of entrepreneurs who own a plastic factory. They developed there the synthetic fibre *Hularo*, which is extremely durable and easy-care and in addition feels pleasant to the touch. When Dekeyser then saw woven furniture from the Philippines at a trade fair, it sparked an idea. Ever since then, Dedon furniture has been manufactured out of synthetic fibres in the East Asian island nation. Other factors contributing to Dekeyser's meteoric ascent are his team-oriented leadership style, a development department with 100 employees, and thoroughly innovative product design. The designers in charge are Dutchman Frank Ligthart, author of the first Dedon furniture, American Richard Frinier, a specialist in garden furniture, and Swissman Nicolas Thomkins, who studied sculpture in Düsseldorf and whose sculptural model **Yin Yang** is reminiscent of dunes formed by the wind, but also of **Luigi Colani's** trailblazing seating designs

from the 1960s. Four kilometres of fibre go into every single chair. It was a very unusual design that inaugurated the Dedon collection. Ligthart's four easychairs form an *Obelisk* when stacked, a design that combines originality with striking visual impact. *Orbit* by Frinier is an oval sofa shell with a cloth canopy as sun shield. Conventional furniture categories blur in these designs. Alongside other, more conventional models that look more like modern versions of colonial furniture, Dekeyser supplies his exclusive clientele with a steady stream of surprises, giving the Dedon brand an unmistakable signature. This is also the case with Frank Ligthart's most recent brainchild: *Leaf*, a lounge chair based on the shape of a leaf which rests on only two supports at the head and foot ends, is back-to-nature design at its finest.

PHOTOS: l.: *Leaf* beach chair by Frank Ligthart
r.: *Obelisk* seating ensemble by Frank Ligthart

MILESTONE: *Yin Yang* garden easychair → page **372**

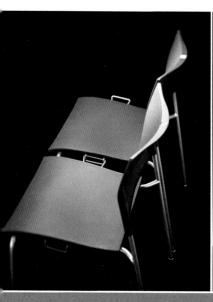 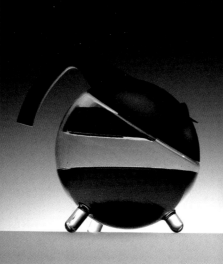 

# Delphin Design

office for product and furniture design, Berlin, founded 1992, **www.delphin-design.de**

Two industrial designers, Dirk Loff from Leipzig, who came to product design via the timber industry and the art academy, and trained toolmaker Thomas G. Wagner from Berlin, have been running a successful design studio in the nation's capital since the mid-1990s. In addition to custom-made interiors, they have also designed a whole range of serially produced pieces including door-handles, jugs, lamps and bathroom fittings. Intelligent, lean solutions – the name (which means "dolphin") exemplifies their design credo. This aim is coupled with wide-ranging experience in working with various materials such as wood, metal and plastic. A co-operation with **Thonet**, manufacturer of the first industrially produced furniture, then makes perfect sense. It began in 2001 with the graceful S 360 chair designed for use in large rooms, whose patented space- and time-saving connector principle won the company wide acclaim and healthy sales figures. There followed the minimalist table system S 1190 with its classic tubular steel aesthetic and, on a completely different note, the large wood table S 1120. Here the stabilizing frame, which usually runs along the edges, was given a Y-form and could thus be "hidden" under the middle of the table. The result is an elegant silhouette due to the illusion of a narrower tabletop. The versatile and delicate series chair S 260 as well, which can be put together securely without tools, fits right into this line of

efficient and elegant designs (all for Thonet). With its award-winning globe-shaped Globo teapot, the Berlin duo not only came up with a striking form but also invented a patented tilt principle so that tea can be served without removing the sieve. And Delphin Design has something to offer coffee drinkers as well: the glass coffeemaker Passero (both for Schott Jenaer Glas, since 2006 no longer available). Here, the hot drink is brewed in a single vessel on the stove. By contrast with the old familiar Bialetti pot, however, the process is visible, can be varied and clean-up is trouble-free. A product that the Delphin team originally developed for themselves is the Display Light lamp. The sturdy polycarbonate light rod, which can be coupled with others of its kind, can be transformed through the insertion and replacement of slides, colour films or natural materials to create a low-key presentation medium.

PHOTOS: l.: S 360 chair for Thonet
m.: Globo teapot for Schott Jenaer Glas
r.: S 1190 table for Thonet

# Deutsche Werkstätten Hellerau

furniture manufacturer, Dresden / Saxony, founded 1889, **www.dwh.de**

Karl Schmidt, entrepreneur and co-founder of the Deutscher Werkbund, became one of the pioneers of modern industrial design. His life's story reflects the many upheavals during what was an eventful epoch. He travelled through England, for example, where both the blessings and blunders of industrialization became evident at a much earlier stage than in Germany. When he saw the work of **Henry van de Velde** at the International Art Exhibition in Dresden in 1897 and came into contact with further protagonists of the movement that was endeavouring to find an alternative to phoney historicism, he knew he had found a home for his creative ambitions. He thereupon founded the Dresdner Werkstätten, a furniture factory that he made into a laboratory for "lifestyle reform" with the help of a team of craftsmen, artists and architects. The project was embedded in the garden town of Hellerau, which boasted a festival theatre and became a centre for expressive dance, an art form that took on enormous importance at the time. One of the main aims of the Werkstätten was to promote an "honest" domestic culture. But social concerns also played a role in Schmidt's model operation. Even before the First World War, he had already introduced the 8.5-hour workday. Designers shared in the company's profits. One of the outstanding furniture designers who worked there, along with Bruno Paul and others, was **Richard Riemerschmid**,

the architect of Hellerau, whose **Music-Room Chair** (Musik-zimmerstuhl) of 1899 transcended the conventions of the genre. His machine-made furniture designed for series production soon became extremely popular and brought its creator both wealth and acclaim. In the meantime, the *Dresdner* and *Münchner Werkstätten* had merged, now calling themselves the *Deutsche Werkstätten* and employing a workforce of around 250. In 1913 no less than 20 artists, among them **Peter Behrens**, were at work on a program for establishing model types for German household items. "Sachlichkeit", a rational approach to design, was celebrating its first triumphs in German homes. In the late 1920s Paul developed the additive furniture program he called the "growing home", one of the precursors of modular furniture (see **WK Wohnen**). The Werkstätten in Hellerau remained an innovative enterprise, distinguishing itself for example in the development of plywood, block board and chipboard. Following German reunification, the company, which had been nationalized by the GDR, returned to private ownership and has made a name for itself since with high-quality interior design.

PHOTOS: l.: *Veneer Chair* by Erich Menzel
m.: *Hellerau* Chair by Richard Riemerschmid
r.: Club chair for Villa Gerl by Hans Kollhoff

MILESTONE: *Music-Room Chair* → page **38**

# Die Collection

furniture manufacturer, Buchen / Hesse and Renningen / Baden-Württemberg, founded 1967, **www.die-collection.de**

Transformable furniture offers all sorts of advantages. Various purposes can be fulfilled without taking up any additional space. This means it's the kind of furniture that's good for small living spaces and convenient to take along when relocating. Die Collection, a manufacturing collective founded in the 1960s, specializes in these domestic miracle-workers. Such pieces are perfectly tailored to the needs of singles, for example, those modern nomads who make frequent moves and like to live in big cities where living space is at a premium. Behind the Die Collection brand are the companies Franz Fertig, a tradition-rich upholstered furniture-maker from the Odenwald region, and Bacher, a producer of tables, chairs and TV furniture based south of Stuttgart. Completing the program is case furniture from Swiss maker Betschart. The relatively difficult task the proponents have set themselves entails having all furniture conceived by external designers who usually bring their own ideas with them. Most of them are German names well-known in the industry such as **Thomas Althaus**, Gabriele Assmann, Alfred Kleene and the duo Volker Laprell and Volker Classen. The designer provenance is not showcased here, however. One of the important pieces is the *Sona* sofa, which does not at first glance reveal that it is replete with possibilities. The *Sino* easychair, which can be easily tilted back or pulled out to lounge length, is just the thing for both avid readers and TV viewers. The additive cabinet system *Uptodate* is a perfect example of a modular concept whose freely selectable widths, depths and heights make for a myriad of possible ensembles. One of its most striking features is the incorporation of upwardly angled sliding doors. An innovative solitary piece of furniture is the *Stretch* sideboard, whose length-changing flexibility supports the idea of open living by affording optical "breakthroughs".

PHOTO: *Uptodate* cabinet system by Thomas Althaus

# Erich **Dieckmann**

artist, architect and furniture designer, born 1896, died 1944

Born in West Prussia, Dieckmann undertook a short course of architecture studies in Danzig and then an even shorter art program in Dresden, and then joined the ranks of those who felt drawn to the institutionalized avant-gardism of the new Bauhaus in Weimar. In 1924, at age 28, he finished his apprenticeship exam at the cabinetry workshop and took over as temporary director the same year. He contributed a built-in cabinet to the "Am Horn" model home in 1923. Dieckmann, who along with **Marcel Breuer** was one of the most productive furniture designers in the early Bauhaus years, designed not only single cabinets but also complete rooms, including a bedroom and a man's study. Apparently, though, he didn't see much of a future for himself at the Bauhaus. When the academy relocated to Dessau, he elected to remain behind in Weimar. He proceeded to take charge of the cabinetry workshop at the newly founded Bauhochschule Weimar (Weimar Academy of Architecture), which under its director Otto Bartning likewise evolved into a centre of "Neues Bauen" (New Building) and "Neues Wohnen" (New Lifestyle). Dieckmann played a significant part in this development, although, or perhaps precisely because, he – like **Josef Albers** – did not switch to the new material of tubular steel and instead pursued his own path. He conceived programs of furniture types with which entire homes could be furnished, including for the Weimar company "Bau- und Wohnungskunst". The academy's "furniture type catalogue" of 1928 thus includes for example furnishings for a rationally designed children's room. His at once constructive and unpretentious designs were by all means innovative, as demonstrated by an armchair with an angular oak frame from 1928 that already presages the formal vocabulary of the 1950s. Although Dieckmann frequently employed high-grade woods, his furniture was still inexpensive thanks to standardization. When the Nazi Party first gained representation in the state government of Thuringia in 1930, the new director had to let the entire faculty go. One year later, Dieckmann became master at the School of Arts & Crafts in Burg Giebichenstein near Halle, where he directed the cabinetry workshop until being relieved of his post again in 1933. This era witnessed his first wicker and tubular steel easychairs (for Cebaso). In the 1930s – he lived in Berlin from 1939 – the now-marginalized designer did freelance work, including as adviser to Reich offices such as the "Beauty of Labour Bureau". Resuscitated today after long years of oblivion, Erich Dieckmann – alongside Breuer and **Ferdinand Kramer** – is considered one of the big names in early series furniture design, whose pieces once again compete with Breuer's for the highest prices at auction.

PHOTOS: l.: *8162* easychair for Cebaso, m.: Children's armchair for the Weimar Academy of Architecture, r.: Wicker chair for the Tannroda Basketweavers' Association

# Stefan **Diez**

furniture and product designer, born 1971, office in Munich / Bavaria, **www.stefan-diez.com**

He caught the public eye with installations such as "Quality Control" in which a robot "inspects" highly valuable Bustelli figurines (2004 for **Nymphenburg**). Diez is one of the shooting stars on the German design scene, but he is by no means an aloof designer-as-artist type. Before his studies he did an apprenticeship as cabinetmaker and spent a year in India, where he built furniture for companies in Bombay and Poona. After passing his exam in industrial design he worked for a few years in the studios of **Richard Sapper** and **Konstantin Grcic**, until he opened his own in Munich in 2002. His office is in the meantime – together with that of his mentor Grcic – regarded as a new force field for creative impulses. His work always starts with models and materials. The Bavarian native demands complete control over the entire development process. It is difficult to find anything extraneous in his designs, but there is nonetheless definitely nothing strained or boring about them. They instead exhibit a subtle interplay between respect for the rules and an utter disregard for convention. His *Friday* chair for example (2003 for Prosedia) is an original interpretation of bentwood à la **Thonet**, but also recalls room sculptures by Grcic and the works of an artist in wood like Hans Wegener. The seating group *Couch* (2005 for **elmarflötotto**) is likewise all about quotations. For what is in formal terms a classic cube-shaped easychair (see

*Kubus* by **Peter Keler**), Diez borrows the filling from the bean-bag chair. Exceptional in this case is the cleverly conceived structure with its inner and outer sack, which allows this lightweight piece of furniture to be manufactured very simply. Big-name manufacturers have by now caught wind of the newcomer. He has designed a coat rack called *Upon* for **Schönbuch**, and for **Rosenthal** the minimalist silverware *Tema*, the *Shuttle* household appliance series and the *Genio* wok set. An important aspect of the latter is the stove-to-table principle. This means that the wok is fit for presentation at the table in its own matching porcelain bowl, with no need to refill the food into a new container. The combination of such antithetical materials as metal and porcelain is part of the appeal of what is actually such an obviously good idea.

PHOTOS: l.: *Big Bin* container for Authentics
m.: *Bent* stool-table-easychair with Christophe de la Fontaine for Moroso
r.: *Tema* silverware for Rosenthal / Thomas

MILESTONE: *Couch* sofa and easychair → page **362**

# Dornbracht

manufacturer of bathroom taps and furniture, Iserlohn / North Rhine-Westphalia, founded 1952, **www.dornbracht.de**

When in the 1990s it began to arrange performances where fashionable creative talents such as Fabrizio Plessi of Italy or Matali Crasset of France realized what were sometimes fascinating and at other times perplexing visions, the bathroom fittings manufacturer from the Sauerland region managed to update its image in the avant-garde direction using artistic means. These activities, dedicated to exploring the "Spirit of Water", elevated the once-humble bathroom to a place where what goes on is no longer considered banal, but rather profoundly human. Hygiene as concept was replaced by buzzwords like "contemplation" and "ritual". Back when Aloys F. Dornbracht began making standard taps in the early 1950s, no one could have predicted that the enterprise would one day assume such a lofty profile. The young company was soon setting its sights on the international market, and evolved into a paragon of the Economic Miracle whose booming sales (in 1970 the equivalent of 5 million, in 2004 around 126 million euros) were readily evident from the continual expansion of the production halls. Complementing the ambitious art events is the outstanding design quality of the products. Design is something Dornbracht discovered in the mid-1980s. The turning point was the single-lever tap *Domani* – in English "tomorrow" – by Dieter Sieger, which would become one of the world's

most decorated taps. International industry greats such as Massimo Iosa Ghini, Jean Marie Massaud and Michael Graves have since contributed their signatures to the high-class product range. The collaboration with the **Sieger Design** studio has proven particularly fruitful. *Domani* was followed by further attention-getting series, among them *Meta*, *Tara* and *Mem*. The new bathroom "Designed in Germany" also featured up-to-the-minute furniture such as the cabinet beam *Space Bar* by Christophe Pillet and the transparent acrylic lounge chair *Wave* by Massaud (→ p.**430**). The *Meta Plasma* cabinet and shelf series by Sieger Design (→ p.**541**) is noteworthy for its strong colours, transparent plastic, and light effects – further elements of the modern hygiene stage whose possibilities are far from exhausted.

PHOTOS: l.: *JustRain* shower, m.: *RainSky E* tap collection
r.: *Domani* tap (all by Sieger Design)

MILESTONE: *Tara* tap → page **258**

# Drabert

office furniture manufacturer, Minden / North Rhine-Westphalia, founded 1889, **www.drabert.de**

This tradition-steeped firm, which began as a locksmith's and metalworking shop, mainly develops office chairs – one of the showcase disciplines of the German furniture industry and one in which the people of eastern Westphalia have decades of experience. As early as the 1920s, long before the topic or even the word "ergonomics" had impinged on public consciousness, Drabert built a tubular steel swivel chair whose form took into consideration the anatomy of the human body and the demands of workaday life. The *Reichspoststuhl* of 1928, known as *RP 28* for short, one of the first office chairs to be designed down to the last detail, is a prototype for its genre, a chair that could once be found more than three million times furnishing German post offices. When choosing the groundbreaking materials – tubular steel and bent plywood – the influence of the just-dawning Bauhaus movement certainly must have played a role, while on the other hand the company had already been producing furniture out of tubular steel itself since the turn of the century. The 1950s brought further innovations. The *4 K* office chair (1954 by **Egon Eiermann**) boasted the first infinitely variable height adjustment, while the *Manager* (1958) was the first chair with a movable backrest. Finally, the tilting backrest in connection with a special seat mechanism in the *Senior* chair (1960) brought a further advance in office comfort. The idea of

a "back-friendly" chair allowing for active sitting began to take shape. Drabert subsequently caused a stir again with its *SM 400* plastic chair (1968 by **Gerd Lange**), whose body-fitting form set the standard that is still followed today. Later on, tip-proof wheels (1970), synchronous tilting mechanisms and single-lever operation (1975) were introduced. In the 1990s the company became a subsidiary of the Dutch Samas Group, Europe's leading office furniture manufacturer, and is now devoting its energies not only to the ergonomically designed workplace, but also to the field of communications, with furnishings for training and conference rooms as well as for waiting and common rooms. Recent office chairs such as *Entrada*, *Salto* and *Cambio* (all by Daniel Figueroa) underscore the design-oriented approach. The conception of the award-winning seminar and conference chair *Tosila* (2004 by Büro Staubach) was based on the results of a recently completed medical study called "Mikromotiv" conducted in conjunction with European research institutes and thanks to which the company was able to demonstrate anew its proficiency in the field of ergonomic sitting.

PHOTOS: l.: *Parlando* chair by the Drabert development team
m.: *Tosila* chair by Büro Staubach, r.: *Drabert 675* chair

MILESTONE: *SM 400* chair → page **168**

# Draenert

furniture manufacturer, Immenstaad / Baden-Wurttemberg, founded 1968, **www.draenert.de**

Tables, chairs to go with them and individual furniture pieces – that sounds like quite a limited, not very exciting product range. But the family enterprise within walking distance of the Lake of Constance has developed an independent and unmistakable profile within just a few decades. The form, especially that of the tables, is oriented on classical Modernism, underscored by the predominant use of metal and glass. An early example is the **Nurglas** set of nesting tables (1972), which have now been taken up again in the program, combined with an ambitious variation in painted glass. The principles of transformation and extension in these designs also express functionalist ideas. But perhaps one can also see in them the Swabian characteristics of meticulousness, precision, inventiveness and joy in experimentation. Typical Draenert tables are *Euklid* (1998) and *Titan III* (2002), a four-person glass table whose extension panels turn it in no time into an eight-person glass table via visible swivel arms. Another successful model is the patented **Eagle** (1995), in which even the pullout panels are made of stone. These kinds of small wonderworks cause the eye to doubt physical laws each time they are witnessed. Behind the clever mechanics is often designer Georg Appeltshauser, who pushed the boundaries of seating comfort in both his doubly adjustable *Linus* chair (2004) and his cantilevered swivelling easychair *Coppa*. Numerous

designs can be credited to founder Peter Draenert, an arts and letters maven who did his doctoral thesis on Hölderlin. The recently deceased senior owner – son Patric has now taken over the business – created the dual corporate profile that unites international style with a regional consciousness. With its very first product, a table on runners called *Schiefer* (Slate, 1968), he introduced the material taken from the company's immediate environment into furniture design. He also initiated the "Steinhof" (Stone Yard), an imposing collection of over 200 unusual stone panels from all over the world. An innovation in a different material – glass – is the organically formed coffee table *Twist* by **Wulf Schneider** (2005): intelligently extendable and with three hand-blown cone-shaped legs, a virtually poetic composition. Similar to **Vitra**, the company takes an intellectual approach to its products. This has given rise, for example, to the Art Collection that has been on offer for several years now, a series of freely designed, limited-edition furniture commissioned from architects, designers and artists.

PHOTOS: l.: *Leonardo* chair by Oswald Matthias Ungers
m.: *Quadra-Tisch* table (Electronic Art Collection) by Walter Giers
r.: *1400 Casanova* table

MILESTONES: *Nurglas* nesting tables → page **194** I *Eagle* pullout table → page **268**

# Duravit

manufacturer of bathroom ceramics and furniture, Homberg / Baden-Wurttemberg, founded 1817, **www.duravit.de**

The striking silhouette of the letter "D" is both promise and program. It might represent for instance "Design" with a capital "D". The letter pops up in every single piece in the bathroom furniture series **Happy D**, while it likewise stands of course for Duravit. Founded in the early 19th century as stoneware and tableware factory, the company grew to become an internationally known brand. From the mid-1980s onward, its style was lastingly moulded by the **Sieger Design** studio, which is also the source of the iconography of *Happy D*. Another product of the same creative minds is the more recent *Ciottolo* collection. Circular or oval-shaped ceramic basins reminiscent of the natural rounded forms of water-smoothed stones are placed individually on wall-hung or freestanding washstands. Apparently, Duravit is aiming at an aesthetic similar to that represented in the other rooms of the house by brands such as **Behr**, **Brühl**, **COR** or **Interlübke**, combining highest-quality fabrication with a startlingly simple formal vocabulary. And in fact the specialists from the Black Forest have succeeded at bringing elementary forms back to the bathroom. This is associated in particular with a certain German name, which however belongs to a Frenchman: Philippe Starck. The designer has just come out with another design called *Series X*, spearheading - like **Bulthaup** in the kitchen – a paradigm change in the bathroom with his free-standing bathtubs for Duravit. The idea is to get back to basics, but on a high stylistic level. The *Caro* collection by **Phoenix Design** and the *Giorno* program designed by Massimo Iosa Ghini have a minimalist look based on the theme of the circle. In the furniture series *In the Mood* on the other hand, myriad visual effects are realized through the use of targeted lighting. *Change* is the first mirror program with light in changing colours that can be adapted to fit the desired mood. The clean lines and original ideas are conceived for the tradition-steeped company by external designers. More recent examples are the multifunctional shower by Jochen Schmiddem or the *Sundeck* bathtub by the EOOS group, which can be covered in a flash to turn it into a lounge chair.

PHOTOS: l.: *Starck Edition 1* washstand
m.: *Ciottolo* washstand by Sieger Design
r.: Multifunctional shower by Jochen Schmiddem

MILESTONE: *Happy D* bathroom series → page 286

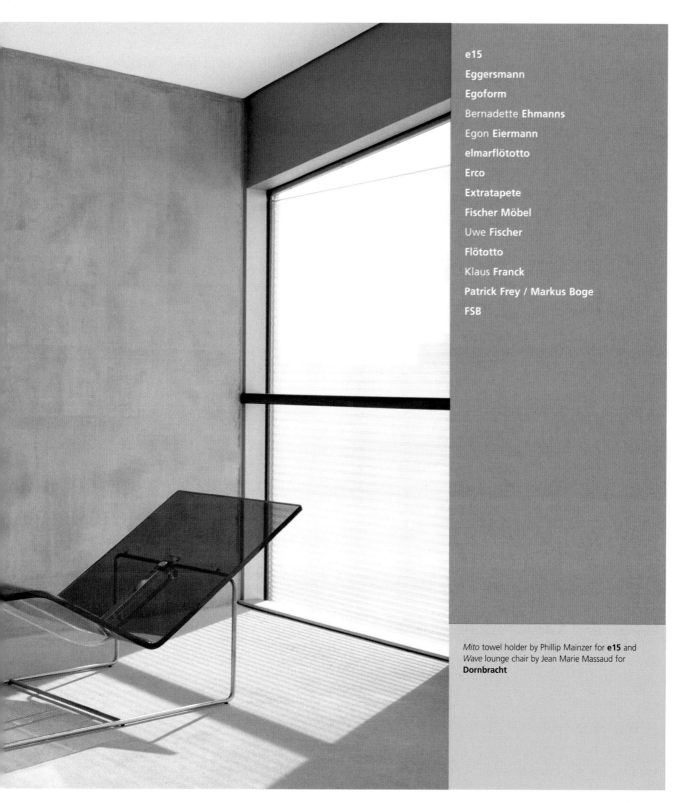

*Mito* towel holder by Phillip Mainzer for **e15** and *Wave* lounge chair by Jean Marie Massaud for **Dornbracht**

# e15

furniture manufacturer, Oberursel / Hesse, founded 1996, **www.e15.com**

The company takes its name from the postal code of the Hackney district of London in which the founders – architect Philipp Mainzer and designer Florian Asche – ran their first workshop. The two had procured old oak bridge piers and made their first four tables out of them. The wood was rough, but warm and authentic, forming a stark contrast to the shiny lacquer-and-chrome aesthetic of the time. What's more, it also formed a counterpoint to the rustic cliché of traditional furniture in oak, a material that has ever since then – along with walnut – been a constant in the company's program. A special feature is the highlighting of the knotholes with black putty. The Germans soon moved their headquarters to a town nearby Frankfurt. The first products Asche and Mainzer made in their new home, in particular the *Bigfoot* table and **Molar** (Backenzahn) stool, already attracted a great deal of attention. Today, they work with a series of external designers including Mark Holmes of Great Britain, Americans Mark Borthwick, Pilar Proffitt and Robert Bristow and Belgians Philippe Allaeys and Hans de Pelsmacker. They deliberately seek out artists to work with. Whether sideboard, bed, desk or bench, it is the consistent clean lines that make for the straightforward appeal of this product range – with noticeable echoes of 1950s modernists such as **Herbert Hirche**. The kind of tension that ensues from forward-looking design

combined with traditional workmanship is a hallmark of the brand. An essential component here is the use of literally hand-picked materials – usually solid European woods, joined by stainless steel, aluminium, leather and in recent years brass and copper as well. The composition and structure of these materials are part of the design, lending the products their singularity. E15 has in the meantime made a name for itself designing public spaces and private interiors, adding garden furniture to its program and also delving into the bathroom arena, where an alliance with specialists Alape and **Dornbracht** has given rise to some new paradigms. This trajectory is far from reaching its end, as demonstrated recently by a new sofa collection based on Oriental relaxation and serenity rituals and complemented by utensils such as trays, carpets and an abundance of comfortable cushions. The departure from all-too-strict asceticism is in evidence in the new catalogue as well, which no longer displays the furniture in a spartan ambience, but rather in the opulently sensual world of a Baroque church.

PHOTOS: l.: *PA02 Noah* bed by Phillippe Allaeys
r.: *Kast Een* and *Kast Drie* shelves by Hans de Pelsmacker

MILESTONE: *Molar* stool → page 280

# Eggersmann

kitchen manufacturer, Hiddenhausen / North Rhine-Westphalia, founded 1908, **www.eggersmann.de**

This medium-sized company is in some ways exemplary of modern German design for living. At home in the traditional furniture-making region of eastern Westphalia, Eggersmann is now in its fourth generation of family ownership. The workforce of 120 represents an operation of a size that can often be found in this industry. The brand's limited public profile is also typical – the few exceptions prove the rule – as is the strong emphasis on quality, as expressed for example in the use of high-grade materials and meticulous workmanship. This is surely one important reason for the fine reputation enjoyed by German kitchens abroad. Eggersmann is a perfect example of this phenomenon as well. Two out of three kitchens made are exported. Insiders know that the purchase cycle for a kitchen is longer than for hardly any other kind of furniture, making it an investment that must be considered very carefully. And here is where Eggersmann has found its market niche, taking advantage of the benefits of industrial production in order to individualize its products – which means that the customer's desires take priority. This is made possible, among other things, by sophisticated logistics at the factory that of course depend on a seasoned corporate culture – a feature found in every company with a design-oriented product policy. Whether functional extras or unusual fittings on the sliding or slide-in doors: special touches are a matter of course here. The company tries to keep ahead by developing new products as well. For example, Eggersmann offered the handle-less kitchen systems that are now beginning to be seen everywhere as early as 2002. The variety of colour schemes and structural variants belie what is actually very stripped-down design. Echoes of the 90-degree severity of classical Modernism can be felt as keenly as can the dominance of horizontals, a characteristic of modern modular furniture systems. The practical symbiosis found here between industrial perfection, traditional craftsmanship and minimalist formal vocabulary, which Martin Kleinhans, owner of **Performa**, has referred to as "technofacture", is perhaps the magic formula for today's innovative medium-sized enterprises.

PHOTOS: l.: Kitchen in walnut block veneer (manufacturer's design)
r.: Kitchen in brushed pine (manufacturer's design)

# Egoform

furniture manufacturer, Westerstede / Lower Saxony, founded 1976, **www.egoform.de**

The business concept was to supply the emerging "lifestyle sector", targeting customers with high design and quality expectations but limited spending power. The company's abstract, rather philosophical name – evoking the idea of self-fulfilment through home design – was intended to signal an alternative to the familiar brands. The mission has been well served by collaborations with various German avant-garde furniture designers, including **Jan Armgardt** and **Stefan Heiliger**. The company's strategy of applying quality craftsmanship in the pursuit of modern design has a tradition going back to the Werkstätten movement (cf. **Deutsche Werkstätten**) and earlier. The dominance of natural materials points to Egoform's roots elsewhere in Germany: the green or ecological movement, several decades later. And we can also trace a much earlier tradition: Commercially, Egoform has followed the direction of the "social" movement prior to World War One, when manufacturers began building sturdy furniture for the middle classes, especially the young. Its designs in solid wood for lounges and kitchens, like the *Chess* table, which comes in 29 standard sizes (plus customized dimensions on request), exemplify the orientation on customer requirements. Wicker furniture, system furniture, chests of drawers and sofas have also entered the program during Egoform's evolution into a full-range supplier. The multi-use adjustable couch *Mio*

(re-issued 2004 as *Vis à Vis*) and the roll-away, swivelling workstation cum dining table *Roll-it* (both by Jan Armgardt) are among the early multifunctional models. In 2001 the trademark rights were sold to the Steinhoff group (likewise based in the Ammerland region), but Egoform products have retained their distinctive profile. From the outset the focus has been on elegant simplicity and functionality, typified in designs like the mobile coffee table *Kayra*. This approach has, of course, absorbed the latest trends. Take for example the bench seats (2006 by Andreas Reichert) in the *Living Soul* collection. They are supplied as a corner seat, either with or without a back. This latest comeback of the tried and trusted corner seat answers a desire of many customers to slide in, pub-style, alongside the others for a cosy meal at home.

PHOTOS: l.: *Chess* table by Andreas Reichert, r.: *Mio* sofa by Jan Armgardt

# Bernadette **Ehmanns**

product designer, born 1953, office in Meerbusch / North Rhine-Westphalia, **www.hey-sign.de**

At first the product designer intended her pieces for purely decorative use. In the late 1990s New York's Museum of Modern Art exhibited Bernadette Ehmanns' felt strips woven into seat cushions. After that her cushions went into production. Indeed, the unexpected accolade from the art scene sparked a renaissance of felt, which had long suffered from the stuffy image of hats and slippers. The underestimated material was now to gain undreamed of popularity. In collaboration with Mathias Hey, Ehmanns built up a collection (under the Hey-Sign label) of products made entirely of industrial felt. Felt lends a highly distinctive visual and sensual quality to bags, carpets, accessories and seating. The appeal of her products comes in part from their soft surfaces, rich colours and light weight. Even the smaller felt items often seem to create a positive ambience in the home, despite their size. For the green-minded, her soft objects have the added bonus of being 100% natural wool. The carpet **Weaving**, one of the early creations in the range, has attained the status of a design milestone. Eight other carpet models now appear in the catalogue. *Square*, for example, consists of individual carpet tiles which, thanks to Velcro interlocking, can be configured and reconfigured with ease to suit changing pattern preferences. Ehmanns' line of small furniture consists entirely of stools. It is as if drawings from a geometry textbook had been transformed into three dimensions. *Posito* is the most ingenious. Its curved segments can be interlocked into different arrangements. More conventional felt products like seat pads, coasters, trivets or placemats also feature in the program. And we can expect to see more designs from Ehmanns. As she says herself, felt has so many applications still waiting to be discovered.

PHOTOS: l.: *Due* cushion, m.: *Big Box*, r.: *Trapee* pouf stool

MILESTONE: **Weaving** felt carpet → page **306**

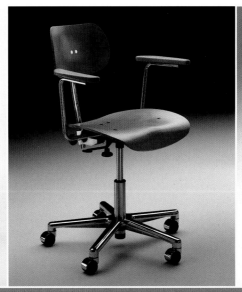

# Egon **Eiermann**

architect and furniture designer, born 1904, died 1970

The architect Egon Eiermann liked to provide total solutions. His contributions to post-war Modernism in Germany include the rebuild of Berlin's Gedächtniskirche (Kaiser Wilhelm Memorial Church) and Bonn's Abgeordnetenhochhaus (high-rise for parliamentarians). Eiermann the perfectionist often conceived his furniture as an integral part of an architectural project. A holistic approach was one thing he shared with his Danish contemporary, Arne Jacobsen. Another was a preference for plywood – although Eiermann actually experimented with this material a little earlier, following in the footsteps of designers like **Josef Albers** or Alvar Aalto. In any case, moulded plywood unleashed a revolution in chair design, and Eiermann played a much bigger role than many realize, given his relative unfamiliarity today. Most of his plywood seating came out immediately after 1950 as Germany endeavoured to make a fresh start in the wake of the country's collapse. As the "Economic Miracle" then took off, Eiermann's seats became a regular feature of public spaces, especially models SE 41, SE 42, SE 68 and SE 18 (all from **Wilde + Spieth**). Marking a clear break with the aesthetics of the Nazi dictatorship, these modern, unsentimental fixtures contributed to the young democracy's search for a new identity to an extent that should not be underestimated. Eiermann's work made a big splash in 1957 at the international building fair Interbau in Berlin. A year

later he again attracted huge attention, this time at the Brussels World's Fair for which he contributed the prize-winning German pavilion, equipping it with items like his ES 57 uplights (later from **Tecnolumen** → p.542). Appropriate materials, structural transparency and quality design were Eiermann's guiding principles. He applied them both to his buildings and his furniture, and passed on this approach to his younger collaborators such as **Herbert Hirche**. One of the most famous designs is the successful SE 18, a folding chair in beech and plywood. Its harmonious proportions and restrained curves, with legs gradually tapering out from the middle, certainly recall Danish designs of that period. In fact Eiermann provided an interface between the German and the up-and-coming Scandinavian modernist movements, a role exemplified in his early basket-chairs, like the E 10 model (today from **Richard Lampert**). The German avant-gardist also kept up with developments in America. Both his SE 42 and his stackable all-purpose chair SE 68, which combines light steel tubing and an ergonomic plywood seat, echo designs by Charles and Ray Eames. For a while Eiermann's work disappeared from the public gaze, but today his chairs, and not forgetting his ingenious cross-braced table frames, are rightfully seen as classics.

PHOTOS: l.: SE 121 chair, m.: S 197 AR office chair
r.: S 38 stool (all for Wilde + Spieth)

# elmarflötotto

furniture manufacturer, Paderborn / North Rhine-Westphalia, founded 1978, **www.elmarfloetotto.de**

The company has become a household name in Germany, where one in three consumers recognizes the **Flötotto** brand name. Elmarflötotto sees itself as an ideas business and has moved far beyond what the non-expert might associate with this name. Its program now embraces original furniture, lamps and various objects that defy easy classification. Take for example the *Fluffizoo* (by **Studio Vertijet**): the playful animal shapes in brightly coloured foam can serve as both a toy and a child's seat. In the late 1970s Anna and Elmar Flötotto took over the family company in its third generation. They soon introduced a fresh approach, setting up a furniture import agency under the Elmarflötotto label and creating their own product designs from time to time. By the beginning of the 1990s, the first collection of Flötotto designs was on the market. And a decade or so later – having completely unexpectedly taken the world by storm with their luminous *Lumibär* and then acquired the Authentics brand – the eastern Westphalian company was producing a regular program. The Elmarflötotto strategy has always been to provide a space for a relaxed, unpretentious kind of avant-gardism. To this end, it has attracted an illustrious circle of creative minds. Predominantly German, the collaborators range from newcomers like **Neunzig° Design** to established pros like **Konstantin Grcic** and Vogt + Weizenegger. Among the most remarkable

pieces of furniture are the flexible, simple yet extremely comfortable plastic chair *Wait* (by **Matthew Hilton**), the container shelving *Big Bin* (→ p.**425**), and the lounge suite *Couch*, whose simple looks belie surprising sophistication (both by **Stefan Diez**). The company's top-sellers have included *Freddy* (by **Hertel & Klarhoefer**), a shelf system in the tradition of *FNP* (by **Axel Kufus** → p.**248**) and *Endless Shelf* (by Werner Aisslinger → p.**266**), which employs a novel network structure. Since the boards come in only two formats, it can be quickly assembled in countless arrangements. Much like the **Koziol** brand, Elmarflötotto has brought together the right design expertise for its project of offering a novel repertoire of shapes and colours that banishes boredom and the clichés of neomodernism. So the lack of a common thread running through the program is no accident, although there is no mistaking a certain fondness for the Swinging Sixties. A swirling example: *Flowerpower*, the ventilator with a difference.

PHOTOS: l.: *Diva* bar stool by Hopf and Wortmann
m.: *Flowerpower* ventilator by Heckhausen and Zetsche
r.: *Fluffizoo* seat and toy object by Studio Vertijet

MILESTONES: *Freddy* shelf system → page **350** | *Couch* sofa and easychair → page **362**

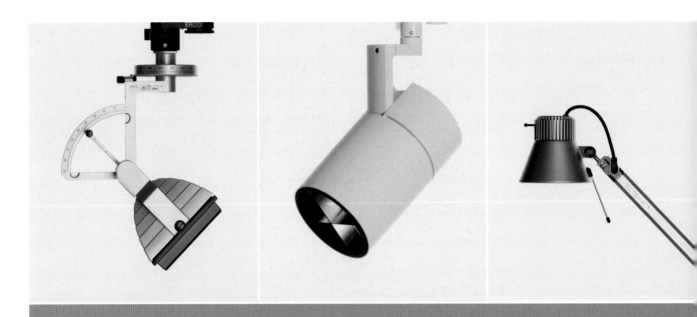

# Erco

lamp manufacturer, Lüdenscheid / North Rhine-Westphalia, founded 1934, **www.erco.com**

In the early 1960s, Klaus Jürgen Maack joined a company that was making high-quality kitchen and bathroom lighting. The new man prophesied to a flabbergasted management the impending collapse of their business if they failed to change course. Thereupon they came up with new systems that soon conquered the then burgeoning market for architectural lighting solutions. The thinking behind Erco's maxim "We sell light, not lights" marks an ingenious paradigm shift. The company has cultivated an intellectual relationship to its product in a similar way to, say, **FSB** or **Wilkhahn**. Erco's rationalism ultimately has its roots in the Bauhaus and in Ulm. **Otl Aicher**, a co-founder of the Ulm Academy of Design, has long worked as a consultant to the company, having previously served **Braun**, Lufthansa and FSB. Erco's communications style remains exemplary. Its soberly intelligent customer journal Lichtbericht has become an icon. Another aspect is the extraordinary continuity of its product range. An expression of the carefully evolved corporate culture is the purpose-built production complex, called the Lichtfabrik (Light Factory), an architecturally acclaimed complex in Lüdenscheid. The company has developed into a specialist for complex lighting requirements. When star architect Richard Meier recently created his glass envelope and museum for the Ara Pacis (the first modern edifice in Rome's historic centre for many years), he

brought in the German high-end manufacturers. Another big project was lighting for the coal washing plant at the Zeche Zollverein mine complex in Essen, now a cultural centre. The industrial heritage site is a showcase for design and architectural excellence. Always internationally oriented, Erco has collaborated with creative minds like British designer Roy Fleetwood or the Dane Knud Holscher. And Italian Mario Bellini designed the extremely versatile modular spotlight family Eclipse, which evokes the appearance of a medium-format camera. But this genre of unadorned technoid beauty is nonetheless a peculiarly German contribution to world design. The sober light machines find their iconographic reflection in the neutral black-white-grey of their maker's corporate design.

PHOTOS: l.: Quinta floodlight, m.: Parscan spotlight, r.: Lucy desk lamp

MILESTONE: *TM* spotlight → page **200**

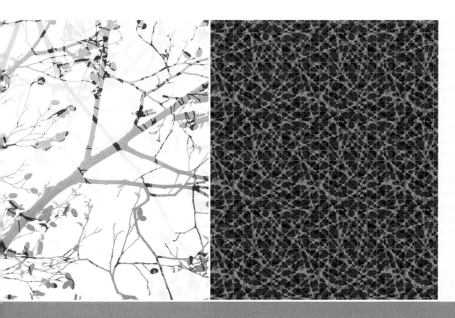
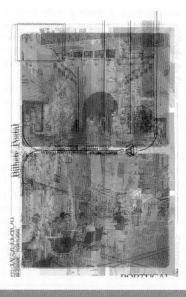

# Extratapete

wallpaper manufacturer, founded 2001, Berlin, **www.extratapete.de**

It all began with a collecting craze. Graphic designers Kathrin Kreitmeyer and Matthias Gerber initially pursued a purely intrinsic interest in the shapes and patterns they found on wrapping paper or old wallpaper scraps – a kind of graphical "objets trouvés". The idea of producing their own wallpaper designs would have been inconceivable, given the costs of the complex production methods traditionally used. Only with the help of a family-run business with a passion for experimentation did this dream become reality. They succeeded in developing a novel technique that was much simpler, allowing small exclusive print-runs, and tapped new markets that no longer depended on the standard distribution channels. And so began their very own collection. The two newcomers found a market niche in an industry which had grown dull. There were few really exciting products, even though German manufacturers like Erfurt or **Rasch** had once rung in the modernist changes in wall coverings. Since 2002 Extratapete has been creating wall coverings in limited editions in East Berlin's Prenzlauer Berg, a quarter buzzing with subcultural energy. The new method, which allows for patterns of up to two metres in length and picture wallpaper in varying formats, has several advantages: not only can the designers produce almost unlimited motifs without being restrained by mainstream taste, but they are also given new scope for trying out variable interior design concepts. As a new format, Extratapete has introduced a series of panorama borders. In addition, they offer four in-house collections which use both graphic and photographic images. Collection One consists of geometric patterns, while Collections Two and Four play with floral motifs, given an abstract feel through special effects like blurring, overlaying or bleeding so that they work well as a background. Collection Three reflects the designers' original approach: randomly reclaimed printed images, like the page of an atlas or a tea towel, are transformed and defamiliarized by being enlarged. What's more, Extratapete has made wall coverings mobile. With the right paste, the non-woven fleece strips can be easily taken down, so wallpaper hanging becomes like picture hanging.

PHOTOS: l.: *Kimiko* wallpaper, m.: *Jo* wallpaper
r.: *Pedro* wallpaper (*Collection 3*)

MILESTONE: *Kollektion 3* wallpaper → page **360**

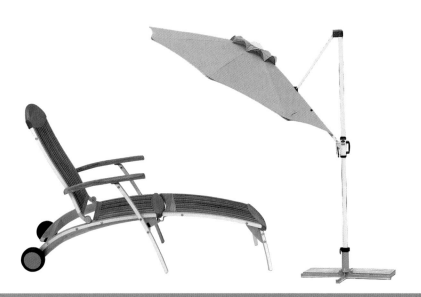

# Fischer Möbel

garden furniture manufacturer, Schlierbach / Baden-Wurttemberg, founded 1984, **www.fischer-moebel.de**

For a long time, garden furniture was sorely neglected by designers. Exotic exceptions, like the *Garten-Ei* (Garden Egg) by Peter Ghyzcy, only prove the rule. But now the Fischer brand has taken its place alongside wickerwork specialist Dedon as a major pioneer in this seasonal segment of the furniture trade. In the 1990s Fischer succeeded in dragging leisure furniture out of its anonymity, thanks to programmes like *La Piazza* (by Karl-Leo Heitlinger) or ***Tennis*** (by Kurt Ranger), giving its products the status of an exclusive collection. The folding *Tennis* armchair is now even regarded as a classic. What set this line apart from the others is the novel combination of a wooden frame in teak, polyester webbing and stainless steel fittings (for the folding mechanism and the rear bar between the armrests). The wide-ranging program now includes a somewhat smaller adjustable armchair, a stackable chair, a lounger, two round dining tables (with stainless steel inserts), a trolley table and a sideboard. An example of pure simplicity is the lounger *Swing*, an in-house design that combines stringency in form and comfort in use, thanks not least to its ample width and adjustable back positions. Its name comes from the accompanying armchair: a cantilevered design in polished stainless steel that adapts the famous archetype for open-air conditions. Outdoor logistics are also well served by the prize-winning variable table *Domido* (2003, by

Kurt Ranger). It can be assembled into five different table sizes, as required: from a small 90-centimetre one to the largest, a dinner table measuring almost three metres in length. The base panels and steel elements easily connect up to form the desired table with a continuous top. The Swedish designer Kerstin Hörlin-Holmquist has used solid teak in her *Eden* series – a furniture architecture that proclaims its traditionalism. Finally, a very novel approach is taken in the lightweight *Air* (2004, by **Wolfgang C. R. Mezger**) – a chair whose dynamically angled seat and back sections are completely shrouded in fabric. The white and silver weave is drawn over like a stocking, lending both comfort and harmony in appearance.

PHOTOS: l.: *Centro* lounger by Karl-Leo Heitlinger, m.: *Futuro* sunshade r.: *Air* chair by Wolfgang C.R. Mezger

MILESTONE: *Tennis* garden furniture → page **256**

# Uwe **Fischer**

product and furniture designer, born 1958, office in Frankfurt / Hesse

After graduating in design, Uwe Fischer was given a choice between the discipline of supplying the mass market and the arbitrariness of one-offs. He chose a middle route and joined up with a fellow student, Achim Heine, to launch Studio Ginbande – a project that (much like **Andreas Brandolini**) was to make some profound contributions to "New German Design" in the 1980s. The objects they created in that period amounted to his manifesto for the rethinking of objects of everyday use. Take for example their idea of folding furniture that disappears into the floor, or their circular children's sofa with inwardly dangling legs (now **Anthologie Quartett**). Probably their best-known design is the accordion-style table-and-benches set called *Tabula Rasa*, which can be extended from one-and-a-half to five metres in length (now **Vitra**). For the German-Swiss manufacturer Vitra they also created the table system Nexus and a space-saving folding stool. Ginbande broke up in the early 1990s, but Fischer has continued designing furniture and lamps. His rotating shell chair *Sina* (1999 for B&B Italia) has been a long-running hit on the market. Fischer, who has also created interiors for museums, trade fairs and restaurants and temporarily held a university chair in Interior Design, has always been interested in the architectural context of his creations and the centrality of light. For the lamp manufacturer **Serien** he developed not only the exalted hanging lamp *Take Five* but also the multi-purpose floor lamp *Jones*, which can be extended upwards for use as an uplight. This functional versatility is at first glance concealed by its sober design. The same is true of a new ceiling lamp in glass, also for Serien, which has a lightweight and sparse construction yet can be fitted, insect-proof, flush with the ceiling. Another strength of this model is the warmth of its illumination, achieved by a differentiated "mixed light". The model comes in thirteen variations and is ideal for smaller rooms that require the right lighting from inconspicuous sources.

PHOTOS: l.: *Jones* lamp for Serien, m.: *Sina* easychair for B&B Italia
r.: *Nexus* table system for Vitra

MILESTONES: *Tabula Rasa* table and bench → page **238** I *Take Five* hanging lamp → page **260**

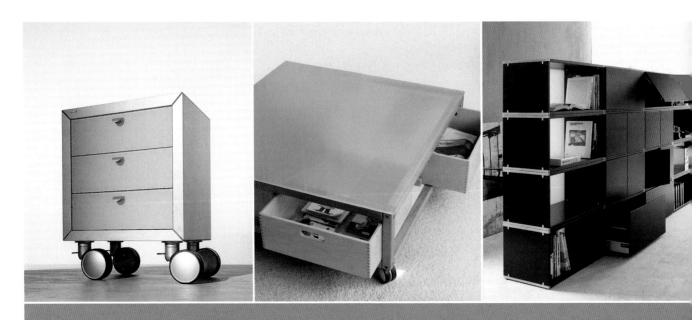

# Flötotto

furniture manufacturer, Gütersloh / North Rhine-Westphalia, founded 1906, **www.floetotto.de**

Founded in the furniture-making region of eastern Westphalia, the company began by specializing in products for the bedroom. It was restructured after World War II to become a "Schulmöbelfabrik", now focusing on the school furniture sector. But by the 1960s there was another change of direction. This time the business developed into a flagship of West German post-war Modernism. Ever since, the company has pursued a characteristic corporate style, supplying furniture for home, school and office. Some Flötotto programs have gone on for decades almost unaltered. Among these perennial favourites are *Profilsystem* (introduced in 1975) and *Personal Colour* (1984). *Profilsystem* in particular demonstrates the principles of system and module, applied here as a solution for every type of room. More recent products include *Lite*, *Unic* and *Kvaro*. When the company began selling a classroom desk ex-works in 1970, it discovered the advantages of direct marketing (launching a webshop as well in 2000). **Elmarflötotto** was then spun off as an independent business. At the end of the 1980s, Flötotto opened its own stores in major city locations. Meanwhile, the brand never lost its huge presence in Germany's schools and universities. However, the company went insolvent in 2002 when the main investor pulled out. It then reverted to a family business and currently employs about 110. As a furniture brand leader in Germany,

Flötotto is a name familiar to one in three people in its home market. Better-off consumers still put its products near the top of their wish lists. All its furniture is still assembled in Germany. This is regarded not only as an important factor in quality assurance but also as an economic advantage: short delivery distances, optimized logistics and rapid response to customer demands. Recently, the company has sought to associate its products with cultural contexts. In 2006, for example, a film premiere was used to launch *Kvaro* (by **Justus Kolberg**). A documentary on the artist duo Christo and Jeanne-Claude was screened in the company's stores. And, in the same year, this classic children's furniture brand marked the thirtieth TV anniversary of the popular German cartoon figure Biene Maja by issuing a special collection for the nursery.

PHOTOS: l.: *System* Lite container, m.: *PS* coffee table
r.: *Kvaro* cabinet system by Justus Kolberg

MILESTONE: *Profilsystem* cupboard system → page **198**

# Klaus **Franck**

furniture designer and graphic artist, born 1932

Actually, he wanted to be jazz player. But Klaus Franck thought it would be better to try something "sensible" and took up architecture, studying for a few terms at Brunswick in the 1950s. After switching to the newly founded Ulm Academy of Design, he never looked back. Those years of intensive study were interrupted by a one-year scholarship in Rio de Janeiro, where he got to know the architect Oskar Niemeyer, and found himself playing gigs with Brazilian musicians. In 1959 the freshly graduated designer wrote a book on exhibitions and began exploring new creative dimensions. His unusual carrier took a new turn from 1962. As the lead interior designer for Lufthansa, Franck's task for seven years was to shape the airline's offices and aircraft interiors. Those years of constant travelling obviously gave him valuable international experience. 1971 then saw him move – after an interlude at **Vitra** – to **Wilkhahn**, a company that had repeatedly reinvented itself and was now looking for some "Ulm" inspiration. Franck, now approaching forty, took charge of the design department, founded just two years earlier. He was given a broad and open-ended brief as an art director in the manner of an **Otl Aicher**. Franck developed a colour scheme, created a new font called *Frutiger*, and advocated the principle that product design should start with an analysis rather than a desired look. A crucial factor behind the success of this all-rounder was his close relationship with the entrepreneur and design enthusiast Fritz Hahne. Franck also returned to university from time to time – as a guest lecturer at various design schools, including the Bauhaus (then still in the GDR). In the early years at Wilkhahn he acted as a mediator between the company and the external designers, almost of all of whom came from the Ulm school. At the end of the 1970s, his inspirational collaboration with colleague Werner Sauer produced what is probably one of the most important Wilkhahn products, the **FS** swivel chair. Other collaborative designs followed, including *Basis*, *Cubis*, *Tubis*, *Thema* and *Modus*, all becoming familiar names in the industry and all winning prizes. Klaus Franck, who later became head of the **Wiege** studio in 1985 before going solo in the 1990s, is a major protagonist of West German Modernism whose unorthodox career belies all the clichés about designers. Today, well beyond retirement age, he still works on his own projects and again finds time for music – as a percussionist in a steel band.

PHOTOS: l.: *Modus* chair collection, m.: *Cubis* easychair
r.: *Versal* chair (all for Wilkhahn)

MILESTONES: *FS-Linie* office chair → page **206** | *x-act* table system → page **278**

# Patrick Frey / Markus Boge

product and furniture designers, born 1973 and 1972, office in Hanover / Lower Saxony, **www.frey-boge.de**, **www.patrick-frey.de**

The little plastic woodpecker, just five centimetres tall and clipped onto the back of a file, brings a bit of colour and wit to the often humour-free zone of the workplace. Patrick Frey and Markus Boge, the originators of this exotic office bird, seek to develop simple solutions and then create products that are easy to use. The idea itself is hardly new, but its consistent application can lead to something novel. The maxim of "simple but not simple-minded" seems to work for Frey and Boge. They both studied design in Hanover until 2002 and, two years later, formed a creative partnership that lasted for three highly successful years. Their twin concept of simplicity was apparent from the outset in two pieces they had submitted for their degrees: The office table **Kant** and the shelving system *Marketing* are both strikingly coherent solutions (both for **Nils Holger Moormann**). In the case of *Kant*, the sharp fold at the back creates additional storage space and adds to stability. The height-adjustable *Marketing*, which can be assembled without tools and was inspired by the principles used in market stalls, proves that modern variations on Germany's ever-popular theme of system furniture are still possible, and in a way that is visually out of the ordinary. A later addition was *Trick Stick* (→ p.**29**), a wardrobe consisting of just three wooden beams that simply leans against the wall, stabilized by its own weight. Other manufacturers soon took note of Frey and Boge. **Magazin**/Manufactum brought out their minimal wall-mounted drawer *Wandsinn*, Bree a shoulder bag, and **Richard Lampert** a serving trolley. The young Cologne company Skia began large-scale production of their eccentric sunshade *Camerarius* with its multiple umbrellas curving upwards. The elegant eye-catching shade-makers have proved a solid commercial success. Other Frey and Boge prototypes are still awaiting a producer, like a stackable chair consisting of two bowed surfaces, which they developed in collaboration with plywood specialist Becker, and a neo-romantic garden bench with integrated street lamp.

PHOTOS: l.: *Marketing* office furniture for Nils Holger Moormann
r.: *Camerarius* sun umbrella for Skia

MILESTONE: *Kant* desk → page **326**

# FSB

door-handle manufacturer, Brakel / North Rhine-Westphalia, founded 1881, **www.fsb.de**

"The invention of the door is just as important as the invention of tools, the wheel or fire", contends architecture critic Wolfgang Pehnt in a book sponsored by the design firm FSB ("Drinnen und draußen" in: *Zugänge – Ausgänge*, ed. by **Otl Aicher** et al. 1987). The makers of stylish door-handles have succeeded in raising the object of their trade above the mundane. They have given an everyday device a cultural, indeed anthropological meaning. It all started, once again, with Otl Aicher, the Ulm-educated mentor of West German design culture as the man who laid down the conceptual guidelines for companies like **Braun**, **Erco** and Lufthansa. A workshop arranged by FSB's manager Jürgen W. Braun in the design-conscious 1980s marked the beginning of a creative process that would ultimately culminate in designer branding. What emerged was an exclusive collection of door fittings conceived as an integral part of a broader communications strategy, just as the far-sighted Aicher had envisioned. The creative process took five years. Every detail was examined and re-examined. From the logo to the corporate typeface, from the adverts to the invoices – nothing was left to chance. The new FSB profile included a highbrow book series dealing with meta-themes like the "language of hands", various architectural issues or the "mythology of functionalism". Sixteen volumes had already been published by the time the company celebrated its 125th

anniversary in 2006. Aicher even laid down four "commandments" for the art of gripping. It might sound like there has been little scope for individual creativity. But far from it: The Weserbergland-based company, one of the biggest in the industry with 1,300 employees, has built up its own universe of door-handles and fittings – a product range that is second to none and extends to backplates, door-knobs, door-stops, furniture items and window grips. The core of the collection contains designs by Johannes Potente, an engraver by trade. His early FSB door-handle models, including the enduring *1034*, apply the soft canons of 1950s and 60s design aesthetics. Today, they are not only best-sellers but can also be found in the permanent collection at New York's Museum of Modern Art. In fact, the museum exhibits all the "authors" who have contributed to the famous German brand: from Mario Botta, Peter Eisenmann and Christoph Ingenhoven, to Erik Magnussen and Jasper Morrison, to **Dieter Rams** and Philippe Starck. With or without authoring, FSB continues to elaborate every detail of door fittings. The latest products introduced by the eastern Westphalian company are its series of glowing LED rosettes, flush-mounted rosettes and "barrier-free" handles.

PHOTOS: l.: *1020* door-handle by Johannes Potente
m.: *1138* door-handle by Dieter Rams, r.: *2339* door-knob by Philippe Starck

MILESTONES: *Bauhaus Door-Handle* → page **52** | *1034* door-handle → page **108**

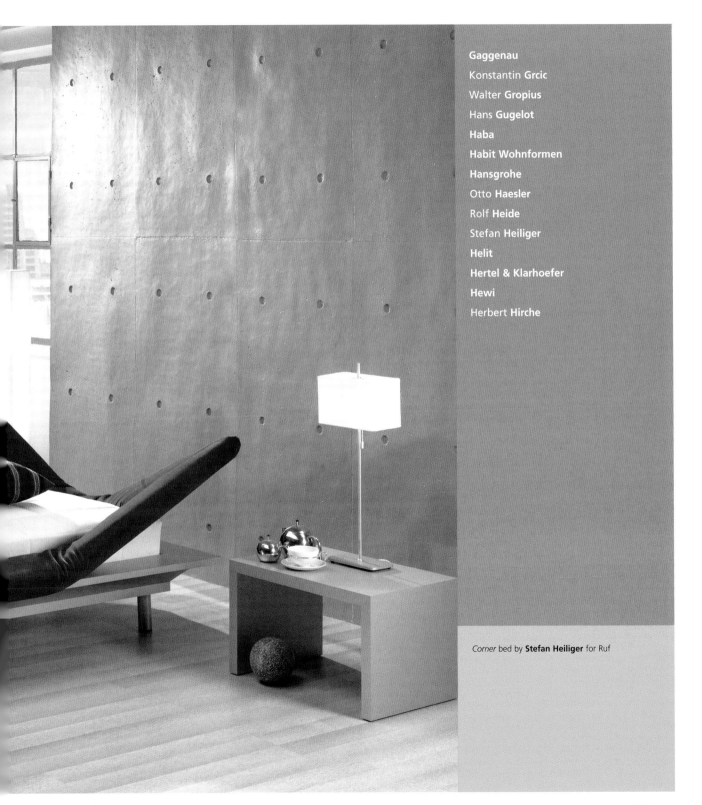

Gaggenau
Konstantin **Grcic**
Walter **Gropius**
Hans **Gugelot**
**Haba**
**Habit Wohnformen**
**Hansgrohe**
Otto **Haesler**
Rolf **Heide**
Stefan **Heiliger**
**Helit**
**Hertel & Klarhoefer**
**Hewi**
Herbert **Hirche**

*Corner* bed by **Stefan Heiliger** for Ruf

# Gaggenau

kitchen appliances manufacturer, Gaggenau / Baden-Wurttemberg, founded 1960, **www.gaggenau.com**

Whether whisper-quiet fans, spacious ovens, air-cleaning catalysts, intelligent cooker controls or air extractor systems – if you are interested in technology-based innovation and design in the kitchen, you cannot ignore Gaggenau. The high-end suppliers from Baden transfer the standards of restaurant-grade kitchens to the modern home. Take, for instance, cooktop zones: they have almost turned the kitchen road map into a philosophy, realizing that timing and organization are crucial to sophisticated cooking. The firm originally grew out of Eisenwerke Gaggenau, which in Imperial Germany built traditional enamelled steel oven housings and later went on to make bicycles. The new business came to specialize in ovens and ranges, like the energy-saving "Sparherde", a series from the late 1920s that expressed the latest functional style of the times. But it was not until the 1960s that Gaggenau really went stylish, mutating into a design-led company. The order of the day was technicism, as defined by **Braun**, and timelessness. This approach has fitted in well with the principle of anonymity, something Gaggenau has adhered to ever since. The company refuses to indulge in designer hype, even though the roster includes stars like freelancer Jacob Jensen (a long-time collaborator with the Danish cult phono brand Bang & Olufsen), who has lent the finishing touches to the styling of many appliances. Yet one can hardly miss the Dane's preference

for smooth surfaces and flush jointing. Gaggenau is a brand with genuine design and technology credentials, uncompromising in its application of quality standards to home kitchen systems. The figures tell their own story. Gaggenau employs over 550 people worldwide and is represented in some fifty countries. Sales in 2004 reached around 130 million euros, with the German market contributing 32 million. The pursuit of design excellence has earned the company numerous awards. The program now comprises ovens, combi-steam ovens, electric and gas cooktops, ventilation systems, dishwashers, refrigerators, freezers and microwaves. In 1995 Gaggenau became a subsidiary of BSH Bosch and Siemens Hausgeräte GmbH, Munich. The brand's original premises now serve as Gaggenau's training centre and exhibition space, including a large cooking workshop. People come here from all over the world: Gaggenau clients, consumers and staff.

PHOTOS: l.: *Vario 200* product series, m.: *SK 535* refrigerator
r.: *EB 388* built-in oven

# Konstantin **Grcic**

product and furniture designer, born 1965, **www.konstantin-grcic.com**

His international reputation as the ultimate exponent of German thoroughness doesn't bother him at all. On the contrary, he thinks it points to the essence of his work. Take the "Ideal House" that Grcic conceived in 2002 for the Cologne Furniture Fair: This mighty cavernous structure consisting of stacked shelves is a massive symbol of rationality and systematization, while also demonstrating the diversity of design options available. His early tables, chairs, shelf units, cabinets and desks seem reserved and sober, but they always hold a few surprises – whether it be their unusual proportions or the materials used, such as compressed wood, corrugated iron or steel. It is no accident that some of the designs, like the secretary desk *Orcus* (for **ClassiCon**), evoke more than a hint of the English furniture tradition. In fact, Bavarian-born Grcic learnt cabinet-making at the John Makepeace School in Devon, studied at London's Royal College of Art, and then worked as an assistant to Jasper Morrison. All in all, a very strong dose of English realism. Grcic has therefore been a conduit for those intercultural influences that have been invigorating German design ever since **Henry van de Velde**. Notwithstanding his self-declared love affair with "everyday and anonymous things", the prestige designer has shown a strong appreciation of the experimental – for instance in his folding coat stand **Hats Off** for **Nils Holger Moormann**. For the same manufacturer he has

also designed other pieces of ingenious minimalism, like the shelf system *Es*, always leaning but quite secure. Grcic is also interested in exploring the application of industrial processes, as seen in his *Chair_One* (for Magis): Sitting on a cone-shaped pedestal, the entire seat was made in die-cast aluminium, something never done before. For this innovation he invented a novel skeletal shape which even today causes dismay in a positive sense. Designs like **Diana** and **Mars** (for ClassiCon) work with variations on the principle of geometric interlocking. The German furniture designer has long grown into an all-rounder. The everyday objects he has created range from drinking glasses (for littala) and kitchen appliances (for Krups) to items as inexpensive as mechanical pencils (for Lamy). The table service *Coup* (for **Rosenthal**) grew from a modest tableware project into a whole system: a collection of 37 porcelain and four glass pieces and a pot that integrates metal and porcelain. The multi-purpose concept is also applied here, where plates can serve as lids, recalling a functionalist tradition in German porcelain.

PHOTOS: l.: *ES* shelf system for Nils Holger Moormann
m.: *Chair_One* chair for Magis, r.: *Grcic* glass series for littala

MILESTONES: *Hats Off* coat stand → page **294** | *Diana* occasional table series → page **332** | *Mars* easychair → page **342**

# Walter **Gropius**

architect, furniture and product designer, born 1883, died 1969

As the founder and first director, he coined the name of what is probably the world's most famous school for art, architecture and design: the Bauhaus. In his programme there in the mid-1920s he demanded a new aesthetic language limited to "typical basic forms". The concept had already been applied in the "Typenmöbel" (modern furniture based on standardized elements) of the **Deutsche Werkstätten**, but in radicalizing it he effectively became the midwife of modern design. Before World War I he worked for two years at the office of **Peter Behrens**. His contribution to the Fagus factory, as early as 1911, produced not only one of the first examples of the new architecture but also some remarkable furniture for its interiors – including delicately ascetic armchairs and settees (today from **Tecta**). What is needed, said Gropius, is the "sparse integration of all the parts without reliance on the old clichés". He saw his interiors like "Direktorenzimmer" (Director's Office, 1923) or "Meisterhaus" (Master's House, 1926) as laboratories of a future lifestyle. He equipped the director's room with his own furniture, including the famous cubic armchair **F 51**, a desk with glass shelving, and a meandering newspaper rack. Without Gropius, the history of furniture would have been very different. After all, in his four years from 1921 as "master of form" in the Bauhaus cabinet-making department he taught the likes of **Joset Albers**, **Marcel Breuer**, **Alma Buscher**

and **Peter Keler**. The way his birthday was always marked by a round of imaginative celebrations illustrates the esteem in which the mentor was held by his students and colleagues. Gropius was a driving force behind the "Neue Sachlichkeit" (New Objectivity). Like his own teacher Peter Behrens, he played the role of a design manager, before the concept really existed. He knew how to exploit the potential of events like the opening of a Bauhaus building in Dessau in 1926. Among his own product designs, which were actually not at all numerous, the cylindrical door-handle **1102** (1922) has come to acquire iconic status. By contrast, his "Einheitsmöbel", a set of standardized furniture created in 1929 for a Berlin department store, has sunk into oblivion even though it anticipated in striking detail some of the universal concepts of the 1950s propagated by **Michael Bayer**, **Herbert Hirche**, **Peter Raacke** and others. Gropius emigrated to London in 1934 where he was head designer at the Isokon furniture company for three years, while also working on his own furniture projects, before moving on to the United States. In American exile Gropius gained enormous fame with his building projects. Alongside Breuer and **Ludwig Mies van der Rohe** he became the majordomo among the architects of his generation. The tea service **TAC 1** (1969 for **Rosenthal**) is a late one-off of exceptional coherence.

PHOTO: Settee and armchair for the Fagus factory, 1911 (re-issued by Tecta)

MILESTONES:  *F 51* easychair → page **48**  I  *Bauhaus Door-Handle* → page **52**  I  *TAC 1* tea service → page **174**

# Hans **Gugelot**

architect, furniture and product designer, born 1920, died 1965, **www.gugelot.de**

As the creator of the radio and record player combination *SK 4* (**Braun** 1956), nicknamed "Schneewittchensarg" (Snow White's Coffin), he launched a new era in home listening appliances in the mid-1950s. But more than this, Hans Gugelot introduced a new cool, technical aesthetic into the modern living room – a paradigm shift equivalent to the introduction of tubular steel furniture in the 1920s. Gugelot came to prominence through his relationship with the Braun company. In the 1950s its products were revolutionized by this pragmatic pioneer. At that time, the Dutchman, who grew up in Switzerland, was also lecturing in product design at the highly influential Academy of Design in Ulm. It was in his department at the design school that the concept of the phono "building blocks" first arose, i.e. the modules that ultimately became the modern hi-fi system. Just as forward-looking, but less well-known, were his furniture designs. He tended to think in terms of interconnected systems, following on from the "Typenmöbel" idea of classical Modernism (see e.g. **Marcel Breuer** and **Deutsche Werkstätten**) – an approach that fitted in seamlessly with ideas being pursued at the Ulm school. In fact, his earlier cabinet system *M 125* clearly shows he had already been applying this concept back in Switzerland. Constructed according to a strict grid, it is the archetype of all variable wall units – shelving being one of the disciplines in

which German furniture designers have most excelled. At the 1957 Interbau exhibition in Berlin his *SK 4* drew wide international attention along with its associated system of tables, desks and beds. M 125 was produced by **Bofinger**, the company that later produced Gugelot's folding wall unit and easy-to-disassemble easychair (today from **Habit**). A number of innovative products, like beverage crates made of plastic or the programmatic stool *Ulmer Hocker*, also emanated from his genius. He went on to design beds and children's furniture. This creative mind said that "thinking what has never yet been thought" constituted the decisive step in the design process, which could not be taught. Although apparently not a particularly gifted teacher himself, his ideas have lived on in his students. They include some major designers of the next generation such as Rido Busse, **Hans "Nick" Roericht** and Reinhold Weiss.

PHOTOS: l.: *GS 1076* armchair for Bofinger (re-edition: Habit)
r.: *PKG-1* audio cabinet for Braun

MILESTONES: **M 125** cabinet system → page **106** I **Ulm Stool** → page **120** I **SK 4 / Phonosuper** phono combination → page **122** **GB 1085** bed → page **126**

# Haba

children's furniture and toy manufacturer, Bad Rodach / Bavaria, founded 1938, **www.haba.de**

It all began with those colourful little building blocks every child knows. They are still to be found in Haba's catalogue, but since those days the old "factory for exquisite wooden playthings" has developed into a supplier of everything children might want in their own room. With as many as 28,000 different items, it offers an unrivalled realm of products. The "Erfinder für Kinder" (Inventor for Kids), in the words of the brand slogan, has a sixteen-strong team for developing and designing innovative products in-house. The program ranges from children's furniture systems and individual pieces, like the versatile foam fun-seater *Reptilo*, to carpets, mirrors and Haba's own assortment of imaginative lamps and clocks, including the slate clock with a face on which kids are invited to chalk up the numbers. Haba pursues a wide variety of child-centred themes, even selling products that are already covered by the big toy-makers like Lego or Playmobil. There is a princess desk along with a football-goal bed, and even a whole ensemble of pirate furniture including a snuggly ship sofa complete with mast and sail. Haba's child-oriented products share a recognizable aesthetic: Graphic and zoomorphic motifs are playfully combined with a vocabulary of elementary geometric shapes. The environmentally conscious choice of materials – dominated by safe laminated woods and plywoods, fabrics, leather, cardboard and felt – also lends a clean modern look we

otherwise associate with avant-garde furniture-makers like **Jonas & Jonas**, **Nils Holger Moormann** or **Performa**. With Haba products, families can create a whole children's universe at home, carefully thought out and functional in every detail. For instance, the legs on Haba furniture can be height-adjusted by means of coloured rings. This means that the tables and chairs can "grow" along with the child.

PHOTOS: l.: *Puck* stool, m.: *Käptn's Corner* bed
r.: *Nautilus* wall cupboard

# Habit

furniture manufacturer, Kürten-Engeldorf / North Rhine-Westphalia, founded 1971, **www.habit.de**

One idea pervades Habit's entire product range: combining simple forms with maximum utility. There is no secret about the origins of this concept. The company's founder, Ulrich Lodholz, was formerly with **Bofinger**, the furniture-makers who became a leading force in the post-war modernist trend in West Germany. So it is hardly surprising to find that – alongside products developed in-house, like the explorable *Living Landscape* (by Tata Ronkholz-Tölle) – nearly all the Bofinger classics found their way, at some time, into the Habit program after the former avant-garde manufacturer collapsed in the economic crisis of the 1970s. Many Habit pieces were designed by the ingenious **Hans Gugelot**, including the archetypal system wall unit *M 125* (no longer in production), the back-to-basics bed *GB 1085*, and the self-assembled easychair *GS 1076* (→ p.**451**) with its springy backrest, which is a prime example of intelligent constructivism. Although Habit's attempt at a re-edition of Helmut Bätzner's *Bofinger Chair* was almost as exciting as its premiere, in the end it had to be aborted due to technical problems. Habit has also produced new versions of furniture from the American Shaker sect, regarded as pioneers of modern minimalism. These items include the comfortable, meticulously reconstructed rocking-chair *F 151*. Focusing on design and marketing, the company from the Bergisches Land region has its products manufactured externally. A number of current designs are in metal, including the garden furniture *Skwer* (by Alfons Bippus and Otto Sudrow), which integrates industrial grids and is totally weatherproof, an office container program, and an aluminium table (by Arnold Bauer) whose extremely pared-down form makes it an all-rounder in its applications. A genuine innovation is the quick-change artist *plug.table* (2005 by Matthias Demacker). The tubular steel legs of this dining-cum-work table can be turned 90 degrees and reinserted into the tabletop to turn it into a low coffee table on U-shaped runners. Reduced to three components, the table can be assembled without any tools. Here, the spirit of minimalism, represented by Bofinger and Gugelot, has been unswervingly translated into a product for today.

PHOTOS: l.: *Alu-Tisch* by Arnold Bauer
r.: container program by Arnold Bauer

MILESTONES: *M 125* cabinet system → page **106**  I  *GB 1085* bed → page **126** I  *Living Landscape* → page **170**

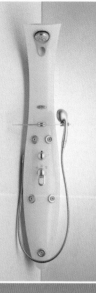

# Hansgrohe

manufacturer of bathroom fittings, Schiltach / Baden-Wurttemberg, founded 1901, **www.hansgrohe.com**

The company from the Black Forest region was the first in the bathroom supply industry to bring in external product designers. Its collaboration with the young Hartmut Esslinger began back in the late 1960s. The founder of the international agency Frog-design made an early career move when he began working with the Swabian firm. His very first design for the company, the compact three-phase shower head *Tribel*, made an immediate impact. It was the first head with a 360-degree swivel – an innovative concept that proved highly marketable and soon won design accolades for Hansgrohe. Since then, awards have mush-roomed. Like its competitor **Dornbracht**, Hansgrohe has also made design an integral part of marketing and corporate culture. Its products are divided into three different brands. Under the name Hansgrohe it sells solid, functional bathroom technology. Pharo stands for deluxe "shower temples" serving a new market for preinstalled shower units – a sector of the industry that Hansgrohe itself has defined. The company's most design-centred brand is Axor, offering a whole series of "lifestyle lines". After Esslinger had shaped the house style into the 1980s, including a major success with the one-hand faucet **Allegroh**, the **Phoenix Design** studio took up the creative reins. Known for its minimalist approach, the Stuttgart studio has authored designs that include taps and mixers like **Arco** and *Talis*.

International star designers Philippe Starck and Antonio Citterio have also contributed complete bathroom collections. But long before the onset of the designer age, the company was already an innovator. At the end of the 1920s it developed a metal hand-shower with a porcelain grip that became a best-seller. In the 1960s Hansgrohe came out with *Selecta*, the first hand-shower with adjustable jets. A more recent development is the advanced showerhead **Raindance**, a hand-shower with a much wider head diameter but shorter handle. It forms part of a complete shower system that uses the latest air whirling tech-niques to offer a continuous spectrum from a hard jet massage to soft rain.

PHOTOS: l.: *Axor Citterio* tap by Antonio Citterio
m.: *Tribel* hand-shower by Hartmut Esslinger
r.: *Helis* shower panel by Phoenix Design

MILESTONES: *Allegroh* tap → page 218 | *Arco* tap → page 250 | *Raindance* shower → page 334

# Otto **Haesler**

architect and furniture designer, born 1880, died 1962

In 1906 he moved from Frankfurt to Celle and set up his own business. It was a time of rapid industrialization and economic expansion in the small town in the Lüneburger Heide region of northern Germany. Local biscuit factory owner and urban developer Harry Trüller became a mentor for young Otto Haesler, supporting his efforts to shape the emerging townscape. Haesler designed a large number of modern buildings until forced to flee by the Nazis in 1934. His clean-lined architecture, which developed out of the critique of Jugendstil, was to feature brief reactionary forays into the home-preservation and neo-classical styles. Haesler's holistic approach was clearly visible as early as 1911 in the Berggartenstrasse housing estate project. Here, he left nothing to chance, even designing the interior decoration and stipulating garden layouts. Pursuing this total design concept in the 1920s, Haesler concentrated on building good but inexpensive housing for ordinary people. His overriding aim was "light, air and sun for all". He became a pioneer of linear "Zeilenbau" developments and supplied models for a rational housing style purged of all superfluous decoration. This even included a thorough reform of the kitchen, as seen in his Celle "Versuchshaus" (pilot house) or in Villa Steinberg. His Georgsgarten development of 1926 was an early and widely praised example of "Neues Bauen" (New Building) and brought him national

recognition. As a member of an association of progressive architects called "Der Ring", he became a leader in the "Modern Movement", comparable to **Ferdinand Kramer** in Frankfurt or **Karl Schneider** in Hamburg. Another housing estate project at Dammerstock in Karlsruhe saw him join forces with **Walter Gropius** to plan the implementation. Here, Haesler used his own furniture designs for the first time, equipping the interiors with *celler volksmöbeln (cvm)* – ""well-built metal furniture at a low price". The Hanover-based artist Kurt Schwitters created the advertising material for these "Typenmöbel" – standardized pieces mainly constructed from lacquered tubular steel frames and plywood boards. He designed chairs, stools and tables with an extremely austere feel. His chair *No. 2*, for example, displays a stripped-down, graphically incisive structure in which the tubing rises as rear verticals and then descends sharply to form the front legs. At the same time Haesler began marketing standardized houses for owner occupancy. His ideas for improving people's homes were sometimes criticized as too dogmatic, but the radical innovator was determined to serve broad sections of society with his designs – something he probably achieved better than any of his contemporaries in those years.

PHOTOS: l.: Entrance hall in Haesler's house
r.: Interior with *celler volksmöbeln*

# Rolf **Heide**

interior, furniture and exhibition designer, born 1932, office in Ahrensburg

His photographs are familiar in Germany. The powerful and sometimes inspiring interiors he once composed for catalogue and adverts by **Bofinger**, **Thonet** or **Duravit** form part of the collective memory of the design-conscious public. Take, for instance, Philippe Starck's one-off bathtub from 1994. It might never have become an icon without Heide's photographic visualization in a rustic ambience. His carefully arranged compositions are sometimes said to be more important than his own furniture designs. But that would fail to recognize his impressive record as a furniture and lamp designer. He has designed products for renowned manufactures such as **COR**, DePadova, Wohnbedarf, **WK Wohnen**, **Vorwerk** and, more recently, **Interlübke**. Having trained in both cabinet-making and interior design, Heide began using his skills in magazine publishing. For the women's title *Brigitte* he regularly composed and shot the "Brigitte-Zimmer" room, offering visions for home furnishing. He moved on to *Schöner Wohnen*, Germany's biggest-selling and, at the time, trend-setting domestic lifestyle magazine. **Peter Maly** and **Siegfried Bensinger** also worked in this role for the periodical. "In the sixties, if you couldn't afford an Eames, as an aficionado of quality you might treat yourself to something from Rolf Heide", wrote a design critic, describing Heide's role with a note of irony. For there is no doubt that he has been one of the outstanding figures of the German design world. Just why the versatile Heide has been so regularly ignored in the literature is hard to understand. Perhaps it is because his profile just doesn't fit the usual job description of a designer. His own pieces include a trolley table (as an alternative to the traditional tea trolley), a playhouse for children, folding chairs (for the home) and a wooden kitchen (for **Habit**). For **Bulthaup** he wrote and designed a book on the kitchen as a living space. "Far too much of what is designed is superfluous", writes the man from northern Germany with a preference for minimalist solutions, reprimanding his fellow designers. Some of his creations are now considered classics, like the *Stapelliege* stacking lounger from the 1960s (now from **Müller Möbelwerkstätten**), the variable *Sofabank* and the modular wall unit program called simply **Container**. Heide, whom colleagues sometimes regard as an "aesthetic pedant", is rigorous in his pursuit of mobile, unconventional and uncomplicated furniture for living. This is exemplified in his *Container-küche* from the early 1990s, which transfers the principle of rolling bookcases from the library to the kitchen.

PHOTOS: l.: *Travo* cabinet and drawers system for Interlübke
r.: *Travo* chair for Interlübke

MILESTONES: *SL* cabinet system → page **148** | *Stacking Lounger* bed → page **166** | *Container* cabinet system → page **184**

# Stefan **Heiliger**

furniture designer, born 1941, office in Frankfurt a.M. / Hesse, **www-heiliger-design.de**

Every self-respecting designer will want to conceive a chair at some time in his or her career. But only a few have made this supreme discipline in the world of design the hub of all their professional creativity, as Stefan Heiliger has done. The fact that he manages to move between the poles of maximized comfort and careful cost control can be understood by looking at his background. Heiliger, whose father was a sculptor, has run a studio for furniture design in Frankfurt since the late 1970s, but before that he worked for several years in the automotive industry. More than once he has been ahead of his time. At the outset of the 1980s he built armchairs with serial spring steel bars, made early use of webbing fabric and developed a folding sofa (1986 for Strässle). This period also saw his first successes with the rocking lounger *Aigner Collection* (for Hain + Thome) and the functional easychair **Spot** (for **WK Wohnen**). Heiliger is an empiricist and experimenter. He first runs tests series to explore the conditions for optimized sitting. If a small-scale model works, he then quickly moves on to life-size pieces. The results of his furniture R&D have found their way into the programs of big-name European brands, including Leolux, Pro Seda, **Rolf Benz**, Strässle and Wittmann. Other important designs include the amazingly sparse functional sofa *1600* (1997 for Rolf Benz) and the sofa bed *Sidney* (1999 for Interprofil),

which turns neatly into a sleeping surface by twisting the seat and back sections. Just in time for the new millennium, the designer brought out his own collection, which contained the round cocktail chair *Basic* and the rocking lounger *Canguro* (later from Leolux). Heiliger's lines and proportions are usually sophisticated and sometimes dynamic. He can produce veritable seating machines, like the armchair *3100* (for Rolf Benz). Here, the adjustment of the back, the angle of the seat and the extension of the footrest can all be coordinated from a single knob. The inventor of form and line has now turned his attention to a new field: the bed *Corner* (2006 for Ruf → p.**446**) has an outer frame with corners that can be turned up. Two people can have breakfast in bed, facing each other, while during the day the bed is transformed into an island of relaxation. Calling into question the entrenched rituals of the traditional bedroom, this multi-purpose bed meets new needs in the modern home.

PHOTOS: l.: *3100* armchair for Rolf Benz, m.: *Akka* easychair for Leolux
r.: *Basic* easychair for Heiliger Collection

MILESTONE: **WK 698 Spot** easychair → page **244**

# Helit

office equipment manufacturer, Kierspe / North Rhine-Westphalia, founded 1897, **www.helit.de**

Originally a blacksmith's workshop, the company switched to bakelite office products in the 1920s. Much later it became a design-led business using a new generation of thermoplastics. In 1961, the founder's grandson Hansfriedrich Hefendehl took command and changed course. Like **Braun** a decade earlier, he cultivated contacts with the Ulm Academy of Design. Walter Zeischegg, who taught product design and geometry, became a permanent consultant to the company. An advocate of systematic design, he helped Helit to develop some 70 products – right up into the 1980s. Zeischegg-inspired products that became familiar worldwide during that era include the hexagonal desktop pen container and the stackable "wave ashtray" **Sinus**. For a long time it was these classics that put the Westphalian company on the map. In the early 1990s the American Gillette group bought out the family business, having already acquired the German design brand Braun. But the Americans soon sold it on, and Helit now belongs to Maped, a leading French maker of school and office products. Since the end of the 1990s the expanding manufacturer has joined the ranks of those putting their cards on designer branding and it now associates its high-end products with interior design ideas. **Wulf Schneider**, for instance, has authored Helit's intelligent presentation systems. One of the latest creations comes from England's star architect Norman

Foster, who has contributed a complete line of desktop utensils. Whether the note box, hole-punch, clock or tape dispenser, on the desk Foster's box-like shapes give the impression of monolithic building blocks. For zanier objects Helit has brought in the Italian Stefano Giovannoni. His little colourful items for office or home – like the magnetic cactus to which paper clips cling, or the see-through hollow fox terrier for holding pens – remind us that work can be fun.

PHOTOS: l.: Desk clock from the collection *Foster* Series by Norman Foster
m.: Serving trolley by F. A. Porsche, r.: Pen container by Walter Zeischegg

MILESTONE: *Sinus* stacking ashtray → page **162**

# Hertel & Klarhoefer

office for architecture and furniture design, Berlin, founded 1999, **www.hertelklarhoefer.de**

Their collaboration goes right back to the playroom. As toddlers they used to build homes for Smurfs out of Lego bricks. Peter Christian Hertel and Sebastian Klarhoefer went on to study architecture in Berlin in the early 1990s. But only toward the end of the decade, each having gained valuable experience in various architecture offices, did the two friends start working together professionally – not, however, in their original vocation but instead in furniture design as a new challenge. In 1999 the two creative minds first presented their shelving concept at their own stand at the Cologne Furniture Fair. The patented unit came on the market in the same year as *webweb* (→ p.**568**), produced by **Zeitraum**, later becoming available in a choice of materials. This all-purpose system, which has something of the magic of Lego bricks about it, can be just as functional in the kitchen as in the office or children's room. It allows for unlimited combinations and takes an honoured place in the long line of impressive shelf units by German designers – the latest ranging from **Endless Shelf** (→ p.**266**) (**Werner Aisslinger**) to **FNP** (→ p.**248**) (**Axel Kufus**), and *Screen* (**Performa**) to **Plattenbau** (→ p.**346**) (**Kaether & Weise**). The Berlin duo's expertise in this field was again demonstrated by their remarkably successful system **Freddy** (2004 for **elmarflötotto**, 2007 as *Freddy Plus*) and more recently by their shelf unit *Daidalos*, named after the

ancient inventor, architect and artist. The latter's tubular steel frame offers stability without diagonals (2006 for **ClassiCon**). The Greek reference here is no accident: Hertel & Klarhoefer say explicitly that they want to create modern classics of lasting value. Indeed, their designs have a cool and matter-of-fact feel that is mirrored in the sobriety of a company name that simply combines their surnames. The two designers have recently been exploring new terrain. For elmarflötotto they created the shiny formica-topped table *Straight* and the stacking bed *Marcel*, a piece of such uncompromising simplicity that it can rival milestones like **Hans Gugelot's** *Minimalbett* (now from **Habit**) or **Rolf Heide's** *Stacking Lounger*.

PHOTOS: l.: *Freddy* shelf system and *Harry* table for elmarflötotto
m.: *Daidalos* shelf unit for ClassiCon, r.: *Marcel* bed for elmarflötotto

MILESTONE: *Freddy* shelf system → page **350**

# Hewi

door-handle manufacturer, Bad Arolsen / Hesse, founded 1929, **www.hewi.de**

The plastic door-handle is a German innovation. And it's a textbook example for what a wide variety of requirements a new invention must fulfil if it is to meet with success. When the button and plastics factory from northern Hesse began producing door-handles made of polyamide instead of metal toward the end of the 1950s, hardware stores – the major sales channel for door fittings at the time – at first reacted warily. It took a change of generations for the new material to come into its own: In the mid-1960s, Rudolf Wilke joined the family enterprise. The son of the founder had occupied himself with plastics during his engineering studies and was therefore not only in a position to assuage retailers' fears, but also able to develop product forms and manufacturing processes suitable for the material's inherent properties. A major order – for the interior fitting of the new university buildings in nearby Marburg – finally assured the newfangled product its breakthrough. The architect wanted to create a total solution, i.e. to closely coordinate forms and colours in the interior design. Plastic was the perfect answer. The year was 1968, a time when Pop Art and the synthetic material of plastic were suddenly gaining social respectability – a trend that Hewi helped to instigate. Rudolf Wilke finally developed the door-handle *111*. This ur-model by no means had a completely revolutionary form, but rather a U-shape singularly appropriate to the

material. It thus fulfilled one important principle of good design, and is today an unusually widely known classic. Wilke took this handle as the springboard for a growing product family, a system entirely along the lines of the Ulm School. The simple formal vocabulary was copied again and again. Later on, after collecting a sizable number of design awards, Hewi substantially expanded its product range. The door-handles were joined by new lines such as bathroom accessories, electronic lock systems and signage. A new focus was on "barrier-free" products, such as the *LifeSystem*, which provides safe and comfortable bathroom use for the disabled. In its original business, door-handles, Hewi has likewise ventured onto new terrain. Now stainless steel plays a key role. In combination with aluminium, it has given rise to yet another innovative design in the *180 C* series.

PHOTOS: l.: *126* door-handle, m.: *DV 499* door-handle
r.: *115* door-handle (from the *111* series)

MILESTONE: *111* door-handle → page **182**

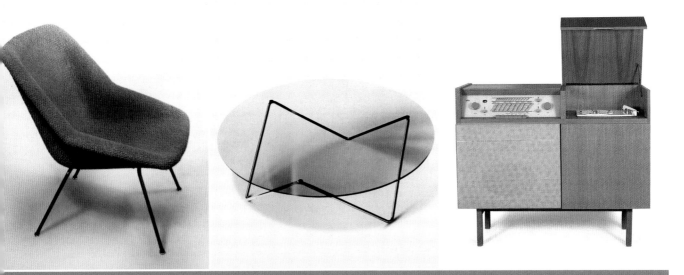

# Herbert **Hirche**

architect, furniture and product designer, born 1910, died 2002

What would have happened if his plans to establish Mannheim as a second Bauhaus-oriented university after Ulm hadn't failed? Notwithstanding this setback, Bauhaus student Herbert Hirche is, next to **Egon Eiermann** and **Hans Gugelot**, one of the key figures in German post-war design, with demonstrated success at adapting classic functionalist concepts to changing lifestyles. The young architect was able to gather a great deal of experience while working in Eiermann's office starting in 1939. After the war he worked for architect Hans Scharoun, wrapped up in projects for rebuilding Berlin. A co-founder of the Verband deutscher Industriedesigner (Association of German Industrial Designers), Hirche helped to shape the domestic world of the "golden" post-war decades; less so in his original occupation than as a gifted teacher as well as a talented furniture and product designer. He saw to it that in the young republic a counterprogram to the prevailing sedate conservatism could develop and prosper. Hirche spearheaded Modernism at a number of prominent firms, among them **Braun** and **Wilkhahn**. In the process, his architectural mindset was probably behind the dominance of the cube in his designs, that rational symbol that is already in strong evidence in early pieces such as his *Tiefer Sessel* (Deep Easychair, made today by **Richard Lampert**) and *Barwagen* (Bar Trolley, for Christian Holzäpfel). The same pared-

down linearity is echoed in his sideboards and his phonographs (for Braun). The Braun *HF 1* television is an icon that seems to escape the otherwise exceedingly brief aesthetic half-life in this field. The flowing forms in his shell and basket chairs, on the other hand, demonstrate the Scandinavian influence that still held sway over the design of this period. Starting in the 1950s, Hirche designed a whole series of modular additive cabinets and shelves, placing him squarely in that very German tradition of systematization. Among the first of these were *DHS 10* (for Christian Holzäpfel), the *LIF* cabinet series and the famed Inwand room divider. These were followed by the furniture ensemble *6000* (for **Behr International**) and an acclaimed multipurpose functional wall unit for **Interlübke**. Other focuses were children's and office furniture (for Christian Holzäpfel). Hirche's flexible and yet highly orderly systems led de facto to the overcoming of the traditional solitary furniture piece. But their main aim was something else again: The versatile pragmatist Hirche wanted to provide people with greater freedom to shape their own environments.

PHOTOS: l.: Shell chair for Walter Knoll
m.: Glass table for the Akademie-Werkstätten Stuttgart
r.: *HM 1* audio cabinet for Braun

Ingo Maurer
Interlübke
Interstuhl
JAB Anstoetz
Jehs + Laub
Jonas & Jonas

*Travo* cabinet by **Rolf Heide** for **Interlübke**
und *Hob* easychair by **Studio Vertijet** for **COR**

463

# Ingo Maurer

lamp manufacturer, Munich / Bavaria, founded 1966, **www.ingo-maurer.com**

He is one of the few greats in his metier, with a distinctive, unmistakable signature running through his entire oeuvre. The lamps created by light poet Ingo Maurer are three-dimensional metaphors. They have names like *Mozzkito* or *Wo-Tum-Bu*, plays on words that are meant, like the lamps themselves, to break up the monotony of mundane everyday life with a touch of cleverly conceived whimsy. *Wo bist Du, Edison, ...?* (Where Are You, Edison, ...?) for example consists of a hologram captured in a lampshade. The principle is the apparent bulb within a bulb. This iconic 20th-century idea has become an ongoing theme with Maurer. The career of the ingenious formal inventor, who has achieved the kind of lasting success on the international stage that few others can boast, began in the 1960s. In those days, "good form" was the measure of all things design-wise. *Bulb* – a bulb within a bulb again – attracted a great deal of attention: a pop object à la Claes Oldenburg with chrome-plated base and crystal shade. Maurer, who went to the USA following studies in graphic art, was strongly influenced by the new art currents there. Back home again, he founded the company Design M, one of the first in Germany to include what is today such an omnipresent Anglicism in its name. Since then Maurer has been designing meta-lamps that not only illuminate their surroundings but also shed light on their own significance. This can be said,

for example, of a successful lamp from the 1980s: *One From The Heart* (→ p.**27**), a heart-shaped floor lamp whose light is reflected back by means of a mirror. In the late 1990s came **Zettel'z**, a hanging lamp whose shade is made up of slips of notepaper. *Birds Birds Birds*, switched on at a touch, was also ahead of its time. Maurer is a master of eliciting the poetry of materials, whether working with layers of silver-coated paper in *Oh Mei Ma*, goose feathers in the flying light bulb *Lucellino* (→ p **158**) or the wire netting he often uses. While the early lamps tended to be handcrafted, he later began to prefer a high-tech look. Maurer's great breakthrough came in the mid-1980s with the much-copied low-voltage halogen system **YaYaHo**, a completely new lighting concept that soon became a classic. Cables traversing the room carry lamps that are reduced to points of light. The nearly immaterialized lighting system seems just as abstract as the "Light Module" from Bega, but at the same time as thoroughly functional as the spotlights produced by **Erco**. *YaYaHo* echoes the virtual world of digital networks that have left rigidity and mechanics behind them. Maurer's product poetry on the highest level represents a style that simply cannot be pigeonholed.

PHOTOS: l.: *aR* floor lamp, m.: *Campari Light* hanging lamp
r.: *Bulb* table lamp

MILESTONES: *Bulb* lamp → page **158**  |  *YaYaHo* ceiling lamp → page **222**  |  *Zettel'z* hanging lamp → page **284**

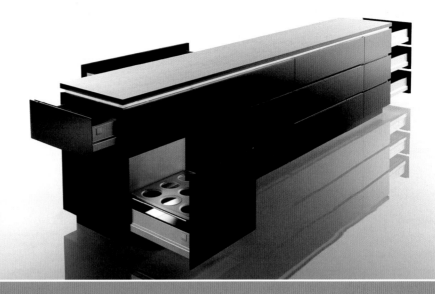

# Interlübke

furniture manufacturer, Rheda-Wiedenbrück / North Rhine-Westphalia, founded 1937, **www.interluebke.de**

The fact that a down-to-earth furniture manufacturer managed to create one of the great German furniture brands, one that almost one out of two Germans are familiar with, is one thing. That this success can be credited to an ambitious design strategy, is another. Coincidence had something to do with both aspects. The company founded by the Lübke brothers from the Westphalian town of Wiedenbrück, originally specializing under the name Gebrüder Lübke in high-polish bedroom suites, discovered in Leo Lübke a visionary entrepreneur who already ventured to bring in a modernist back in the 1950s: **Michael Bayer**, a university lecturer in the neighbouring town of Detmold. Bayer first revised the corporate identity, and then the entire product range. His comprehensive Interlübke furniture system ultimately gave the company a new and memorable brand name. The next decisive step was taken at the beginning of the 1960s, when the endless cabinet system *SL* (by Team Form) gave the eastern Westphalia company its ticket onto the international stage. Later, the new Team Form AG also designed the walk-in *Aparo* closet as well as the *Studimo* shelf grid. A further milestone in company history, and a very typical product of its time, is the functional wall by **Herbert Hirche** that caused such a furore in the late 1970s. Here, some of the most important functions of the home are hidden behind sliding doors. Leo Lübke had in the meantime

hired the young **Peter Maly**, first as art director for catalogues and trade fairs, and later as designer as well. His incisive Duo cabinet system from the 1980s already excited considerable interest. The company responded to an intervening crisis period, reflected by an unfocused profile and poor balance sheet, by overhauling the entire product line starting in the year 2000. **Rolf Heide** contributed the *Travo* cabinet system (2002, → p.**456**), which can be hung up, stood up or stacked up at will, as well as a revised version of the *SL* wall unit. The product offensive also included the *Case* container trolley and *Cube* cabinet system by **Werner Aisslinger**, as well as two new designs by Maly. With the highly variable *Medio* hi-fi furniture and the *Contrast* shelf system, in which horizontals dominate, the old master managed to create yet further new furniture types. Finally, the *EO* cabinet system with its multicoloured interior lighting (2001, by **Wulf Schneider** and Stephan Veit) brought the firm enormous publicity. This light cube featuring a programmable coloured light show was the first piece of furniture able to react to the owner's mood.

PHOTOS: l.: *Aparo* wall unit system by Team Form AG (detail)
r.: *Cube* cabinet system by Werner Aisslinger

MILESTONES: *SL* cabinet system → page **148** I *EO* cabinet system → page **318**

# Interstuhl

chair manufacturer, Messstetten-Tieringen / Baden-Wurttemberg, founded 1930, **www.interstuhl.de**

Under the literary-sounding motto "The Lightness of Sitting", and with an elaborate light installation, the manufacturer from the Schwäbisch Alb region made a splash at the Orgatec 2006 office furniture show with one of the largest exhibition stands, thus demonstrating a whole new self-confidence and the ambition to establish itself amongst the leading brands in the industry. When the company celebrated its twenty-millionth chair in 2004, this was merely a station along the way. With a current annual production of 800,000 chairs, the next record is already in sight. The family enterprise from southern Germany, which burgeoned in the late 1950s with work chairs for seamstresses working in the textile industry, has boasted impressive production figures for a long time now. It fits in well with this picture that the company's Bimos brand is the market leader in industrial work chairs – products which however have no public profile. Although Interstuhl chairs have always kept up with the latest innovations in ergonomics, with features such as lumbar support or synchronized mechanics, the brand name, by contrast with companies such as **Drabert** or **Wilkhahn**, has never been associated with innovative design. The corporate profile, which also entailed a high level of environmental awareness, was not visible in the products. It was not until models such as *Xantos* came out (by **Reiner Moll**) that first-class engineering and con-

struction were coupled with a distinctive look. The folding chair *X & Y* (by Emilio Ambasz) and the *Converso* universal chair (by Claudio Bellini) are on a comparable design level. Finally, **Silver** (2004, by Hadi Teherani, Hans-Ulrich Bitsch and Ulrich Nether), an aluminium-shell office chair that packs a considerable optical punch, gave the brand image a real boost. The status object became a favourite prop for TV productions. Less spectacular, but just as groundbreaking, were designs such as **Sputnik** (2005, by **Votteler & Votteler**) and *Axos* (2006, by Reiner Moll), which aim at opposite market poles. While Sputnik can offer an optimal price/performance ratio thanks to clever structural refinements, *Axos* is a chair geared for the executive suite, combining elegance with deluxe comfort. A new concept for custom chairs has now been introduced under the label "interstuhl manufactur", bringing fine materials and surfaces into play to offer the kind of extravagance that has been completely unknown up until now in the office chair realm.

PHOTOS: l.: *X & Y* chair collection by Emilio Ambasz
m.: Sofa (*Flirt* furniture collection), r.: *Mitos* office chair

MILESTONES: *Silver* → page 330 | *Sputnik* office chair → page 358

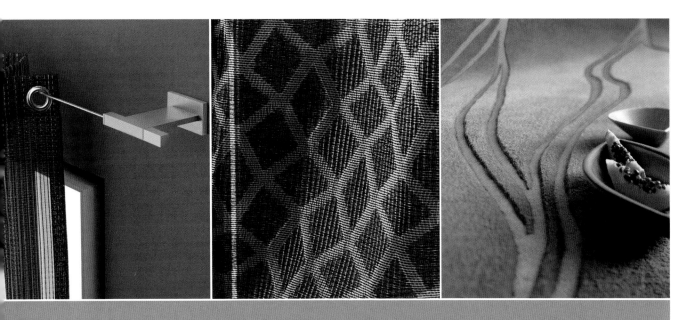

# JAB Anstoetz

fabric editor and carpet manufacturer, Bielefeld / North Rhine-Westphalia, founded 1946, **www.jab.de**

By means of aggressive marketing, which combines the company name with the face of Ralph Anstoetz, the Westphalian firm has emerged from anonymity into the limelight during the last few years. This entailed a metamorphosis from a more traditional fabric editor to a supplier catering to a clientele looking for high style and quality of life. It was only logical that design would play a large part in the new corporate image. After all, the possible applications of textiles in interior design are virtually endless: from drapes to upholstery, from tablecloths to carpets. The JAB Group, which encompasses the Bielefelder Möbelwerkstätten as well as the design brand **Carpet Concept**, is a full-service supplier in this realm and, with some 1,300 employees and a turnover well over the 200-million-euro mark, an industry leader. Specialties including a horsehair collection or high-tech textiles such as the extremely easy-care Color Protect furniture covers, demonstrate the company's desire to provide exclusive products on a high level of technical sophistication. As an incisive unique selling proposition to help stand up to the global competition, the firm created a design ambience in the 1990s that is very difficult to copy. An important step toward documenting its creative competence was the **_Design Edition_** in 2000. Here, designer carpets were promoted on a scale never before seen in the industry. Carpet series in which the rectangle formed the framework for a wide variety of interpretations were supplied by Rodolfo Dordoni of Italy, Ross Lovegrove of England, Pascal and Mikael Mourgue of France and the Germans **Konstantin Grcic** and **Peter Maly**, all of them members of the champions' league in their metier. The collaboration with Marty Lamers of the Netherlands, a designer/artist and longstanding employee of **Ulf Moritz**, was also part of this strategy. This association resulted in the 2004 _Showroom_ collection, which features surprising combinations of materials and has since been re-issued three times. The unusually comprehensive _Metropolitan_ curtain rod system conceived by Maly and his partner Carsten Gollnick set new standards with its variability and formal stringency. Other designers who have supplemented the range of contemporary carpets, winning awards in the process, are Elke Klar, **Christian Werner** and **Studio Vertijet**.

PHOTOS: l.: _Metropolitan_ curtain rod system
m.: _Cross_ fabric, r.: _Wave_ carpet

MILESTONE: **_Design Edition_** carpet collection → page **310**

# Jehs + Laub

office for product and furniture design, Stuttgart / Baden-Wurttemberg, founded 1994, **www.jehs-laub.com**

"The weather, the bars, the beautiful furniture. We wanted to move to Milan immediately." Markus Jehs and Jürgen Laub still go into raptures when they talk about their first visit to the Salone del Mobile. As it turned out, they ended up first completing their studies in industrial design in Schwäbisch Gmünd, wrote a joint dissertation in the early 1990s and then soon set up a studio in Stuttgart instead. But their experiences in Italy bore fruit, because the clientele for the lamps and chairs they were soon presenting at international furniture fairs included several big-name Italian firms such as Cassina, Nemo and Ycami. "The way the Italians work suits us very well", explains Jehs. "Once a design has been chosen, no effort is spared to make the idea a reality." The results include the sofa group Blox (for Cassina), a seating architecture in which the theme of the cube, one of the idioms of postmodernism at the latest since **Peter Keler**, has been reinterpreted in a masterful fashion. The *S 555* chair (for **Thonet**) derives its appeal from the contrast between its rectangular surfaces and the three-dimensional indentations at pelvis height. In the meantime, the Swabian designers' fine reputation has also spread northward. For the well-known Danish manufacturer Fritz Hansen, the Stuttgart natives designed a shell-based easychair called *Space Chair*. Jehs + Laub demonstrate an amazingly deft touch when handling the basic three-dimensional shapes. This thoroughly "German virtue" is something they put into practice in a way that's all their own and on various scales, whether in their coat rack programs (for **Schönbuch**) or the *Size* series (for **Renz**) of office tables and cabinets of monumental simplicity.

PHOTOS: l.: *Space Chair* easychair for Fritz Hansen
m.: *Corona* hanging lamp for Nemo, r.: *4000* collection for Thonet

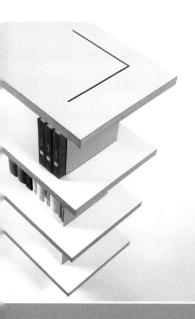

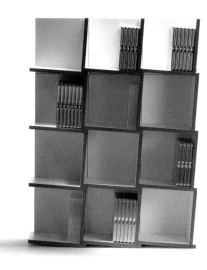

# Jonas & Jonas

furniture manufacturer, Vilsbiburg / Bavaria, founded 1998, **www.jonasundjonas.de**

The *Tri* shelf unit (by Markus Honka), whose signature optical feature is its offset boards, is built by simply sticking the pieces together. Height and width are virtually unlimited. It consists of only a single element type and needs no special parts: an astoundingly constructive brand of minimalism. "Ideas come when you walk through the world with your eyes wide open", Hubertus Jonas explains. The graduate in business administration with long years of experience in the furnishings industry founded a design-oriented company in Lower Bavaria with his wife, Ellen, into which to pour the sum of their experiences and contacts. Each job begins with an exacting briefing in which the spirit and purpose of the planned design are discussed in detail. After that, nothing takes place without the designers' input. The entire development and further development of the products is coordinated closely with their authors, who usually come from Germany. A leitmotif is furniture that can be easily assembled and rearranged – if possible without tools – to quickly adapt to the needs of the user. The focus is on shelves and tables. A unique furniture range has come about in this manner within just a few years, distinguished by ingenious ideas, formal rigour and modern materials – an unobtrusive avant-gardism similar to that found in the products of **Kaether & Weise**, **Nils Holger Moormann** or **Performa**. Particularly worthy of note are designs such as the two quite different standing desks Piensa and **Nudo** (by Bernd Benninghoff and Karsten Weigel) along with *Wallflower* (by Markus Honka), a mini-shelf made of bent plastic that leans against the wall supported on metal legs, casually but with guaranteed stability. The *Lizz* folding table (by Martin Dettinger and Christian Hoisl) is as easy as can be to fold and unfold. *Grupo* (by Meier Thelen) introduced an entire system of small furniture pieces. These objects are once again all about flexibility and easy operation, ongoing themes at Jonas & Jonas.

PHOTOS: l.: *Flat* shelf module, m.: *Wallflower* by Markus Honka
r.: *Tri* shelf module

MILESTONES: *Nudo* standing desk → page **316**

Kaether & Weise
Kahla
Kaldewei
Peter Keler
Keuco
Justus Kolberg
König + Neurath
Koziol
KPM
Ferdinand Kramer
Axel Kufus
Kusch + Co
Gerd Lange
Jürgen Lange
Leise
Lepper Schmidt Sommerlade
Glen Oliver Löw
Loewe

*Plan* bathroom collection by **Reiner Moll** for **Keuco**

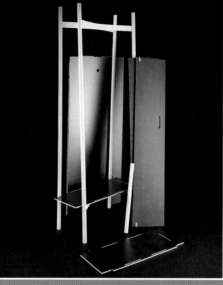

# Kaether & Weise

furniture manufacturer, Lamspringe / Lower Saxony, founded 1998, **www.kaetherundweise.de**

That the **Plattenbau** shelf unit (2004) was recently chosen as "Best of the Best" by the Design Centre of North Rhine-West-phalia, is surely just as much a success factor as the fact that the attractive and endlessly extendable piece of furniture has apparently become a favourite prop of German film directors. It already had two starring roles in its very first year of existence, in the films "Elementarteilchen" (The Elementary Particles) and "Die Wolke" (The Cloud). The Florian Petri shelf with the wonder-fully ironic name ("Plattenbau" is a term used to refer to Eastern-Bloc-style prefabricated concrete apartment blocks), which is simply snapped together out of 4-mm-thin high-pressure lami-nate panels, offers irrefutable proof that, in the wake of hits such as **Axel Kufus'** FNP (→ p.**248**) (1989), **Werner Aisslinger's** Endless Shelf (→ p.**266**) (1994) and **Performa's** 03 (2003), the history of the intelligent shelf system made in Germany is by no means over. When the two master carpenters Andreas Kaether and Stephan Weise – specialists in shop fittings who were on the lookout for an additional economic mainstay – offered designer Thorsten Franck some advice in materials in the late 1990s, what resulted was a project for furniture design. Their very first pro-gram, Franck's Build-in-a-minute furniture series, attracted attention and even found its way into design museums. Pieces such as the Build-and-file shelf made of wooden poles and

coated plywood panels, or the three-legged table trestle Sidestep, made from a single panel (and able to support up to 700 pounds) are paradoxically both incredibly stable and remarkably light-weight, making them ideal for easy transport. This kind of furni-ture, just the thing for today's peripatetic lifestyle, stands for a new, unpretentious brand of Modernism. That the pragmatic, ascetic attitude reflected therein can also be found at other companies today, such as **Nils Holger Moormann** or **Jonas & Jonas**, who have also done their part in promoting the plywood renaissance, is something the two carpenters from southern Lower Saxony take no pains to deny. They are broadening their product range step by step. It now features a closet and a new idea for the children's room: "Rutschi", the portable slide that can simply be docked onto a chair.

PHOTOS: l.: Sidestep table trestle (Build-in-a-minute collection) and Easystool stool, m.: Lockaway cabinet (Build-in-a-minute collection) r.: Flat Mate folding chair

MILESTONE: **Plattenbau** shelf system → page **346**

# Kahla

porcelain manufacturer, Kahla / Thuringia, founded 1844, **www.kahlaporzellan.com**

This Central German brand, which managed to survive the collapse of the GDR, is a positive exception to the rule and at the same time exemplary of the breathtaking rollercoaster ride of German economic history. Founded in the kindergarten days of the industry, the company – after taking over **Arzberg** and Hutschenreuther – would grow to become Germany's largest porcelain manufacturer by the end of the 1920s, only to be turned into a state-run operation behind the "Iron Curtain". The "people's" state combine included 17 plant sites and a workforce of 18,000. After a failed attempt at privatization in the early 1990s, Günther Raithel, an ex-**Rosenthal** manager, succeeded at turning things around. The seasoned industry expert combined investments in new technology, leaner processes and inventive marketing with a vision: a new beginning based on design-conscious product development and a facelift to the corporate image, including a new logo. Even rivals in the West are astounded at the 50 design awards the firm has collected in just a decade. Today, the brand, together with Arzberg and Rosenthal, again stands for the great German tradition of modern porcelain manufacture. This can be credited primarily to house designers Cornelia Müller, Barbara Schmidt and Mirjami Rissanen, who are responsible for conceiving most of the products. Schmidt's Allround service alone has received several prizes. Circle and wave are the formative design elements here. The white household and hotel porcelain is, as its name says, a variable and comprehensive program. By contrast, her service Update, another award-winner, consisted at first of just a few basic pieces, but has in the meantime grown. In Elixyr, a more recent design, symmetry and asymmetry enter into an exciting dialogue. The various services are offered in both purist white and various patterns. What they all have in common is simplicity and multifunctionality, which means that pieces such as plates, bowls and saucers can be used and combined for various purposes – principles once propagated at the Bauhaus and in Ulm. Müller's Abra Cadabra is another extremely versatile service, from little bowls with lids to whimsical saucers or the decorative platter. A new idea stems from Finnish designer Rissanen: a graceful peacock feather as universal leitmotif creates an aesthetic link between the various porcelain series.

PHOTOS: l.: *Touch!* collection, r.: *Abra Cadabra* collection

# Kaldewei

bath and shower tray manufacturer, Ahlen / North Rhine-Westphalia, founded 1918, **www.kaldewei.de**

The company name is by now synonymous with a traditional material: enamelled steel. The combination of steel, the stuff of which the industrial revolution was made, and white enamel, which has moulded our image of what a modern bathroom should look like, possesses unrivalled qualities even today. In addition to offering good flow properties and being nearly one hundred percent recyclable, steel enamel baths have an extremely hard surface that is only surpassed by that of precious stones, a feature that is ideal when it comes to hygiene. The Westphalian enterprise, today the world's leading manufacturer of bathtubs, started out as a producer of raw goods for the enamel industry such as washtubs and milk jugs. The company began in the mid-1930s to fabricate steel bathtubs. At the end of the 1950s, the first tub without a welded seam represented an innovation that would become the new gold standard within the space of just a few years. Kaldewei is today the only manufacturer in the industry with its own enamel development department and its own production. Today's product range encompasses well over 200 models, with systematic thinking a key concept behind the collections. Complete solutions and clever details for both the high-end small bathroom and the capacious luxury oasis are on offer, along with furnishings for hotel bathrooms the world over. With the discovery of the bathroom as a place for contemplative

withdrawal and relaxation, in which we like to surround ourselves with harmonious accoutrements, the design aspect automatically came to the fore. Kaldewei now collaborates with two premier design studios: **Phoenix Design** in Stuttgart, which can boast wide-ranging experience in bathroom design, and Sottsass Associati in Milan. The Italians are enlisted in particular for premium models such as the Kusatsu Pool, a deep sitzbath that is oriented on Japanese bathing culture, and the *Mega Duo Oval*, whose interior figure-eight shape is combined with an oval, rectangular or hexagonal exterior form.

PHOTOS: l.: *Mega Duo Oval* bath by Sottsass Associati
m.: *Vaio Duo* bath by Phoenix Design
r.: *Megaplan* shower tray by Sottsass Associati

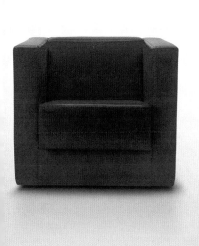

# Peter **Keler**

artist and furniture designer, born 1898, died 1982

His block chair of 1925 is a three-dimensional manifesto. The reduction to a simple cube – even more radically than Josef Hoffmann and **Walter Gropius** before him and Le Corbusier with *Grand Confort* after him – identifies the model as a minimalist type. From the functionalist point of view, what is today referred to as the "Bauhaus Cube" (re-edition from **Tecta**) represents the natural counterpart to the cubic shapes in both a building's exterior and interior design. But Keler was neither architect nor theorist. In the early 1920s, the Holstein native was part of the artists' circle in Worpswede. Heinrich Vogeler, enamoured of the English Arts and Crafts movement, had transformed his house there into a "total work of art" and therewith defined the avant-garde colony as a project for *Lebensreform* (lifestyle reform). Keler's extensive oeuvre expresses this vision of overhauling all aspects of life, with clear political overtones. He worked as painter, graphic artist, photographer and furniture designer, and later taught architecture and visual arts as well. This broad spectrum of activities, never legitimized by an academic degree, was typical of the spirit of renewal that shaped the era. He was soon making his way, like his Worpswede artist colleague **Wilhelm Wagenfeld**, to the Bauhaus in Weimar, an irresistible magnet for aesthetes like himself. There, he studied in the workshops for cabinetry and mural painting. His cradle

(re-edition from Tecta) made out of elementary forms and painted in primary colours is both a theoretical statement and a practical piece of furniture. Keler, who went on to design a children's swing, children's chair on runners and additional furniture, also had a hand in the forward-looking, striking planar treatment of the wall of a passageway at the Weimar Bauhaus in 1923. Later, he worked as a freelancer, until he became one of those ostracized by the Nazis as "degenerate" artists. After 1945, the versatile talent returned to Weimar, which was now located in an East Germany shaped by "socialist realism". He became professor of "Optical Pedagogy". Like **Marianne Brandt** and **Erich Dieckmann**, he was one of the "second rank" of Bauhaus figures whose work was long forgotten and then rediscovered in our era of design recycling and at least partially re-issued.

PHOTOS: l.: *D1* easychair (re-edition from Tecta)
m.: *Bauhaus Cradle* (re-edition from Tecta), r.: *Kubus* chair

# Keuco

manufacturer of bathroom taps and furniture, Hemer / North Rhine-Westphalia, founded 1953, **www.keuco.de**

Manufacturers in the industry know full well that bathroom furnishings enjoy an extremely long life cycle. So it makes economic sense to focus on this circumstance, like this Westphalian firm has, and produce only durable products. The company name is composed of the first letters of the name of Paul Keune, who in the early 1950s founded a metalworking operation in the centre of the German fittings industry. Just a decade later, he was already specializing in high-grade accessories for the bathroom, a decision that would prove to be a prescient one. Following a period of rapid expansion, the company, which today boasts the most advanced goods distribution centre in the industry, developed into the international market leader for bathroom fittings. As customers increasingly came to demand harmonious furnishing concepts, co-operations with manufacturers like **Villeroy & Boch** and Grohe were initiated. After acquiring a manufacturer of mirrored cabinets and a kitchen and bathroom furniture-maker, however, the company was finally in a position to offer its own brand of complete bathroom ensembles. Keuco already began working with **Luigi Colani** in the 1970s, the maverick who was at the time in the process of revolutionizing modern German design for living virtually single-handedly. Projects with what are as a rule somewhat less eccentric creative talents are today an integral component of the corporate strategy. The results can definitely stand up to comparison with brands such as **Erco** or **FSB**, although the Sauerland-based company does not make much ado about the fact that it can boast an above-average design culture. Keeping the names of the designers behind the products anonymous is likewise part of a strategy in which everything is subordinated to the high profile of the brand itself. The extraordinarily fruitful, nearly two-decade long relationship with the office of **Reiner Moll** is thus largely known only to insiders. The collaboration has resulted in bestsellers such as the *Alea* series and the minimalist *Plan* program, probably the most comprehensive of its kind. The Keuco-Moll team has always been a source of innovative precedents, whether in the case of *Aquamove*, the world's first hydraulically adjustable showerhead, or *Bella Vista*, an LED-lit cosmetic mirror that casts a sometimes shockingly honest light on what it reflects.

PHOTOS: l.: *Edition 300* single-lever tap
m.: Rotating cabinet (*Plan* collection) by Reiner Moll
r.: Cosmetic mirror *Bella Vista* by Reiner Moll

# Justus **Kolberg**

furniture designer, born 1962, office in Hamburg, **www.kolbergdesign.com**

"Simple, but not banal!" Justus Kolberg sums up his design aspirations in a motto that is just as reduced as the message it contains. The Schleswig-Holstein native demonstrates what he means by this maxim in his works, for example the new *Hook* coat rack series (for **Schönbuch**) or the *Kvaro* cabinet system (for **Flötotto**, → p.**442**), a straightforward all-round furniture program based on the square, as successor to the legendary *Profilsystem* (→ p.**198**). It was clear as early as 1991 that an unusual career was in the stars for Kolberg when he was named "Design Champion" based on his dissertation. He began by first travelling to Italy, where he saw a well-designed chair in a large series at Castelli and was seized by an urge to try his hand at the ultimate design discipline. After a few years working for furniture-maker Tecno and in the **Wiege** design offices, Kolberg went out on his own in the late 1990s. Today he is creating cutting-edge office furniture with the help of Danish designer Erik Simonsen, and is much prized in professional circles for his pared-down, coherent concepts. The up-and-coming talent is not yet well-known to a wider public, although several journalists have already paid him a visit. Kolberg belongs to the school of trouble-shooters. He works away at structural details, engineering and the connections between parts until the optimal solution is attained. These painstaking efforts can usually no longer be seen in the finished chair. His first major hit was the *slim-line 08* folding chair (1992, for Tecno). It was followed by the elegant **Confair** conference furniture (1994, for Wilkhahn), the *Verso* table program (2000, for **Renz**) and the *Phoenix* swivel chair (2002, for **Kusch + Co**), along with wooden and garden chairs. These works for prestigious international companies in the field of furniture for commercial properties have almost without exception been crowned with design laurels. The secret behind Kolberg's success, which he describes as "achieving elegant simplicity by applying sensitive intelligence" once again sounds simple, but nonetheless requires no copyright.

PHOTOS: l.: *Verso* container for Renz, m.: *More* collection for Howe
r.: *Confair* office furniture collection for Wilkhahn

---

MILESTONE: **Confair** office furniture collection → page **264**

# König + Neurath

office furniture manufacturer, Karben / Hesse, founded 1925, **www.koenig-neurath.de**

Still family-run today, this company from southern Hesse already began establishing its brand back in the 1960s. The acquisition of the Christian Holzäpfel company – a prime innovator in the field of German furniture design – in the 1970s was followed by rapid internationalization in the 1980s, coupled with the introduction of novel products. Ever since *King Alpha* came out (1980, by Frogdesign), one of the first multifunctional office systems, design has also played a role in the corporate philosophy. The brand carved out a profile for itself as full-service supplier on a high level, offering informative Internet portals as part of the mix. The current collection ranges from the portable leaning aid *Quick* (which can be folded up like a metal scooter), to container programs and variable table and desk systems, to complete office furnishings solutions. The concepts come from both the company's own in-house design and development team as well as from external designers – who are not showcased, though. Notable among these are Hans-Ulrich Bitsch and Hadi Teherani, whose *Standby Office* mobile office unit (2000) represents a response to the increasing flexibility demanded in the working world, as does the multi-award-winning *Re.Lounge* easychair and table program by **Burkhard Vogtherr** (2002, with Jonathan Prestich). The latter, which today offers two easychair and two table variations, has an unusually low seating height that makes it ideal for ad-hoc meetings in a relaxed atmosphere, as well a congenial addition to the home. Tensa from the year 2000 set an exclamation mark on the hotly contested terrain of swivelling office chairs with its "dynamic torsion system". Soon to follow in the industry's showcase discipline was *Skye*, best in class in terms of offering a wide range of seating angles, all the way to a near-reclining position. Other company innovations include the *DO IT* table system, which comes with flexible dividing walls to fit a number of different work situations. Today, with over 1,300 employees at four production sites, the enterprise with headquarters in the Wetterau region generates the highest sales volume of all German office furniture manufacturers.

PHOTOS: *Kineta* office chair by Simon Desanta
r.: *Do IT Team Office* office furniture system by Cornelius Müller-Schellhorn

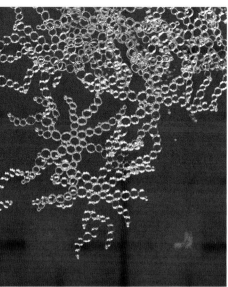

# Koziol

manufacturer of household, gift and furnishing items, Erbach / Hesse, founded 1927, **www.koziol.de**

A humidifier dubbed *Balduin* takes the form of a friendly, ergo-nomically shaped ghost, while tape dispenser *Elvis* has the swinging hips of the legendary rock 'n' roller. Dirty dishes are cheerfully tackled by dish brushes *Tim* and *Tweetie* with their stubbly punk hairstyles. With a large dose of irony and subtle allusions to everyday culture, the products made by this company in southern Hesse, which has adopted the hard-to-contradict guiding principle "Design ist Dasein" (Design is Being) are full of surprises, but of course viewed with suspicion by those who stand guard over proper design etiquette. Good manners are hardly at risk, though, when wit and bright colours are celebra-ted here in high style. The "Ideas for Friends", as marketing-conscious company owner Stephan Koziol calls his collection of internationally coveted gift and household items, are admittedly not exactly exercises in purism. Their charm lies precisely in their highly original and sometimes off-beat look, the plastic of which they're made being right in step with the times and demon-strating convincingly that whimsical playfulness is not at home only south of the Alps. In the late 1920s company founder Bernhard Koziol had a workshop for carved brooches and ivory figurines. In the mid-1930s he switched to the new injection-moulded plastics, obviously a far-sighted move. Finally, in the early 1950s, the Odenwald firm came up with a worldwide best-seller: the water-filled "snow globes" with their frozen scenes over which snow flurries fall when the ball is shaken. Having now gone far beyond this still-popular souvenir classic, Koziol is today pursuing an entirely new product line under the label "spheres": furnishing objects for the business world. One of the successful products in this range is the series of room dividers made of variously structured coloured squares that can be freely interhung to form surfaces of any size. Images of the Bauhaus and Ulm inevitably come to mind upon contemplating this utterly simple, yet highly variable, system. The transparent walls of colour create spatial situations and influence the atmosphere within them. Also new is a lamp collection, including the hanging lamp *Josephine*. Its name and plastic skirt, which comes in a range of shimmering colours, represent yet another tongue-in-cheek cultural quote.

PHOTOS: l.: *Balduin* humidifier
m.: *Amoebe* room divider/deco element by Harry & Camilla
r.: *Josephine* hanging lamp (manufacturer's design)

MILESTONE: *Fusion* room divider → page **354**

# KPM

porcelain manufacturer, Berlin, founded 1763, **www.kpm-berlin.de**

Looking back over the two-and-a-half centuries that KPM has been in existence is like a course in art history: playful rococo succeeded by harmoniously proportioned classicism and effusively elegant Jugendstil, and finally the programmatic simplicity of the Modernism that found its centre in the Berlin of the early 20th century. This stylistic ebb and flow is likewise embodied in the designers that left their mark on KPM products. The list ranges from state master builder Karl Friedrich Schinkel, to tableware reformer Trude Petri, to Italian design master Enzo Mari, who came to the company on the Spree River in the mid-1990s as artistic director and left behind a service called *Berlin* as calling card. Ever since Prussian King Friedrich II acquired what was at the time a state-of-the-art workshop from a Berlin merchant in the mid-18th century, the brand with the blue sceptre has remained true to its craftsmanship tradition (joined by only six other enterprises worldwide). This is why, even today, each and every piece is unique. Porcelain manufacturers need artistic personnel for the design and painted décor of the pieces. These artists can be regarded as the prototypical designers and thus the trailblazers for today's ideas of form. Sculptor Friedrich Elias Meyer, for example, created both figurines and a number of services in the second half of the 18th century. Whether a fat-bellied coffeepot, sugar bowl or soup tureen, these were formal templates that still set the standard today. Among them, Meyer's *Neuglatt* tableware from 1769 has – as the name already hints – an amazingly clear and hence modern look. Following a period of enthusiasm for antiquity and then the reign of commercially profitable historicism, KPM made a fresh creative start around 1900 by espousing the avant-garde Jugendstil trend. Witnesses to this period include the *Ceres* service by Theo Schmuz-Baudiss. In the late, Bauhaus-inspired 1920s, ceramicist Trude Petri then succeeded at conceiving icons of the "*Neue Sachlichkeit*" (New Objectivity) that swept décor-laden Wilhelminian preciousness right off the table. In particular the **Urbino** service from 1931 masterfully combines lightness with severity, looking even more radical than, for example, **Arzberg's** *1382* tableware (→ p.**90**) from the same year. Enzo Mari picked up on the same attitude once again toward the end of the century.

PHOTOS: l.: *Area* vase and flower pot collection
r.: Teapot (*Berlin* service) by Enzo Mari

MILESTONE: *Urbino* porcelain tableware → page **86**

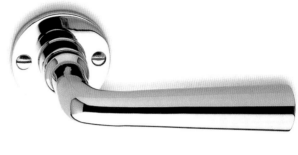

# Ferdinand **Kramer**

architect and furniture designer, born 1898, died 1985

At 18, Kramer, son of a Frankfurt businessman, was a soldier lying in a trench near Verdun. He would later be locked up in an insane asylum for refusing to obey orders. After successfully fleeing that institution, his architecture studies took him to Munich and gained him entrée into diverse intellectual circles. Because of his left-wing views, he was known to many as "Red Ferdinand". But this didn't stop him from designing furniture for a friend who was a baron. He was disappointed by the Bauhaus, where he studied for a short time, but he did make friends there with artists including Gerhard Marcks. Kramer took up work on the "New Frankfurt" under City Architect Ernst May in the mid-1920s, designing buildings made of concrete, iron and glass, including an old people's home (together with Mart Stam), a central garage with petrol station and a few apartment blocks with standardized floor plans measuring 50 square metres "for subsistence-level living". His main job was to come up with suitable furnishings and household goods for the new municipal buildings, including the kind of streamlined, angular, type-based furniture that would be both affordable and functional (to be made by unemployed cabinetmakers). Kramer, one of the key proponents – along with **Erich Dieckmann**, Otto Haesler, **Karl Schneider** and others – of the new rational domestic lifestyle outside of the Bauhaus, also developed small, high-performance

coal stoves, as well as lamps, door-handles, space-saving sitzbaths and furnishings for city-run kindergartens. He rose to fame with the **Kramerstuhl** (*Kramer Chair*), a modern piece using the bentwood technique (for **Thonet**). The designer/ activist also lectured at the Frankfurt Art Academy on issues surrounding "functional architecture". Always a man with a mission, Kramer spent his whole life trying to simplify the world. This goal is witnessed by inventions such as a foldable metal dish shelf, a combined clothing and linens closet, as well as "knock-down furniture" designed for self-assembly and disposable umbrellas made of coated paper that he developed while in American exile. After being banned from his profession due to his political views and Jewish wife, the avant-gardist was forced to start over again in America, where, despite numerous projects, he never managed to gain a career foothold. Upon returning to his home-town, he became director of architecture at the rebuilt Goethe University.

PHOTOS: l.: *Kramer Table*, r.: *Door-handle* (re-edition from Tecnolumen)

MILESTONE: *Kramer Chair* → page **68**

# Axel **Kufus**

furniture designer, born 1958, office in Berlin, **www.kufus.de**

"Side holds rail, rail holds shelf, shelf holds rail, rail holds side". What sounds like a piece of modern poetry is actually a brief description of a shelf called *Flächennutzungsplan* (Land Use Plan), better known as **FNP** (1989, for **Nils Holger Moormann**) – a key product for Axel Kufus. It is at once a symbol of the magic of simplicity, of the living tradition of modular furniture of German design and of the way of thinking of its creator. The Essenborn designer became famous through completely different kinds of designs, such as a blue easychair that looks like a mop or the *Kellerfensterschrank* (Cellar Window Cabinet) in which a concrete cabinet fitted with metal grates stands atop raw tree boughs (in collaboration with sculptor Ulrike Holthöfer). These are products from the eccentric days of "New German Design", unwieldy object collages with which young designers defied the functionalism that had dominated the field up until the mid-1980s. Kufus, who had already long been a professor of product design, was just taking up design studies in Berlin, a centre of the revolt that was stirring. The path he ultimately chose was decisively shaped by his previous training, however. A carpenter with a master craftsman's diploma, he is viewed by many today as the German Jasper Morrison. But one might also see him as a representative of primal German design virtues. His designs betray a profound knowledge of materials and their properties,

coupled with a sense of how to pare down material needs and limit himself to straightforward, soft-spoken forms. This is functionalism on a high level, the kind of design one might call Utilism International, the name of the company Kufus founded together with Morrison and Andreas Brandolini. His products usually have laconic names, such as the *Egal* shelf (1989, for Nils Holger Moormann) or *Kufus* table (for **Magazin** → p.**492** ). What's impressive about them is often the combination of a surprising idea with creative trenchancy, such as in the easy-to-dismantle *Stoeck* plywood chair (1993, for Atoll). This penchant for dissecting came in handy for a much more complex project: the *Office Kitchen*. The modular structure of this multi-award-winning office kitchen of tomorrow (2000, for Casawell, i.e. **Alno**) makes it extremely adaptable despite very modest space needs. Now the Berlin-based designer is the first non-Frenchman to be invited to design furniture for the exclusive state-run Mobilier National in Paris, an accolade for which he showed his appreciation with the series *Dreimöbel* (Three Furniture), a desk, shelf and side unit that display unparalleled simplicity.

PHOTOS: l.: *Lader* chest of drawers for Nils Holger Moormann
m.: Desk (*Dreimöbel* collection) for Mobilier National Paris, r.: *Stoeck* chair for Atoll

MILESTONE: *FNP* shelf system → page **248**

# Kusch + Co

furniture manufacturer, Hallenberg / North Rhine-Westphalia, founded 1939, **www.kusch.de**

When the gigantic Congress Center opened in Hamburg in 1972, Kusch chairs were ready to receive guests in the huge conference hall. In 1997, when the Commerzbank in Frankfurt commissioned what was then the tallest office tower in Europe, the bankers ordered furniture from Hallenberg for their new building. Kusch, a specialist in furnishings for offices and commercial properties, has a workforce of 500, two plants and an annual production of 350,000 chairs and tables. Although one of the larger operations in the industry, it is still a family-owned company. Even today, Kusch is still rightly proud of its production expertise. In the first year of World War II, the young self-made man Ernst Kusch set up a sawmill. He was soon successfully producing chairs such as the straightforward and indestructible model *100*. By the early 1950s, the firm already had its own fleet of delivery trucks. In the swinging sixties, **Luigi Colani** developed sitting sculptures for the Sauerland company that were not only conspicuous for their erotic curves, but also for their poster-bright colours and innovative foam technology, as witnessed for example by the lounge chair ***TV-relax*** (re-issued in 2006). Booming sales were achieved with other models, such as the *1000,* the first German-made plastic chair, as well as the "million-selling" chair *2000* (1963, by Edlef Bandixen), which was produced for three decades. During this time – good design

was now a corporate strategy – the founder's son Dieter Kusch took the helm, guiding the company onto international markets (and then handing over the reins to the next generation in the year 2000). With the round chair *Soley* (by Valdimar Hardarson), the "furniture piece of the year" in 1984, the company rushed on ahead of the competition, as was also the case with the *7100* bench (by Jorgen Kastholm), an early seating program for airport waiting rooms. In the 1990s, this new field of endeavour brought fruitful collaboration with Argentinean designer Jorge Pensi, whose bench system *¡Hola!* scooped up twelve awards. The furniture-makers from Hallenberg are naturally proud to have made the top of the list of 100 best firms in the "design ranking" twice in the company's history. Robert de le Roi, director of product development and himself responsible for a series of designs, maintains close contact with the external creative talents, among them prominent German furniture designers such as Udo Feldotto, **Justus Kolberg** and Uwe **Sommerlade**, who contributed the all-purpose chair *Scorpii*, a typical Kusch model with its purist look and highly variable functions. What's also special about the company is that designs by senior head Dieter Kusch can still be found in the current product range.

PHOTOS: l.: *Ronda* easychair program by Jorge Pensi
m.: *¡Hola!* stacking chair by Jorge Pensi, r.: *Trio* stacking chair by Robert de le Roi

MILESTONE: ***TV-relax*** lounge chair → page **172**

# Gerd **Lange**

furniture and product designer, born 1931, office in Kapsweyer / Baden-Wurttemberg

He is part of the generation born around 1930 that brought forth a whole series of outstanding creative personalities – including such disparate ones as **Luigi Colani** and **Peter Maly** – and which shaped the identity of German design, especially to foreign eyes, with a profile that still predominates today. One can search in vain, however, for a uniform, immediately recognizable signature uniting all of Gerd Lange's various designs. On the contrary, he would deem such a facile, fashionable uniformity to be superficial. One of the prime aims of the avowed functionalist is instead the long service life of his products. This demand for dependability also extends to his own person. He has been working for some of his clients, such as Steelcase Strafor, for several years now. After completing his state exams in the 1950s, Lange has always been self-employed. He already began at that time to work as a team with his wife and manager, Renate. He opened his studio in a former mill in the village of Kapsweyer in the Palatinate region in the early 1960s. His spacious workplace, far away from the hustle and bustle of city life, gives the early riser the peace and quiet he needs to indulge in his laid-back work style. His workday is shaped to a great extent by the elaborate creation of models. He has gained industry-wide fame especially through his chairs, but by no means wants to be reduced to the identity of mere chair-maker. Excursions onto other terrain included a coffee maker (for AEG) and plastic shelves (for Wogg). In 1965 he designed the *Farmer-Sessel* (Farmer Easy-chair, for **Bofinger**), a simple and inventive wooden peg construction. Two years later, it was followed by the stackable *SM 400* plastic chair, which is produced by *Drabert* in Minden, where it is still today a highlight of the collection. Later he created *Flex*, the first plastic chair with wooden legs (for **Thonet**). A man like Gerd Lange never retires. He is still making individual pieces of furniture and overseeing the re-design of his chairs in the Old Opera in Frankfurt.

PHOTOS: l.: *Flex* chair for Thonet
r.: *Flexturn* office chair program for Thonet

MILESTONE: *SM 400* chair → page **168**

# Jürgen **Lange**

furniture designer, born 1940, office in Grafenau / Baden-Wurttemberg

Aigner, **Behr**, **COR**, Daimler-Benz, IBM, **Interlübke**, Knoll International, Philips, Porsche, **Rosenthal**, **Schönbuch**, Steelcase, **Thonet**, **Walter Knoll**, **Wilkhahn**, Wittmann, **WK Wohnen**. This alphabetical list of his clients, which could be extended considerably, constitutes an impressive gallery of major brands. Jürgen Lange studied in Braunschweig with Arno **Votteler** in the early 1960s and then took a job in his office. He went out on his own in 1968, at a time when the number of design offices was still very modest. The north German native is hence a member of the generation of wartime children who were swept up in the optimism of the second wave of Modernism. The aim of his work, which has resulted in a whole host of patents, has always been to create machine-made series products. But he did not build his reputation on domestic and office furniture alone, but also based on such endeavours as design consulting and exhibition stand conception. He sees his job as acting as co-ordinator between corporate management, engineering and marketing, with the most important and likewise most difficult task consisting of "not losing sight of the people for whom the products are being made". His longstanding clients include coat-rack specialist Schönbuch, whose current program contains two of his pieces, including the long-lived *Trio*. With *Change* and *Headline* (for Behr) he wrote important chapters in the history of the many-sided German cabinet system. The latter features a clever pivoting "function column" that enhanced the flexibility factor even further. He created *Paneel* for the same manufacturer, a variable hanging system based on an idea that is more relevant today than ever. Other key designs include the functional secretary *Privé* (for Rosenthal) and the *Studio* upholstery program (for Walter Knoll). The *domino* cabinet system (with Harriet Schwab, for Interlübke) with its slatted sliding doors, perforated back walls and cable conduits is ready to face the media-infused everyday world of tomorrow. For form inventor Lange, the necessity of design lies in our continually changing lifestyles.

PHOTOS: l.: *Headline* cabinet and shelf system for Behr
m.: *Privé* secretary for Rosenthal, r.: *Studio* sofa system for Walter Knoll

MILESTONE: *Trio* coat rack → page **240**

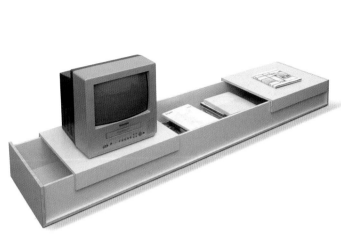

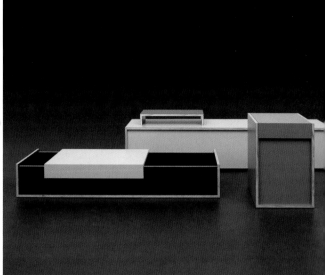

# Leise

furniture manufacturer, Frankfurt a.M. / Hesse, founded 2007, **www.leise-leise.com**

That Knut Völzke developed a design brand in his dissertation is really nothing out of the ordinary. But that he then went on to put his theory into actual commercial practice is by all means something special. The results were on view at the Cologne Furniture Fair in 2005, where the maverick aroused a great deal of interest. Völzke works under the Leise brand, a name that means "quiet" and stands for objects that do not loudly and aggressively impose themselves on the public consciousness. Famous role models for this reserved attitude can be found in German design history, as well as for the conceptual strategy behind it. One of the guiding spirits when it comes to marrying rationality to inventiveness is German design pioneer **Ferdinand Kramer**. Leise's modest-sized program, which began to take shape back in 2005, comprises a series of small-scale designs that one can rightfully refer to as case furniture. These containers have an extremely stripped-down look and are constructed according to a unique principle: A mitred U-shaped body is closed at the ends by two side panels atop which likewise U-shaped lids and sliding elements can be placed. The material is not off the rack, either. Völzke uses specially made panels of native coniferous woods whose fine grain is just as exclusive as the high-grade colour laminate coating. Leise-brand minimalism is accompanied by a surprising level of multifunctionality in these small furniture pieces – a versatility that can be attributed to the simplicity of the concept. The lid elements, which close flush with the side panel strips that project over the top plane, thus forming a flat surface on top, can be used for various purposes: not only as sliding covers for the diverse container formats, but also as a tray or occasional table. The other objects as well, all of which make do without any holes or knobs as handles, are not designated for any one specific function. They can in addition be mixed and matched, for example by being stuck together. The colours stand for Mondrian-like planarity, while the unpainted contour at the edges describes the objects' clean-lined geometry. This graphical aspect at the same time expresses the modular idea on which these pieces are based. Every single object is both storage space and body in space.

PHOTOS: *Julies* object and container furniture

# Lepper Schmidt Sommerlade

office for furniture design, Kassel / Hesse, founded 1992, **www.lss-designer.de**

Design is observation, communication, environment, culture – but "not art". Christian Lepper, Roland Schmidt and Uwe Sommerlade, three designers who studied in Kassel and have been running an office there for the past one-and-a-half decades, see themselves as mediators. The busy trio specializes in furniture, interior design and exhibitions. What they all have in common is their training as cabinetmakers. They view open lines of communication with clients as one of the key conditions for successful design. This maxim has allowed them to build an impressive list of references, including major German manufacturers like **Brunner**, **Kusch + Co**, **Rosenthal** Einrichtung and **Thonet**, along with Italian firms such as Rossin and Tonon, and US furniture-maker Haworth. The design studio based in northern Hesse designed the model *A 1700* for neighbour Thonet, a cleverly conceived table system without apron in which the skilfully set legs can be quickly released and attached again. They had already attracted attention with two additional tables: *Faldo* (for Kusch + Co) and Sleight (for Brunner). The trio is not interested solely in formally coherent ideas. Design for them is instead a question of deep-going development work. They hold several patents for these kinds of technical diving expeditions. It thus comes as no surprise that they have also been successful at inventing new sitting machines. But there is nothing apparatus-like about their *S-con* (for art collection) and *Drive* (for Brunner) swivelling office chairs. Their elegant look is meant to upgrade the otherwise drab workplace. Now, the table and chair experts have also tried their hand at a further field of endeavour. "LSS" conceived a special hanging lamp called *Phil* for client Klein & Co. in which the two transparent sides of the champagne-cooler-sized shade are placed two centimetres apart to leave the customer plenty of room to exercise his own creativity.

PHOTOS: l.: *Carry* chair for Brunner, r.: *A 1700* table for Thonet

# Glen Oliver **Löw**

furniture and product designer, born 1959, office in Hamburg

Immediately after the Leverkusen native completed his studies at the University of Wuppertal and had his diploma in industrial design in hand, he felt drawn to the design Mecca of Milan. In this wellspring of modern furniture, he proceeded to do a second degree at the Domus Academy before becoming assistant to Antonio Citterio. It was the mid-1980s and only initiates already knew that Citterio, whose partner Löw soon became, would rise in the ensuing years to become one of the most in-demand designers. At Citterio & Partners, the big names in the industry crossed paths, among them Bieffe, Flos, Iittala, Kartell and **Vitra**. Löw's picture-book career also added several chapters there. The Rhineland native was soon working for multinationals such as Hackman of Finland and Steelcase in the USA, for whose chair *Think* he developed a patented sitting-and-leaning technology. Finally, he began to work on polishing the image of prominent corporations: The branch concept for Commerzbank (1996) and the interior design of the Smart car dealerships began on his drawing board. In the year 2000 he was appointed professor of industrial design at the Academy of Fine Arts in Hamburg, where he also established a studio to do work for companies such as Steelcase and **Thonet**. Among his best-known pieces are the practical *Battista* folding table, the *T-Chair* office chair (1990, for Vitra → p.**551**) and the *Mobil* container trolley (1992, for Kartell),

which set off a worldwide trend for translucent plastic. Löw, like his longstanding partner, stands for an urbane, very cool, neo-modern direction in furnishings. He by no means shies away from confronting the German design tradition head-on. This is demonstrated for example by his *S 60* easychair (2001, for Thonet), an up-to-date variation on the recurring theme of the cantilevered chair, which has in the meantime progressed through the series *S 70*, *S 80* and *S 90*.

PHOTOS: l.: *S 70* chair for Thonet, m.: *Battista* folding table for Kartell r.: *S 60* chair for Thonet

# Loewe

TV and phonograph manufacturer, Kronach / Bavaria, founded 1923 in Berlin, **www.loewe.de**

At the end of 2006, the press reported that three million euros would be paid out to the around 1,000 Loewe employees: as compensation for salaries that had been delayed in times of crisis. So this is hardly a run-of-the-mill company, but still one with a typical German story. It's a story of technical inventions, competitive pressure from the Far East, and design. The company from the Upper Franconia region was one of those brands that emerged back when radio and television were just taking their first steps. As early as the 1930s, the Berlin company was already trying to put a television set into series production, and then in the "golden" decades after 1945 – now in a south German location – it enjoyed a meteoric rise. Loewe stood time and again for the latest technology, such as with the first portable tape player in the early 1950s and the video recorder – still with monstrous dimensions – just a decade later. In the 1980s, when Japanese manufacturers seemed to be rapidly taking the technological lead, the company once again put all its cards on innovation: with the first stereo television set, for example, the first Btx decoder series or the *Multitel TV 10*, which combined television and telephone and was probably too far ahead of its time. Another novelty hit the right chord, however: The ***Art 1*** television set, designed by Alexander Neumeister, inaugurated the futuristic-looking media statue as new aesthetic type and

was just as groundbreaking an accomplishment as **Herbert Hirche's** model *HF 1* (for **Braun**, → p.**130**) back in its day. But it was above all a milestone for Loewe itself, for the decision to employ an external designer had paid off richly. While almost every other German company in the industry was forced out of the market, the formula of design plus innovation proved to create the perfect niche. Since the late 1980s, the **Phoenix Design** studio has been supplying the concepts for the multimedia future found in the German living room, emulating the best Braun tradition of rational purism while pursuing a formal vocabulary as consistent as that of Apple or Bang & Olufsen. They are also responsible for introducing the centrally positioned power button, now a signature feature of Loewe products. Television and hi-fi systems such as *Spheros*, *Xelos* or *Individual* are dovetailed to create an integrated system, while also offering exclusive details such as a bi-directional remote control. The intelligent set-up solutions, such as the attachment of the television set to a metal pole spanned between floor and ceiling, likewise extend our entrenched media-consumption habits. The first television set that can be designed by the purchaser has been on offer since 2005 – the aptly named *Individual* series. There are well over 400 variations to choose from.

PHOTOS: l.: *Individual* system, r.: *Spheros 42 HD C* plasma television

MILESTONES: *Art 1* television set → page **230** | *Mimo* television set → page **336**

*Tattomi* lounge/easychair by **Jan Armgardt**
and **Ingo Maurer** for **Mobilia**

# Magazin

furniture store and manufacturer, Stuttgart / Baden-Wurttemberg, founded 1971, **www.magazin.com**

At the beginning of the rebellious 1970s, instructors at Stuttgart Art Academy tried out experimental forms of teaching, challenging the role of the designer. A group of reformist instructors founded the *Institut für angewandte Sozialökologie* (Institute for Applied Social Ecology) which, among other goals, had the aim of analysing and further developing the functional uses of consumer products. In order to gain experience in the business world and to become financially independent, they opened a backyard store: Magazin. Its founders, including designer and long-time manager Otto Sudrow, were committed to the tradition of classical Modernism they knew from the Academy. As was the case with the design critics of the early 20th century, this was a project for general enlightenment: Common sense was to enter the home in a modern variety of "lifestyle reform". To this very day, the project, which originally derived from political economy and the founders' criticism of product aesthetics, remains unique. Magazin's product range was to consist of existing capital goods, because they guarantee the utmost in quality at the lowest price. They discovered what they were looking for at industrial fairs and in catalogues. The first products on offer included work lamps, lab chinaware, restaurant glassware, butchers' knives, untreated muslin for filtering processes, factory shelves, postmen's bags and metal pails – things they turned into useful consumer goods. The store's owners also came up with products of their own. After the first catalogue appeared in 1980 printed on grey recycled paper, Magazin rapidly expanded to become a nationwide furniture store with a significantly increased range of supplies. Today, there are the stores in Stuttgart and in Bonn. Magazin joined arms with the mail order firm Manufactum in 2001, a move that opened up totally new perspectives. In the meantime, Magazin offers a comprehensive choice of goods for nearly all areas of home furnishing and decoration. But the rationalist ideas of the founding era are still evident today in the matter-of-fact tone of all articles and explanatory texts. The number of Magazin's novel creations, soon to include a table series by **Axel Kufus**, has increased considerably. To name just a few: the multipurpose MDF sofa bed (by Michael Mettler) or the numberless radio-controlled wall clock. The program's intellectual background remains evident in the fact that shelves reappear time and again. Some of the new innovative products in this exciting line include *Mein_Back* (by Hannes Bäuerle, Claudia Miller and Alexander Seifried) – constructed from transport boxes – and *1hoch3* (by Dominik Lutz), a connector system using only one component.

PHOTOS: l.: *Kufus* table by Axel Kufus,
r.: *Bankbett* (Bench Bed) by Gerhard Wollnitz

MILESTONES: *2200 / Olympic Chair* → page **98**  I  *Mein_Back* shelf system → page **356**

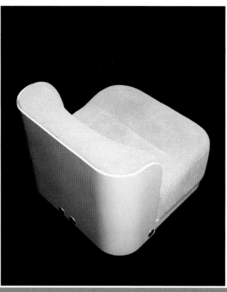

# Peter **Maly**

furniture and product designer, born 1936, studio in Hamburg, **www.peter-maly.de**

When he received his first orders from furniture manufacturer Ligne Roset in the 1980s, the French were expressly interested in his systematic approach and his understanding of technology. His work is in fact today regarded as the epitome of German rationality, and Bohemian-born Maly would hardly disagree. Following his training as a cabinetmaker and interior designer, Maly worked in the 1960s for Germany's largest and – at that time – trend-setting interior design magazine, *Schöner Wohnen*, a publication that he influenced, and which in turn influenced him. The newcomer gained immediate popularity with his monthly *Skizzenbuch* (Sketchbook) in which he solved the interior design problems of his millions of readers. Styling the photographs showing staged modern living areas – then still a novelty – gave him the experience he needed to form the basis of his career. At the same time he was working as a journalist, he also created his first furniture concepts, first for **Tecta** and **COR**. Here, the young Maly encountered the charismatic entrepreneurs Axel Bruchhäuser and Helmut Lübke. Beginning in 1971, he worked freelance as one of the first art directors in the industry, designing trade fair stands, catalogues and ads, first for **Interlübke**, and later for almost all of his customers. This might explain a perfectionism that goes far beyond actual product design. Hamburg-based Maly accompanies a project from A to Z, including all

presentations and advertising campaigns. Finally, the mid-1980s saw his breakthrough as a designer: with the *Maly-Bett* Bed (Maly Bed, for Ligne Roset), the *Zyklus* easychair (for COR), and the *Duo* cabinet system (for Interlübke), commercially successful products for three large companies that simultaneously hit the market. Even though basic forms like the square became a leitmotif for him, his main catchwords have always been 'functional' and 'durable', an approach that combines the innovative with the conservative. Harmonious designs like the *737* chair (for **Thonet**), where Maly fought for the belted seats, are a good example. In the meantime, the champion of German furniture design has also left his matter-of-fact mark on other areas, including lamps (for **Anta**), pianos (for **Sauter**), fireplaces (for **Conmoto**) and carpets (for **Carpet Concept** and **JAB Anstoetz**). Chairs and cabinet systems remain his trademark, however, among them epoch-making programs like *Menos* (for **Behr**) or *Quadrat* (for **Christine Kröncke** → p.**415**), a system that hasn't aged a bit in a quarter century.

PHOTOS: l.: *Circo* easychair for COR, m.: *Trinom* easychair for COR r.: *737* chair for Thonet

# Martin Stoll

chair manufacturer, Waldshut-Tiengen / Baden-Wurttemberg, founded 1870, **www.martinstoll.com**

The Swabian manufacturer that has been part of the Dutch Samas Group since 1999 grew large with the workhorses amongst chairs: the office swivel chair. The first one in Germany was built in 1920. It wasn't until Martin Stoll junior founded his own company in the late 1970s, quickly presenting his model S – the first chair with a patented active pelvis support – that the chapter of design was opened in the southern Black Forest. The young businessman turned to Arno **Votteler** for help, who developed models for the company well into the 1990s. Their joint debut product – widely used for instance by German discounter Aldi as a cashiers' chair – has been just as long-lived as that store chain. Other designers also contributed important models, including in the 1990s Matteo Thun of Switzerland (*Collection L*) and Swabia-based **Reiner Moll** (*Collection K*). For the managerial set, Martin Stoll offers the series *Executive Office* (by Albert Holz), a system exhibiting a minimalist geometry that is reminiscent of early Bauhaus constructivism. The most recent chair series, *Collection E* (by Uta and Andreas Krob), on the other hand enters uncharted territories. Instead of the usual additive construction, the designer realized an integral concept that allows a glimpse of technical details that generally are not visible. Add to that a world premiere: the first office chair that allows the sitter to regulate the grade of its hardness or softness. This Swiss-made design was realized in cooperation with the Berlin engineering office Brüske, which spent two years developing the technology. Using a slide, the aggregate state of the seat can be changed from, for example, "French comfortable" to "Scandinavian sturdy". *Collection W* (by Helmut Staubach, 2003) demonstrates avant-gardism of another kind: black leather on a tubular steel framework. This elegant and simple waiting room furniture is clearly reminiscent of classical Modernism. Waiting-room chair Lenio also has a rectangular base, but here an S-shaped seat shell "hovers" above the robust wooden framework. This makes for an exciting formal contrast and a comfortable seat as well.

PHOTOS: l.: *Collection E* office chair by Uta and Andreas Krob
m.: *Lenio* chair by Dominique Perrault and Gaelle Lauriot-Prévost
r.: *Collection W* Konferenz chair by Helmut Staubach

# Mawa

manufacturer of lights and home accessories, Langerwisch / Brandenburg, founded 1977, **www.mawa-design.de**

The lighting for a library, a theatre or a former city council build-ing that needed about four-thousand new lamps: Light planning, if need be on a large scale, has meanwhile become one of the Central German company's specialties. The name is derived from that of its founder Martin Wallroth, an entrepreneur with an un-orthodox vita. A native of the northern German town of Lübeck, Wallroth broke off his theology studies and instead became a survival artist in the subculture of 1970s Berlin, developing an affinity for technical issues. So it wasn't much of a surprise when, toward the end of that decade, he was successful with a concept of his own: acrylic watches, a product for which he founded a one-man firm on Oranienstrasse in the Berlin district of Kreuzberg. Slowly but surely, Wallroth created a design-oriented line of products for the home. Today that assortment ranges from wine and CD shelves, a collection of coat racks and lamps, to wall clocks, including one named the "Bauhaus Clock". About two dozen people work in Wallroth's firm, which includes a development team and a highly specialized metal workshop. Recently, the "technomanufacture", which is now housed in an attractive site in the Brandenburg countryside, reinvented itself once again. MAWA has now made a name for itself by putting back on the market lamps like the floor lamps by Fridtjof Schliephacke and Günter Ssymmank (→ p.**23**) as well as a series of designs by **Wilhelm Braun-Feldweg**, whose wall lamp **Britz** is a paragon of ingenious simplicity. In addition, the company has come up with quite a few extremely innovative developments of its own, for example the anti-glare hanging lamp **Fridtjof 1**, or the economical, dustproof wall lamp *Quadrat* with its cleverly conceived illumination technique. It was due to the many custom-made designs that lamps and lighting became the company's main business within the space of just a few years, although its profile is still shaped by the personality of its founder: flexibility incarnate.

PHOTOS: l.: *Bankers* wall clock by Arne Jacobsen
m.: and r.: *Wittenberg* lighting system (manufacturer's design)

MILESTONES: *Britz* wall lamp → page **146** | *Fridtjof 1* hanging lamp → page **314**

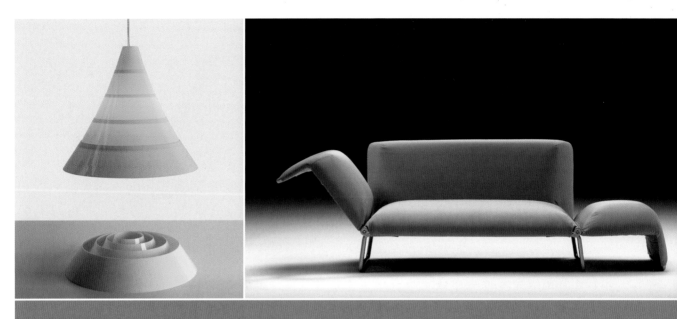

# Gioia **Meller Marcovicz**

furniture designer and entrepreneur, born 1955, office in Venice / Italy, **www.gioiadesign.com**

The daughter of a photographer and an art director with German-Hungarian roots began her career as a fashion designer in Munich before establishing herself with her own fashion label in London. After years of successful work, she finally turned her back on that hectic metier and studied furniture design. The fact that fashion designer Issey Miyake bought one of her sofas on the spur of the moment at the presentation of her final project at London's Royal College of Art gave her unexpected publicity. From the early 1990s on, Marcovicz worked freelance for renowned furniture-makers. And many are surprised – given her professional beginnings – at the amount of attention she lavishes on the sophisticated technology of her furniture. They are by no means decorative furnishings only; rather, it is their versatility that makes them convincing. This is true of the complete garden furniture collection **Dia** (for **ClassiCon**) as well as for the *Plug in* sofa bed (for Wittmann) with its tubular steel frame and integrated floor lamp. Time and again, Marcovicz manages to combine timeless harmony with clever details. Finally, she founded the company Gioia. Under this label, the European designer, who has moved to Venice in the meantime, markets lamps and furniture like the glass folding table *Tio*. A unique mixture of convertibility, elegance and quotations from the history of domestic design marks her small collection of lamps.

The model *Primo*, which is available as a floor, table or wall-mounted version, is reminiscent of the 1950s with its long variable neck and plastic conical-shaped shade. The hanging lamp *Bee*, which sheds direct and indirect light with its five concentric shades that can be locked in place, is a bow to Danish designer Poul Henningsen. Her winged sofa *Sigmund* is almost a classic already, a resting place for modern souls that can be transformed in no time into a chaise longue or sleeping area.

PHOTOS: l.: *Bee* hanging lamp, r.: *Sigmund* multifunctional sofa

MILESTONE: *Dia* garden furniture collection → page **288**

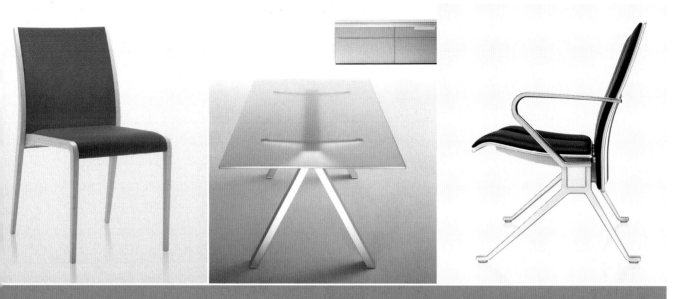

# Wolfgang C. R. **Mezger**

furniture designer, born 1951, design office in Eislingen / Baden-Wurttemberg

"Materials that are used correctly are beautiful," is his declaration of love for the physical substrate of his work. Wolfgang C.R. Mezger has an eye for the basics, but also for the fine finishing touches. Three-quarters of his customers come from the office furniture sector, a fastidious clientele that wants only the best, but not at high prices. In this respect, Mezger is regarded as the man for the optimum, a man who is happy to push the technical envelope and who places an emphasis on aesthetic longevity. For **Brunner** he designed the "architect's chair" *Milano*, a chair that combines a clear structure with exceptional stability. Even more successful is *Milanolight*, which features plywood bent at a record-breaking radius. That model was followed by *Fina*; light as a feather and with an extremely thin seat shell, it draws its optical elegance from its technical finesse. There is hardly a design without a well-thought-through, though usually unobtrusive detail. The extremely robust *Take* bench (for Brunner), constructed according to a modular system, centres on a tandem beam that was particularly time-consuming to manufacture, but which makes the system amazingly flexible. For the US company Davis, he created the wooden shell chairs **Lipse** (licensed to **Walter Knoll**) and *Circus*, whose armrests have been cleverly integrated. A clearly defined vision is necessary in order to achieve inventive form and construction. For Mezger, that means creating a small scale model before he tackles the original size. The son of the owner of a model-building shop first learned typesetting, then went on to study industrial design at the University of Design in Schwäbisch Gmünd – a period that left its mark on him. For years, he worked as a freelancer for **Hans "Nick" Roericht** and taught design classes. In the early 1980s, he finally decided against an academic career, and set off down the hard road to independence. Today, he has long since arrived in the executive suites, where he is regarded as a specialist in furnishing the offices of managers. His *Focus* program (1988, for **Renz**) was a surprise with its consistently modular design. *Icon* (2000, for Walter Knoll) is an office system in a class of its own with its minimalist attitude and maximum legroom. A key detail is the supporting desk rail that hides all the wiring but itself remains invisible, so it won't be in the way when, one day, electric cables are a thing of the past. Mezger knows that a designer must plan for the future because, as he says, "technology ages faster today than furniture does".

PHOTOS: l.: *Act* chair for Brunner, m.: *Icon* office system for Walter Knoll r.: *Take* bench system for Brunner

MILESTONES: *Lipse* chair system → page **324** | *Milanolight* chair → page **352**

# Miele

household appliance manufacturer, Gütersloh / North Rhine-Westphalia, founded 1899, **www.miele.de**

When the Gütersloh-based company showed signs of approaching a crisis a few years ago, that didn't at all fit the image of the A-student who lays claim to being quality leader in the hotly-contested market; an A-student who boasted a considerable turnover of two-and-a-half billion euros in 2005/2006, with 15,000 employees in ten plants (eight of them in Germany). Today, Miele's world is back to normal, the company having increased its turnover by a full 12 percent since then. Miele stands for continuity and the non-existence of problems. The products' longevity and technical perfection are the foundations of Miele's success. This is symbolized by the tireless washing machine behind whose sleek-looking exterior lurks an abundance of high-tech power. But this basic trend can be found in the matter-of-fact design of all the other products as well: the lack of "design" in the sense of fashionable gadgets is a consistent characteristic. The best example for homogeneity as a program is provided by the built-in appliances for kitchens. In all the appliances today, stainless steel, black glass and uniform controls are as much a succinct feature as the horizontal lines. This is true for ovens, for steamers and for coffee machines alike. And due to this uniformity, all of the appliances are easy to combine. Since the 1970s, Miele has boasted a design department whose success isn't documented as much in an endless series of awards, but in continuous innovation – often hardly visible to the eye. A precondition for this success is the close co-operation between product design on the one hand and development and construction on the other. It's part of the tradition of the integrated concept that **Braun** was the first to apply consistently. And the same as with the modern automobile, optimal handling is the main design criterion, from opening the appliance to the question what kind of unintentional mistakes could crop up. Across the globe, the unobtrusive appliances from Westphalia are regarded as the luxury cars among kitchen appliances and as a prime example for what is expected from the label "Made in Germany".

PHOTOS: l.: *Miele@Home InfoControl*
m.: *Navitronic TouchControl* built-in appliances, r.: *Side-by-side* refrigerator

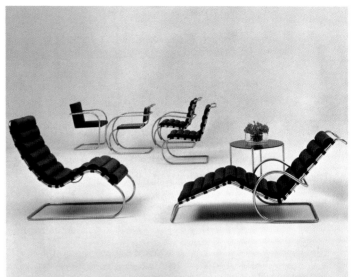

# Ludwig **Mies van der Rohe**

architect and furniture designer, born 1886, died 1969

Although the son of an Aachen stonemason never took any official final exams, architecture as a profession seemed to be his destiny. After learning a great deal about construction in his father's business, the 19-year-old went to Berlin, where he worked in the offices of Bruno Paul and **Peter Behrens**, both central figures in the reform movement. Mies was admitted to the circles of the wealthy and educated, some of whom were collectors who aroused his interest in modern art. The early 1920s saw his first skyscraper designs. A bachelor again after a failed marriage, Mies the modernist abjured any kind of "trivial embellishment". But even in his revolutionary open floor plans – most of them for villas – he never departed from the basic structure of a middle-class way of life, which included the separation of the men's from the women's area, as well as some sort of shield from the staff. Furniture was merely a by-product of his construction work. The Weissenhof residential estate project in Stuttgart (1927), his German pavilion for the World Fair in Barcelona (1929), as well as the Villa Tugenhat in Brno (1930) represent milestones in architectural design. His international career began with the "cantilevered chair" – totally without back legs – he presented in Stuttgart, originally a concept by Mart Stam, which Mies honed. He called the easychair he designed for the World Fair, **MR 90**, a "monumental object". His use of

strip steel was uncommon, but its relatively heavy weight enabled him here to engineer the chair's striking scissors-shaped base. Although his furniture was at first produced only in limited editions, it inaugurated a new style, as did the glass-topped table with the visible cross-frame and the chaise longue with its row of parallel bulges. The importance of his furniture is underlined by the many knock-off products, by the originals' successful re-marketing and the continuation of his ideas by prominent designers like Franco Albini or Poul Kjaerholm, and even the anti-designers from Archizoom. Mies von der Rohe is usually named in connection with the Bauhaus, but he had already developed all the essentials before he became its last director in 1930. Efforts at coming to an arrangement with the Nazi dictatorship failed. In the late 1930s, he emigrated to the USA, where he headed up the architecture department at the Illinois Institute of Technology. He was a much sought-after architect worldwide up until the day he died and is regarded, along with **Marcel Breuer** and **Walter Gropius**, as one of the grand masters of the "International Style".

PHOTOS: l.: Upholstered furniture collection for the Ester House in Krefeld
r.: *MR* collection and *Brno* chair

MILESTONES: **MR 10** chair → page **70** I **MR 90 / Barcelona** easychair → page **74** I **MR 50 / Brno** chair → page **80**

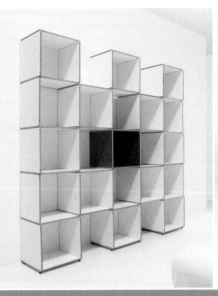

# Mobilia

furniture manufacturer, Burgthann / Bavaria, founded 1961, **www.mobilia-collection.de**

The name just about says it all. During the experiment-happy 1960s, the Frankonian firm put mobile and multifunctional furniture on a market that no longer had room for rigid concepts of domestic life. They were innovators, in the same league as **Bofinger** or **Otto Zapf**. Especially the upholstered furniture by architect Hans Hopfer, reminiscent of Bauhaus and the Ulm School in its simplicity and systematic approach, dissolved established furniture categories, replacing them with more flexible forms. The product names in those days are a telling expression of that development. Hopfer's early *Bausystem* (Construction Kit) sleeper sofa was followed by *Mobiliante* and *Player*, two cushion puzzles that can be changed and expanded and thus adapted to people's individual needs. The "sofa land-scape" *Lounge* took the principle of flexibility one step further: only three basic elements allow virtually endless seating and lounging arrangements. In the 1970s, pyramid-shaped stackable so-called construction kits by Hopfner and the firm's founder Peter Biedermann offered an elementary alternative to traditional wardrobes and cabinets. During the next decade, when design was the buzzword of the day, Werner Dechand took over management and expanded the program by adding original designs like *Stick* (by Eduard Erenski), a coat rack that leans against the wall, a minimalist table frame by **Rolf Heide** and a

few designs by **Jan Armgardt**, including *Tattomi*, a "jack-of-all-trades" easychair/sofa/bed that attracted a great deal of attention and still is at the heart of the collection today. After Werner Dechand's sudden death, his sons Andreas and Markus took over the company that still stands for courage and principles. That includes loyalty to the designers, a loyalty that spans the generations. For instance, Patricia Hopfer, Hans Hopfer's daughter, is now also part of the Mobilia "family". Current products are the transparent chaise longue *MC 1* (by Olaf Kitzig), made completely from a single piece of acrylic, the astonishing *falter* folding furnishings that function without fittings or hinges, as well as the *Stapler* connector shelves (both by dreipunkt4). The latter are made of a single simple component that is used for the base, top, side frames and backs, making for an extremely flexible shelving system that is the veritable incarnation of the Mobilia collection's founding idea.

PHOTOS: l.: *MC 1* lounge chair by Olaf Kitzig
m.: *Stapler* shelf system by dreipunkt4, r.: *Falter* table by dreipunkt4

MILESTONE: *Tattomi* lounge chair → page **232**

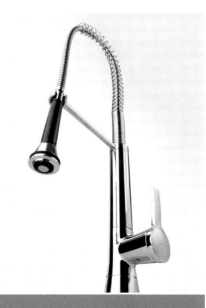

# Reiner **Moll**

furniture and product designer, born 1947, office in Schwäbisch Gmünd / Baden-Wurttemberg, **www.molldesign.de**

His studio – awarded "Design Team of the Year" in 1991 – has been one of the most successful for more than 30 years. All the same, Reiner Moll is not a star designer who regularly pops up in the media: his qualities are of quite a different nature. The Swabian adopted his analytical approach from his teacher Karl Dittert, whose roots go back to the Bauhaus. Moll believes, to put his professional concept in a nutshell, that "design is never an end in itself". Every single time, you have to redefine the purpose. That's why communication is so important, not only amongst the 12 studio employees, but also with the manu-facturer. A network of informers supports this process. And in the end, that's how products like the three-legged table *Stand up* (2004 for Hiller) emerge, a table that, when folded using a proprietary mechanism, is extremely narrow. The company's range of endeavours is just as universal as its basic approach: The product line spans ceiling lamps to heating boilers. For Moll, furniture soon became the central topic. His contact with **Wilk-hahn** in the 1970s resulted in the "century chair" *Binar*, the first chair with a clamped-on base. Projects for **Bisterfeld+Weiss**, **König+Neurath**, **Planmöbel**, **Renz** and others followed. The office chairs *Axos* and *Xantos* (for **Interstuhl**) are more recent success stories. Villeroy & Boch is one of Molldesign's long-time customers, a manufacturer for whom the firm has not only

designed bathtubs and basins (***Virage*** 1993), but also bathroom furnishings, including the versatile series *Bellevue*. Also of note here is the formally restrained bathroom series *Plan* (for **Keuco** → pp.**470** and **476**), one of the most extensive on the market. For that same manufacturer, the clever Swabian designed *Aqua-move*, the first hydraulic shower tap as well as the incredibly clear LED cosmetic mirror *Bella Vista* (→ pp.**476**). Sometimes Moll is asked to do a study, like that by chipboard producer Pfleiderer, which resulted in the first four-part kitchen in 1990. The tubular steel chair *Xenar* (1995 for Interprofil) is an unabashed homage to the Bauhaus era. The chaise longue *Dreipunkt* (2005 for Dreipunkt) on the other hand embodies a technically oriented style; it's an all rounder with four motors that goes from a com-pletely flat reclining surface to a full-fledged armchair. Versatile Moll, himself the prototype of an industrial designer, places an emphasis on longevity – for aesthetic, ecological and economic reasons.

PHOTOS: l.: *EL 300* easychair for Erpo International
m.: *Binar* chair for Wilkhahn, r.: *Tallo* kitchen tap for Villeroy & Boch

MILESTONE: *Virage* washstand → page **262**

# Möller Design

furniture manufacturer, Lemgo / North Rhine-Westphalia, founded 1987, **www.moeller-design.de**

Friedrich-Wilhelm Möller, a cabinetmaker and interior designer by profession, made quite a few detours before he began to design furniture. But in the early 1960s he was a freelance representative for **COR** and **Interlübke**, and that took him straight to the heart of the business. The wealth of experience he gained during those years probably contributed to the creation of his upholstered furniture program *Conseta* (for COR). At that time, his innovative modular system was groundbreaking and today, four decades later, it is still a best-seller. Despite his continued achievements, however, COR parted from its long-time associate in the late 1980s. So Möller founded his own design-oriented furniture company, which he rapidly put on the road to success. His formula includes guidelines that all come from the textbook of "good form" and are all oriented toward values that for a century have been at the top of the list in German design. Furniture should be long-lasting, maintain its aesthetic punch over the years and, last but not least, be geared toward the people who use it, measuring up to their standards and meeting their needs. Such a concept also incorporates the notion of a feeling of cosiness and security. Möller's catalogue includes upholstered furniture, cabinet systems, tables and beds. The comfortable and simple bed *Yomo* – one of the company's first designs – as well as the 1986 pivoting glass table *Gironda* and

the 1993 wardrobe *Para,* which is based on a classic country-style wardrobe, are among Möller's outstanding designs. Design awards like the one for the *Mia* bed in 2000 confirm the soundness of the eastern Westphalian's strategy. Möller's son has headed the company since the founder's death in 1996. One of the family business's characteristics is the fact that all of its furniture, which is produced in Swabia, is designed on site by a creative team of currently ten designers.

PHOTOS: l.: *Gironda* pivoting glass table by Friedrich-Wilhelm Möller
m.: *Plain* cabinet, r.: *Kanjo* wardrobe

MILESTONE: *Conseta* sofa system → page **152**

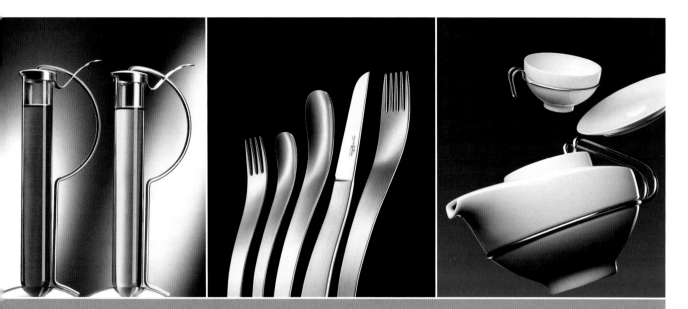

# Mono

silverware and household goods manufacturer, Mettmann / North Rhine-Westphalia, founded 1895, **www.mono.de**

Founded around 1900 as a manufacturer of goods made out of Britannia alloy, the family company first made waves beyond the local scene in the 1930s when it provided the Olympic silverware for the Olympic Village in Berlin. It wasn't until two decades later, though, that Mono really reinvented itself. Despite the boom during the years of Germany's "Economic Miracle", the silverware industry encountered difficulties toward the end of the 1950s. At the same time, success stories like that of **Braun** and **Rosenthal**, both founded on design, were making the rounds. Herbert Seibel, Mono's manager and a grandson of the original founder, decided that his company would set itself apart from others through "good form", by which he meant most of all no frills or embellishments. The result was the **mono-a** silverware series – designed by **Peter Raacke** – which was an instant hit. It became a best-seller that made the label known overnight as a synonym for good German silverware design – along with **Pott,** a firm that Mono is meanwhile allied with. The line of products for the table was completed with teapot warmers, candlesticks and accessories (by Fried Ulber) as well as further Raacke silverware designs, including a version for children. Later on, the modular teapot *Classic*, made of glass and metal, spearheaded a new style. A new type of product was being created here, something the company from the Bergisches Land region

managed time and again, even in fringe areas. Accessories like the mug pendant *Dolce* (by Mikaela Dörfel) or the *Concave* glowing bowl (by Franz Maurer) are tiny innovations at the table that make the company what it calls a "co-designer of life". The *Geminii* series (by Mikaela Dörfel) was a novelty in china and stainless steel. This combination was uncommon and for Mono it meant embracing a new material. Since the 1980s – following Alessi's example – Mono has steadily expanded its product line. Teapots were added to the silverware, along with espresso cups, candlesticks, nutcrackers, apple peelers and other well-crafted useful things. Organically shaped products renouncing edges and corners from the 1990s like the silverware *mono-filio* (by Ralph Krämer) or a set of candlesticks (by Fried Ulber) are as simple today as they were then. The *Zeug* silverware pattern (by Michael Schneider) and the knife set *Cubus* (by Fried Ulber) are veritable prototypes.

PHOTOS: l.: *Mono-jardino* oil and vinegar cruets
m.: *Mono-filio* silverware by Ralph Krämer, r.: *Geminii* service by Mikaela Dörfel

MILESTONES: *mono-a* silverware → page **136** l *Mono Classic* teapot → page **210**

  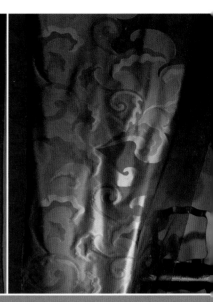

# Ulf **Moritz**

textile designer, born 1939, studio in Amsterdam / Netherlands

Thin copper wire and black linen thread twist around tufts of horsehair. Black glass beads glisten on transparent ground. Ulf Moritz has considerably expanded the notion of material or fabric. The only thing that is typical about his work, he once said, is that he does not repeat himself. Moritz won't be pigeon-holed and is regarded as Germany's most creative home textile designer. Like **Luigi Colani**, **Peter Maly** and **Dieter Rams**, he belonged to the war generation that had a strong influence on post-war Modernism and the image of German design. In the late 1950s Ulf Moritz studied at the Krefeld School of Textile Engineering. Georg Muche, for years head of the Bauhaus weaving mill, was one of his teachers. For Moritz, who was born in Poland, the beginning of his career in 1960 went hand in hand with an important move: to Amsterdam, where he has lived ever since. In the 1960s, he worked for a Dutch fabric manufacturer. A decade late, while teaching at Eindhoven's School of Design, he had his breakthrough as a freelance designer. Companies like **Christine Kröncke**, Felice Rossi, **Interlübke** and Montis were now his customers. He began working with Sahco in 1986, a co-operation that is still of prime importance today. Year after year, Moritz presents a collection of exceptional designs for that company, and he is also responsible for shaping Sahco's corporate image. This just goes to show how far the creative potential in a lasting relationship between designer and manufacturer can be stretched. Toward the end of the 1990s, Moritz embarked on a successful foray in a new direction with the *Walls* wallpaper collection (for Marburger Tapetenfabrik). In the meantime, he has also designed sofas and chairs (for Team by Wellis and others) and vases (for Leonardo). But his main focus remains fabric, where he is not only the leading producer of ideas, but also manages, thanks to his profound knowledge of manufacturing technology, to create affordable products.

PHOTOS: l.: *Cosima* fabric collection, m.: *Fairy Tale* fabric collection
r.: *Fabiana* fabric collection (all for Sahco)

# Müller Möbelwerkstätten

furniture manufacturer, Bockhorn / Lower Saxony, founded 1869, **www.muellermoebel.de**

**Jan Armgardt**, **Siegfried Bensinger**, **Rolf Heide**. The fact that three major German furniture designers have worked with the northern German company for decades says a great deal about its long-term strategy. It wasn't until the 1960s that the cabinetry workshop that had produced furniture for the previous 30 years began serial production. Today, the company, which is based near Bremen and focuses on interior fittings and serial production, offers around 600 products. Müller Möbelwerkstätten already began in the 1970s to work with external designers. The *Penelope* sofa bed and an ingenious table trestle (both by Jan Armgardt) were among the early designs. In the mid-1980s, the furniture collection was assigned to the newly created sister company Emform, and since then the company has positioned itself among the limited ranks of the design-conscious – explicitly acting on the assumption of a "German understanding of design and quality". Clear-cut forms and the renunciation of any fashionable transience are, of course, part of this understanding. The use of modern, unobtrusive materials such as aluminium and plywood gives the furniture an inter-national flair, as does the concept of mobile living: exemplified, for example, by a cradle (by Hannes Weber and Nikolaus Hartl) that can be dismounted and easily transported. The fundamental basis for the concept, however, is working with capable designers, generally Germans. The *Skala* shelving (by Siegfried Bensinger) is an example of an upmarket system, with combinable elements that form a regular grid pattern and boast a new type of drawer and door front – a basic shelf solution with sides all of the same thickness. Even nitpicking formalists are bound to enjoy the care-ful co-ordination of width, height and depth as well as their pro-portional relations to the shelves' thickness. Such consistency calls for a more than average degree of accuracy. The combination desk/mobile container from the *Swing* program (by Jan Armgardt) on the other hand is directed at the increasing need for flexibility in our everyday lives. Finally, the *Modular* program (by Rolf Heide), which includes the famous **Stapelliege** (Stacking Lounger), shows that even the unconventional can be lasting.

PHOTOS: l.: Sideboard/bar (*Swing* program) by Jan Armgardt
m.: *Skala* shelf by Siegfried Bensinger
r.: *Container* cabinet system (*Modular* program) by Rolf Heide

MILESTONES: *Stacking Lounger* → page **166** | *Container* cabinet system → page **184**

# Nils Holger Moormann

furniture manufacturer, Aschau / Bavaria, founded 1992, **www.moormann.de**

He has for a long time cut an unconventional figure on the German and European design scenes, well-known as a producer of purist furniture and an opponent of dress codes. The unwieldy man who hails from the foothills of the Alps has managed to put a new and contemporary face on German domestic funct-ionalism. It was he who provoked an unpretentious plywood/ chipboard Modernism that young companies like **Jonas & Jonas**, **Kaether & Weise**, **Performa** and **Sanktjohanser** now also espouse. He entered the trade, however, from quite a different angle: In the early 1980s, Nils Holger Moormann dropped out of law school to embark on a new profession. After several hard and lean years, his breakthrough came with two products. The first was Wolfgang Laubersheimer's **Verspanntes Regal** (Tense Bookcase) made of sheet steel, which thrilled industry experts and is today regarded as a new German furniture classic. The *Schuhkippe* shoe cabinet followed, an instant hit at the cash register. This new kind of cabinet, with a depth of only 16 cm, is exemplary in its simplicity for Moormann's product concept, as is the *Zoll D* shelf, a modular system made of aluminium sheeting. "The basic idea", the German Design Award jury wrote, "is the greatest possible reduction in material, processing and joining together of the individual parts". Moormann is renowned for taking even young, as yet unknown designers seriously, so

proposals come in by the basketful. He invests not only money, but also his heart and soul in the development of new products. In the **FNP** shelf system (by **Axel Kufus**), a best-seller, one can see the amount of thought that went into creating this minima-list but at the same time highly flexible hardboard construction. The same is true for the lightweight plywood table **Spanoto**, the coat rack **Hats Off** and the Es shelf that **Konstantin Grcic** thought up to make life easier for librarians and scholars. The **Kant** desk (by **Frey & Boge**), the top of which folds at the back, made him popular with pencil pushers as well. The modular wall shelf *Erika* (by Storno) is one of the newer products, as is the paperback rack *Buchstabler* (by Tom Fischer) and the garden object *Walden* – Moormann's own monumental contribution to life outdoors. All of these objects have a very dry aesthetic, comparable to a fine wine. Moormann has also made himself a name with an ingenious masterstroke: he conducted a plagiar-ism lawsuit against Ikea through all the courts – and won!

PHOTOS: l.: *Zoll D* shelf by Lukas Buol and Marco Zünd
m.: *Schuhkippe* shoe container by Hanspeter Weidmann
r.: *Buchstabler* shelf by Tom Fischer

MILESTONES:   **Tense Bookcase** → page **228**  I  **FNP** shelf system → page **248**  I  **Spanoto** table → page **274**  I  **Hats Off** coat rack → page **294**
**Kant** desk → page **326**

# Torsten **Neeland**

furniture and product designer, born 1963, office in London / Great Britain, **www.torsten-neeland.co.uk**

Torsten Neeland, who studied industrial design in Hamburg, succeeded at the end of the 1990s – after relocating to London – in ascending to the firmament of sought-after star designers of the Grcic generation. What followed were such diverse products as *LiberTea*, an eight-part tea preparation set (for **WMF**), the *Stav* silverware pattern (for Auerhahn), the *Crossover* bathtub shelf with mirror and reader-friendly bookrest (for **Dornbracht**), and finally two occasional tables (for **Anthologie Quartett** and Mouvements Modernes). In recent days, Neeland has turned his attention to the theme of light, turning out highly innovative designs in a terrain where, contrary to popular opinion, the possibilities are far from being exhausted. One example is *Hybrid* (for Mouvements Modernes), a formally reduced coat rack in the form of a console that does double duty as light source. Four lamps are installed within a frame, generating an indirect ambient light. The back wall has an application of invisible paint that reacts to black light, with different light colours to choose from. The floor lamp *uv-1* for the same manufacturer functions, like *Hybrid*, with invisible paint and black light. Additional original lighting creations include *Cut* and *Tank* (both for **Anta**). The latter is a wall lamp made of a covered, ring-shaped neon tube that casts indirect light on the wall. The intensity of the light can be adjusted manually. The light field can also be

changed, switching between flat and circular. Furthermore, colour filters can be applied to support or change the mood of the room. Here as well, Neeland has created an interactive product whose impact can be influenced by the user. The designer, who has made his home in London, sees himself as moving along the interface between art and technology. He has recently conceived not only domestic interiors but also stage settings for an English dance company, as well as fine-tuning the corporate visuals for firms such as **COR**, **Duravit** and **Interlübke**.

PHOTOS: l.: *Cut* table lamp for Anta
m.: Stool/occasional table for Anthologie Quartett
r.: *LiberTea* teapot for WMF

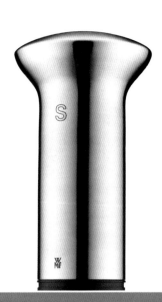

# Neunzig° Design

office for furniture and product design, Wendlingen / Baden-Wurttemberg, founded 1994, **www.neunzig-grad.com**

The duo of Barbara Funck and Rainer Weckenmann, who chose to name their company after the 90-degree angle, are interested in imbuing our everyday world with "more colour, warmth, joy and meaning". This is done based on an analysis of current needs and traditional as well as changing behavioural habits, all the while taking advantage of the latest in technology. At the same time, they always keep sight of the "heart of a product" and heed the well-known designer maxim that "beauty often lies in simplicity". The result they are striving for is a relaxed relationship between object and user. At least that's how the theory goes. In practice, the two industrial designers who studied in Schwäbisch-Gmünd have already implemented these principles in conjunction with prominent manufacturers including Belux, Boffi, Ideal Standard, Osram and **WMF**. In their studio, an old railway station with a view of the Neckar River, such products have been created as the *Basic* salt shaker (for WMF), which, although clean-lined and modern, also has something archaic about it. The stable salt container is extra large and has a special shape that prevents the salt from clumping. And the matte upper section is dishwasher safe. For the same manufacturer the two also designed the award-winning **Velvet** silverware pattern and a few more products for better eating and drinking. Additional focuses are lamps and bathroom furnishings, such as

the *Ceramix 60s* tap complete with temperature display (for Ideal Standard) and the washstand *Folio* (for Boffi), a sculpture for the bath whose asymmetrical, slanted basin looks expressionist but is in reality highly functional.

PHOTOS: l.: *Moskito* chair for elmarflötotto
m.: *Big Size* hanging lamp for Belux, r.: *Basic* salt shaker for WMF

MILESTONE: *Velvet* silverware → page **296**

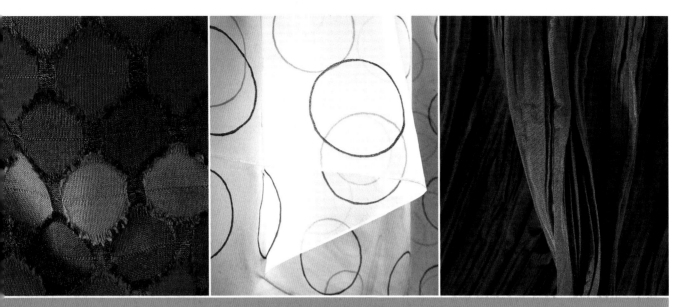

# Nya Nordiska

fabric editor, Dannenberg / Lower Saxony, founded 1964, **www.nya.com**

With more than 700 decoration and upholstery fabrics for the home as well as commercial properties, this company with subsidiaries in Paris, London, Como and Tokyo is one of the industry giants. But it all started on a modest scale. After 20 years as an apprentice and journeyman in European fabric-printing shops, and then a post as art director at a Swedish print shop, Heinz Röntgen founded his own fabric editing company in the mid-1960s. At first he offered a small selection of fabrics based on Scandinavian models – hence the company name, which means "new things from the North". What was coming out of Denmark, Sweden and Finland in those days was considered ultra-modern and shaped domestic styling worldwide. Functionalism and a simple, natural quality were the properties associated with these designs – still leitmotifs even today. In 1974 Röntgen's later wife and business partner Diete Hansl joined the company, a trained textile saleswoman. Upon the death of the company founder in 2003, she took over the management, joined by her children Marcus Hansl, Remo Röntgen, Sybilla Hansl and Bernhard Hansl. The senior executive is now in charge of designing the collection, along with Sybilla Hansl and designer Alice Pieper. The founder designed a large portion of the fabrics himself; with a great love of experimentation, he developed unusual patterns, incorporating new kinds of thread and manufacturing tech-

niques. Following the move to Dannenberg on the Elbe River, Nya Nordiska increasingly opened up to international design currents in the late 1970s. Well over 100 awards document how persistently a uniform creative line has been pursued in a metier whose design independence is often underestimated. The common misconception that nothing much of lasting value is produced in this fast-paced industry is effectively laid to rest by success stories like that of the polyamide fabric series *Lia*. With this hit decorative fabric, Nya Nordiska became the first fabric editor to be recognized with a German Design Award, in silver. Every year, Nya Nordiska brings out a new collection produced in Europe exclusively for its own agency, guaranteeing both innovation and exclusivity.

PHOTOS: l.: *Clou* fabric, m.: *Mega Pearl* fabric, r.: *Tiziano* fabric

MILESTONE: *Lia* fabric collection → page **242**

# Nymphenburg

porcelain manufacturer, Munich / Bavaria, founded 1747, **www.nymphenburg-porzellan.de**

Bowl with hare – this work by Hella Jongerius attracted a great deal of media attention. The Dutchwoman, known for her originality and chutzpah, slightly modified the famous animal figures and thus created a subtle quotation reaching back more than two hundred years. When the first porcelain began to be manufactured in the mid-18th century, Bavaria's Elector Max III Joseph supported the fledgling enterprise. But it was only after a move and expansion that the hoped-for success could be won. Soon the ingenious sculptor Franz Anton Bustelli was turning out his famous figurines, which, usually used as table decoration, still have a share today in shaping Nymphenburg's worldwide reputation. Under the direction of Albert Bäuml the company enjoyed a new artistic flowering around 1900. The brief heyday of Jugendstil marked – as with so many other porcelain makers – Nymphenburg's entry into the modernist era, which would however be interrupted from time to time by retrograde currents such as the neobaroque wave. Young artists joined the firm in these times of change. Among them were landscape painter Hermann Gradl, who at only 18 won a Grand Prix at the 1900 Paris World Exposition. The influence of the reform movement could not be dodged, however, not least due to the proximity of the *Münchner Werkstätten*. Reform efforts at Nymphenburg were personified by figures like Adalbert Niemeyer, who in 1906

– one year before he became a co-founder of the Werkbund – designed the sleek service dubbed *No. 820*. Its most conspicuous, and difficult-to-craft, feature is a cubic border. The era of classical Modernism at Nymphenburg was shaped to a great extent by Wolfgang von Wersin, whose forms exude noble restraint and are never trivial. In his *Lotos* service, von Wersin demonstrated his adeptness at designing in three dimensions along with his commitment to timeless modernity at a high level. The whisper-thin, gently curving shapes are the quintessence of perfection. The painted décor underscores the flow of line, lending the service an elegant and distinguished air. Of equal standing to Trude Petri, for example, or Hermann Gretsch, the rationalist left his mark on the Nymphenburg line until well into the 1960s. Thereafter a Rococo revival temporarily put an end to the era of creativity. In recent days well-known artists and designers such as Jongerius, American Ted Mühling and Munich-based **Konstantin Grcic** have been exploring what artistic potential still lurks undiscovered in the realm of white china.

PHOTOS: l.: Eggcup (*Konstantin Grcic Collection*)
r.: *Lotos* porcelain tableware by Wolfgang von Wersin

MILESTONE: *Fish Service* porcelain tableware → page **40**

# Herbert **Ohl**

furniture designer, born 1926, lives in Darmstadt / Hesse

He is one of the war children generation of designers who – like **Hans Theo Baumann** or **Otto Zapf** for example – is to thank for the fact that the second wave of Modernism was able to gain a foothold in the young and prosperous post-war Federal Republic of Germany. After studying architecture – with **Egon Eiermann**, among others – he began to work independently in the mid-1950s and lived until the end of the 60s in Ulm. At an early phase the active designer was already attracting notice with his unusual and analytical acuity, developing out-of-the-ordinary concepts such as the "Kugelkino" spherical cinema. It thus came as no surprise when in 1966 he was appointed director of the Academy of Design in Ulm, the closing of which he thus experienced first hand. Ohl and **Richard Sapper** were the first German designers to set up permanent business contacts with Italy. He has even more in common with his somewhat more famous colleague, such as the unconditional rationality of his designs, the constant urge to transcend limitations and the fact that he never copies but has continually been copied by others. Ohl worked for a few years for automaker Fiat. One of his main fields of activity besides automobiles and construction systems was furniture. His Italian clients included companies such as Arflex, Fantoni and Matteograssi. For Fantoni he developed among other things the intelligent worktable *Evolution 2* and

the grip-less cabinet system *24 Grad*, whose hinges are one of his wonderworks. Important designs that came onto the German market are *Multipli* (for **WK Wohnen**), a cabinet system that is as comprehensive as it is variable, and the chairs *Swing* (for **Rosenthal**) and *Circo*. Typical for the unerring pioneer is the *O-Line* chair collection with its unusual use of nylon webbing (for Arflex, and *Nuvola* as a further development for **Wilkhahn**) as well as a wire chair that he, against all the rules, developed to series maturity in his garage with the help of a master metal-smith from Odenwald. A citizen of the world, Ohl has never taken a narrow view of things. While teaching in Chicago, for example, he developed a "World Peace Tower", which was exhibited at the famous Athenaeum.

PHOTOS: r.: *Circo* chairs for Lübke
l.: *Nuvola* furniture program by Herbert and Jutta Ohl for Wilkhahn

MILESTONE: *O-Line* easychair → page **196**

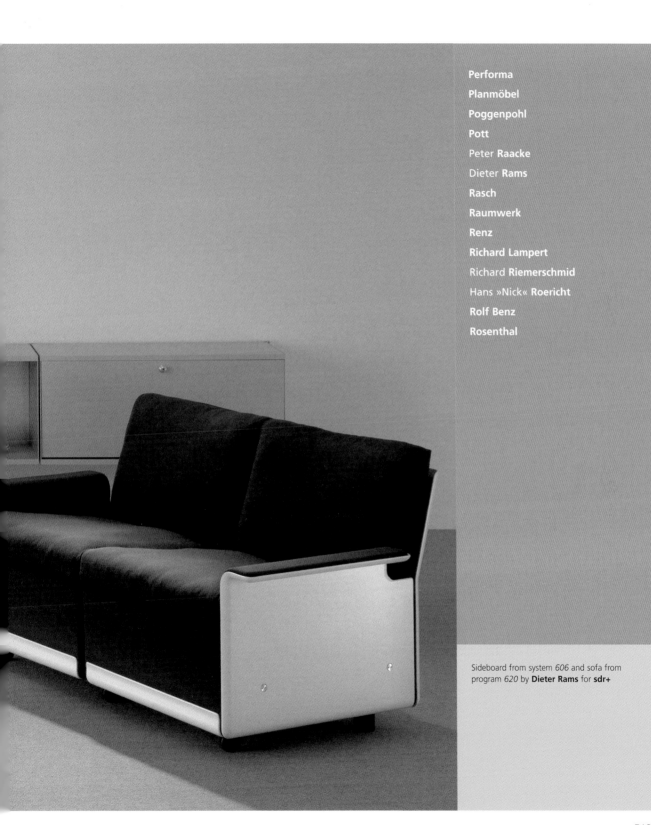

**Performa**

**Planmöbel**

**Poggenpohl**

**Pott**

Peter **Raacke**

Dieter **Rams**

**Rasch**

**Raumwerk**

**Renz**

**Richard Lampert**

Richard **Riemerschmid**

Hans »Nick« **Roericht**

**Rolf Benz**

**Rosenthal**

Sideboard from system *606* and sofa from
program *620* by **Dieter Rams** for **sdr+**

# Performa

furniture manufacturer, Pleidelsheim / Baden-Wurttemberg, founded 1987, **www.performa.de**

"Behind our designs is not a style, but a way of thinking", is how Martin Kleinhans puts it. The trained cabinetmaker, who originally worked as a mechanical engineer and is thus a career changer like **Nils Holger Moormann**, also discovered like his colleague a penchant for designing furniture. In the late 1980s he began to act on his impulse. A decade later, now with production director Matthias Eckert as partner, he made the decision to put out his own collection. It now comprises some 20 products. One that was already shown at the 1997 Cologne Furniture Fair was a shallow wall container up to three metres in length. It is disarmingly simple and has a linoleum skin that is mitred all around. This exacting craftsmanship lends the piece the look of a block in space, which, although angular, is not hard due to the softness of the material. The same interesting combination of clean lines and soft, pleasant touchability can be found in the square-shaped **Performa** coat rack, which comes in linoleum or rubber. The height at which clothes are hung can "grow" with the children. It is probably no coincidence that Performa furniture sells especially well in Switzerland, where ascetic form has always been appreciated and quality honoured. The ten-person company from the Stuttgart area regards itself as a "technofacture": a small manufacturer that unites meticulous craftsmanship with exact reproducibility based on modern

software. Word of this concept has gotten around by now, so that a major manufacturer like **Wilkhahn** recently decided to profit from the Swabians' expertise by producing their highly acclaimed *DIN A* container series. The latest products include the *Screen* shelf, which takes up the theme of the modular shelving system, adding another surprising variation to the long line of forerunners such as *FNP* (→ p.**248**) (by **Axel Kufus**), *Endless Shelf* (→ p.**266**) (by Werner Aisslinger) and *Plattenbau* (→ p.**346**) (by **Kaether & Weise**). Due to its simple structure, borrowed from reinforced concrete buildings, no screws are required. Especially when used as a room divider with transparent frosted plexiglass for back and side walls, the 03 exudes an almost magical glow. But at the same time it is made to be put together simply at home, with no need to get out the toolbox. Now the Swabian form and idea incubator has developed a completely new furniture type: the "slideboard" **Nuf** (from Beyonddesign). This modular sliding cabinet, suitable for both home and office, is the most flexible storage solution since the invention of the chest.

PHOTOS: l.: *Screen* shelf, r.: *6.0* wall container

MILESTONES: *Performa* coat rack → page **320**  l  *Nuf* cabinet system → page **374**

# Phoenix Design

studio for product design, Stuttgart / Baden-Wurttemberg, **www.phoenixdesign.de**

The founding duo Andreas Haug and Tom Schönherr, former colleagues at Frogdesign, do not aim to impose their own expressive signature on their clients. They are interested instead in task-specific solutions oriented on the desired target group. Their brand of high-end minimalism with undeniable reverberations of classical Modernism results in sophisticated, cosmopolitan products. Whether mobile phone, stereo system or faucet, all of their designs are first submitted in prototype form to not only be seen but touched, a service that makes it that much easier for clients to articulate concrete requests. This intensive dialogue frequently gives rise to innovative products and unusually long-standing working relationships, such as with bathroom fittings manufacturer **Hansgrohe**. Creating a strong brand profile is not something that can be done overnight. It comes about as a process in which the manufacturer and designer must work hand-in-hand. **Loewe**, a company with a highly developed design culture, was one of those to take this route – which is often a meandering one. Over the space of an entire decade, various design features were worked out that guarantee a high recognition factor but which are far more than skin-deep. What resulted was a variety of different Loewe television sets that all have one thing in common: The Phoenix team namely crystallized the upscale brand into a single central hallmark. A control

button placed squarely in the middle of the lower edge of each television set identifies the set as unmistakably Loewe. Homogeneity and individuality don't have to be contradictions: For Lamy, Phoenix developed an exclusive pen series called *Accent* in which the grips can be switched according to taste and preferred pen-holding position.

PHOTOS: l.: *Raindance* shower for Hansgrohe
r.: *Individual* television set for Loewe

MILESTONES: *Arco* tap → page **250** | *Mimo* television set → page **334** | *Raindance* shower → page **336**

# Poggenpohl

kitchen manufacturer, Herford / North Rhine-Westphalia, founded 1892, **www.poggenpohl.de**

What is probably the world's most famous kitchen-maker started out furnishing high-class "daughters' rooms" in the pared-down Werkstätten style. In 1905, when Jugendstil was already passé, the company brought out a kitchen cabinet with a separate upper cabinet standing on small legs. This was already an early precursor of the linear kitchen that would one day replace the traditional buffet. In the 1920s, when the gas range and electric appliances were on the rise and living space was at a premium, Poggenpohl developed the "reform kitchen", a clearly articulated white cabinet cube whose signature feature was the semi-circular "functional handle" with a round glass plate as base. The program – like Bruno Paul's "growing apartment" – was an example of the transposition of the "Neue Sachlichkeit" (New Objectivity) onto German everyday life. This is the era when the ten layers of paint applied to every kitchen cabinet became a seal of quality. The principle of the "add-on kitchen" finally prevailed at Poggenpohl in the late 1950s. Under Walter Ludewig, who directed the company from 1940 to 1987, it transformed itself into one of the leading international kitchen manufacturers and one of the best-known brands in the furniture industry. In the "Economic Miracle" years, the add-on programs were expanded and perfected, for example with the introduction of the grip rail. The experiment of the "spherical kitchen" (1970) by

**Luigi Colani** was a tempting utopia, but remained an isolated episode. At the end of the 1980s Poggenpohl was purchased by a Scandinavian corporation. The kitchens are still produced in Germany, however, by a workforce of almost 500. A total of 75% are destined for export, well over the industry average. With programs such as +*Integration*, an effort to fuse design, high-tech and new media that was introduced in 2004, new visions are now explicitly geared toward a design-conscious target group. Along with Bulthaup, Poggenpohl is today jockeying for the leading role in terms of conception. The central theme that has crystallized out is the kitchen's gradual shift in meaning from a monofunctional room to a focal point of the home with versatile uses. In 2005 this idea was given concrete form in *Plusmodo* designed by Jorge Pensi of Spain, a program that stands as a model for the finely orchestrated dialectic of presentation and concealment. A recently published design study has now confirmed that the kitchen will soon take on the role of the living room, with daily life revolving more and more around the dining table. The Porsche Design studio is already working on applying findings like these to creating the luxury kitchen of the future.

PHOTO: *Plusmodo* kitchen

# Pott

silverware manufacturer, Mettmann / North Rhine-Westphalia, founded 1904, **www.pott-bestecke.de**

The Pott brand stands for transcending the traditional silver cutlery that, alongside the "fine china" has long established itself as the prime status symbol on the middle-class dining table. By introducing no-frills forms and "honest" industrial materials, the company created – comparable to reform brands like **Thonet** or **Arzberg** – a product type with a whole new identity. Its success at transferring the virtues of classical Modernism onto objects of daily use that exhibit a high design standard made the enterprise from the Bergisches Land region a model brand in its metier. No one could have predicted this development at the time the company was founded, when Carl Hugo Pott was running a small workshop specializing in the "damascene" technique for decorating knife blades. It was only after son Carl Pott entered the family business around 1930 that a few silverware patterns began to be produced. Pott Jr., inspired by the rationalist spirit of the times, pursued a fully new line. One of his very first silverware series, with the fittingly unpretentious name *2716*, attracted international acclaim. These eating utensils were of spartan simplicity and went well with the new tableware created by Hermann Gretsch or Trude Petri. Although the model received an award at the 1937 Paris World Exposition, many dealers refused to carry Pott's unconventional wares. He nonetheless held fast to his Bauhaus-influenced ideas. The reward came in the 1950s,

when traditions were being discarded right and left and modernity was the order of the day. Now Lufthansa ordered its onboard eating utensils from Pott, and designs by like-minded souls such as Hermann Gretsch and **Wilhelm Wagenfeld** expanded the range. The entrepreneur often invested years of development in new types of knives, forks and spoons. Carl Pott designed the majority of his models himself, receiving a sizeable number of design awards for his efforts – back when they still meant something. When the family failed to produce a third-generation successor, the company was acquired by the firm Seibel Designpartner and has since then been allied with **Mono**, a dream liaison of two brands from the German design aristocracy that, despite certain overlaps, seem to complement one another harmoniously. The catalogue was expanded to include works by young designers. Even though the new house designer Ralph Krämer allowed himself a bit more freedom when crafting his award-winning *Picado* cheese knife, the up-and-coming talents are nonetheless still measured according to the purism Pott is known for.

PHOTOS: l.: *2716* silverware by Carl Pott
m.: *Marisco* oyster knife by Ralph Krämer, r.: Sugar bowl and creamer

MILESTONES: *Model 33* silverware → page **204** | *Picado* parmesan knife → page **254**

# Peter **Raacke**

product and furniture designer, born 1928, office in Berlin

Although his career biography is closely intertwined with the Academy of Design in Ulm, where he taught as visiting professor in the early 1960s, he defies all the stereotypes associated with that school. He has always proceeded in a pragmatic and often unorthodox manner, placing a great deal of importance on an extended concept of functionality that takes into consideration the cultural and human context. Trained as an artist-blacksmith and enameller, the highly gifted artist actually wanted to become a painter. He studied in Paris in the 1950s and then travelled through the USA, where he came into contact with Bauhaus émigrés. In 1958, now a university lecturer, he was a co-founder of the *Verband Deutscher Industriedesigner* (Association of German Industrial Designers). His first series products were combi-cookers he designed in the mid-1950s (for Haas & Sohn), precursors of the white built-in appliances that would later become standard, giving the modern kitchen a technical, clinical aura for over half a century. Raacke then became interested in experimenting with "pure" form. The ***mono-a*** silverware pattern he designed toward the end of the 1950s for the company of the same name is one of the very few designs that one can with confidence call "timeless". Although this word certainly does not apply to the same degree to the following series *Oval* and *Clip* (1973 and 1982, for **Mono**), they, too, are exceptionally striking.

He likewise pursed a radical path in his work with Voko, at the time probably the most innovative office furniture manufacturer, for which Raacke developed the first organizational furniture. The *Zeitgewinn* system (1957), a construction kit consisting of cubic furnishing elements with characteristic, seminal feet of rectangular steel tubing, formed a blueprint for the office world for decades to come. Raacke collaborated with Voko for about a decade (succeeded there by Karl Dittert), until he took his leave of strict functionalism and turned his ardour toward the pop and protest culture instead. The unconventional thinker achieved a modicum of celebrity at the end of the 1960s when he developed the first furniture program made of corrugated cardboard: the ***Papp*** series including the famous *Papp-Otto* easychair. Raacke, who initiated so much and yet is only well-known within the industry, is also regarded as a pioneer of environmentally friendly design, aiming at forming so-called "design chains": a catch phrase referring to the aspiration to repeatedly recycle products and materials.

PHOTOS: l.: *Papp-Otto* easychair, r.: *Zeitgewinn* furniture system for Voko

MILESTONE: ***mono-a*** silverware → page **136** | ***Papp*** furniture → page **156**

# Dieter **Rams**

furniture and product designer, born 1932, lives in Kronberg / Hesse

Whenever the topic of German design in the latter half of the 20th century comes up anywhere in the world, his name is bound to be mentioned sooner or later. Dieter Rams' career began in the mid-1950s when, at only 23, he was hired by **Braun**, whose revolutionary design concept he had a share in shaping, alongside **Hans Gugelot**, **Herbert Hirche** and others. He was director of the design department for over three decades, starting in 1961. Design principles that came directly from the Ulm school, and indirectly by way of the Bauhaus, were incorporated in the new product generation, demonstrated for example by the dominance of the cube. The replacement of the radio with the modular stereo system – realized for the first time in the model *studio 2* – in connection with a radically stripped-down exterior that can be traced largely to **Otl Aicher**, gave Braun devices the status of archetypes that would set the trend in this field for decades to come. The penetration of undisguised technology into the domestic realm alone was a premiere. The carefully arranged, colour-coordinated control buttons and knobs on the fronts of the hi-fi amplifiers Rams designed became telling icons and status symbols. He also supplied the furniture to go with these devices, as did Gugelot and Hirche. A working relationship with the Zapf/Vitsoe (later Vitsoe) company, which specialized in modern assembled furniture, gave rise to designs such as the

RZ 60 wall shelf. This was the forerunner of model *606*, a classic among modular furniture systems (today made by **sdr+**). Grids and the additive principle were applied to a diverse range of furniture types, whether small pieces like the *740* stacking stools and *010* nesting tables (→ p.**537**) or more elaborate systems like the *980* container program (with Thomas Merkel). Rams' *RZ 62* easychair is likewise based on a cleverly conceived system. All elements including the sides and backrests are easy to remove and can thus be replaced as necessary. There followed chairs, easychairs, tables, coat racks and shelves on wheels, which, like the Braun appliances, always maintain a neutral look. Dieter Rams is the very incarnation of late functionalism in his straight-lined version of the trend, often viewed as typically German. This is just the style against which the next generation would rebel. He himself sees in the level of discipline he demands of design a legitimate means for fighting increasing wastefulness and premature aesthetic obsolescence.

PHOTOS: l.: *FS 80* television set for Braun
m.: *RHa* desk lamp (with Andreas Hackbarth) for Tecnolumen
r.: *980* container program (with Thomas Merkel) for sdr+

# Rasch

wallpaper manufacturer, Bramsche / Lower Saxony, founded 1897, **www.rasch.de**

It was the sole comprehensive product program to come out of the famed Academy of Art and Design in Ulm, and, what's more, the only item that has been in production without interruption since its inception in 1928. This lasting success was by no means a sure thing for the person who initiated the program. Wallpaper manufacturer Emil Rasch, who originally came up with idea for the *Bauhaus Wallpaper* project, took the marketing into his own hands after the retail branch had responded with extreme reserve to the severe graphic wall design he was proposing. He placed ads that formed the key to the final breakthrough, providing an example, even after 1933, alongside **Arzberg**, **Pott** and others, for the partial survival of the "Neue Sachlichkeit" (New Objectivity) during the Nazi era. Following the Second World War, when Modernism was helping to lend the young West Germany an identity, Rasch continued to pursue his progressive line. He produced artists' wallpapers and joined forces with a dozen like-minded manufacturers, including **Braun** and **Rosenthal**, to propagate "good form". Among the most popular products of the 1950s were the "abstract" patterns typical of the time that came from the pen of English designer Lucienne Day. Rasch continued to put the "zeitgeist" up on walls everywhere throughout the 1960s and 70s. The *Avantgarde* collection by graphic artist Klaus Dombrowski of Essen took its cue from American Pop Art, introducing large-scale patterns into the German home. In the late 1980s Rasch finally made the design wave just part of the furniture: in the *Zeitwände* collection German and international designers including Ron Arad, Ginbande, Ettore Sottsass and Borek Sipek were let loose to put their postmodern spin on the once mundane world of wall coverings – an early case of the designer product. Even though this collection sooner found its way into museums than into the home, market leader Rasch, whose turnover (2005: 115 million euros) is rising more rapidly abroad than in Germany, had effectively established itself as an innovative brand. The product launch was accompanied by a highly acclaimed advertising campaign in which more or less well-known designers posed in front of plain white walls. The Pop-inspired *Colorflage* collection by **Markus Benesch** has of late set another avant-garde accent. Designed for a younger target group, the *Colors of Berlin* series by Berlin graffiti artist Oliver Kray can of course be pasted up by adults as well.

PHOTOS: l.: *Bauhaus Wallpaper*, m.: *Fiori* collection
r.: *City* wallpaper by Lucienne Day

MILESTONE: *Bauhaus Wallpaper* → page **78**

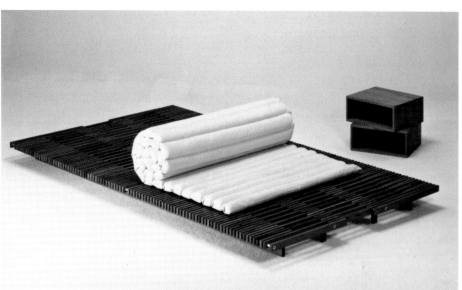

# Raumwerk

furniture manufacturer, Stuttgart / Baden-Wurttemberg, founded 2000, **www.raumwerk-stuttgart.de**

In the beginning were Swabian master craftsman Heinrich Schuhmacher and Japanese designer Toshio Odate. To make furniture according to their own notions, carpenter and architect Joachim Bürklein and his wife, architect Inge Hebeda, set up their own operation on a former farm. There, models are converted into prototypes one-to-one, from idea sketch to graphic fine-tuning on the computer, with individual elements repeatedly taken out and made in different variations until they approximate as closely as possible the original idea. "It is of existential importance to us to exert an influence on the design from start to finish, and to work directly with the chosen material", explains Bürklein. Wood is the main material of choice, not least due to its sensuous qualities, but other materials such as acrylic, aluminium, steel and polycarbonate can also be found. One of their favourite material combinations is wood with white satinized acrylic glass, as seen in the sideboard, the nightstands and the *Klippklapp* chest of drawers. Raumwerk furniture can usually do more than first meets the eye: by folding out, twisting open, stacking, sliding – changes that can be carried out at a touch and open up unexpected functions. The *Gästebett* (Guest Bed, 2001), for example, is no run-of-the-mill ponderous sofa bed, but rather a transparent wood structure that can be folded up to create a bench. The concave surface thus formed serves for sufficient seating comfort. In the lightweight *Postbett* the under-bed drawers are concealed from view by an "optical illusion": They are behind the slats that are part of the frame, which at the same time serve as handles with which the hidden drawers can be slid out diagonally. The incisive structure of parallel slats, the fine oiled pearwood and the subtle detailing lend this piece its typical Raumwerk flair.

PHOTOS: l.: *Regal 2006* shelf, r.: *Gästebett* bed

# Renz

office furniture manufacturer, Böblingen / Baden-Wurttemberg, founded 1882, **www.renz.de**

In the over 120-year-long company history, the specialization in office furniture is a relatively new development that was not originally envisioned. The trend was set in the mid-1970s with a dining table that was also sold as a desk. This hint was followed up in the early 1980s with *Contur* (by Heiner Gölz), the first program designed for the executive office. Here, the course was already set for the firm to become a major player with an international clientele. As is common in the industry and particularly in the Swabia region, the company would remain under family ownership. Since the 1990s, the design studio of **Wolfgang C. R. Mezger** has put its stamp on the product range, beginning with the furnishing system *Tao* (1990), whose key structural feature consists of upwardly tapering metal legs and which was later expanded into an entire executive program. It was followed by *Cosmo* (1992), with slanted legs and an amoeba-shaped table, and later the team workplace *Telos* (1998). In the ensuing years Hamburg designer **Justus Kolberg** realized a whole series of furniture groups, including the *Verso* management-level series and the O-shaped, intelligently linked *Segno* conference tables (both 2000), as well as the *Tema* team workplace program (2004), a keeper of order that fuses systematic design, fine craftsmanship and industrial rationality. In Kolberg's *Sono* system (2006) clean lines and transparency find entrée in the boardroom. The studio **Jehs + Laub** has also created two new programs for Renz. *Size* (2004) consists of office tables of monumental simplicity and in *Lane* (2006) an L-shaped tabletop that is apparently bent out of a single piece is set atop a cabinet element, forming a flexible duo and demonstrating that clarity and softness do not have to be a contradiction.

PHOTOS: l.: *Size* desk collection by Jehs + Laub
r.: *Sono* office system by Justus Kolberg

# Richard Lampert

furniture manufacturer, Stuttgart / Baden-Wurttemberg, founded 1993, **www.richard-lampert.de**

When design experts Richard Lampert and Otto Sudrow joined forces in the early 1990s in Stuttgart to plan a program of high-end designer furniture, it soon became evident that the legacy of two German architect/designers would play an important role for them: **Herbert Hirche** and **Egon Eiermann**, two protagonists of the West German post-war Modernism that had one of its centres in Baden-Wurttemberg. Hirche worked in Stuttgart. He was behind the **Tiefer Sessel** (Deep Easychair, 1953), which was recently re-issued: a design of architectural severity that carries on the tubular steel aesthetic of the Bauhaus era with confident virtuosity. Eiermann, sometimes referred to as the "German Eames", was soon represented in the product range by half a dozen different designs including basket furniture like the goblet-shaped, well-proportioned **E 10** easychair and the lightweight, formally appealing **Santa Lucia** rattan chair, as well as the famous **Table Frame with Cross-Bars** (in two versions) that university lecturer Eiermann designed for himself and his students and which would become the very image of the architect's table. The basic idea behind Eiermann's iconic table is revisited in two related pieces. The first is a standing desk after a concept devised by Sudrow that takes up the same structural principle as found in the table frame. The second is an example of the classics brought down to a size fit for the younger set.

The desk for homework and play can easily accompany a pupil all the way from the first form to graduation (2006 by Peter Horn). The swivel chair that "grows with it" comes from the same designer. From the start, the re-editions were not meant to stand on their own, but rather to be complemented by ambitious new designs. Today - Sudrow has since left the company – the products on offer include an archetypical solid wood bed (2003 by Katja Falkenburger), the versatile occasional furniture *Unit* (2003 by Eric Degenhardt) and the *Rollwagen* (Rolling Trolley, 2004 by Patrick **Frey** and Markus **Boge**). The *Seesaw* swivel chair (2000 by Peter Horn) affords a pleasant springiness thanks to a seat carried downward in a wide arch: a cantilevered chair on wheels like nothing that went before. Horn is also the author of the lightweight *Stapelstuhl* (Stacking Chair, 2003) for every occasion, which is inexpensive to boot – likewise a maxim of classical Modernism, but one that the old masters by no means always heeded.

PHOTOS: l.: *Seesaw* swivel chair by Peter Horn
r.: *Unit* occasional furniture by Eric Degenhardt

# Richard **Riemerschmid**

artist, architect and furniture designer, born 1868, died 1957

"With their educational talent, materials surpass the best teachers", is one of his guiding principles. Richard Riemerschmid's solid chairs, usually made of untreated wood in which the grain is allowed to fully come into its own, stand in stark contrast to the addiction to grandiosity that otherwise marked his era. Initially, he took inspiration from country-style furnishings. Simple, clear-cut structures in which no attempt was made to hide the joints became Riemerschmid's signature, both in individual pieces and later in inexpensive industrial series, which as "machine-made furniture" soon grew in popularity both in Germany and abroad. The programs he developed for the Dresden-based **Deutsche Werkstätten** are regarded by some as representing the birth of modern furniture design and made Riemerschmid – like **Peter Behrens** – one of the first sought-after designers. With his reform furnishings he was able to realize a dream turnover some years of over one million Reichsmarks, from which he received a certain percentage. He moved to Dresden in 1903, where he designed and planned in close co-operation with entrepreneur Karl Schmidt the Hellerau garden city, a centre of the "Lebens-reform" (lifestyle reform) movement. The graduate of the Art Academy had already taken his leave from painting by the mid-1890s. This was when the magazine *Jugend* first came out, for which he designed covers. The Jugendstil style that took its name from this periodical naturally did not fail to have a certain influence on Riemerschmid; however – similar to Behrens, **Henry van de Velde** and Bruno Paul – he tended toward the drier variant typical for Germany, inspired strongly by the Arts & Crafts movement. His *Service mit Blattdekor* (Service with Leaf Decor) for the Meissen Porcelain Factory (1903) of all things is a good example of this style. Later, he devoted all his energy to fighting against superfluous ornament. The Munich-based designer created a comprehensive oeuvre encompassing individual furniture pieces and furnishings for entire homes as well as china, glasses, beer steins, lamps, wallpapers and carpets. Furniture remained his chief focus, however, in particular chairs and cabinets, whose formal development he was instrumental in driving forward. His *Musikzimmerstuhl* (Music Room Chair) is regarded as the masterpiece of this early inventor of form. Later, the busy designer was involved in the founding of the Deutscher Werk-bund and worked once again as architect, developing wooden houses with standardized elements and decorating passenger ships.

PHOTOS: l.: Beer stein with pewter lid for Villeroy & Boch
m.: Buffet for Fleischhauer & Söhne
r.: Armchair for the W. Otto House, Bremen

MILESTONES: *Music Room Chair* → page **38** | *Service with Leaf Decor* → page **44**

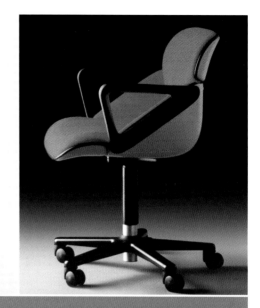

# Hans »Nick« **Roericht**

product designer and design researcher, born 1932, lives in Ulm, **www.roericht.de**

Even today, he still recommends the "emancipation of designers from the colourful world of merchandise". Hans "Nick" Roericht studied at the Academy of Design in Ulm in the late 1950s, where he acquired his analytical credentials. In his 1959 dissertation he developed the **TC 100** stacking tableware (made today by **Rosenthal**), the first of its kind and an incunabula of functionalism for the table. It has been produced now for more than 40 years, a longevity that is probably attributable to the fact that it is easy to store and still looks good. Following stays in the USA, Roericht founded at the end of the 1960s the office Produktentwicklung Roericht / Designresearch, which would become one of Germany's most successful studios for product design and design consulting and make Roericht a sought-after man. Lufthansa, for example, enlisted him to create on-board eating utensils (1971). In the early 1970s he was appointed professor at the University of the Arts in Berlin. Within his person he synthesized the critical Ulm approach with elements of the student movement – a mixture that was seminal for the design upheaval of the 1980s. Concurrently with his teaching duties, Roericht worked for companies such as Lufthansa, Pirelli and Rosenthal and took on projects to "humanize the working world" or "furnish a home for the mentally handicapped". What was probably his most intense working relationship, with

**Wilkhahn**, began at the beginning of the 1970s. He developed chair programs for the office furniture manufacturer as well as a whole series of studies dealing with topics such as "New Conference Concepts", "Future Wilkhahn Products" or "The Future of Sitting". Pioneering office furniture came about almost as an afterthought. His designs for Wilkhahn include the 190 conference easychair (1976) and the 840 waiting rooms chairs put together out of modular elements (1979). Finally, his examination of how people sit at the desk led to the concept of the leaning aid for more active sitting. This groundbreaking mobile furniture type would go into production some two decades later as **Stitz**.

PHOTOS: l.: *Cumuli* sofa system
r.: *190* swivel and conference easychair program for Wilkhahn

MILESTONES: *TC 100* stacking tableware → page **140** I *Stitz* leaning aid → page **252**

# Rolf Benz

furniture manufacturer, Nagold / Baden-Wurttemberg, founded 1964, **www.rolf-benz.de**

"When you buy Rolf Benz, you buy guaranteed taste", is how an executive at the firm sums up the brand promise. The path from crafts enterprise nestled in the Black Forest to the largest German manufacturer of upholstered furniture, which already made a splash in the early 1970s by placing nationwide ads, is one of the dream careers of the West German economy. In 1959 trained upholsterer Rolf Benz founded a furniture frame factory in Nagold, and then five years later brought out his own line of furniture under the acronym "bmp" (Benz Möbelprogramme). The very first product, a rational sofa ensemble with matching side tables called *Addiform* (by Rolf Benz → p.**23**) brought the young company its first accolades. The facilities had to be expanded because in just four years the workforce had swelled from about 30 to almost 300 (in 2004 there were 750 employees). A focus on quality and an unrivalled retail marketing program are still the key instruments for the company's success today. The Swabian mentality - Mercedes-Benz is not far away – likewise does its part. BMP ventured its first formal experiments in the early 1970s, such as the Riesenkissen (Giant Cushions, by Will Eckstein), which truly deserved the name "lounge landscape" and was an eye-catcher at the firm's first appearance at the 1971 Cologne Furniture Fair. In the design-enamoured 1980s, sofa groups with natural wood frames were increasingly joined by asymmetrical upholstery shapes and leather sofas in simple proportions perceived as "classic", which now shaped the brand image. Exemplary of this style is the model *6500* (1985, by Mathias Hoffmann). In 1987 the company changed its name to Rolf Benz, highlighting its repositioning as upscale label. Since then, the corporate strategy has entailed intense collaboration with freelance, usually German, designers, among them Georg Appelshauser, **Norbert Beck**, **Anita Schmidt**, **Stefan Heiliger**, Mathias Hoffmann and **Burkhard Vogtherr**. The spotlight is not on their names, however, but on comfort aspects and the "timeless" line. In the 1990s the company developed into a full-range supplier. Finally, Hülsta took the reins and the founder withdrew from the scene. The formula for success seems to still be working: The anniversary sofa *Dono* (2004 by Christian Werner) brought not only design kudos but also spectacular sales figures. Norbert Beck then created in model *540* (2007, → p.**393**) yet another surprising variation on the transformable sofa. Chair *620* by the same designer offers for the first time an online configuration program for customers to create a custom model according to their individual needs.

PHOTOS: r.: *522* sofa by Christian Werner
l.. Chair (Program *620*) by Norbert Beck

MILESTONES: *8950* table → page **290** | *Dono* sofa system → page **348**

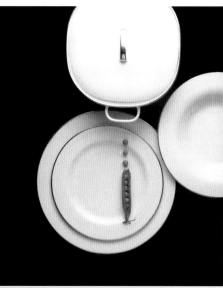

# Rosenthal

porcelain and furniture manufacturer, Selb / Bavaria and Espelkamp / North Rhine-Westphalia, founded 1879, **www.rosenthal.de**

In 1960 Rosenthal opened its first Studiohaus shop in Nuremberg. It is still following the same principle today: The first design chain store in the world sells only products a jury has selected as examples of good design. And the Studio Line products introduced in parallel can only be purchased at a Studiohaus. Rosenthal was the first company in the world to seek contact with international designers, a strategy that would not be adopted on a widespread scale until the 1980s. At the same time, the company forged alliances with other German design-oriented firms such as **Braun** and **Rasch**. The product range reaches from Bauhaus Modernism à la **Walter Gropius**, to American, Scandinavian and Italian designs, and on to **Luigi Colani**. Originally established in the late 19th century, the enterprise based in the Franconia region had expanded substantially by the outbreak of the Second World War. An "art department" had been set up even before World War I. But design only became an issue after the founder's son Philip Rosenthal, a non-conformist, democrat and visionary, took charge in the 1950s. The *Form 2000* service from 1954, from the drawing board of US designer Richard Latham, was the starting shot. It was followed by the *Berlin* service by **Hans Theo Baumann** in the post-war rationalist mode. As time went by, the world's largest supplier of high-grade tableware, which was taken over by Wedgwood in the late 1990s, expanded its offerings,

adding glassware, silverware and furniture. A furniture plant in Espelkamp was purchased in the early 1970s. Big-name furniture designers were commissioned from day one, such as **Burkhard Vogtherr**, who conceived one of the early collections, the table-and-easychair ensemble dubbed *Hombre*. There was not only series furniture, but also artistic works in limited editions, corresponding to the Studio Line. Nail artist Günther Uecker created alongside his early-1980s reliefs also an individual furniture piece he called *Lettera*, a standing desk for quickly jotting down ideas. Of the some 2,000 employees working for Rosenthal AG today, only 45 are located at the furniture plant. One of the focuses is office furniture, such as the *Cetera* conference table system *Cetera* (by **Lepper Schmidt Sommerlade**), the great advantage of which consists in the individually removable table legs. Behind the concept for the *Controller Serial Network* is the vision of integrating all the technology in a room, including even the most detailed conference table systems, into a single control, while maintaining flexibility. An interesting piece from the collection of solitary furniture creations is *Flying Carpet* (by Simon Desanta), a lightweight, springy easychair whose free-form shape affords a great variety of sitting options.

PHOTOS: l.: *Form 2000* service by Richard Latham
m.: *Moon* service by Jasper Morrison, r.: *Suomi* service by Timo Sarpaneva

MILESTONES: *Berlin* porcelain → page **132** | *TAC 1* tea service → page **174** | *Flying Carpet* easychair → page **236**

*Circo* easychair by **Peter Maly** for **COR**
and *Vivace* grand piano by Peter Maly for **Sauter**

# Sanktjohanser

furniture manufacturer, Uffing / Bavaria, founded 1992, **www.hubertmatthiassanktjohanser.de**

The furniture produced by Sanktjohanser is simple and cubic, with precise edges and perfect surfaces. Only on second glance does the refinement come to fore with which the form always fulfils the function, usually in a new and unexpected way. The folding stool, for example, is not only one of the lightest in weight of its species, but is also a startlingly adaptable and portable piece of furniture. Likewise exemplary of the firm's creativity is the **Socialbox**, a one-of-a-kind tilting cabinet suitable for a variety of uses and the incarnation of what the pioneers of classical Modernism once proclaimed as open living. The combination of clarity and deeper meaning, something that would surely have found favour with **Otl Aicher**, coupled with a selection of materials in which wood, multiplex and felt play important roles, gives rise to unconventional designs that are aesthetically convincing and yet just the opposite of obliging. If the often-misused term "design philosophy" ever makes sense, then here. The manufacturer from Pfaffenwinkel belongs to a new German domestic aesthetic whose clear-cut and sometimes rather dry charm is being moulded by young brands like **e15**, **Nils Holger Moormann** or **Performa**. Sanktjohanser offers something for nearly any type of living space. From the multi-purpose *Slow* chair and the sleek *Dinavier* dining table, to various shelf systems, occasional tables and beds, to the universal furniture

called *Socialbox*. "Design for me has to do mostly with seeing, with an ability to perceive things clearly", says Hubert Sanktjohanser, son of a carpenter, who after completing secondary school learned a trade and started his own company in the 1980s. Since 1992 he has been living and working with his wife, an architect, and their three children in the combined home and workshop they planned and built together in a village in the foothills of the Alps. There is the kind of silence here that is conducive to "getting to the bottom of things" – although this is by no means a purely rational process, but often more like a chain of associations.

PHOTOS: l.: *Slow* chair by Hubert Matthias & Anda Sanktjohanser
m.: *Falthocker* (Folding Stool), r.: *UKW* shelf

MILESTONE: *Socialbox* universal furniture → page **368**

# Richard **Sapper**

product designer, born 1932, lives in Milan / Italy

His *Tizio* table lamp (for Artemide) from the early 1970s is a finely calibrated balancing act. This original game with counter-balances made the lamp one of the mega milestones of design history and a veritable symbol of design itself. Sapper, one of the most successful of international designers, has again and again sent ripples through the world of design from his home base in Italy. With his teaching activities in Stuttgart he is in addition a great role model, having shaped the aesthetic of our everyday lives for over half a century. Of the Munich-born designer, whose career began at Mercedes-Benz, colleague Ettore Sottsass once said he was incapable of producing a bad design. Sapper's products are precise, functional, innovative and often highly complex. He always endeavours to find solutions and to "give form a meaning". There is almost nothing the busy designer has not put his hand to at some point in his life. With his mentor, the Italian Marco Zanuso, the young Sapper developed radios and television sets of extremely innovative design in the 1960s (for Brionvega). The same period saw one of the first fully plastic chairs, the *K 4999* for children (for Kartell), which soon stood as model for countless "adult" counterparts. The same team was responsible for the *Lambda* metal chair (for Gavina, 1964), which is made out of ten thin punched steel sheets. The office chair named after him from the late 1970s, the *Sapper* (for

Knoll), likewise has exemplary status. Other furniture, usually for the office, was conceived for companies including B&B Italia, CAP, Castelli and Molteni, as well as an entire home office collection for Unifor. In the 1980s the Thinkpad laptop series for IBM and the *9091* water kettle (for Alessi) were the postmodern icons that gave the object of daily use a whole new standing. With the lightweight *Aida* garden furniture (for Magis), the dean of design then went on to lend restaurants and private outdoor celebrations a touch of elegance. Sapper, who in recent years has once again worked often in Germany, is perhaps the best example of the synthesis of German perfectionism with Italian sensuality.

PHOTOS: l.: *9090* espresso pot for Alessi
m.: *Aida* stacking chair for Magis
r.: *TS 502* radio for Brionvega (with Marco Zanuso)

MILESTONES: *K 4999* children's chair → page **150** | *Tizio* table lamp → page **188** | *9091* water kettle → page **214**

# Sauter

piano maker, Spaichingen / Baden-Wurttemberg, founded 1819, **www.sauter-pianos.de**

In the early 19th century, back in the days of Romanticism and Classicism, Vienna was the centre of the music world. And this is just where the company founder learned his trade seven generations ago, with a master from whom Beethoven ordered his piano. Sauter is thus anything but an ordinary company; rather, it is the oldest existing piano manufacturer in the world. Despite consistent high quality, the competition from the Far East at some point became a constant menace. The best way for the company to distinguish itself on the market was then to do nothing less than rethink piano design from the ground up. It was high time anyway to give the grand piano a look more in keeping with the contemporary aesthetic. Few had dared as yet to venture onto this hallowed ground, with the exception of **Luigi Colani** and his typically eccentric model (for Schimmel). The one chosen to take up the challenge was **Peter Maly**, who at the end of the 1990s created the grand piano *Vivace* (→ p.**528**). He devised a new and subtle flow of line, with truncated radii replacing the traditional curves. A row of stainless steel intarsia squares accents the new line given this king of all instruments. The following model, *Ambiente*, then broke several of what used to be considered hard and fast rules of the metier. Conspicuous here is the wide arc of the lid, which, instead of forming the usual "S" now describes a parabolic curve. The novel silhouette

takes its impact to a great extent from the integration of the feet in an enclosing apron formed by a chrome profile set at some distance from the body. What Maly achieved in the luxury segment was echoed by **Reiner Moll** in the compact class. In his model *Vision* shadow grooves running all around the perimeter bring the clean-lined box form to the fore. Maly subsequently managed to create nothing less than a modern icon with his up-right piano *Pure*. Its name says it all. In the good German design tradition, this piano is all about avoiding anything extraneous and thinking carefully about the positioning of all of the some 8,000 parts. Design plus state-of-the-art technology while renouncing all electronics. This is the formula the Swabian manufacturer applied to attain its USP, transporting this resonant object in our domestic environment into the design here-and-now.

PHOTOS: l.: *Ambiente* concert grand piano by Peter Maly
r.: *Vista* piano by Molldesign

MILESTONE: *Pure* piano → page **312**

# Anita **Schmidt**

furniture designer, office in Bretten / Baden-Wurttemberg

For insiders, she is virtually synonymous with well-designed up-holstered furniture. Many of her models are currently in production, although the road to success was not always a direct one. Anita Schmidt followed up her philosophy studies with an apprenticeship in the furniture industry. In the early 1970s she then went out on her own, specializing in the genteel culture of sitting. She has done work for many leading brands, including Begana, De Sede, Hülsta, Laauser, **Rolf Benz**, Straub and **Walter Knoll**. Schmidt has an unfailing sense of what customers want. At Rolf Benz, a manufacturer for which she developed half a dozen models, she made curvaceous lines popular. The *2800* lounge chair conceived by the seating designer from the Kraich-gau region, for example, seems to float on thin air. A comparable success story – and one that has endured for over one-and-a-half decades – is the model *322* (1989 for Rolf Benz), looking with its slanting aluminium feet like the very picture of the "designer sofa". With over 40,000 units sold, this is one of the company's best-sellers, now reissued in leather as "2007 Classic of the Year". A design with a double meaning is the sofa *Kissen* (1986 for **WK Wohnen**), which looks just like what its name indicates, a cushion, but is actually a full-fledged sofa bed. The well-travelled designer is always open to new ideas. While watching a blacksmith at work in Turkey she was inspired to try

using iron in her work and developed on the spot in a small village prototypes for a furniture system that later went into series production (WK Wohnen, 1987). Although more of an exception as furniture type, *Bosporus* in a way sums up many of the qualities this designer brings to her work: It is practical, versatile and just a bit playful.

PHOTOS: l.: *2800* sofa for Rolf Benz, r.: *622* sofa for Rolf Benz

# Karl **Schneider**

architect, furniture and product designer, born 1892, died 1945

Although a cultural award in his hometown has been named after him, he is one of the designers who have fallen into oblivion. Karl Schneider was a "rebel against the diehard conventionalists" wrote an art journal in 1929. After working in **Walter Gropius'** office before the First World War, he then realized countless construction projects in the style of "Neue Sachlichkeit" (New Objectivity) in Hamburg between the wars: from villas to factories and ultramodern filling stations, to cinemas, department stores and gigantic workers' housing complexes, the model homes for which he furnished himself. New York's Museum of Modern Art displayed his building for the Hamburg Art Association in its 1931 "Modern Architecture" exhibition as a prime example of the "International Style". The private villa he designed in 1928 for a timber plant owner named Bauer on Hamburg's Oberalster Lake – a composition of nesting cubes – had a linear kitchen and wall-to-wall cabinets. In 1930 he presented a complete program of furniture types, including a tubular steel easychair typical of the day as well as chairs with moulded wood runners and curving forms that presaged later designs by Alvar Aalto or Bruno Mathsson. The combinable cabinet elements, such as the buffet he named *KS 81* in the shorthand Bauhaus manner, already seem akin in their severity to the sideboards **Herbert Hirche** would create in the 1950s. As

member of various architecture associations, such as the avant-gardist "Ring" and the "Volkswohnungsbau" (AVOBAU), he was a proponent of classical Modernism, one of the central themes of which was how to handle the general lack of living space. He is the perfect example of how widespread this movement already was at the time in Germany. The free spirit turned Hamburg into one of the centres of the "Neues Bauen" (New Building) and "Neues Wohnen" (New Lifestyle), just as **Ferdinand Kramer** had in Frankfurt and **Otto Haesler** in Celle. Schneider is also a case study for the expulsion of an intellectual elite from their home country. Ostracized by the Nazis as a "cultural Bolshevist", he was compelled to emigrate to the United States.

PHOTOS: l. and r.: *Typenmöbel* (type furniture) for the Schneider House, Bahrenfeld

# Wulf **Schneider**

interior and furniture designer, born 1943, office in Stuttgart / Baden-Wurttemberg, **www.profwulfschneider.de**

The quintessential element in his occupation is after all the human being. If products are not "accepted", then they have missed the point. That's why sensual components and current perceptual patterns must always be taken into consideration. "This was made just for you", should be the message. The aim of this holistic approach would ultimately be a "product culture" – a very German-sounding essence. As early as the end of the 1980s, Wulf Schneider already wrote a book on the "sense and nonsense" of the designer environment. After studying interior and product design in the 1960s and holding executive positions in business as well as a design professorship, he liked to expound upon the fundamentals of product design. The eternal quest-ioner, who has been working as a self-employed designer since the mid-1970s, has found a clientele that shares his demanding approach. He has been developing chairs for **Thonet** since the early 1980s, which regularly received awards even before design prizes started wildly proliferating. Among them are the models *S 320* and *S 570* as contemporary syntheses of wood and steel, as well as *290*, a patented chair in only three parts, with the seating area cut out of the backrest piece. There followed the multipur-pose easychair **S 3500**, a tubular steel design with a classic Bauhaus flavour whose easy-to-remove seat cushion multiplies the comfort factor. Schneider also developed intelligent furniture

for **COR**: The *Clou* upholstered cubes (1994 → p.**419**), a reinter-pretation of the modular sofa, unite a range of practical com-bination options with unusual proportions and armrests that remind some of ears. Six years later came *Arthe* (2000 for COR), a sofa with joints. Finally, Schneider conceived whole furniture programs such as *Team*, a series of seven swivelling and canti-levered chairs (for Arts Collection), and the conference ensembles *No Limits* and *High End* (for **Sedus Stoll**). A furniture system that brings the sense of sight into play in a completely new manner is the lighted cabinet **EO** (2001 for **Interlübke**) in which the brightness and colour of the illumination can be modified. The round fireplace *Emotion* (for Skantherm) also has a pleasant surprise in store. It has the first panoramic glass pane that not only radiates heat optimally but also affords a good view of the fire from "all" sides.

PHOTOS: l.: *Arthe* sofa for COR, r.: *S 320 P* chair for Thonet

MILESTONE: *EO* cabinet system → page **318** I *S 3500* easychair → page **368**

# Schönbuch

entry hall furniture manufacturer, Bad Königshofen / Bavaria, founded 1960, **www.schoenbuch-collection.de**

The entryway is an area of the home that is often neglected today by architects and designers, and even by the residents themselves. But, as was the case with the likewise long-forgotten bathroom, which is now experiencing a renaissance, this underestimated transitional zone harbours plenty of design potential. This is the mission of a company whose name was taken from a forested region that lies between Stuttgart and Tübingen. Schönbuch, originally a woodworking operation, outsourced its production in the 1980s and has for almost half a century specialized in intelligently designed entry hall furnishings. Early on, the corporate strategy already involved continuous working relationships with external designers like **Thomas Althaus**, **Ulf Moritz**, Andreas Weber and **Jürgen Lange**, who with his model *Trio* delivered a best-seller that evidently has no aesthetic expiration date. In this typical niche field, high demands are exacted not only by what is usually a narrow space, but also by the non-standardized dimensions, which often make it impossible to take advantage of what is on offer at furniture stores. After a change in ownership, the company began at the end of 2004 to consistently build on its creative USP in this fringe area. Part of this push was a model campaign with designs by young, usually German designers. Among the new products for the contemporary entry way is *Up and Down*, a meandering

cross between shelf and classic coat rack by Munich designer Carmen Stallbaumer. Another nice piece to come home to, but of an entirely different sort, is the hanging console *Hesperide* by Carsten Gollnick of Berlin, a horizontal shadowbox in wood and leather. The **Jehs + Laub** studio from Hanover contributed two designs to the rejuvenated assortment, *Stripes* and *Match*, both strictly right-angled box systems that are simple yet surprisingly variable.

PHOTOS: l.: *Stripes* cabinet system by Jehs + Laub
m.: *Line* wall-mounted coat rack by Apartment 8
r.: *Match* entryway program by Jehs + Laub

MILESTONE: *Trio* coat rack → page **240**

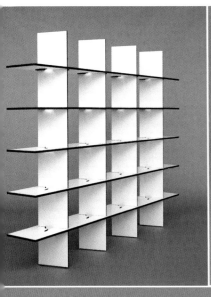
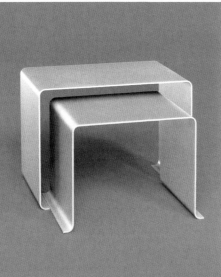

# sdr+

furniture manufacturer, Cologne / North Rhine-Westphalia, founded 1995, **www.sdr-plus.com**

It all started with a shock. When in 1995 the legendary furniture firm Vitsoe, famous for a longstanding partnership with **Dieter Rams**, closed its doors, Rams' furniture designs were suddenly no longer available. Six prominent German furniture stores reacted spontaneously by getting together and purchasing the licensing rights. Plans were made to continue producing the pieces under the acronym sdr – for "System Furniture Dieter Rams". The plus stands for the ambition to further develop the designs. House designer Thomas Merkel in particular has revised Rams' designs in a congenial manner, contributing his own input in the process. A start was made with four product lines: the *606* shelf system, *620* easychair (**RZ 62**), *570* table and *710* cabinets. Due to popular demand, the conference table program *850* was also reworked and continues to be sold very successfully. To complement the program, the *980* container system (→ p.**519**) was then reintroduced in the late 1990s, a co-operation between Rams and Merkel. A guideline behind the entire product range is the principle that the various programs are conceived not only as discrete systems, but can also be combined with one another. According to the well-known credo that Rams espoused for four decades as head designer at **Braun**, all furniture should be designed in such a way that it does not shout out its presence, but rather melds into the background,

standing at the ready to serve when needed. This is regarded at sdr+ as an essential requirement for a lifelong human-furniture liaison. Another advantage to this approach is that the "neutral" designs fit into nearly any environment. There is also a system behind the names: They indicate the year an item was designed. Therefore, the *010* nesting tables were developed by Rams and Merkel in the year 2001, and two years later came the *030* coat racks. All of the pieces are made in Germany, both to guarantee high quality and to be able to react rapidly and flexibly to customer wishes.

PHOTOS: l.: *020 Twister* shelf by Dreiform
m.: *010* nesting tables by Dieter Rams and Thomas Merkel
r.: *030* entryway program by Thomas Merkel and Dieter Rams

MILESTONES: *606* shelf system → page **142** I *RZ 62* easychair → page **144**

# Sedus Stoll

furniture manufacturer, Waldshut / Baden-Wurttemberg, founded 1871, **www.sedus.de**

With eight European subsidiaries (four of them production sites) and an export ratio between 40 and 50%, this company with its headquarters on the Swiss border is one of the leading brands in the office furniture industry. Today Sedus Stoll is a full-range furniture purveyor, a status it reached for one thing by acquiring the Klöber and Gesika companies, the latter ideally complementing the product portfolio with desks, containers and cabinets. Sedus Stoll's origins can be traced to a single product: the office chair. In the mid-1920s the firm introduced Europe's first sprung swivel chair and, just a few years later, swivel castors as well. In the 1970s the focus shifted more and more toward anatomically adaptable chairs, and the company opened its own design department. Today, the pool of knowledge Sedus Stoll has gathered on correct sitting is one of its core competencies. Its most successful product turned out to be the *Paris* swivel chair, sold over one million times. Designer Michael Kläsener has made some vital contributions to the current extensive office chair line, from the entry model *Yeah!* to Lisboa in the business class. **Wulf Schneider** conceived the flexible table systems *No Limits* and *High End*, which provide variable configurations and quick assembly and breakdown to optimize work meetings. The *Corner* series by English designer Peter Wilson, by contrast, upsets our visual habits with its asymmetrical easychairs covered in bi-coloured leather. Sedus Stoll develops its catalogue based on sociological studies aiming at elucidating the relationship between the various worlds of home, work and leisure. The new products in the *Place 2.5* system are derived from the studies' findings and are designed, e.g. to enrich the performance-driven office environment with emotional resonance from the leisure-time world. Creative ideas are called for here, such as the portable leaning aid *Smile* (by Emil Lohrer), whose height can be adjusted just like a bicycle seat. At the heart of the aforementioned system is a table, or "system bench", called *Invitation*, a variable tool that encourages creative and playful uses. "Work is child's play" is a fitting motto for the campaign, which is geared toward activating people's spontaneity and sense of fun. *Turtle Club*, the brightly coloured plastic hemisphere by Italian Matteo Thun, goes a long way toward relieving the workaday world of some of its stultifying earnestness.

PHOTOS: l.: *Time Out MS* folding table by Mathias Seiler and *Let's Fly* chair by Team Papenfuss, m.: *Turtle Club* easychair by Mattheo Thun r.: *Smile* leaning aid by Emil Lohrer

# Seefelder Möbelwerkstätten

furniture manufacturer, Seefeld / Bavaria, founded 1983, **www.seefelder.com**

The head office in the lake-dotted landscape of Upper Bavaria already has an appeal all its own. Originally a subsidiary of **Brühl**, the Seefelder Werkstätten became independent at the beginning of the 1980s and soon developed an attractive, by now quite wide-ranging production program, which today runs the gamut from modern upholstered pieces to stools and dining ensembles all the way to coffee and pullout tables and carpets. Another new start was necessitated by a restructuring following insolvency and subsequent take-over by marketing director Gabi Meyer-Brühl and production manager Heinz Schrewe, two thirty-somethings who stand for a forward-looking orientation. The focus of the current product line is on sofas, such as the model *Joy*, an ingenious pullout couch in which the perpendicular backrest and armrests lie down flat to form a reclining surface. *Joy* was developed by the company itself, although normally working with external designers is the corporate policy. The enthusiastically received **Janus** folding table with its patented mechanism (by Luzius Huber and Florian Steiger) is likewise an example of miraculous expansion. It not only doubles its length, but also changes colour. Additional folding artists are the sofas *Shift* and *Layla*. They are at once sofa, bed and recamiere (both by Volker Laprell and Volker Classen), achieving their metamorphosis through an invisible mechanical substructure – each in a

different way. A plethora of possibilities is likewise offered by the upholstered puzzle called *Play* (by **Jan Armgardt**). One of the newer sofas, also by Armgardt, is *Alfa*, as sleek as it is adaptable, changing its appearance, chameleon-like, to match its surroundings. Consisting of a modular system of six combinable basic units, its composition, cover and cushions can be exchanged to give it a look that is by turns classic, opulent or cosy.

PHOTOS: l.: *Shift* multifunctional sofa by Volker Laprell and Volker Classen
r.: *Alfa* sofa by Jan Armgardt

MILESTONES: *Janus* table → page **338**

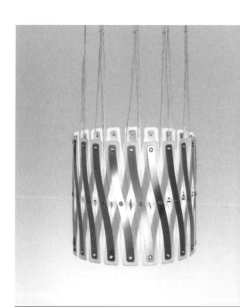

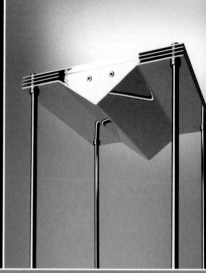

# Serien

lamp manufacturer, Rodgau / Hesse, founded 1983, **www.serien-lighting.de**

It isn't hard to guess which era this company dates back to – the experiment-happy and sometimes playful 1980s. The multi-award-winning series *Zoom*, the brainchild of Floyd Paxton, with lamps that can be pulled apart like an accordion and then pushed together again, tempts anyone who sees them to have a go. Whether large or small cylinders, compact table lamp or stately chandelier, the diameter can be altered between 20 and 130, respectively 40 and 260 centimetres, which of course results in completely different light effects. **Uwe Fischer's** hanging lamp *Take Five* is similarly variable. Lamp manufacturer Serien has made a name for itself by offering original, well-thought-out designs. One of the more recent products is *Poppy* (by Ulrich Beckert, Georg Soanca-Pollack and Peter Thammer), a flowerlike shape made up of several stems and calyxes that open when the lamp is switched on. Wall and ceiling lamp have 15 arms, the chandelier even double that amount. The "leaves" of the lamp shades are made of a bi-metal that expands when heated, resulting in a surprising "blooming" effect. The lampshades are of hand-blown glass whose transparency only becomes evident when the lamp is turned on. Another innovation is the unusual *Propeller* ceiling fan (by Yaacov Kaufmann). Just one glance is enough to confirm that this fan is utterly unlike the others and, what's more, it also functions as a lamp. The advantage is a

beautiful closed form without the usual blades – an object that does not reveal its identity as machine. Some Serien products started out on the drawing boards of company founders Jean-Marc da Costa and Manfred Wolf, for example the *Basis* uplight, an aluminium construction that impresses with its clean lines, delicate dimensions and effective lighting performance. Even more minimalistic is the *SML* series, a flat rectangle as wall or ceiling uplight and downlight. The name reveals its special feature: both versions come in sizes S, M and L.

PHOTOS: l.: *Zoom* lamp by Floyd Paxton
m.: *Poppy* chandelier by Ulrich Beckert, Georg Soanca-Pollack, Peter Thammer
r.: *Basis* lighting series by Jean-Marc da Costa

MILESTONE: *Take Five* hanging lamp → page **260**

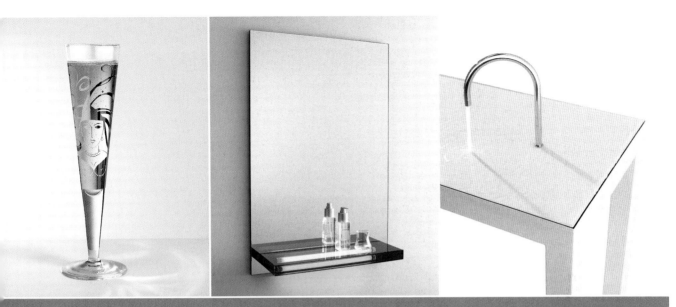

# Sieger Design

studio for product design, Harkotten Castle near Sassenberg / North Rhine-Westphalia, founded 1965, **www.sieger-design.com**

He is the creative force behind washstands, bathtubs and showers, soap rests, sink heaters and entire bathrooms. If things go on like this, it might one day be hard to do anything in the bathroom without encountering design by Dieter Sieger. In the beginning, there were no signs that such omnipresence would one day come to pass. Sieger did an apprenticeship as a bricklayer before going on to study architecture. He has built numerous houses and, as a sailing enthusiast, has also constructed and furnished luxury yachts. The upward climber, in whose family business sons Christian and Michael now work, has set up a studio in the baroque palace of Harkotten between Bielefeld and Münster – a stark contrast to the frequently cool aesthetic of his own buildings. His designer colleague **Luigi Colani** once resided here as well, with whom he has at least one thing in common. Sieger, too, has long since become his own trademark. His third career began for Sieger Senior in the early 1980s. The busy man started conceiving bathroom fittings that were by turns strictly modern or lasciviously luxurious. Sieger's first product design, the modular *Lavar-Set*, was followed by the precisely calibrated, geometrically formed *Domani* plastic tap series, winner of many design awards. The Sieger company was soon branching out from the bathroom into the rest of the house and can now boast products including glasses (for Ritzenhoff), tableware (for

Arzberg), a coffeemaker (for **WMF**) and even a television set (for Sony). Virtually the house designer for **Dornbracht**, with designs including the retro tap *Tara*, and designing pieces for Alape as well, Sieger Design has however remained true to its roots. Today the sons are putting up some competition for their father by editing their own collections. The result is a brand of avant-garde luxury that is designed to answer a variety of needs for the upmarket lifestyle, from furniture to porcelain to outfitting the gentleman with ties and cufflinks.

PHOTOS: l.: *Champus* champagne flute for Ritzenhoff
m.: *Meta Plasma* bathroom accessories for Dornbracht
r.: *Betty Blue* washstand for Alape

MILESTONES: *Tara* tap → page **258**  I  *Happy D* bathroom series → page **286**

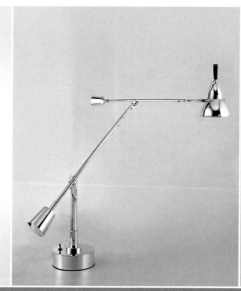
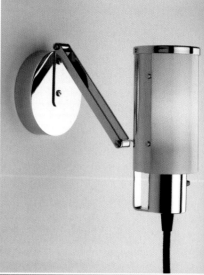

# Tecnolumen

lamp manufacturer, Bremen, founded 1980, **www.tecnolumen.com**

The elegant pivoting wall lamp made of glass and metal that one can easily picture in a 1920s bar setting was the invention of **Wilhelm Wagenfeld**. Tecnolumen is the only authorized manufacturer of the table lamp that – sometimes called the Wagenfeld and sometimes the Bauhaus lamp (reissued as **WA 24**) – became a classic and can surely be counted among the all-time design icons. Such Bauhaus products are one focus of the Tecnolumen product range, and the other is on lamps related to the design concepts the Bauhaus stood for. This also includes some anonymous creations, e.g. the unusual BH 23 table lamp, held in place by a counterweight. As **Marianne Brandt** worked with similar constructions, for example in the *HMB 25* ceiling lamp she collaborated on with Hans Przyrembel in 1925, it is assumed that there is some connection between the two. Also in Tecnolumen's program is Brandt's **Tea-Extract-Pot**, with which she made unadorned basic geometric shapes presentable on the parlour table. The "New Frankfurt" that was likewise a part of the "Neue Sachlichkeit" (New Objectivity), is represented by a door-handle designed by ingenious tinkerer **Ferdinand Kramer**, who furnished the new living quarters of the city with pared-down pieces. Frenchman Eduard-Wilfried Buquet can apparently also be counted among the avant-gardists of those years, having patented the flexible connectors he invented for his unique table lamp, which has now been reissued as a halogen lamp. Tecnolumen has also reintroduced designs that arose in the spirit of the second wave of Modernism after 1945, among them the sleek ceiling uplight *ES 57* that **Egon Eiermann** designed for the German pavilion at the Brussels World's Fair in 1958, which derives its appeal from the symmetry of shade and base cones. The *RHa* desk lamp (by Andreas Hackbarth and **Dieter Rams**) from the 1980s holds its own in terms of stringency with successful table lamps like *Tizio* by **Richard Sapper** (→ p. **188**) or **Tobias Grau's** *Soon* (→ p.**308**). More recent products include the table and hanging lamp *TL / HL WS 04* with white opalized glass cylinder, and *Lightworm*, a table lamp that consists of nothing more than a bendable metal base. These minimalist designs are the work of Walter Schnepel, Tecnolumen's founder.

PHOTOS: l.: *ES 57* floor lamp by Egon Eiermann
m.: *EB 27* desk lamp by Eduard-Wilfried Buquet
r.: Wall lamp (*WNL 30* collection) by Wilhelm Wagenfeld

MILESTONES: **WA 24** table lamp → page **54**  |  **Tea-Extract-Pot** → page **56**  |  **HMB 25** hanging lamp → page **62**

# Tecta

furniture manufacturer, Lauenförde / Lower Saxony, founded 1972, **www.tecta.de**

When Axel Bruchhäuser left East Germany in the 1970s and came to the West, he first tried to contact the masters of functionalism, tracked down Dutchman Mart Stam in Switzerland, visited **Marcel Breuer** in New York and found the family of the Russian El Lissitzky in Siberian exile. He acquired his first licenses at the time, which would form the foundation for the Tecta program, to which the young **Peter Maly** also made an important contribution at this early stage. Bruchhäuser was not only active as archaeologist of Modernism, but also as executor of wills. Numerous designs were first machine-made at Tecta, such as Breuer's glass case and the **F 51** easychair by **Walter Gropius**. For Breuer's practical folding easychair, the straps originally developed by Grete Reichert out of "Eisengarn" thread were specially reconstructed. Bauhaus furniture still makes up a sizeable portion of the company's sales, including a famous tubular steel chair by **Ludwig Mies van der Rohe**, whose mother of all cantilevered chairs from 1927 is also in the catalogue (with natural cane seat and back by Lilly Reich), and a container and "bicycle lounger" by Marcel Breuer. The collection also includes less familiar Bauhaus names such as Erich Brendel, who added a folding table and cube-shaped, likewise folding, tea trolley to the list of functional pieces. **Peter Keler** achieved a modicum of fame with his *Kandinsky* cradle (1922) and *Kubus* block chair

(1925). Further facets of classical Modernism have long since been added to the mix, such as the *D 5* cantilevered chair by Sergius Rügenberg, an employee of Mies van der Rohe. Also among the constructivist gems of the between-war period is Lissitzky's midnight blue plywood chair (1930). His *Tisch des Ansagers* (Announcer's Table) was also reissued, the asymmetrical panels of which became a leitmotif amongst the Tecta tables. Interesting contributions of more recent vintage come from **Stefan Wewerka** and the American couple Alison & Peter Smithson. Bruchhäuser and his team are also behind several designs, such as the *B 20* cantilevered chair. Here, early 20th century avant-gardism enters a liaison with the vanguard design of today.

PHOTOS: l.: *K 40* occasional table by Marcel Breuer
m.: *D 5* easychair by Sergius Ruegenberg,
r.: *M4 R* console trolley (manufacturer's design)

MILESTONES: *F 51* easychair → page 48 | *B 9* nesting tables → page 64 | *Einschwinger* chair → page 212 | *Kitchen Tree* kitchen furniture → page 220

# Thonet

furniture manufacturer, Frankenberg / Hesse, founded 1819, **www.thonet.de**

The world-famous bentwood furniture maker Thonet is still a family-owned enterprise even today, currently operated in the Hessian town of Frankenberg in the fifth generation. The story began with cabinetmaker Michael Thonet from the Rhineland, who developed the bentwood technique in the early years of the 19th century and was then summoned to Vienna by Prince Metternich, where he made his first industrially produced furniture. His chairs were easy to take apart and transport and inaugurated modern mass production in this field. His famous coffee house chair *No. 14* alone was sold more than 30 million times by the Second World War. Thonet had this model to thank for the fact that it was already a multinational enterprise by 1900. The industrial aesthetic plus minimalism, including a sparing use of materials, were the distinguishing features of the first tubular steel chairs from the 1920s, a uniquely German innovation that revolutionized the world of furniture design and with which the Thonet name is likewise closely associated. The *S 43*, the first cantilevered chair by Mart Stam, the *B 32* (today *S 32*) by **Marcel Breuer** and the *MR 10* (today *S 533*) by **Ludwig Mies van der Rohe** are all still produced today. After 1945, when many factories lay in ruin, part of the family remained in Vienna (today Thonet Vienna) and the rest carried on the tradition in West Germany. Tubular steel and wood for a long time remained the dominant materials. Every decade gave birth to its own set of classics as the company continued to rely on collaboration with prominent designers: from Eddie Harlis, who in the 1950s designed the optimistic *S 664*, to Pop designer Verner Panton, all the way to contemporary international stars such as Norman Foster or Alfredo Häberli, but also including numerous Germans like Ulrich Böhme, **Gerd Lange**, **Glen Oliver Löw**, **Peter Maly**, **Wolfgang C. R. Mezger** und **Wulf Schneider**. Accents were set with the technically sophisticated *S 360* chair (2001 by **Delphin Design**) as well as with the *S 4000* upholstered furniture program (2001 by **Jehs + Laub**) and the *A 660* easychair by James Irvine, which brought the bentwood technique up to date using aluminium and net webbing.

PHOTOS: l.: *A 660* chair by James Irvine, m.: *225* chair (manufacturer's design) r.: *S 3000* easychair by Christoph Zschocke

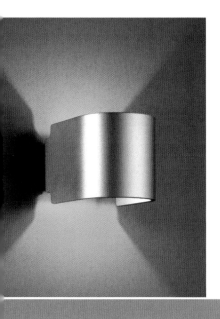

# Tobias Grau

lamp manufacturer, Rellingen / Schleswig-Holstein, founded 1984, **www.tobiasgrau.com**

Tobias Grau is of the opinion that the "need for individuality" is increasing, calling for "unconventional and non-commercial" concepts. This doesn't mean of course that he is lacking in commercial savvy. His first foray as lamp designer was already so successful – immediately crowned by a design award – that he came to the decision to concentrate his energies in this field. The holder of a degree in business administration, who gathered his design experience as an autodidact (including during a stay in the USA), Grau established a company on a Hamburg factory floor in the mid-1980s, first specializing in furniture and interior design. In addition to interiors for fashion stores and offices, he also brought out his first lamp collection at the end of the 1980s. A decade later the rising entrepreneur built an imposing, elongated company headquarters on the outskirts of Hamburg in a striking oval shape, which just three years later already had to be expanded. It was above all the positive reaction to the low-voltage lighting system *Luja* in the early days that formed the occasion for building his own brand. Grau, whose company now employs a workforce of about 90, can draw on a long roster of specialists amongst his suppliers, who number in the hundreds. This allows him to enjoy an unusually wide scope when it comes to choosing materials. With development times between one and two years, the designs are marked by a high level of

technical refinement and distinctive forms. This can be seen, for example, in the floor and wall lamp *George*, whose glass body recalls a car headlight, or in the snake-like table lamp **Soon**. One of the more significant innovations of late is the *Go* series. The office floor lamp *Go Floor* captivates with a pared-down look that hardly betrays the power lurking within. It combines stunning design impact with high-performance indirect light. The result of what are actually quite contradictory features is an effective mixed light that is pleasantly diffused throughout the room.

PHOTOS: l.: *Simple* wall lamp, m.: Floor lamp (*George* collection)
r.: *Projekt X* hanging lamp

MILESTONE: *Soon* table lamp → page **308**

Sofa *370* by **Christian Werner** for **Rolf Benz**

# Henry van de **Velde**

artist, architect and furniture designer, born 1863, died 1957

"Beauty has power over every activity", van de Velde wrote in 1899 in a popular article. The Belgian architect and theoretician, who studied in Antwerp and Paris, was one of those polyglot personalities who became pioneers of new design in the reform fever that swept through Europe in the years around 1900. Under the influence of the English arts & crafts movement, van de Velde turned his attention to the applied arts and became one of the prominent early representatives of Jugendstil. His house in Uccle (1895) already exhibited the light, elegant flow of line that distinguished his style and can also be found in furniture like the *Bloemenwerf* chair. Soon the young architect was well-known in Germany as well, especially through the contracts coming from Berlin, such as the ones for furnishing the gallery of art dealers Keller & Reiner and the premises of the Havana Company in the finest Jugendstil. These interiors weren't merely a feast for the eyes and an attraction for customers, but also an attempt to suspend the hierarchy of the arts by putting art in the service of everyday life. The Nietzsche follower created his furniture in the spirit of free design and as a total work of art – but in spite of that, he remained a realist. "As long as an industrial magnate is doing well, he won't approach an artist", he wrote in a letter to **Walter Gropius** in 1915. "And if he comes when he isn't doing well, he goes to the artist like going

to the devil to sell his soul, which is determined to do anything to fill his threatened purse." Eventually van de Velde was called by the writer and culture critic Count Harry Kessler to be the director of the School of Applied Arts in Weimar (from whence the Bauhaus would later emerge, for which he recommended Gropius as director). Here he was to create profane temples for the New Weimar in keeping with the ambitions of lifestyle reform, a goal he realized for the first time in the Nietzsche Archive (1903). The integrated furniture took up the flow of line evident throughout the room. Other projects followed, including museum buildings in Dresden and Hagen. He was subsequently caught up in the schism within the Deutscher Werkbund, of which he was a co-founder: the industrial faction, including **Peter Behrens**, pleaded for standardization, which he, as a representative of the artists' group, vehemently argued against. Treated with hostility due to his foreign origins, he left the cosmopolitan city of Weimar at the beginning of the First World War and emigrated to Switzerland.

PHOTOS: l.: *Bloemenwerf* chair
m.: *Villa Stern* salon tables for Julius Stern
r.: *Villa Esche* easychair for Herbert Esche

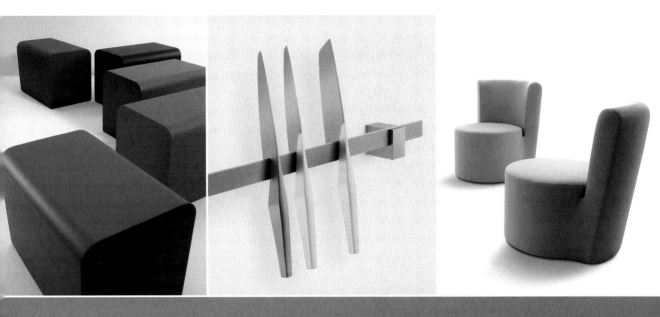

# Studio Vertijet

office for furniture and product design, Halle / Saxony-Anhalt, founded 2000, **www.vertijet.de**

They develop the idea first and then an understanding of the consumer. The park bench *Freestyler*, which is in a form that resembles a surfboard, is ideal for young people who meet out of doors. The *Ponti* beer garden table was created for "individuals lacking a garden". The *Rahm'ses* bookshelf is designed to help those who move often or like to change their decor. Made out of only four main elements, an infinite number of configurations is possible, and thanks to small locking pins, tools aren't necessary. Studio Vertijet comprises interior designer Antje Hoppert and designer Steffen Kroll. The studio quickly became a household name for 'people in the know' and is now counted as a top address in German home design. It is always one of the first names mentioned when young, successful German furniture designers are discussed. In just a few years, the Saxons have opened up a new field starring their own furnishings. They designed carpet collections, for example, for well-known manu-facturers like **JAB Anstoetz** and **COR**. For the latter this was a premiere. It was the upholstered furniture for COR in particular that attracted the attention of those in the business and also went over well on the market. With ***Scroll***, they managed to raise the conversion factor of the common sofa to an even higher power. The *Nuba* sofa by contrast gives the impression of a monument to seating, as if it were chiselled out of stone.

Hoppert and Kroll even succeeded at what no one thought possible: inventing a new variation of the cantilevered chair in *Hob* (→ p.**462**) (all 2003, for COR). This is not the only creation of theirs that takes full advantage of what a material is capable of: the *Neo* chair likewise takes the possibilities to their limit. The application of a new 3-D technique was critical in this case, allowing for the extreme bends and small cross sections. The chair resembles a naturally growing tree in structure. A classic furniture type, which appeared to be out of fashion, experiences a Renaissance here.

PHOTOS: l.: *Cosy* seating furniture for elmarflöttoto, m.: *Soon* knife series r.: *Ovo* easychair for COR

---

MILESTONES: ***Design Edition*** carpet collection → page **310** I ***Scroll*** sofa system → page **322**

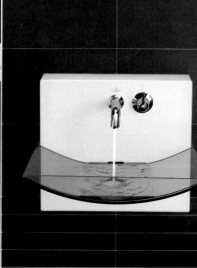

# Villeroy & Boch

manufacturer of porcelain and bathroom furnishings, Mettlach / Saarland, founded 1748, **www.villeroy-boch.com**

When iron caster François Boch began making ceramic crockery in 1748 in the Lorraine village of Audun-le-Tiche, no one suspected that the enterprise would one day attain worldwide fame. Half a century later, his son Jean-François Boch acquired an old monastery in Mettlach on the Saar River, which was an outstanding location for the transport of goods and raw materials and is still to this day company headquarters. The product history of Villeroy & Boch – which today encompasses not only tableware, tiles and bathroom furnishings, but also an incredibly wide-ranging universe of cutlery, glasses, gift articles and kitchen sinks – reflects the major artistic currents of the times. During the reform years around 1900, well-known artists worked for Villeroy & Boch, including **Peter Behrens** (→ p.**15**) and Joseph Maria Olbrich (→ p.**13**). A basin and pitcher by **Henry van de Velde** represented the tempered version of Jugendstil then prevailing in Germany. While a simple service designed around 1930 stands for the trend toward "Neue Sachlichkeit" (New Objectivity), the *Kugelgeschirr* (Sphere Service, by Helen von Boch) from the early 1970s became an icon of the Pop era. The 1970s also saw the company take a crucial step in the area of bath collections. Designer **Luigi Colani** was asked to create a completely new style for the bathroom, turning the one-time "water closet" into a comfortable and integral part of the home

– a process that still continues today. Later on, studios such as Frogdesign and Conran & Partners also created bath collections for the company. The partnership with **Reiner Moll**, who is today probably the most important designer working for Villeroy & Boch, began in the late 1980s at a motorway rest stop between Stuttgart and Ulm, where he met the executive director of product development. Moll's design for a washstand that could be cut to the desired length, called **Virage**, laid the groundwork for a relationship that would last even beyond changes in management. Numerous products followed, such as *Bellevue*, one of the most successful bath collections, and the *Arcora* series of kitchen sinks. Designs oriented toward specific target groups, innovative technology and high-grade materials: this is the strategy that has allowed the ceramic company set in a bend of the Saar River to attain its standing as one of the leading brands in the industry, in particular in bathrooms and tableware. A current contribution to modern dining culture is the service *New Wave*, whose wilfully curved forms are guaranteed to capture attention.

PHOTOS: l.: Wash basin and pitcher by Henry van de Velde
m.: *New Wave* service, r.: *Liaison* washstand

MILESTONE: *Virage* washstand → page **262**

# Vitra

furniture manufacturer, Weil am Rhein / Baden-Wurttemberg, founded 1934, **www.vitra.com**

For the outsider they often are hard to tell apart. Two enterprises fall under the Vitra brand: a European-league manufacturer specializing in office furniture and an economically independent museum that devotes itself specifically to seating furniture. Under the management of Alexander von Vegesack, the museum component has made great contributions to the history of home design. Like no other company in the business, the German-Swiss enterprise maintains an intellectual relationship to its products. Rather than developing a monolithic corporate image, it has relied on a heterogeneous and multicultural approach. Vitra first took flight in the late 1950s with designs by Americans Charles and Ray Eames. A decade later, the *Panton Chair* by Verner Panton of Denmark caused a sensation and started a new trend. The designers who have worked for Vitra since the 1990s are among Europe's design elite: from Italy, Mario Bellini and Antonio Citterio, from England, Jasper Morrison and Norman Foster, from France, Philippe Starck and the brothers Ronan and Erwan Bouroullec and, recently, **Werner Aisslinger** from Germany. The company in addition manufactures important creations by the French modernist Jean Prouvet. Behind the firm's design and corporate identity strategy is an unusual entrepreneur. Rolf Fehlbaum is a leading figure in the industry. His "edition" of experimental seating furniture at the end of the 1980s, issued in small series, put Vitra in the limelight. Included were "classics" such as Shiro Kuramata's easychair made from metal netting and Frank Gehry's glued cardboard *Grandpa Chair*. The American Gehry also designed the building for the Vitra Design Museum. The exalted architecture kicked off a program in which half a dozen prominent architects set various accents on the company grounds, among them the minimalist Tadao Ando and the deconstructivist Zaha Hadid, virtually unknown at the time, who designed the garage for the fire brigade. At the turn of the new century, Vitra built an administration building for tomorrow, incorporating the concept of open, flexible and completely networked offices.

PHOTOS: l.: *DKR* chair (*Wire Collection*) by Charles Eames
m.: *T-Chair* office chair by Antonio Citterio and Glen Oliver Löw
r.: *Taino* chair by Jacob Gebert

# Burkhard **Vogtherr**

furniture and product designer, born 1942, office in Mulhouse / France, **www.vogtherrdesign.com**

The intelligent table *Maxmax* which he just created for **Rosen-thal** makes all the necessary but unattractive technical utensils such as notebook adapter, battery charger et cetera invisible. This design brings Burkhard Vogtherr back to his roots. His first creations were likewise for Rosenthal, including a futuristic bed-closet-cell with a built-in hi-fi system. After the completion of his training as a carpenter, the native of Baden first studied industrial design. At the end of the 1960s he won the German prize for "Good Form", the first ever awarded. His winning design was for a phonograph system housed inside plastic spheres. Now that he had caused a stir with this "sound atomium", he turned his attention next to the phenomenon of the chair. The Alsace-based German designer would soon become one of the most sought-after specialists the world over for seating opportunities of every kind. He has worked for leading international furniture makers like Arco, Arflex, Bushy, Cappellini, Dietiker, Fritz Hansen and Wittmann, but also for the German manufacturers **COR**, **Drabert**, **Klöber** and **WK Wohnen**. Since the 1970s he has developed a large number of swivelling office chairs for companies including Drabert and the American manufacturer Davis. By the early 1980s the star had already managed without much ado to achieve his breakthrough in Italy. Arflex bought his slim and distinctive **T-Line** easychair. He created further designs for

the same company that stand in pleasant contrast to the wide-spread expressionist rage of those years, such as the easychairs *Felix*, an individual take on the theme of the box, *Armilla*, a puzzle put together out of triangles, and finally *Leo lea*, a tribute to the clarity of classical Modernism whose lightness surpasses even that of the originals. Vogtherr's sensible stylistic idiom is probably one of the most important reasons why his order books are always full. In the early 1990s he created for Cappellini a table-chair-bed ensemble called *Small Room*, a work every bit as committed to simplicity as the recent *Lance* table (for Arco), a solid structure whose wood version is supported by V-type legs reminiscent of a traditional trestle.

PHOTOS: l.: *Libra* sofa for COR, m.: *Spin* office chair for Fritz Hansen r.: *Armilla* easychair for Arflex

MILESTONE: *T-Line* easychair → page **224**

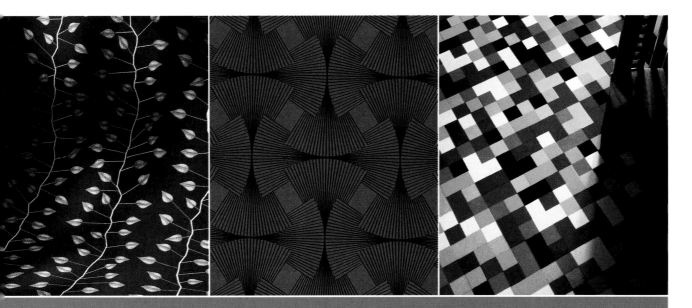

# Vorwerk

carpet manufacturer, Hamelin / Lower Saxony, founded 1883, **www.vorwerk-teppich.de**

Artist Rosemarie Trockel and architect Jean Nouvel, Pop icon Roy Lichtenstein and theatre director Robert Wilson all have something in common. They and many other prominent creative talents have dabbled in carpet design. Although our gaze is directed downwards a substantial percent of the time, meaning that the conditions under our feet shouldn't be beneath our consideration, modern carpet design was for a long time a niche business. That is, until the Vorwerk company – known for durable vacuum cleaners and tasteful wall-to-wall carpeting – decided to fill this vacuum in the industry in the 1980s. Like **Rosenthal** and **FSB**, Vorwerk proceeded by hiring well-known artists, architects and designers for its designer carpet project. What resulted were product lines such as *First Edition* and *Dialog Art Collection*. The company from the Weser Hills even managed to bring back the kind of flowered rugs that had long gone out of fashion – with up-to-date designs including a rose pattern by Robert Wilson. With its *Classics* line, Vorwerk has been doing practical research into historical design for several years. The reintroduction of creations from German design pioneers begins with Jugendstil. Patterns by **Peter Behrens** and **Richard Riemerschmid** show the high graphic level achieved in this short but highly creative epoch. Finally, a resounding response was obtained with an edition of carpet designs by the "Bauhaus women", who invented

the modern carpet practically single-handedly in the weaving mill of the famous art academy. The abstract designs by artists like Getrud Arndt, Kitty Fischer or Gunta Stölz, heretofore only known from books and museums, resonate with the same intense aura as the artworks of those years. A new and ambitious collection is ***Ulf Moritz*** by Vorwerk. Using materials like mohair, linen, various wool and woolmix products as well as high-quality Antron yarns, the celebrated designer has created worlds of sensuous colour.

PHOTOS: l. and m.: *Dialog Flower* Edition carpets
r.: *Dialog First Edition* carpet by Gerhard Richter

MILESTONE: *Bauhaus Carpet* → page **50**

# Votteler & Votteler

offices for furniture design, Freudenstadt / Baden-Wurttemberg and Hemmingen / Lower Saxony, **www.vottelerdesign.de**

Industry insiders know Arno Votteler as an authority on office furniture. He started working with his son in the 1990s. Votteler senior, born in 1929, was shaped by a childhood in the "wood-craft workshop" of his father as well as by an apprenticeship as carpenter. Son Matthias, who studied business administration and is likewise a designer, prefers instead the constructional potential of metal – preferences that complement each other. Due to ever tighter budgets, designers increasingly have to take on the responsibilities of a producer, for example negotiations with suppliers, for which the son's qualifications in this area proved to be helpful. In the early days of his career, Arno Votteler could rely on intellectual mentors like his professor **Herbert Hirche** or the furniture-company founder **Walter Knoll**, the result being that the young boy from the Black Forest quickly developed a polyglot personality: first working for the London office of Gutman, then in 1957 running the Gutman branch in Stuttgart and finally in the early 1960s opening his own studio. Later on, he worked, among other things, as a university lecturer in Brazil, the USA, India and China. His clientele likewise became ever more varied. For instance, at the end of the 1960s he developed for the dockyard Blohm & Voss not only a system of modularly furnished cabins, but also an architectural grid for the deckhouse. During this phase Arno Votteler won Planmöbel as

client, for which he developed over the course of a quarter of a century various office series, among them the long-running hit *Concept*. Similarly intense co-operation began towards the end of the 1970s with **Martin Stoll** with the model *S*, the first swivel chair with active pelvic support. Parallel to this he developed a series of chairs for **Bisterfeld + Weiss** (→ p.399) as well as furniture for hotels and retirement homes. This was a period that witnessed a departure from pure functionalism, expressed for example in the posh *Ponte* line for the executive office (1985 for RTR), a furnishings system based on the bridge principle. At the same time, Votteler held the post of director of the Institute for Interior and Furniture Design he had founded at the Academy of Fine Arts in Stuttgart, also known as the "Weissenhof Institute". Father and son, as the firm Votteler & Votteler, are known for their persistent fine-tuning of every design, paired with a pronounced sense of what is feasible. The highly integrated *Sputnik* swivel chair and the lightweight plastic chair *Bullauge* (both 2005, for **Interstuhl**), which got its name from distinctive circular recesses that resemble portholes, are some of their newer products.

PHOTOS: l.: *350* easychair for Walter Knoll
m.: *Sputnik* office chair for Interstuhl, r.: *Bullauge* chair for Interstuhl

MILESTONE: *Sputnik* office chair → page 358

# Wilhelm **Wagenfeld**

product designer, born 1900, died 1990, **www.wilhelm-wagenfeld-stiftung.de**

He was one of the first in his craft. Wilhelm Wagenfeld became famous through the lamp with transparent glass base and round white opaline glass shade that he created with Karl J. Jucker at the Bauhaus in the mid-1920s. The small, delicate table lamp looks as simple as a street lamp: a symbol for the early German brand of minimalism and today a synonym for Bauhaus classic. The design product par excellence. When Wagenfeld called the best characteristic things can have their "undemanding" nature, what he meant is that objects of everyday use should be serviceable, inexpensive and at the same time attractive. The trained silversmith created a multitude of useful items that were at once ambitious and unassuming, made from glass, metal or plastic. The hallmark of all of them is their high design quality, such as his bent inkpots (for Pelikan) or the silverware series *83* (for **Pott**) and *Form 3600* (for **WMF**). His days as Bauhaus student already began in the early 1920s under Lazlo Moholy-Nagy in the metal workshop, where he worked with **Marianne Brandt**. He later became the workshop's director after the Bauhaus relocated to Dessau. While many Bauhaus artists were forced to leave Germany after 1933, Wagenfeld was able to carry on with his work, teaching at the Art Academy in Berlin and other institutions. For Jenaer Glass he experimented with what was up until then considered a cheap material – moulded

glass. The fireproof covered bowls he developed towards the end of the 1930s became kitchen icons, as did the stackable *Kubus* glass storage containers. After the Second World War, Wagenfeld drew on his previous success and began to work for companies like **Rosenthal** as well as **Braun**. In the mid-1950s he designed a record player for the phonograph maker that was integrated into the famous compact system *SK 4* (→ p.**122**) and was also part of his own portable *Combi* radio/record player, whose front he provided with bevelled lines and soft edges. This device comes across as surprisingly modern even today. The pragmatic thinker achieved one of his greatest triumphs on the German dining table: with a butter dish as well as salt and pepper shakers (for **WMF**) he dubbed *Max and Moritz*.

PHOTOS: l.: *83* silverware for Pott
r.: *Kubus* stacking containers for Vereinigte Lausitzer Glaswerke

MILESTONES: *WA 24* table lamp → page **54** I *Max and Moritz* salt and pepper shakers → page **114**

# Walter Knoll

furniture manufacturer, Herrenberg / Baden-Wurttemberg, founded 1925, **www.walterknoll.de**

After a trip to America, Walter Knoll founded a furniture company in the mid-1920s under his own name. The son of a Stuttgart upholsterer, he had been managing his father's business with his brothers for almost 20 years when he was inspired by the 'New World' and the Bauhaus style to take off in a new direction. He was thus virtually predestined to undertake, among other things, the furnishing of the avant-garde Weissenhof housing development in Stuttgart. His "Antimott" program replaced springs and plush upholstery with elastic straps. The aluminium armchairs designed to furnish zeppelins were pioneering. Shortly before the Second World War, Walter Knoll's eldest son, Hans, moved to the United States and founded the company Knoll International, which was to shape the fortunes of modern furniture. In the 1950s the latest pieces looked organic and Scandinavian. New methods for processing wood and metal enabled curvatures and eliminated the constraint of the right angle. In 1974 the firm's products were presented for the first time at the Milan Furniture Show. "Informal" and "relaxed" were the catchwords for the furnishing style of this and the following decade. Knoll managed to produce pieces in step with the taste of the times and simultaneously to push beyond it with a high level of formal quality. As reward for this persistently pursued strategy, the company started to receive large orders.

The office furniture division began to gain in significance, under the brand name of Walter Knoll Office. An endlessly additive seating system was developed for Berlin's Tegel Airport in 1975. With large jobs like this one, the company was able to prove its competence in the field of commercial furnishings, making a name for itself outside Germany as well with status-lending programs for foyers, consulting areas and executive offices – a field in which designer **Wolfgang C. R. Mezger**, among others, became a noted specialist. In 1993, neighbouring company **Rolf Benz** took over. Markus Benz, the oldest son of the founder, became managing director, sharpening the profile of a collection known for its clean to classic lines. Since that time Walter Knoll has grown worldwide and introduced more than 70 new products. High quality and comfortable functionality are a matter of course. All pieces are the work of noteworthy German and international designers. The Vienna office EOOS, Norman Foster and Pearson Lloyd of England as well as Ben van Berkel of the Netherlands figure prominently in the product range, which, particularly in the more recent pieces, exhibits a clear architectural character.

PHOTOS: l.: *Jason Lite* chair by EOOS
m.: *Oscar* easychair by Pearson Lloyd
r.: *FK 6725* chair by Preben Fabricius and Jörgen Kastholm

MILESTONE: *369* easychair → page **124**

# Weko

office furniture manufacturer, Cologne / North Rhine-Westphalia, founded 1925, **www.weko-bueromoebel.de**

The family business working out of the cathedral city, already in the third generation, not only paved the way for the desk container in the 1960s, but also for colour ergonomics and environmentally friendly furnishings. In the mid-1990s came a new corporate identity, including design consistently oriented on classical Modernism. Weko developed purist modular furniture, calling its various collections *"Baureihen"* (Construction Series, a term taken from Gert Wessel) because they were to take up the style of the Dessau Bauhaus. Altogether five different series were created. *Baureihe b* consists of chairs whose runners describe a rectangle and which do not deny for a minute their reliance on the creations of old masters such as **Marcel Breuer** or **Ludwig Mies van der Rohe**. *Baureihen c, e* and *m* offer minimalist cabinet programs pared down to the essentials, likewise implementing Bauhaus maxims. Finally, *Baureihe t* adds a flexible table. The multi-award-winning program is based on a uniform construction principle. The foundation of every series is formed by a single tubing cross-section and system node that are the same in every furniture component, which makes components freely combinable. This is an up-to-date interpretation of the principles espoused by the modern movement between the wars. *Baureihe e*, for example, is a construction kit furniture system with units that, positioned either on top or next to each other, create a very homogeneous impression rather than looking like stacked elements. For formal and ergonomic reasons, and naturally to preserve the clean lines, there are no visible fittings or grips. Doors and drawers open automatically with a gentle press.

PHOTO: Desk and *Baureihe e* modular cabinet

MILESTONE: *Baureihe e* cabinet system → page **340**

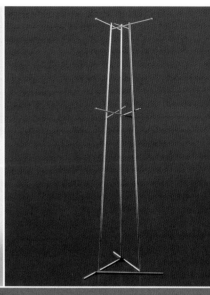

# Christian **Werner**

interior and furniture designer, born 1959, office in Hamburg, **www.christian-werner.com**

"Designers create everyday helpers", says Christian Werner, and indeed the white elements of his container series *Everywhere* (for Ligne Roset) seem like servants who know how to adapt to any situation. This storage system contains over thirty elements. It is the best-selling case furniture offered by the French manufacturer, for which Werner has designed over fifty stores as well as the C-shaped *Pop* easychair, an invitation to relax. Werner wrote his dissertation as a student of **Dieter Rams**. That was in the wild 1980s, when he still belonged to the circle of "New German Design". He eventually quit as long-time assistant of **Peter Maly** in order to move on in his own creative development. But first he learned from Maly how to go beyond mere furniture design and to also shape not only interiors but with them the image of the respective client, a capability that is not very widespread in the industry. A native of Berlin, Werner is one of the most successful furniture designers of the last few years, attributable to the way he he is able to relate his creations to changing lifestyles. This is exactly what was required for the *Dono* sofa (2004), which became the number one sofa from **Rolf Benz**. What's new about it is the enclosing shelf, to which the cushions are clamped on. Sofas today are personal areas for many activities. Therefore one needs a place to set a wine glass, mobile phone or book. The *6900* sofa, for the same manufacturer, follows a different concept. It provides a large area to lie on that is enclosed by a thin, different-coloured shell. The play of proportions, contrasts and recurring radii lends it the homogeneousness, almost architectural character of a quiet room for withdrawal and contemplation. Within a year of the 6900, further sofas and easychair models followed: the *310, 370* (→ p.**546**) and *522* (→ p.**526**). Werner was also responsible for designing the successful Swabian manufacturer's stand at the Cologne Furniture Fair. Over time, Werner's activities have stretched beyond pure furniture design, for instance, with his seven prize-winning carpet designs for the **Design Edition** from **JAB Anstoetz**.

PHOTOS: l.: *310* easychair for Rolf Benz, m.: *Pop* easychair for Ligne Roset r.: *Meret* coat rack for Schönbuch

# Stefan **Wewerka**

architect, artist and furniture designer, born 1928, lives in Magdeburg / Saxony-Anhalt

Chairs without seats, crooked chairs, chairs that disappear into the wall, chairs that – because they only consist of one half – do not become whole until set next to a mirror, or chair fragments that lean against one another for support. These are works from the studio of object artist Stefan Wewerka, which propagates the thesis: "One has to have a slant in order to go straight ahead." The architect and later action artist, designer, jewellery and film maker from Magdeburg began his career in the mid-1950s with the construction of an unusual youth hostel as well as with visions for an "earth architecture". In the 1970s, when he was closely involved with the Fluxus movement, the independent thinker suddenly came up with his first industrially produced furniture. He found in entrepreneur Axel Bruchhäuser, owner of the **Tecta** furniture company, a partner who was open to the idea that furniture can be art, with every piece an experiment. Bruchhäuser was also in the position, with his staff, to put even unusual ideas into production. From the beginning of the 1980s – Wewerka had at this point occupied himself with furniture objects for twenty years already - he created for the Westphalian enterprise a highly complex collection, which includes cabinets, tables and chairs as well as dressers, lamps and sofas. In the process he developed his own geometric, asymmetrical formal vocabulary. Within it are combined surprising proportions and references to functionalist Modernism, whether to **Mies van der Rohe** in the **Einschwinger** (a three-metre-long steel tube bent into a chair) or to Gio Ponti in the *B4* chair made of black-stained ash. High points in Wewerka's conceptualism are the *Cella* unit for small apartments and the multiply pivoting **Küchenbaum** (Kitchen Tree) all-in-one cooking station. These ensembles are just as sculptural as they are versatile, exemplifying Stefan Wewerka's about-face from anti-establishment artist to functional consolidator, spanning the astounding arc from constructivism to deconstructivism. With his *B1* easychair, the ingenious designer created out of two sawed-up chairs a new model that allows for many different sitting positions.

PHOTOS: l.: *Anlehnung* chair sculpture
m.: *Dreibeiner B1* chair for Tecta
r.: *B3* cantilevered chair for Tecta

MILESTONES: *Einschwinger* chair → page **212** | kitchen furniture *Kitchen Tree* → page **220**

# Wiege

furniture and product design, office in Bad Münder / Lower Saxony, founded 1985, **www.wiege.com**

The development department of the famous office furniture manufacturer **Wilkhahn** had by the mid-1980s turned itself into an independent design studio. Under the direction of former head designer **Klaus Franck**, this quickly became an internationally oriented project. The studio today focuses on product and interior design as well as trade fair stands. The bulk of the orders no longer come from the former parent company, but in the realm of office furniture, Wiege is still their most important supplier of ideas. The studio thus developed for Wilkhahn not only the newest generation of cantilevered chairs, but also a series of swivelling office chairs such as *Modus*, *Neos* and *Solis*, in which the emphasis is on ergonomics allowing for dynamic sitting. The complex structure typical for individually adjustable swivel chairs was consciously avoided here. A clean-lined design makes the functions readable and enables their intuitive use. The *Cana* chair, which can be transformed into a comfortable office lounger, serves other needs. Further solutions for the work routine include the table program *Minamo* for the Japanese manufacturer Kokuyo and the flexible *Suonada* room division system for the Turkish office furniture manufacturer Koleksiyon. The team of ten working under the management of Michael Englisch and Jochen Hahne offers the whole development repertoire from idea to model construction and sees its major task as steering clients on a smooth course between "the short cycles of the fashion currents" and the necessity of a "clear design attitude", with themselves as bastion of the latter.

PHOTOS: l.: *Sito* office chair for Wilkhahn, m.: *Challenge* chair for Tonon r.: Desk lamp (*Easy* lighting collection) for Wofi

MILESTONES: *Confair* office furniture system → page **264**

# Wilde + Spieth

furniture manufacturer, Esslingen / Baden-Wurttemberg, founded 1831, **www.wilde-spieth.com**

This carpentry enterprise has been in operation for over 100 years, specializing in rolling shutters at the beginning of the last century until architect **Egon Eiermann** asked in 1948 if he could also order some chairs. It was the beginning of one of those productive partnerships between a designer and a business that obviously came together at the right moment. Seven different models had already been developed by 1950, still in the post-war era. In the decade that followed, about a dozen more were added. Some of them have been on the market since their creation, including the plywood chair *SE 68* (1950), the folding chair *SE 18* and the folding table *S 319* (both from 1952). Others were reissued, e.g. the three-legged chair *SE 42* (1948). By the time of Eiermann's death in 1970, more than 30 series models had been developed. Those that became famous were especially the tubular steel and plywood chairs from the early years, which in their unpretentious functionalism stood for the future and became incunabula of the post-war modern trend. Contrary to their classical modern forerunners, however, which Eiermann and others borrowed from, they found their way into everyday life. Sales of Eiermann's furniture rose so sharply that at the beginning of the 1960s it was necessary to build a factory in the industrial area of Esslingen in order to keep up with demand. The manufacturing of shutters was soon left behind. A speciality

of Wilde + Spieth is the music chair series, which likewise came from Eiermann's drawing board and is still produced today. He was obviously familiar with the needs of professional musicians. Special features like height and seat slope adjustments, air holes, as well as firm seat cushions have long passed the test in the orchestra pits of this world. Already back in the 1950s, the company took additional modern architects on board. These included Paul Schneider-Esleben, **Herta-Maria Witzemann** and former Eiermann employee **Herbert Hirche**, whose stackable tubular steel chair with cane seat (1957) was designed for restaurants as well as homes. After successfully weathering a bankruptcy, Wilde + Spieth celebrated its anniversary year in 2004 – Eiermann's 100th birthday – by making a fresh start with leaner structures. One of those who treasure Eiermann's work is the American architect Daniel Libeskind, who uses chairs designed by the German neo-functionalist in his buildings and will soon be represented himself in the Wilde + Spieth catalogue with a chair that bears his name.

PHOTOS: l.: *SE 41* swivel chair, m.: *SE 330* café table
r.: *S 319* folding table (all by Egon Eiermann)

MILESTONES: *SE 42* chair → page **102** | *SE 68* chair → page **104** | *SE 18* folding chair → page **110**

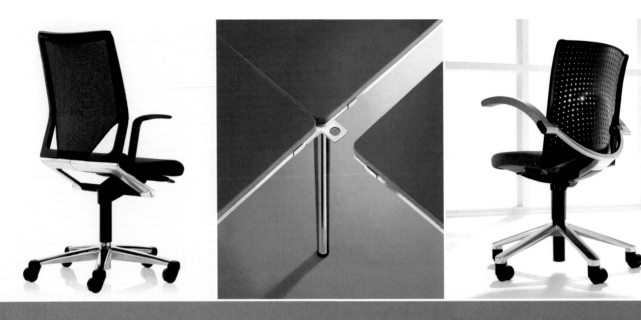

# Wilkhahn

office furniture manufacturer, Bad Münder / Lower Saxony, founded 1907, **www.wilkhahn.com**

The **FS** office chair was a sensation when it was presented at the beginning of the 1980s. This cross between a swivel and rocking chair, equipped with novel mechanisms and a flexible shell seat, did not exhibit any ergonomic weaknesses and yet avoided the apparatus-like look of some of the competing models. Wilkhahn, once one of over one hundred chair factories in the area, which acquired its wood from the surrounding beech forests, transformed itself in the 1950s into a design-oriented company – a question of survival. Its rescuer was named Fritz Hahne, an ambitious entrepreneur who took not only his inspiration, but also the new corporate identity from the Academy of Design in Ulm. **Klaus Franck**, one the FS creators, is also an Ulm graduate and Ulmer designer, like **Hans "Nick" Roericht** and **Herbert Ohl**. The Ulmers dedicated themselves to the office chair, making what had largely been an ignored genre part of the design terrain. Over the years the enterprise in southern Lower Saxony became the place to be for the elite of the rising industrial and furniture design industry in Germany. Its profile was honed through numerous innovations which included shell chairs and bench systems and the use of new materials such as webbing. Highly innovative standout products include the **Stitz** leaning aid (by Hans "Nick" Roericht), which fosters the natural urge to move and is hence healthier for the body than sitting still, as well as the *Nuvola* armchair with its transparent webbing (by Jutta and Herbert Ohl p. 511). The neighbouring **Wiege** studio designed the *Solis* program, which also took up the theme of dynamic sitting and aimed at intuitive operation. A completely new product segment is computer monitor units such as *Consultable*, *Interactable* or *Interwall*, tables with integrated displays as well as freestanding or hanging monitor walls that were developed for varying work situations and will gradually replace the clipboard. Another trailblazing design was the team office system **Confair** (by Fritz Frenkler, **Justus Kolberg**, Andreas Störiko and Wiege), an original that has since found many emulators in the industry. Wilkhahn, a high-end supplier that maintains stringent ecological standards, has long acquired an international clientele. Frequent travellers will already have noticed this: *Tubis* bench seating can be found in the airports of Hong Kong, Milan and Munich. But the fact that the company still relies on tradition is demonstrated by *Sito* and *Cura*, new, up-to-date interpretations of the cantilevered chair.

PHOTOS: l.: *Modus* office chair by Klaus Franck, Werner Sauer, Wiege
m.: *Contas* table by Wiege, r.: *Picto* office chair by Wiege

MILESTONES: *FS-Linie* office chair → page **206** I *Stitz* leaning aid → page **252** I *Confair* office furniture system → page **264**

# Herta-Maria **Witzemann**

architect, furniture designer and author, born 1909, died 1999

One of her early works was the "Notwohnung" (Emergency Living Quarters) for Ferdinand Porsche, which she furnished in cool Bauhaus style. Later she became known through projects such as her interiors for the Stuttgart Television Tower and the Chancellor's Bungalow in Bonn. The residence of the head of government defined the official style of the republic. The native Austrian advanced to the rank of star interior designer, a role she self-confidently filled. Witzemann studied during the Second World War in Vienna and Munich and was already working independently in 1948. A professor of furniture-making from 1952, she would become an influential figure during the 1950s, acclaimed even beyond Germany's borders. In 1957 she received a silver medal at the Triennial in Milan, at the time the most important international design show. Like her contemporaries who were also active in the southwest, **Egon Eiermann** and **Herbert Hirche**, she designed furniture for **Wilde + Spieth**, including the *SW 50* easychair with clean-lined L-shaped upholstery atop tubular steel and the *SW 88* garden chair, whose cane back and seat are carried by a scaffolding of metal bars. A classic is the bistro table *SWF*, which is still in production today. Together with her aforementioned male colleagues, Witzemann was a contentious protagonist of post-war modernism in the German Federal Republic, propagating her position in books with titles like *Deutsche Möbel heute* (German Furniture Today) or *Morgen wohnen wir schöner* (Better Living for Tomorrow, with Mechthild v. Kienlin), which ensured that the concept of good form reached the general public. As a member of the Erwin Hoffmann Foundation, set up by the **WK** federation, she wanted to "educate the wider populace about the cultural and social significance of the home".

PHOTOS: l.: *SWF 1* table, m.: *SWF 2* table
r.: *SW 88* garden chair (all for Wilde + Spieth)

# WK Wohnen

furniture manufacturer and advocacy group, Dreieich / Hesse, founded 1912, **www.wkwohnen.de**

Legally, WK Wohnen is an association; practically speaking, it is the oldest manufacturer of German designer furniture. The membership roster lists approximately 130 furniture stores, which exclusively carry the WK furnishings line. They are in contact with some 50 manufacturers and a similar number of designers. The association has working for it the crème de la crème of the German furniture design scene, including **Thomas Althaus**, **Jan Armgardt**, **Siegfried Bensinger** (who functioned as art director for a time), **Egon Eiermann**, **Rolf Heide**, **Stefan Heiliger**, **Peter Maly**, **Wolfgang C. R. Mezger**, **Anita Schmidt**, **Burkhard Vogtherr** and **Herta-Maria Witzemann**, just to name a few. The enlightened idea of "the art of the home" – later called "lifestyle culture" – developed shortly before the First World War, when the Deutscher Werkbund was working to reform the domestic environment. A group of German furniture stores united in order to manufacture high-quality series furniture emulating the precedent set by the Deutsche Werkstätten. In the beginning, the exclusive manufacturer was the **Behr** company. The association's statutes proclaim its commitment to "spreading good taste", following the precepts of the Deutscher Werkbund. In the post-Bauhaus period, flexible extendable furniture systems were added to the program, which could be combined into an "Aufbauheim" ("Assembled Home", by Paul Griesser). Thus WK

Wohnen became an early agency for modular furniture systems, an ongoing theme in German furniture design which was carried forward by designers including Georg Satink (1952, *WK-Satink*) and Peter Maly (1987, *Muro*). While the reaction to lean times after the Second World War was the development of simple furniture under the label *WK-Sozialwerk*, the company soon thereafter participated in the neo-modern trend sweeping through West Germany with functional designs that were successfully presented in 1958 at the Brussels World Fair and elsewhere. Later on came the rocking chair *Nonna* (1973, by Paul Tuttle), a hybrid made of bentwood and metal. The stretchable **WK 698 Spot** easychair (1989, by Stefan Heiliger) is regarded as an incunabula of the form-happy postmodern era. Milestones of more recent vintage include the *WK 600* sofa (by Thomas Althaus), the clever pullout table *814* (by Dietmar Joester) and the rocking lounge chair *Balance* (by Stefan Heiliger). All the same, the label has seldom stood out with conspicuous avant-gardism. One of the advantages of WK-Wohnen, more important than ever these days, is the co-ordinated offer of a complete line of furnishings exuding a well-tempered functionalism.

PHOTOS: l.: *Balance* lounge chair by Stefan Heiliger
r.: *WK 600* sofa by Thomas Althaus

MILESTONE: *WK 698 Spot* easychair → page **244**

# WMF

metalware and coffeemaker manufacturer, Geislingen / Baden-Wurttemberg, founded 1853, **www.wmf.de**

By the time the First World War broke out, the company had developed into the largest employer in the German Southwest with 6,000 workers, a number that isn't all that far from today's figure (5,300 in 2003). One of the most successful products in imperial times was the silver-plated cutlery, for which the company had a patented procedure. In artistic terms as well, the incredibly diverse product range experienced its first heyday during the Jugendstil period around 1900. At the end of the 1920s, WMF secured the exclusive rights to V2-A steel, better known as 18/10 stainless steel and registered under the trademark "Cromargan", a material well-suited for the production of household appliances and kitchen utensils. Thus the Swabians were the first to manufacture durable, stainless high-grade steel goods at a reasonable price. Easy-care and durable, Cromargan soon made its way into German kitchen cabinets in the form of pots and pans, bowls and cutlery. But it was only after the Second World War that WMF experienced the hoped-for boom in stainless steel household goods. The name **Wilhelm Wagenfeld** was closely connected with this development. Already well-known in the industry, the designer united absolute functionality with smart 1950s style, seen e.g. in his salt shakers and in egg cups that are stackable and made from a single piece. His *Form 3600* silverware by contrast had a sharp-edged angular form, attracting attention above all due to the unusually short knife blade. After a time it seemed like the label would sink into the mainstream, but in the 1980s WMF again started placing emphasis on original designs, which in postmodern times didn't always have to be as irreproachably functional as with the stricter Wagenfeld. Famous international designers such as Matteo Thun and Dieter **Sieger**, but also the fashion designer Pierre Cardin and the Danish product designer Ole Palsby, who alone created six different silverware patterns, contributed to the renovated profile of the WMF assortment. The collection includes glasses, candlesticks, spoons, saucepans, vacuum jugs and gift articles as well as very successful coffee machines. The products are sold in WMF shops usually located in city centres – a concept learned from **Rosenthal**. The strategy of offering designer products continues, featuring for example the *Lounge* bar accessories by James Irvine (→ p.**36**) and the *Kult* table accessories by Sebastian Bergne.

PHOTOS: l.: Shakers from the *Kult* table accessory series by Sebastian Bergne m.: *Merit* silverware by Fred Danner, r.: *Concept* bread basket by Ole Palsby

MILESTONES: *Nr. 1/2* cocktail shaker → page 36 I *Max and Moritz* salt and pepper shakers → page **114**

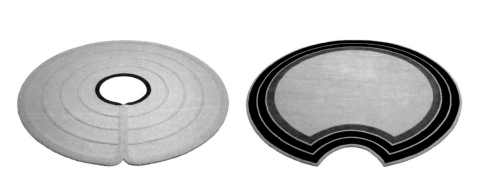

# Sigrid **Wylach**

textile and furniture designer, studio in Wuppertal / North Rhine-Westphalia, **www.unikate.cc**

Around 1960 the native Berliner studied at the *Werkkunstschule* (School of Arts & Crafts) in Hanover, a city that was redeveloped after the war with a rationally planned grid of streets through which wafted the spirit of the second wave of Modernism. Afterwards she worked in the **Vorwerk** carpet studio as designer and pattern drawer. In the late 1960s she gathered experience as an adviser for Bayer AG, one of her key tasks being to plan various exhibitions. Among them was the series called *Visiona*, a name typical for the times, for which the Leverkusen chemical company engaged high-calibre international designers around 1970 during the Cologne Furniture Fair. There, the young Sigrid Wylach presented carpet designs that she was soon manufacturing in her own workshop. Numerous orders from banks, hotels, embassies and industrial enterprises followed. One order stood out from all the rest: the project to develop a new carpet collection for an existing furniture collection, an unusual concept. Because it was for Knoll International – ever since the 1950s a byword for modern interior design in the rational "International Style" – the project carried great significance. Wylach found herself developing carpets to complement important furniture classics like **Ludwig Mies van der Rohe's** cantilevered chair, Eero Saarinen's famous Tulip chair and Warren Plattner's impressive wire furniture. Their aesthetic dialogue with the giants of Modernism is still convincing even today. At the same time, the carpets (which are today sold by Markanto) can exist quite independently from Knoll International, which uses them worldwide in its various branches.

PHOTOS: l.: *White Flower* carpet, m.: *Beach* carpet
r.: *Palazzo* carpet (all for Knoll International, reissued by Markanto)

# Otto **Zapf**

furniture designer, born 1931, office in Kronberg / Hesse

The son of a cabinetmaker family, who studied mathematics and physics, originally wanted nothing to do with the banal everyday world of furniture. But things turned out differently. In the late 1950s, Otto Zapf and the Dane Niels Wiese met at the Furniture Fair in Cologne. Both were excited about the Bauhaus, the radically redesigned **Braun** products and the idea of system-atization. They had seen the model homes by the world's leading architects exhibited in 1957 at the Berliner Interbau show and decided to establish a furniture company in the spirit of the "International Style" that prevailed there. Vitsoe/Zapf would become, like **Bofinger** or **Behr**, a germ cell of the modern furniture trend that sprouted in West Germany. Some of the early products are based on designs by **Dieter Rams**. In the 1960s, after his alliance with Vitsoe and Rams had come to an end, Zapf made a name for himself with variable and idea-rich living concepts, which regularly appeared in the magazine *Schöner Wohnen*, one of the must-reads for modern domestic trends. The *Comodus* easychair with removable cover followed, as well as the even more unconventional *Softline*, a cabinet and shelf system with snap-on, snap-off surfaces. At the time Zapf was the first furniture designer with his own showroom and later his own factory. He attracted attention in the early 1970s with his "lounge landscapes" *Pillorama* and *Pollorama*: modular, multifunctional and ground-covering systems of upholstered elements in which the Ulm sense of order and the relaxed lifestyle of the late 1960s generation entered into a liaison. At the beginning of the 1980s he experienced the "American Dream": Knoll International furnished the administrative building of a telephone company with the *Zapf Office System* designed a decade earlier. 7,500 workplaces were set up, at the time the largest single furniture order ever and the beginning of a long, fruitful co-operation with the upscale American manufacturer that opened the doors of large offices to Zapf. This project also represented the breakthrough of systematic design in the workplace, ushering in a completely new, holistic office concept. Zapf, the design entrepreneur, who continues to commute between Hesse and the USA, once again caused a furore in the mid-1980s, with the *Wingset* shelf system (at first for **Vitra**, later for **Habitat**), adding another highlight to his innovative oeuvre. The 1990s then saw *Contur*, a plywood chair with a stretched "tongue" in the backrest, a simple instrument for continuous relaxed sitting.

PHOTOS: l.: *Arcadia* sofa for Knoll International
r.: Module from the *Sofalette 83* seating system for Knoll International

MILESTONE: *Softline* cabinet system → page **186**

# Zeitraum

furniture manufacturer, Munich / Bavaria, founded 1990, **www.zeitraum-moebel.de**

What the company with a core team of only seven members and some eight external producers was able to put into operation in the space of just a few years is a good example of a well-funct-ioning publishing house system. One can see certain parallels to **e15** not only in this sense, but also in the quality-oriented principles and the preferential use of natural materials – both in furnishings and the catalogue – although the Zeitraum team can justifiably claim the creative copyright on this marriage of wood and Modernism as well as on the associated image. The young Munich entrepreneurs have managed to bring about a whole new awareness of materials, as for example **Performa** has done on other terrain. The product line comprises cabinets, shelves, chairs, tables, beds and small furniture. The focus is on solid wood and the consistent handling of its variety and irregularities. Stylistic models were, in the beginning, the simple furniture of the Shakers, of the Biedermeier era and of other cultures, inclu-ding sometimes a piece from the flea market. The bulk of designs still come today from the firm's founders Peter Gaebelein, Birgit Gämmerler and Peter Joebsch. But for a long time now other designers, who are with few exceptions of German origin, have been shaping a broader stylistic idiom. For example, the side table *Cube* (by Formstelle) has laminated inserts in "pepper red" and "ice blue". Much Zeitraum furniture is universally applicable,

like the chair *Sit* (by Catharina Lorenz) or the patented shelf sys-tem *webweb* (by **Hertel & Klarhoefer**). These classics are now joined by the *Noon* series of cylindrical lights (by El Schmidt) and the *Side Comfort* upholstered furniture ensemble (by Formstelle), soft sleek cubes that can be ideally combined among themselves or in connection with the cabinet furniture. The firm's concept also encompasses a professional corporate identity, which has been rewarded by a great deal of attention in the press.

PHOTOS: l.: *Webweb* shelf system by Hertel & Klarhoefer
r.: *Cena* table and *Sit* chair by Catharina Lorenz

Index **according to Product Groups**

## BATHROOM TAPS AND WASHSTANDS AND ACCESSORIES
1983 *Allegroh* tap
1991 *Arco* tap
1992 *Tara* tap
1993 *Virage* washstand
1998 *Happy D* bathroom series
2003 *Raindance* shower
Manufacturers: Dornbracht, Duravit, Hansgrohe, Kaldewei, Keuco, Villeroy & Boch

## BEDS
1956 *GB 1085* bed
1968 *Stacking Lounger* bed
Manufacturers: e15, Interlübke, Möller Design, Performa, Raumwerk, Sanktjohanser, Zeitraum

## CABINET FURNITURE
1950 *M 125* cabinet system
1963 *SL* cabinet system
1971 *Container* cabinet system
1971 *Softline* cabinet system
1975 *Profile System* cabinet system
1996 *Menos* cabinet system
2001 *EO* cabinet system
2003 *Baureihe e* cabinet system
2006 *Socialbox* universal furniture
2007 *Nuf* cabinet system
Manufacturers: Behr International, Bofinger, Christine Kröncke, Deutsche Werkstätten, Die Collection, e15, Egoform, Flötotto, Interlübke, König + Neurath, Leise, Möller Design, Müller Möbelwerkstätten, Nils Holger Moormann, Performa, Planmöbel, Renz, Sanktjohanser, Sedus Stoll, Tecta, Weko, WK Wohnen, Zeitraum

## CARPETS AND TEXTILES
1920 *Bauhaus Carpet*
1988 *Lia* textile collection
2000 *Weaving* felt carpet
2000 *Design Edition* carpet collection
Manufacturers: Carpet Concept, JAB Anstoetz, Nya Nordiska, Rolf Benz, Vorwerk

## CHAIRS AND BENCHES
1830 *Schinkel* garden chair
1859 *No. 14* chair
1899 *Music-Room Chair*
1901 *Behrens* chair
1927 *Kramer Chair*
1927 *MR 10* chair
1929 *32* chair
1930 *MR 50 / Brno* chair
1931 *ST 14* chair
1936 *2200 / Olympic Chair*
1949 *SE 42* chair
1950 *SE 68* chair
1953 *SE 18* folding chair
1954 *S 664* chair
1964 *Bofinger Chair*
1966 *Papp* furniture system
1967 *Floris* chair
1968 *SM 400* chair
1969 *Santa Lucia* chair
1980 *FS Line* office chair
1982 *Einschwinger* chair
1983 *Consumer's Rest* chair
1986 *Solid* chair
1987 *Tabula Rasa* table and benches
1991 *Stitz* leaning aid
1996 *Time Documents* chair
2002 *Lipse* chair system
2002 *Silver* office chair
2004 *Milanolight* chair
2005 *Sputnik* office chair
Manufacturers: Anthologie Quartett, Bisterfeld + Weiss, Bofinger, Brunner, Christine Kröncke, ClassiCon, COR, Draenert, Deutsche Werkstätten,

Die Collection, Drabert, e15, Egoform, Kusch + Co, elmarflötotto, Flötotto, Habit, Interstuhl, Magazin, Mobilia Collection, Nils Holger Moormann, Sanktjohanser, Sedus Stoll, Seefelder, Thonet, Vitra, Wilde + Spieth, Wilkhahn, WK Wohnen, Zeitraum

## CHILDREN'S FURNITURE
1964 *K 4999* chair
1966 *Papp* furniture system
1972 *Zocker* sitting device
Hersteller: Anthologie Quartett, elmarflötotto, Flötotto, ClassiCon, Kaether & Weise

## COAT RACKS
1987 *Trio* coat rack
1998 *Hats Off* coat rack
2001 *Performa* coat rack
Manufacturers: ClassiCon, Jonas & Jonas, Nils Holger Moormann, Performa, Schönbuch, sdr+, Thonet

## DOOR-HANDLES
1922 *Bauhaus Door-Handle*
1952 *1034* door-handle
1970 *Series 111* door-handle
Manufacturers: FSB, Hewi

## FIREPLACES
2004 *Balance* fireplace
Manufacturer: Conmoto

## GARDEN FURNITURE
1830 *Schinkel* garden chair
1968 *Garden Egg* garden easychair
1992 *Tennis* garden furniture
1998 *Dia* garden furniture collection
2007 *Yin Yang* garden easychair
Manufacturers: Conmoto, Dedon, Fischer Möbel

## KITCHEN FURNITURE AND APPLIANCES
1926 *Frankfurt Kitchen*
1972 *KF 20* coffee maker
1984 *Kitchen Tree* kitchen furniture
1997 *S 20* kitchen system
Manufacturers: Alno, Braun, Bulthaup, Eggersmann, Gaggenau, Miele, Nils Holger Moormann, Poggenpohl, Tecta, WMF

## LAMPS
1924 *WA 24* table lamp
1925 *HMB 25* hanging lamp
1930 *6632* desk lamp
1962 *Britz* wall lamp
1966 *Bulb* lamp
1972 *Tizio* table lamp
1975 *TM* spotlight
1984 *YaYaHo* ceiling lamp
1993 *Take Five* hanging lamp
1997 *Zettel'z* hanging lamp
1998 *Screen* lamp
2000 *Soon* table lamp
2000 *Fridtjof 1* hanging lamp
Manufacturers: Anta, Anthologie Quartett, ClassiCon, Erco, Ingo Maurer, Mawa, Nils Holger Moormann, Rolf Benz, Serien, Tecnolumen, Tecta, Tobias Grau

## OCCASIONAL FURNITURE
1925 *Albers* nesting tables
1926 *B 9* nesting tables
1933 *S 179* serving trolley
1956 *Bar Trolley*
1973 *Nurglas* nesting tables
1994 *Confair* office furniture system
2002 *Diana* occasional table series
Manufacturers: Bofinger, ClassiCon, COR, Draenert, e15, Egoform, Flötotto, Habit, Inter-

lübke, Jonas & Jonas, Magazin, Müller Möbelwerkstätten, Nils Holger Moormann, Performa, Raumwerk, Renz, Rolf Benz, Sanktjohanser, sdr+, Sedus Stoll, Tecta, Thonet, Vitra, Wilkhahn, Wilde + Spieth, WK Wohnen, Zeitraum

## PHONOGRAPHS AND TELEVISION SETS
1956 *SK 4 / Phonosuper* phono combination
1958 *HF 1* television set
1959 *studio 2* hi-fi system
1985 *Art 1* television set
2003 *Mimo* television set
Manufacturers: Braun, Loewe

## PIANOS
2000 *Pure* piano
Manufacturers: Sauter, Wilde + Spieth

## ROOM DIVIDERS
1994 *Confair* office furniture system
2004 *Fusion* room divider
Manufacturers: König + Neurath, Koziol, Performa, Planmöbel, Sedus Stoll, Vitra, Wilkhahn

## SHELF SYSTEMS
1932 *Eiermann* shelf
1960 *606* shelf system
1984 *Tense Bookcase*
1989 *FNP* shelf system
1994 *Endless Shelf* shelf system
1996 *Wonder Boxes* shelf
2004 *Plattenbau* shelf system
2004 *Freddy* shelf system
2005 *Mein_Back* shelf system
2006 *Socialbox* universal furniture
Manufacturers: ClassiCon, e15, elmarflötotto, Flötotto, Jonas & Jonas, Kaether & Weise, König + Neurath, Magazin, Mobilia Collection, Müller Möbelwerkstätten, Nils Holger Moormann, Performa, Planmöbel, Raumwerk, Sanktjohanser, sdr+, WK Wohnen, Zeitraum

## SILVERWARE
1959 *mono-a* silverware
1976 *Model 33* silverware
1991 *Picado* parmesan knife
1998 *Velvet* silverware
Manufacturers: Alfi, Mono, Pott, WMF

## STOOLS
1955 *Ulm Stool*
1966 *Papp* furniture system
1996 *Molar* stool
2000 *Soest* Stool
Manufacturers: e15, elmarflötotto, Kaether & Weise, Nils Holger Moormann, Performa, Sanktjohanser, sdr+, Vitra, Wilde + Spieth, WK Wohnen, Zeitraum

## TABLEWARE AND ACCESSOIRES
1891 *No. 1/ 2* cocktail shaker
1899 *Fish Service* tableware
1903 *Service with Leaf Decor*
1909 *Behrens* kettle
1924 *Tea-Extract-Pot*
1931 *Urbino* porcelain tableware
1931 *Form 1382* porcelain tableware
1953 *Max and Moritz* salt and pepper shakers
1959 *Berlin* porcelain tableware
1959 *TC 100* stacking tableware
1967 *Sinus* stacking ashtrays
1969 *TAC 1* tea service
1981 *Mono Classic* teapot
1982 *9091* water kettle
1989 *Achat* thermos
2006 *Form 2006* porcelain tableware
Manufacturers: Anthologie Quartett, Arzberg,

Helit, Kahla, Koziol, KPM, Mono, Nymphenburg, Pott, Rosenthal, Villeroy & Boch, WMF

## UPHOLSTERED FURNITURE
1920 *F 51* easychair
1925 *B 3* chair
1928 *B 35* easychair
1929 *MR 90 / Barcelona* easychair
1948 *E 10* basket chair
1953 *Deep Easychair with Footstool*
1956 *369* easychair
1959 *Quinta* upholstered furniture system
1962 *RZ 62* easychair
1964 *Conseta* sofa system
1968 *Living Landscape* upholstered furniture system
1968 *TV-Relax* lounge chair
1969 *Orbis* easychair
1975 *O-Line* easychair
1976 *Sinus* easychair
1984 *T- Line* easychair
1984 *Zyklus* easychair
1985 *Tattomi* easychair
1986 *Flying Carpet* easychair
1989 *WK 698 Spot* easychair
1999 *Soft Cell* chair and lounger
2002 *Scroll* sofa system
2002 *Lobby* sofa system
2003 *Mars* easychair
2004 *Dono* sofa system
2005 *Couch* sofa and easychair
2007 *Yin Yang* garden easychair
2007 *S 3500* easychair
2007 *Plupp a.p.* functional sofa
Manufacturers: Anthologie Quartett, Bofinger, Brühl, COR, ClassiCon, Dedon, Deutsche Werkstätten, Die Collection, Egoform, elmarflötotto, Habit, Interstuhl, Kusch + Co, Mobilia Collection, Möller Design, Rolf Benz, Seefelder Möbelwerkstätten, Tecta, Thonet, Vitra, Wilkhahn, WK Wohnen

## TABLES AND DESKS
1925 *Albers* nesting tables
1926 *B 9* nesting tables
1934 *S 285* desk
1953 *Table Base with Cross-Bracing*
1966 *Papp* furniture system
1973 *1600 Nurglas* nesting tables
1987 *Tabula Rasa* table and benches
1994 *Confair* office furniture system
1995 *Eagle* pullout table
1996 *Spanoto* table
1996 *x-act* table system
1998 *8950* table
1999 *Sax* table
2000 *Nudo* standing desk
2002 *Kant* desk
2005 *Janus* table
Manufacturers: Brunner, Draenert, Christine Kröncke, Drabert, e15, Habit, Kaether & Weise, König + Neurath, Magazin, Mobilia Collection, Möller Design, Nils Holger Moormann, Performa, Planmöbel, Renz, Rolf Benz, Rosenthal, Sanktjohanser, sdr+, Seefelder Möbelwerkstätten, Tecta, Thonet, Vitra, Weko, Wilde + Spieth, Wilkhahn, WK Wohnen, Zeitraum

## WALL OBJECTS
1930 *1930 Light Switch*
1969 *Uten.Silo* wall storage unit
1981 *ABW 41* wall clock
Manufacturers: Berker, Braun, Mawa, Vitra

## WALLPAPER
1930 *Bauhaus Wallpaper*
2005 *Kollektion 3* wallpaper
Hersteller: Extratapete, Rasch

## Credits

Published by DuMont Buchverlag,
Cologne 2008

© 2008 normal buch, Bonn
All rights reserved

Exclusive rights for the German-speaking
countries: DuMont Buchverlag, Cologne

Idea and concept: Bernd Polster and Olaf Meyer

Text and editing: Bernd Polster

Art Director: Olaf Meyer

Graphic design assistant: Marc Mougeotte

Editorial assistants:
Stephan Heuken, Nicole Lammerich,
Marc Mougeotte, Florian Rühmann,
Marijke Schwarz, Nadja Wahl

Text and photo research:
Stephan Heuken, Nicole Lammerich,
Marijke Schwarz

Coordination: Nicole Lammerich

Translation into English: Jennifer Taylor, Steve Cox

Editorial coordination:
Uta Grosenick

Proofreading:
Thomas Fidelak (www.context-id.info),
Annegret Hunke-Wormser

Production:
Marcus Muraro

Printing: GZD, Ditzingen

ISBN: 978-3-8321-7776-8

Printed in Germany

## Photographs:

The photographs in this book are used with the kind permission of the designers and companies featured as well as the below-named institutions, who retain the rights to such photographs.

Photo Cover: *B 3* Chair © Knoll International. Photographer René Gruszka

Photo p. 42: © Galerie Ulrich Fiedler, Cologne

Photo p. 140: Stacking Tableware TC 100, dissertation by Hans "Nick" Roericht, 1959 photograph Wolfgang Adler, City Archives of Ulm. © Ulm Museum/Academy of Design Archives

Photos pp. 156 and 157: © Photographer Roman Raacke

Photos pp. 230 and 231: © N+P Industrial Design GmbH, 1992 / www.neumeister-partner.de

Photos pp. 73, 103, 129, 145, 154, 155, 159, 160, 161, 165, 171, 173, 177, 187, 192, 193, 235, 271, 273, 281, 295, 417 left and right, 524 middle, 554 left, 563 right and back flap (*Molar* stool by e15): © Agentur Comwork, Cologne

The following photos were made available to us by Quittenbaum Kunstauktionen, Munich (www.quittenbaum.de): Aicher, Otto: p. 380; Baumann, Hans Theo: pp. 132–133, 391; Bollhagen, Hedwig: p. 402; Brandt, Marianne: p. 404; Gropius, Walter: pp. 52–53, 174–175; Kramer, Ferdinand: p. 481; Riemerschmid, Richard: pp. 38, 44–45, 524 left and right

For the works of Albers, Josef: pp. 58–59, 382; Behrens, Peter: pp. 15, 42–43, 46–47, 395; Gropius, Walter: pp. 17, 48–49, 52–53, 174–175, 450; Richter, Gerhard: p. 553; Riemerschmid, Richard: pp. 15, 38–39, 44–45, 524; van der Rohe, Mies: pp. 17, 70–71, 74–75, 76–77, 80–81, 499; Stiletto Design (alias Frank Schreiner): pp. 216–217; Wagenfeld, Wilhelm: pp. 54–55, 114–115, 122–123, 555; Wewerka, Stefan: pp. 212–213, 220–221, 559: © VG Bild-Kunst, Bonn 2008

All other illustrations are company photographs of licensed products

For the products from Braun: pp. 122–123, 130–131, 138–139, 190–191, 208–209, 380, 405, 451, 461, 519 and back cover (coffee maker *KF 20*): © Braun GmbH, Kronberg

**We would like to thank** all of the designers and companies presented in this book for their extraordinarily helpful response to our requests for information and materials, without which this book would not have been possible.

Our sincere gratitude as well to **Mr Askan Quittenbaum** from Auktionshaus Quittenbaum (www.quittenbaum.de) for his constructive collaboration in getting this book off the ground. **Mr Dietrich Klatt** of the Otto Haesler Foundation in Celle (www.haesler-ini.homepage.t-online.de), **Professor Eberhard Pook** of the Karl Schneider Archives in Hamburg (www.karl-schneider-archiv.de) and **Ms Simone Oelker-Czychowski** and **Ms Nicola von Albrecht** likewise made valuable contributions to this book.

We would like to draw attention in particular to the very helpful cooperation of **Mr Sven Vorderstrase** from the Comwork agency (www.comwork.net) and the associated company **Markanto** (www.markanto.de).

Special thanks are due to **Mr Helmut Lübke**, former chairman of the Verband der deutschen Möbelindustrie (VDM – Association of German Furniture Manufacturers), who initiated the previous book: *Möbeldesign Deutschland. Die Klassiker.* His sudden death was a shock to us all. We are thus all the more indebted to **Ms Ursula M. Geismann**, who carried on guidance of the project for VDM, as well as the association's managing director **Dirk-Uwe Klaas** for their help and cooperation.

For further information on German design for modern living, please visit the Internet port **www.formguide.de**.